Beyond Doer and Done To

In *Beyond Doer and Done To*, Jessica Benjamin, author of the path-breaking *Bonds of Love*, expands her theory of mutual recognition and its breakdown into the complementarity of "doer and done to." Her innovative theory charts the growth of the Third in early development through the movement between recognition and breakdown, and shows how it parallels the enactments in the psychoanalytic relationship. Benjamin's recognition theory illuminates the radical potential of acknowledgment in healing both individual and social trauma, in creating relational repair in the transformational space of thirdness. Benjamin's unique formulations of intersubjectivity make essential reading for both psychoanalytic therapists and theorists in the humanities and social sciences.

Jessica Benjamin, Ph.D., is a psychoanalyst and supervising faculty member at New York University Postdoctoral Psychology Program and the Stephen Mitchell Relational Studies Center in New York. She is author of the Routledge title *Shadow of the Other*.

"Among the most influential and most widely read of psychoanalytic writers, Benjamin in her latest work perfects her brilliant, trail-blazing articulation of intersubjective recognition theory. In *Beyond Doer and Done To* she elucidates the relations of complementarity, acknowledgment, rhythmicity, the Third, mutual vulnerability, doer-done to relations, trauma, dissociation and witnessing. She has provided a theory of recognition and its vicissitudes, recognition between mothers and infants, therapeutic healing recognition, and recognition relations among couples, families, and even the warring peoples of the world. This magnificent interdisciplinary synthesis breaks through intellectual barriers and will inspire generations of psychotherapists, psychologists, philosophers, feminists, social theorists, and activists."

—**Lewis Aron**, Ph.D., Director of the New York University
Postdoctoral Program in Psychotherapy & Psychoanalysis

Beyond Doer and Done To

Recognition Theory,
Intersubjectivity and the Third

Jessica Benjamin

Routledge
Taylor & Francis Group

LONDON AND NEW YORK

First published 2018
by Routledge
2 Park Square, Milton Park, Abingdon, Oxon OX14 4RN

and by Routledge
711 Third Avenue, New York, NY 10017

Routledge is an imprint of the Taylor & Francis Group, an informa business

British Library Cataloguing in Publication Data
A catalogue record for this book is available from the British Library

Library of Congress Cataloging in Publication Data
Names: Benjamin, Jessica, author.
Title: Beyond Doer and Done To : Recognition Theory, Intersubjectivity and
the Third / Jessica Benjamin.
Description: Abingdon, Oxon ; New York, NY : Routledge, 2017. |
Includes bibliographical references and index.
Identifiers: LCCN 2016048054| ISBN 9781138218413 (hardback : alk. paper) |
ISBN 9781138218420 (pbk. : alk. paper) | ISBN 9781315437699 (e-book)
Subjects: LCSH: Recognition (Psychology) | Intersubjectivity—Psychological
aspects. | Interpersonal relations. | Psychoanalysis and feminism.
Classification: LCC BF378.R4 B46 2017 | DDC 153.1/24—dc23
LC record available at https://lccn.loc.gov/2016048054

ISBN: 978-1-138-21841-3 (hbk)
ISBN: 978-1-138-21842-0 (pbk)
ISBN: 978-1-315-43769-9 (ebk)

Typeset in Times New Roman and Gill Sans
by Florence Production Ltd, Stoodleigh, Devon, UK

Contents

Acknowledgments

As this book has been written over almost two decades, there are any number of individuals and members of my community to whom I am most grateful. My colleagues in the Relational and Independent orientations of the New York University Postdoctoral Program have contributed a home base over these years, as have members of the faculty of the Stephen Mitchell Relational Studies Center.

I am especially grateful for my late wonderful friend Ruth Stein who was a great interlocutor and support for my work. And to Lew Aron with whom I drafted a first paper on the Third and who has continued to read what I've written throughout, while developing his own ideas, so many of which have been invaluable in helping me clarify my own thinking.

Rachel Kabasakalian McKay took on a very special role in helping me write this book. She agreed to be my editor, shepherd and "midwife," thinking through each part and how to assemble the whole, constantly analysing and clarifying ideas, creating coherence. She deserves my utmost gratitude, and more, recognition for making the completion of this book possible.

Kim Bernstein provided uniquely helpful critical reading and editing of some of the more refractory chapters of this book.

I give thanks also to friends who gave generously of their help: Hazel Ipp who has read and supported much of this work with a tough mind and a warm heart. Galit Atlas who courageously collaborated on the writing of "Too-Muchness," offering insight, reading and assimilating vital parts of my theory and helping me clarify important ideas. Eyal Rozmarin who affirmed my theoretical endeavour by pulling together a whole collection of essays on my work. Andrew Samuels who gave much helpful advice. Gila Ashtor who shared with me new perspectives on critical theory. Serefina Bathrick whose wisdom brings to life so many therapeutic insights. Philip Bromberg who has been in equal parts affectionate arguer and enthusiast. Martha Bragin who shared enormous insights from her work with victims of social trauma all over the world. Elsa First, who could hold the child's mind and the big social picture together, was always ready to think with me. A number of colleagues who have commented on one or more chapters with support and useful criticism: Beatrice Beebe, Celia Brickman, Andrea Celenza, Stephen

Frosch, Sue Grand, Orna Guralnik, Barbara Kane, Susan Kraemer, Steven Knoblauch, Susan Mailer, Phil Ringstrom, Eyal Rozmarin, Maura Sheehy, Malcolm Slavin, Donnell Stern, Melanie Suchet, Charles Spezzano. My Monday and Wednesday groups with whom I discussed all of this through years of writing the early chapters, and more recently my Tuesday group who read much of this manuscript.

And my deepest gratitude to my patients who have shared their stories and reflected so much of mental life and living back to me.

During the period when I wrote this book I had an unusual opportunity to put my ideas on acknowledgment and thirdness into practice, and so learn from people who generously shared their experience.Two who personally guided and inspired me on a transformational journey into new territory with their own power-ful visions of the Third: the late Eyad el Sarraj, a leader of extraordinary strength who offered profound understanding and courage in the face of violence; and Yitzhak Mendelsohn, psychosocial activist, who could contain with compassion the complexities of social trauma and conflict as well as healing. My comrades in the Acknowledgment Project, in particular Uri Hadar, along with Judith Thompson and Adin Thayer, who helped me to think and organize, made so much possible. As did the members of ILAS in Chile who shared their work and histories with me. And my thanks to Irris Singer who gave me the opportunity to work on her project *Moving Beyond Violence*, along with Bassam Aramin and Itamar Shapira from whom I learned so much. Pumla Gobodo-Madikizela gave me a chance to reflect these experiences in light of her vital conceptualization of perpetrator–victim relationships and the possibilities of reconciliation.

The Lotte Koehler Foundation who awarded me the Hans Kilian prize in meta-humanistic studies in 2015 gave me an extraordinary kind of encouragement and recognition that allowed me to devote myself to finishing this book, for which I am so grateful. I thank Lotte Koehler of the foundation, a prescient early supporter of the idea of recognition, its role in both psychoanalysis and infancy studies. In addition, Jurgen Staub and Pradeep Chakarat of the Kilian Center at Bochum University for their incredibly meaningful support and challenging, enlivening discussions.

Lastly thanks to: my children, Jake and Jonah Rabinbach, for their loving pre-sence in my life, for what I learned from and with them about playing and growing up, for sharing their merriment and vitality, and later their encouragement. Andy Rabinbach, who was there at the inception of these ideas and shared so many years of caring for family and writing together. And Barry Magid, my own personal magpie, who tucked whole chunks of my theory into his warm nest and produced them when needed, along with pieces of the family silver. His loving companion-ship and playful, critical mind have carried me through the whole process, especially the toughest moments.

Chapter 1 first appeared as "Beyond doer and done to: An intersubjective view of thirdness," *Psychoanalytic Quarterly*, Volume LXXIII, Issue 1, January 2004, pp. 5–46. Reprinted with the permission of John Wiley & Sons, Ltd. This version was taken from the volume *Relational Psychoanalysis Volume IV*, eds Aron & Harris, 2012, published by Routledge.

A portion of Chapter 2 was originally published as "Enactment, acknowledgment and the bearing of badness," in *When Hurt Remains: Relational Perspectives on Therapeutic Failure*, edited by Asaf Rolef Ben-Shahar and Rachel Shalit (published by Karnac Books in 2016), and is reprinted with the kind permission of Karnac Books.

The clinical segment in Chapter 3 appeared in somewhat different form in the article on "The necessity of the analyst's acknowledging failure," *International Journal of Psychoanalysis*, 90: 441–450 2009, reprinted by kind permission of John Wiley & Sons.

Parts of Chapter 4 were originally published in "Revisiting the riddle of sex," in *Dialogues on Sexuality, Gender and Psychoanalysis*, edited by Irene Matthis (published by Karnac Books in 2004), and is reprinted with the kind permission of Karnac Books. Some parts were published in the article "The too-muchness of excitement: Sexuality in light of excess, attachment and affect regulation," with Galit Atlas, in *The International Journal of Psychoanalysis*, 96, 39–63, 2015, for which I am grateful for permission to publish by John Wiley & Sons.

Parts of Chapter 5 were first published as "From enactment to play: Metacommunication, acknowledgment and the third of paradox," *Rivista di Psicoanalisi* (2016). Reprinted by kind permission of the journal.

A portion of Chapter 7 was published as "Non-violence as the respect for all suffering: Thoughts inspired" by Eyad el Sarraj, in *Psychoanalysis, Culture and Society*, Vol. 21:5–20 2016 and is published with kind permission of Palgrave-MacMillan.

Introduction

Recognition, intersubjectivity and the Third

I.

This book develops the basic ideas of an intersubjective psycho-analysis organized around the idea of recognition. In contrast to the time when I first strove to formulate a theory of intersubjectivity—that wide-angle perspective that describes psychic processes and the growth of minds in terms of their reciprocally knowing interaction—it is now a dominant rather than marginal view in psychoanalysis (see Benjamin, 2016a). Intrapsychic theory, focused on the properties of one mind, has been modified and reoriented in light of the notion of intersubjectivity. We now think in terms of the interpenetration of minds, conscious and unconscious, even mirror neuron to mirror neuron. The implications of an intersubjective psychoanalysis have been revolutionary. They extend not only to clinical process, where the awareness of the analyst's participation and use of her own subjectivity has reorganized our practice, but more broadly to our entire view of human development and social bonds.

Whereas in my earlier work (especially Benjamin 1988; 1995a) I tried to articulate some of the concepts that would enable a turn to intersubjectivity—which was newly born and in formation—in this book I am reflecting on the consequences of a practice and theory elaborated subsequently by a broad group of psychoanalysts. Many but not all of them identified with "the relational turn" in North America. This book proposes a theoretical framework that illuminates those consequences, those that have emerged from the study of early development as well as relational practice. Centering on recognition, it aims to integrate thinking about mutuality and bi-directionality of relationships in both the analytic and developmental process of change.

Embracing the inspired contributions of thinkers representing a range of approaches to intersubjectivity I hope to illuminate the larger stakes of the contemporary psychoanalytic project: its unique way of thinking about self and other, mind and affect, the psychic life of social subjects. Consequently, I hope that these propositions will reach across the disciplinary barriers and enable non-psychoanalysts to access the social and philosophical implications of intersubjective psychoanalysis (see Benjamin, 2016). This intention is congruent with my original interdisciplinary starting point in the critical theory of society—a social theory aimed at unmasking hidden pathologies of power and domination—as well as my current concern with the processes of social healing and witnessing of collective trauma (indeed, in light of current events, with non-violent resistance). As important as those concerns are however, there is no doubt that this book arises from, and gives primary attention to, my clinical experience as a psychoanalyst and my practical personal experiences as a mother. A mother, I should add, who studied mother-infant interaction and before that was passionately involved in the second wave generation of feminism, which sought to change the relations of mothering and working as well as psychoanalytic theory.

At the time that I was first developing my thinking about recognition in the 1970s, discovering the vital new field of studies in mother-infant interaction was electrifying. It seemed to offer confirmation of something I had looked in vain to find in the field of psychoanalysis itself—a demonstration of how we get into each other's minds, and indeed do this long before speech (Bullowa, 1979). Studies of mother-infant interaction provided concrete illlustrations of how recogniton works in action as well as a new scaffolding for the idea of intersubjectivity (Trevarthen, 1977; 1979; Sander, 1983; Stern, 1985) previously considered philosophically (Habermas, 1972). It was now possible to develop a theoretical framework in which the action of recognition appeared as the basic element or building block of relationships; we could think in terms of relationships that transpire between two essentially similar minds that are nonetheless continually challenged, and often destabilized by each other's difference and disjunction.

A developmental micro-analytic approach to intersubjectivity begins with the embodied, emotional, rudimentary self interacting not with an abstract Other but another, more developed person. This interaction will necessarily include the infant's effect on her caretaker; it will be a two way street. Likewise, in the analytic process, we consider the reciprocal effect each partner has on the other's psyche, and as in development we study the interaction by which recognition process works. In philosophy the notion of a self constituted through reciprocal recognition postulates that the affirmation of independence depends on the expectation of mutual care or shared concerns (Honneth, 1995; 2007). Still, as with the notion of the self formed by a regulatory social order or through exclusion of the other (Butler, 1997; 2000), the significance and qualities of the other as an independent subject not defined by us may not receive their due (Benjamin,1998; Oliver, 2001). The matter of how we come to appreciate the other's separate existence, how we evolve through a relationship where each is the other's other seems to be the rightful concern of a psychoanalytic theorizing of intersubjectivity.

In starting with a *psychological* view of intersubjectivity, the self is seen developing in relation to an other (henceforth the "mother") who not only provides recognition, but is dependent on the self's agency and responsiveness to create a working pattern of co-created action. If intersubjective capacities are to be realized, the child must be involved in creating a mutually differentiating system, an exchange of recognition. Ideally, the mother will be recognized as part of a mutual dynamic of reciprocal responsiveness and understanding. This system is the ianuguration of what I will be conceptualizing as the Third.

By starting with this psychoanalytically conceived intersubjectivity we may highlight the otherwise obscured reality: that the first other, woman as mother, was originally viewed through the patriarchal lens as a vehicle for the (male) self's development. The way in which the self is changed by having to struggle with the other's difference is, from a feminist perspective, necessarily part of a reciprocal process whereby the self is the other's other, the one who confronts the other with the need for accommodation and differentiation as well as the possibility of enlivening responsiveness. This is to say that the emphasis on mutual responsiveness and transformation as being psychologically vital tries to conceptualize the presence of two different minds mutually affecting each other regardless of their inequality or asymmetry—thereby leaving a potential space for equality and symmetry.

II.

Recognition as an organizing idea may be thought of in two ways: first, as a psychic position in which we know the other's mind as an equal source of intention and agency, affecting and being affected; and second as a process or action, the essence of responsiveness in interaction. The position of recognizing other minds was certainly not assumed in the original theorizing of psychoanalysis, which began with the intrapsychic topography and mechanisms of the individual mind. It has not gone unremarked in post-modern thought that positioning the analyst as the one who knows this topography and these mechanisms undid psychoanalysis's most radical discovery: the Unconscious as the limit upon the subject's claim to (self) knowledge (Laplanche, 1997; Rozmarin, 2007). However, the intersubjectivity of relational analysis throws doubt on more than the analyst's interpretive certainties or "keys to the kingdom"—the formulations viewed by earlier generations of classical analysts as unlocking the unconscious templates of neurosis. More radically, intersubjective theory throws the analyst into the non-linear system of two subjects, each presumed able to destabilize the other's self-certainty or be destabilized at any moment, so that meanings are emergent (Hoffman, 1998; Stern, 2009).

Thus, conceiving an intersubjective psychoanalysis meant positing the presence of two knowing and not-knowing subjects in the room—each one potentially engaged in recognition of the other's alterity, the other's different center of perspective, or perhaps equally unsettled and engaged in avoiding that recognition. Of key importance to my take on this is that such recognition involves an affectively meaningful experience of the other as not simply an object of need to be controlled or resisted, consumed or pushed away, but another mind we can connect with. Which is to say, experiencing the other as a responsive agent who can reciprocate that desire for recognition versus an object of need or drive to be managed within our own mental web. Crucially, these two psychic positions, corresponding to intersubjective and intrapsychic theories, are best conceived not as exclusive but as interrelated phenomenologies of psychic life. Indeed the oscillations between them correspond to our shifts in relational states between feelings of self being *with* an other self and self being in complementary relation *to* an object (Benjamin, 1988).

Throughout this book I shall be referring to the position of "the Third." It is the position in which we implicitly recognize the other as a "like subject," a being we can experience as an "other mind." The Third refers to a position constituted through holding the tension of recognition between difference and sameness, taking the other to be a separate but equivalent center of initiative and conscious-ness with whom nonetheless feelings and intentions can be shared. Sharing begins in the earliest pre-verbal interactions: the creation of alignment in intentions or resonance of feeling, a degree of symmetry or sense of sameness even among unequal partners. But in the face of our inevitable incongruence such alignment can only be maintained paradoxically, by tolerating the inevitable interactive shifts from alignment to misalignment and back.

Breakdown of this basic recognition position is a common and pervasive phe-nomenon, however. The two sides of sameness and difference, congruence and incongruence, fail to be upheld by the crossbeam of the Third. This breakdown spells collapse into twoness, a relational formation in which the other appears as object or objectifying, unresponsive or injuring, threatening to erase one's own subjectivity or be oneself erased. This relational formation, based on splitting, takes shape as the complementarity of doer and done to, but there are many other permutuations: accuser and accused, helpless and coercive, even victim and perpetrator.

The second meaning of recognition pertains not to psychic position but to expressive behavior, to dynamic process, to responsiveness in action. Acts of recognition confirm that I am seen, known, my intentions have been understood, I have had an impact on you, and this must also mean that I matter to you; and reciprocally, that I see and know you, I understand your intentions, your actions affect me and you matter to me. Further, we share feelings, reflect each other's knowing, so we also have shared awareness. This is recognition. So far, I have found no other word that serves to sum up this whole congelation of meanings of how we impact and know one another, even though numerous other words can and have been used to describe facets of it. As the basic building block of connection and the primary form of linking between two persons, recognition is, consciously or unconsciously, going on all the time. As with breathing in and out, we may not stop to notice it unless the oxygen supply wanes and we start to look for a way out—or lose consciousness. Psychically, that way out is dissociation (Davies & Frawley, 1994; Bromberg, 1998; Howell, 2005). Of course, recognition is all about such noticing (or not); about the fact that we are wired to be sensitive and responsive to what the other is doing, to the other's response to our doing, to the way they "make me feel," the way I "make them feel," and whether I feel like they are doing something *to* me or *with* me, and vice versa.

And this matter of vice versa is a question for itself: whether we are recipro-cating according to the same terms, struggling to find our terms, or mismatching on different terms; whether our mental gears are meshing or jamming. In short, the question is whether doing is *with* or *to*: doing *to* me implies that complemen-tary twoness of opposing doer and done to, while doing *with* suggests that shared state of fitting in, coordination, or purposeful negotiation of difference that will be called thirdness. In light of infancy research, thirdness originally appears as a dynamic coordination, in which matching, mismatching, and return to matching of shared direction can be charted as a non-linear relation far from an exact mirroring or synchrony. It is not an action–reaction pattern. Though this process depends largely, but not wholly, on the attunement of the parental figure, such early interaction already reveals the importance of reciprocity in interaction.

In adapting these studies of earliest interaction to clinical theorizing I often use the image of a dance of two partners oriented to a shared but unscripted choreo-graphy as a metaphor for the Third. The shared expectation of a co-created dynamic pattern that both partners orient to could, of course, also apply to the overly tight coordination of doer and done to patterns of reactivity—the ones that reflect misattunement and failure to get it (Stern & Beebe, 1977), that lock us into reactivity. These observations allowed us to conceptualize the open-ended move-ment of co-created Thirds as distinct from such reactive patterns. Like the ideas of potential space in Winnicott (1971a) and the emergence of unforeseen or unbid-den experience in Stern (2015), the idea of thirdness tries to capture the original idea of free association as an opening to the not yet known, what arises without coercion and constraint. Recognition in interaction is not a steady-state or stable condition but an ongoing process involving shifts in and out of thirdness.

I have stressed throughout my writing that the formulation of intersubjectivity and the capacity for recognition does not obviate the persistence of an intrapsy-chic life organized around complementarity, subject and object, and splitting as described by Klein in her notion of the paranoid-schizoid position. Of course this intrapsychic mental organization can become more dominant when recognition fails, but it is always part of our psychic make-up. What I have added, following Winnicott, is that the alternative goes beyond Klein's intrapsychic depressive position of holding opposites in tension (ambivalence). There is a position of inter-subjective relating, the Third, in which the self reaches and feels reached by the real other predominates. The shifts between intrapsychic and intersubjective relating may be seen as ongoing, part of a continuing tension in the self. This formulation means that in theorizing recognition we must conceptualize not a static condition but a continual oscillation between relating to the outside other and the inner object (Winnicott, 1971a).

Intrapsychic relating to the object allows for the splitting that infuses the com-plementarity of doer and done to, in which the dominant form is coercion or sub-mission, in which action and response are not freely given. Ironically, each person may feel coerced by the other, as if pushed into their assigned role, neither in control. Where then is goodness, where badness? The complementarity of victim and victimizer, even when congealed in manifestly clear relations of domination, so often generates confusion. Invariably, doer–done to relations involve some dissociation of what is felt, experienced, known. As we have come to wider understanding of trauma in the form of non-recognition, dissociation has increasingly become part of our general understanding of the psyche. This widens our scope to how ongoing forms of doer–done to relations leave the self without access to thirdness and failure of recognition leaves parts of self in the closet.

Even when individuals have secure areas of intersubjective relating, the movement from felt awareness of the other as subject to dissociative relating to the object, from emotional contact to disconnection, are part of ordinary dyadic fluctuations. Such oscillations may be encompassed in the larger movement whereby we create the Third, as we learn to restore connections after minor or major disruptions. This larger movement is observable in the study of early interaction, where the process of disruption and repair between parent and infant helps form the ability to tolerate and integrate moments of disjunction and difference (Tronick, 1989). The process of restoring recognition that we observed in earliest interaction, the successful reorganization and recreation of attuned coordination after moments of mismatch or frustration could thus be translated into a larger principle: recognition depends on mutual correction, and the ongoing adjustment or repair of disruption becomes the platform of thirdness.

Relational repair (as opposed to the self's internal repair of the object's goodness) involves the caregiver acknowledging—in deeds and communicative gestures—the violations of expected patterns of soothing or responsiveness. This process of repair serves to create a sense of the *lawful world*, a central category of experience. In the lawful world, the other's behavior is not simply always predictable but more importantly confirms when the unexpected or painful wrongness occurs as well as the need to put things right. And what cannot be put right, yet another violation of expectancy, is also acknowledged. The mental representation of lawful world refers not to juridical law, but to a belief in the value and possibility of intelligible, responsive and respectful behavior as a condition of mental sanity and interpersonal/social bonds; it is associated with differentiated respect for the person of the other. This idea of *acknowledgment* and how it creates the sense of the lawful world will be threaded throughout these essays.

This idea has assumed even greater importance for me since the election of 2016 and the inauguration of Trump has been taking place as I write this introduction. We have seen how the manipulation of political processes by an individual who deliberately, violently transgresses against the lawful world—with its attendant respect for all persons—has led to a collective reaction to a psychically traumatic social violation. The sentiments of shock, fear and grief expressed in our consulting rooms as well as in public reflect the experience of loss of the lawful world.

In this light the idea I have developed in my chapter on collective trauma and witnessing may be especially relevant, the idea that associated with the doer–done to complementarity is a powerful fantasy, "Only one can live." It informs both the individual and collective mind, organizing what Freud saw as Oedipal competition into a life and death struggle—Cain and Abel comes to mind—in which only one can survive. While everyone may be subject to this fantasy at times of fear and stress, when the social Third breaks down, or when certain groups organize around this fantasy, it becomes a dominant structure, there appears to be no exit from the stark alternatives of kill or be killed, annihilated or harming. Resisting this fantasy requires some version of the Third, a vision of a lawful world in which self and other, Them and Us, can be recognized.

III.

I believe that in formal terms the same process of acknowledgment is crucial in social and clinical dimensions of interaction. The process evolves through early experience with accommodation, attunement, understanding into later more complex forms. The demand to cope with disruptions and difference, face the consequences of failures of recognition for self and other, accommodate even as one is being accommodated to—all these should appear in statu nascendi, in early relational repair in infancy and early childhood. In the chapters that follow I will show how clinical psychoanalysis has given us a unique perspective on relational repair and trace the vicissitudes of intersubjective breakdowns and healing through acknowledgment.

Central to my formulation of recognition theory, the idea of acknowledgment is exemplified in psychoanalytic practice where its function is to restore the space of thirdness. What characterizes this space is the sense that each partner can feel and think independently without feeling the push-pull of complementarity. This process, more complex than it might first appear, has been well articulated by North American relational analysts who have explored how analysts may make rooms for their own tendencies to dissociation, their feelings of shame or badness, and in that sense, their lack of mastery and control. That lack of knowingness is associated with a theorizing of dissociation (Stern, 1997) and the awareness of mutual interpersonal vulnerability that infuses the analytic relationship, even when not consciously formulated or spoken of (Aron, 1996). The emphasis on our own propensities for dissociating in tandem with or separately from our patients has changed our work (Bromberg, 2006; 2011). Realizing that the analyst's vulnerability can be expressed in the very need to be the healer, we are poised to accept the fallacy of positing the Third as an ideal state of relatedness that can be sustained (Benjamin, 2000a; 2000b). It becomes ever clearer how analysts are charged with negotiating the tension between withdrawal into self-protection and acknowledging the presence of dissociated feelings of pain and shame by recognizing the other's intentions, or by reaching shared understanding. The difficulty is that dissociation within both patient and analyst (or both together), the unconscious movement between different self-states, can often only be recognized in hindsight.

From this vantage point, I discuss the analytic process of repairing the Third, which works both by restoring rhythmicity or recognition as well as by working with the collisions that result from the complementary impasses of doer and done to. The relational discourse on enactments or collisions, the analysis of repetition and repair of the simulated past injuries, has mushroomed—even as it remains relatively unknown to much of the more traditional psychoanalytic world, despite relational efforts to integrate and mediate different positions (see Cooper, 2010). In the clinical discussions, I will consider how we engage relational repair, how we both formulate and show procedurally our awareness of how each of our minds work and re-create a sense of a lawful world. In light of the intensified focus on trauma and its enactment in the analytic situation I will consider the tension between the experience of mutual vulnerability and the analyst's asymmetrical stance of witnessing and acknowledging the suffering a patient has endured. Further, how this acknowledgment is complicated by the inevitable dissociation as well as the unconscious circuity and symbolic scrambling with which the past manifests in the present.

The project undertaken in these essays was to formulate these issues—some of which appear rather differently in different psychoanalytic cultures—in a conceptual framework of recognition and thirdness that spans the arc from infant development to the analytic dyad to social and collective trauma. The breadth of this framework corresponds to the idea of recognition as a multi-faceted concept; hence it articulates different facets of thirdness in relation to a variety of inter-subjective relations, different registers of the Third position as they appear developmentally, clinically and socially. I have attempted to elaborate the Third as a position that itself develops, from the very basic interactive patterns—rhythmicity—into more complex, symbolically mediated forms of shared reflection, dialogue and negotiation of difference. Hence, we experience the Third as both rhythmic and differentiating, each aspect enhancing the other, even though one may be foregrounded at a given moment. The Third has its developmental trajectory toward greater complexity and differentiation in which it is important not to privilege any one moment.

IV.

Given this broad framework, I can now imagine my reader wondering: "How is this theory of recognition related to other theories of knowing minds?" One might wonder about the relationship of recognition theory to the widely used ideas regarding mentalization and affect regulation (Siegel, 1999; Fonagy et al., 2002; Schore, 2003; 2011; Hill, 2015). Affect regulation theory, as developed by Schore and Siegel, stresses the implicit communication between our right brains that organizes mental states and directly influences our level of physiological arousal, while mentalization theory, formulated by Fonagy and Target (1996 a & b; Fonagy et al., 2002) stresses the reflective aspect of understanding and being understood by others' minds, enabling the distinction between inner and outer reality. Together these theories show how the complex and vital process of mental development is mediated in infancy and early childhood: the specific consequences of being soothed and understood, having pain and joy reflected back, in ways that stabilize the child's affect state and create symbolic capacities.

As I see it, the adult action of reflecting back feeling—showing that I get what you are experiencing, which now therefore becomes a communication to me—constitutes the basic 1.0 version of recognition. Initially, then, recognition makes action into communication, and this action on both sides is required for the child to be coherent, regulated, to have defined emotions as well as agency, as well as to later think about what is in the mind of the other and her own mind. In my conceptualization, affect regulation and mentalization are effects of the caregiver's recognizing action on the growth of the mind, and conversely build the capacity to act in this way with others.

But what if such recognition, such intersubjective relatedness, were to be seen as an end in itself? By focusing on what we must be able to do to regulate affect or evolve mentalization, we are still concerned with cultivating the mind. One might still want to ask to what end? Daniel Stern, whose contributions spanned early infancy studies and later a general theory of mind, formulated the process of recognition in terms of the need for intersubjective orientation and relatedness, which are necessary for their own sake. Knowing and being known from the "inside" can also be seen as an essential motivation separate from the basic need for attachment, which is associated with safety (Stern, 2004). I am inclined to add that although the safety of being held and nourished is distinct from the inter-subjective relatedness of knowing other minds, when those needs are split the self also tends to be split between security and recognition. In some instances parts of self must be dissociated, unrecognized, in order to be safe; in others, safety is sacrificed in order to feel known. And this leads to an important point: a person may develop the capacities for mentalization and self-regulation even while organizing the self in terms of such splits. The full experience of knowing and being known while trusting in the lawful world, such as we aim for in psycho-analysis, requires overcoming these splits.

If we accept this way of thinking about recognition as a motivating need—a need that "drives" the psyche (to use an outmoded phrase) since without it we are alone and unsafe—then we may end up not far from Freud's (1930) original powerful insight that the child renounces parts of his psyche to stay connected to the parent (authority figure), to keep mother or father's love. Recognition of one part is renounced to attain safe inhabiting of another. The alienation of self from its own needs through splitting and dissociation follows upon the denial of recognition; these alienating forms aim to get around the withholding of the needed caregiver attention, that which alone stabilizes the psyche. If too much of what a child initiates is rejected and refused, rather than recognized and responded to, the ability to respond to other minds will be impaired as vital parts of self have been dissociated: e.g. experiences of excitement, pain, fear have become disavowed, "Not-me" in Sullivan's term (1953). This, in short, is the phenomenology of our psychic life as it evolved in the history of psychoanalytic theorizing of object relations. In this way an important bridge was built between

attachment vs. intersubjectivity

early mental development and clinical experience, and as it turns out, social relations in general.

Simply, we may say that object relations theory assumed, but did not formulate, a tacit phenomenology of recognition. It described internal relations that could only develop on the basis of a broad spectrum of interactive experience whereby one's feelings and actions are affirmed or disconfirmed. Once we shift to an inter-subjective perspective, however, the intent of those actions (as we see when they are affirmed, not alienated) appears to be that of sharing what we each reciprocally apprehend about the other's mind or feeling. Recognition as affirmative response to the other may proceed along diverse avenues we shall explore later: matching the other's intentions and rhythms, empathizing with and understanding their narratives and dilemmas, witnessing their suffering and injury, acknowledging to them one's own vulnerability or wrongdoing, identifying with them in one's own mind, granting the other's dignity and common humanity, validating the rightful order of things, making space for difference and otherness.

The essential point on which recognition theory focuses is the reciprocal response to each other's minds, regardless of its specific form—the awareness of the other as subject rather than object. And this connectedness to the other as a being with an equivalent center of initiative and feeling, as expressed by Buber's (1923) terminology of I and Thou as opposed to I and It, may be its own end, a need unto itself, because without it the self cannot actually feel its full "I-ness." In this sense it is an indispensable basis for our having any good sort of life or mind at all, both condition of being and end in itself. Recognition defies the distinction between ends and means.

Recognition theory is an effort to weave together insights held by many quite different thinkers regarding the need to know and be known by other minds. As Hegel first posited, it is in this way that the conscious self comes to truly live its sense of selfhood. The need to feel one exists "inside" the other's mind is a primary psychoanalytic metaphor, through which Bion expressed from a somewhat different angle, the desire for being known. The idea of mutual recognition as the basis for intersubjectivity exceeds the concept of mutual influence, which describes a process observed from the outside and points towards the experience inside: the appreciation of being mutually affected, the shared realization of impact, "Zing, what you do to me." This powerful motivation to share experience not only for safety or some other end's sake becomes an experience of desire, something the subject "owns" as hers. It begins the moment the toddler says "I Want that" and seeks recognition through the other's desire. Desire makes us a subject, and the essential desire is to be met by the other's desire.

The distinct meaning of this desire for mutual recognition might be clarified if I express this idea from the perspective of the caregiving mother rather than the child, whose development and affect regulation she supports. The mother, as I shall argue, is ideally motivated by desire as well as her child's need. Given some measure of reciprocal responsiveness, you love what you do for the other as much as you love what the other does for you. Your love establishes the other's subjective existence for you as well as your own. Then again, as a lover, your acts form part of a circuit of desire, the Third of love, through which it arises. I would contend that the patient comes to analysis to find her *own* love as much as to be or feel loved: to be "*in*" love"—in its thirdness. Important is, as McKay (2016) has formulated, that the felt experience of mutual recognition supplies not only the bread of being understood but the roses of "us two" discovering something together, being present for and aware of knowing each other.

V.

From the beginning, the idea of mutual recognition generated controversy in the world of psychoanalysis; it became the flashpoint of a long debate. First presented developmentally, its translation into the clinical field required much work (see especially Aron, 1996). Did it mean that the analyst's subjectivity should be revealed to the patient, or that it is known implicitly whether revealed or not (Hoffman, 1983; 1998; Aron, 1996)? Or did it refer to our already integrated notions of the analyst's ("counter transference") identifications (see Gerhardt et al., 2000)? How should or do we think about mutual identification, the unconscious ways in which our minds come to mirror one another, the way our projective processes become entangled and interact? And how could the relationship between mothers and infants be seen as mutual when it is so asymmetrical; indeed, can it rightfully be said that the infant's reciprocal responsiveness means that the relationship contains mutual recognition?

I will present my view of what is at stake in this debate, but let me first interpose a preliminary move—perhaps this term, mutuality, needs to be deconstructed. That is, the binary of mutuality with its opposite, usually taken to be asymmetry, needs to be broken down or "sublated" (transcended but preserved in new form). In making a case for mutuality, I will be following Aron (1996) and elaborate how its notion is enlarged (not diminished) by the opposing term of asymmetry. That is, I will show how we can arrive at a third position that holds the opposites in tension. The beginning of reciprocity in the mother and infant relationship, with its huge disparity in capacities, already illustrates the dialectic of mutuality and asymmetry.

The idea is that even unequally matched partners can yet be reciprocating, share mutual understanding or feeling based on the intentionality of recognition—procedurally, pre-verbally as well as symbolically. Let me illustrate this point about asymmetrical interactions by previewing a central thread of this book, the giving and receiving of acknowledgment. If, for instance, I (in my capacity as analyst) offer an acknowledgment of some failure of responsiveness or of some violation of the other's rightful expectation, this giving and receiving depends upon a mutual understanding of what is intended; further, the healing action depends upon a reciprocal appreciation by the other of what I offer. Without that appreciation, the other is not genuinely feeling, sharing and integrating the acknowledgment. So acknowledgment, though unidirectional, becomes an opportunity for generating mutual recognition between different subjects, felt as such.

In this way acknowledgment and recognition may be formulated as distinct and mutually supporting actions. Or, we could say that the acknowledgment becomes an instantiation of recognition that relies on a deep reciprocal knowing what the other is about. While this principle is observable in psychoanalytic practice, it may well hold good in other relations: a child with a parent, an injured party with the one responsible for witnessing, if not for having injured. To generalize, there needs to be reciprocal affirmation of the action through which one person's experience is validated and known. That is the meta-level of the communication, which is represented as "This other person is reaching toward me, receiving my message, making it right with me—even, holding my pain in her heart." When agreement or resonance is achieved by acknowledging some failure of understanding or attunement it simultaneously halts the toggling back and forth of projection, the complementary doer–done to relation. For instance, in witnessing, This other mind now resonates with the vibration of my pain: we are together in the rhythmicity of the Third (Gobodo-Madikizela, 2013).

VI.

The argument for finding oneself by going out into the not-self and returning to a now different and altered self (marked by the alterity it has encountered) points toward the underlying movement of intersubjectivity. To realize this transformation not primarily as loss but rather as enrichment of self requires the movement between self and not-self that mirrors the more universal movement between oneness and thirdness. The other, the not-self, is the one we need in order to realize this movement. Developmentally, we need the other to share our state in order to contain and so experience excitement, joy, arousal and not merely relief from suffering. To heal psychologically, we need the other's witnessing and empathy, but also to create conditions for mutual sharing of positive affect so as to inflect even the witnessing of suffering with the opening into mutual transformation. It is necessary to encounter in the other some specific version of that same desire for self-affirmation through knowing and being known. Mutuality is necessary insofar as the self needs to give as much as it needs to receive.

Growing up and living in an acquisitive, instrumental culture, dominated by fantasies of material wealth and fears of loss, the very idea of giving to the other, surrendering to the thirdness of mutuality, is easily translated into submission and self-loss. Even psychoanalysts are prone to imagining that their patients only need be given recognition, empathy and understanding, of which they were doubtless deprived, and to miss the strength that comes from giving, being a reciprocally responsive other who can go out into the other's mind and return enriched, able to formulate their own understanding. Now more than ever, when we are poised to witness the avalanche of greed, fear, and authoritarianism in the seat of the American government, it seems to me important to realize the power generated by the position of being able to give recognition, to respond and bear witness. Regardless of whether one occupies the position of demanding or giving recognition, as we realize the interdependence of these moves we realize both sides serve to uphold universal claims for dignity, are needed to protect those who are denied dignity.

I do not therefore accept the splitting that detaches the healing of wounds or empathy for suffering from the opportunity to be recognized in expressing desire. This reciprocal interaction, jointly experienced, creates a shared Third that transforms both giver and receiver. For this reason I will contend that the mutuality of shared transformation is at the core of psychoanalysis and is fundamental to our interaction.

Thinking in these terms of the reciprocal affirmation of intent by different partners might clear the confusion generated by a common misunderstanding of recognition: misconstruing the idea of recognizing the other's subjectivity to mean that the patient "must" recognize the analyst's personal expressions of subjectivity (Orange, 2010; see Benjamin, response, 2010; see Gerhardt et al., 2000; Benjamin 2000b). As I will discuss (Chapter 3), in psychoanalytic theory recognition pertains to what makes someone's independent subjectivity qua other mind apparent. For example, the analyst's empathic acknowledgment of the patient's unique suffering becomes an opportunity for the patient's recognition that the analyst is not identical with his (feared) mental object who has failed to empathize.

The analyst who can persevere as the patient presents the part of himself that does not feel able to take in recognition or nourishment, contains the painful disbelief in her understanding, her goodness, her intention to heal. She thereby "survives destruction" in Winnicott's (1971a) famous phrase, meaning the analyst is recognized as a separate subject, an outside other. When the analyst or the mother seems to grasp the intention behind repudiating feelings or negating fantasies ("I don't need you") without retaliating or collapsing, she distinguishes herself from the manifestation of the patient's or child's fearful projections. The analyst shows she is feeling the impact and receiving the communication, without falling into the reactivity of the complementary position (or at least not staying in it). The analyst is thus distinguished from the intrapsychic object and the patient is able to separate from his fantasy of being too powerful and destructive. In this way the distinction between the intrapsychic and intersubjective reality is highlighted.

This all-important distinction, in Winnicott's terms (1971a), in which the contrast between the equally essential modes of intrapsychic and intersubjective (inner fantasy and shared external reality) is established, restores the third position in the relationship. Both partners might now share the space of thirdness based on two differentiated subjects facing each other, one of whom is trying to be responsible for much of what goes on between them. This process is the primary meaning of recognizing the analyst (other or mother) as subject.

This paradigm of recognition and destruction, inaugurated by Winnicott, became the essential platform for the more general social-philosophical point of my understanding of recognition, which differentiates it from many other thinkers (Benjamin, 1988; 1990/95). It demonstrates that liberation comes not only through *being* recognized but also *doing* the recognizing. In psychoanalytic terms, to recognize the other as an independent source of confirmation and be freed from frightening or aggressive projections—which ultimately cause one to feel monstrous, damaging or damaged—is essential to emotional liberation. This freedom involves a shift for both analyst and patient into a mutually created Third, which entails a simultaneity of recognition and acknowledgment.

Acknowledgment means that the self can own rather than dissociate—project into the not-me what it needs to contain as part-of-me—its own vulnerability or harming. Now, it can recognize the other as a separate self rather than turning her into a container for the not-me. Winnicott proposed that it is this freedom that makes room for the possibility of loving the other who has stayed present to receive the communication; you are outside, you survived, now you can be loved. *That is an enduring idea that to me seems eternally new and freshly revealed.*

VII.

What amazed me when I first discovered this argument for recognizing the other, instead of merely seeking recognition for the self, was the way it resonated with the problem of recognition as set forth by Hegel. Since Hegel's original dialectical formulation continues to underpin my version of recognition theory, it seems worth recapitulating the connection. While this philosophically central discussion of recognizing the other has been less accessible and integrated in psychoanalytic theory than in philosophy, it seems to me essentially connected to the recent psychoanalytic discussions of trauma and the Other in recent literature (see Grand & Salberg, 2017). Without it, the laudable expansion of psychoanalytic attention to gender, race, and class lacks a theoretical scaffold and may devolve into place-holding. Recognition theory, as I have formulated it, is meant to offer one possible scaffold. In addition, its deconstruction of authority relations (knowing subject, known object) is of equally crucial importance for the psychoanalytic relationship (Benjamin, 1997).

As I explained in *The Bonds of Love* (1988), Winnicott's (1971a) idea of liberation from the bind of non-recognition—the inability of the omnipotent mind to contact an outside other—shed further light on the philosophical parable of the master-slave relation as put forth by Hegel in *The Phenomenology of Spirit* (1807; see O'Neill, 1996). Or conversely, we might say that Hegel had, well before Freud's theorizing of narcissism, described the self that is trapped in omnipotence —a self without reflection by the other, lacking exactly that intersubjective relatedness without which we are psychically alone.

Hegel's analysis of dependence and independence of the Self (self-consciousness as he referred to it) could be imbricated with the psychoanalytic description of the ego that does not want to recognize the outside world, is afflicted by helplessness and dependency on those who would shape it according to their dictates. This is a text with an endless number of readings, but as I have come to think about it, Hegel at first demonstrates logically how the desire to be recognized would drive the need for mutuality, would *require* the reciprocal action of each self-aware consciousness reflecting back the other. Since the self cannot be adequately reflected back by an object, it must find another equal self to do this, meaning, a self which it can recognize in return. In effect, it must perforce recognize the other as a like subject. However, as we find in the psychoanalytic relationship, this condition is circular, as it would imply that we have *already* experienced an other who neither retaliates nor collapses.

As to Hegel, he simply states that the tension according to which each Self must give the Other recognition breaks down, and the two terms—recognizing and being recognized—are split apart. This splitting, were it not logically determined by the dialectical movement of breaking apart and reassembling in new form, would in any case appear to reflect historical truth. One Self (henceforth master) receives the recognition while the other Self (henceforth servant or slave) gives it. While there have been numerous interpretations of why Hegel thinks this must happen, we may reduce it to two essential and interconnected conditions. First, the Self finds it intolerable to bear the vulnerability of being dependent on an other subject whom he does not control, indeed who is independent and can demand the same recognition as the Self. Second, the Self is trying to master and deny the vulnerability of its organic bodily existence. If one wishes to escape dependency on the other, one must face death, that is, stake one's life and deny fear, overriding the vulnerability of the flesh. Alternatively, if one tries to escape death, one accepts the truth of one's vulnerability in exchange for enduring the servitude of dependency. So, the first choice becomes the way of the master, the second the way of bondage (slave/servant).

As I proposed in *The Bonds of Love*, following Kojeve's (1969) famous interpretation, this parable of master and slave is relevant for the intersubjective framing of psychoanalytic theory. In Freud's ego–object paradigm, the subject would be seen as the ego who strives to master the object, would ultimately renounce need for the maternal object in order to separate itself from early helplessness and dependency, that is, to become like father. As a critical analysis of the Oedipus complex reveals, mastery and independence based on repudiating passivity produces the male subject as a position of reversal: the woman/mother who was powerful and needed when one was an infant is now reduced to a devalued or denigrated maternal object. In this way, the male subject circumvents facing her as an other, as an equivalent subject. He denies dependency on the other whom he subjugates.

With this version of oedipal theory in mind, I proposed that we read the Hegelian paradigm as a commentary upon the vicious circle of gender that anchored patriarchal domination. A real break with this paradigm of domination would then require a conception of development as an intersubjective process in which differentiation is not primarily a result of repressing the love relation; but also, would not require oedipal socialization into the heterosexual complementarity of male subject, female object. An intersubjective theory of differentiation might rather take as starting point the Winnicottian move that postulates survival of the object/other as a condition of the mother's transformation into subject. Such a move would be conditional on the original male subject taking back the projection of his own helplessness and vulnerability, accepting his own relation to "nature." This means acknowledging his commonality with the maternal body that stands for mortality as well as his dependence for life on that embodied subject (Dinnerstein, 1976).

But this is only one moment of the necessary movement. The other, equally important, moment is that the one who was formerly the female object (oppressed, property), resists being consumed and reduced, asserting her separate existence; to risk her own death without taking life, without violence and reversal of the complementarity, reaching for the Third. This would be the difference the other can make. We can, I believe, adapt this paradigm of change for racial enslavement. As the complex struggle for liberation from these complementary doer–done to positions evolves, it becomes apparent how necessary it is to think in terms of a Third. This Third then can transcend reversal: not the slave denying her own vulnerability but confronting the master with his, thereby asserting mutual vulnerability and need for recognition without denying dependency.

Why is that obvious proposal not so obvious? Why is the propensity to maintain splitting in reverse so common, the obvious deconstruction of binaries so difficult? For victims to avoid the fate of power reversal, in which they re-enact the traumatizing violence they have been subject to (if only by hurting themselves), they, too, must renounce the projection of their helplessness into the other. But the internalization of the master as the image of freedom or the ideal of Power is not so readily expunged; to whom should we then address the unconscious demand for recognition and identification (see Fanon, 1967)? And how meaningful is a demand for racial or national liberation that maintains female subjugation?

In the political arena, the social demand for recognition that absorbed the master's model of denial and projection of shameful vulnerability and powerlessness—forcing those unwanted parts into the image of the degraded or subjugated Other—has often led to tragic reversals of complementarity where victims mimic former abusers. To grasp how unconscious idealization and envy of the master's permission to transgress led to victims becoming perpetrator, we must venture into the tangled vicissitudes of the doer–done to complementarity. It may sound easy in theory but in practices these states of aspiring to power and exposure to vulnerability are dissociated, the terror and shame of openly baring the weak self or harming self are so great. Keeping these states unlinked and behind the veil protects us all from pain and confusion.

In the analytic setting, working with such reversals of shame and vulnerability that are the legacy of trauma and non-recognition, of injuries not modified by the opportunity for intersubjective repair, has been our great challenge. Feeling oneself thrust in the role of seeming abuser, feeling unable to extricate oneself from being victimizer or victim, can be extremely painful for the analyst. However, analysts have also the opportunity to learn a great deal about the repetitions of the doer and done to relation, since developing intersubjective theory and making the relational turn. Intersubjective relations of acknowledgment and repair counter the intrapsychic realm of splitting and so enable us to step out of the relations of doer and done to. The point of this book is to make that learning available for both clinical and social use.

VIII.

The challenge to a psychologically oriented recognition theory was articulated by Butler (1997). Her starting point is, following Foucault, a social self whose dependency for recognition always already places it in a submissive relation to an alienating, subjugating regulatory system (see Butler, 1997). Lacking a notion of a psychological self with some inherent tendencies, it might seem that the social self could submit and sacrifice to maintain belonging without soul and body rebelling. But precisely this rebellion—in the form of hysterics' bodily resistance to the pain of self-denial in the patriarchal order—gave birth to psychoanalysis. Psychoanalysis insisted that parts of self that were denied would demand some expression, perhaps equally painful; that the process of splitting off desire for the other, the basic needs for safety and agency, always has violent repercussions. The psychoanalytic project always did and still does imply the possibility of alternative relations that articulate and transform the conflict between belonging (socially recognized identity) and recognition of desire. While Butler appears to suggest that dependency necessarily entails subjugation, Allen (2008) argues that while human beings "so crave recognition that we take whatever kind . . . we can get, even . . . capitulating to our own subordination," it does not follow that other possibilities, such as mutual recognition, do not exist (p. 84). What is important, Allen suggests, is that we see recognition as a temporal process involving break-down and restoration of tension between recognition and destruction. The temporal perspective is vital for a psychoanalytic view because in so many instances we are driven to circle back, repeat past failures in new forms, but in this way we are also opening up possibilities for repair.

Whereas those oppressive identities that offer the appearance of recognition at the price of feeling real suck us into the zone of rigid complementarities,[1] resistance and critique of those constrictions inform the successful struggles for recognition—of difference, queerness, multiplicity. These struggles have cleared considerable

1   The implications of intersubjectivity in relation to social identity or groups claiming redress for their identity are more problematic than conventional political discourse often admits, since Identity can be a form of alienating recognition even as the subject seeks to use it to secure a sense of self and belonging. In the political arena the appeals to national identity may be linked to the adulation and submission to the leader cum ego ideal elucidated by Freud (1921) as mass psychology, ideas further elaborated by post-Freudians (Adorno, 1956; Marcuse, 1962). I began (Benjamin, 1988; 1998) by trying to grasp the psychoanalytic social psychology of non-recognition, both its effects—the alienation of our powers and desires—and its origins in psychic development as interwoven with the sexual organization of social life, culminating in my intervention in the feminist debate around the nature of the subject (*Shadow of the Other*, 1988).

space for alternative social attachments in which known identities can be deconstructed and their components used as building materials for the self. Identifications that function as submission in one register, can be reconfigured in the intersubjective register of thirdness. As we shall see, the ability to play implies a relationship to difference that supersedes undifferentiated psychological relations of coercion. To be able to "stand in the spaces" as Bromberg (1998) put it, to disidentify with any one voice as "I," in Rivera's (1989) terms, depends on intersubjective relations that validate that multiplicity. The aim of maintaining social solidarity while tolerating the tension of conflicting identifications parallels the psychoanalytic process of allowing multiple self-states to exist without one negating the other. Understood in this way, recognition and appreciation for the other, or the other within, overcomes the act of appropriation; identification with the different other serves as a form of empathy that actually destabilizes the subjugating forms of social dependency that constrict what counts as intelligible, human, worthy.

This emphasis on psychological difference and multiplicity[2] points us toward the crucial distinction between recognition theory rooted in a psychoanalytic perspective and one that derives from the sphere of the political. Questioning the common understanding of offering political recognition to the other as affirmation of social identity, Oliver (2001) articulated the problem of regarding the other as if her subjectivity did not already exist apart from the subject's dubious power to confer recognition upon it. The other is not in actual fact the subject's projection, however he may relate to her as if she were. With a different point of departure, Markell's (2003) work also points to the problem of projection. He traces the failure of the demand for recognition to conceptually include the master subject's acknowledgment of the unbearable weakness within himself that *he* has been denying, that is, the vulnerability that the master projectively offloads. Lacking is not merely the master's recognition of the slave as equal but a kind of self-knowledge, an acknowledgment of something about himself: the suffering heretofore imposed upon/admitted only by the slave. But if this is so, then rectification would demand a further step beyond the master taking on board some weakness he could not previously bear. This proposition is illustrated by Markell, following Cavell, with reference to King Lear's suffering and disorientation as a consequence of his repudiation of Cordelia, and his final acknowledgment of his dependency to her. We should note that intersubjective repair demands performing an action *directed toward* the other in which acknowledging the violence of projecting weakness must also include that he is the cause of the other's suffering.

To these considerations of recognition I would add: If the other is the one who is meant to be liberated by this admission of responsibility, and who may have rightly demanded it, doesn't it follow that acknowledgment cannot be sundered

---

2   We have seen how the play with identities in the last decades have allowed the emergence of a vision of a lawful world in which there is greater trust in "pussies" of different stripes.

from recognition? Doesn't such acknowledgment also simultaneously constitute a recognition of the other's worthiness at the same time as an admission of the subject's unworthy action? When the movement of this transforming action from self-knowledge to acknowledgment becomes *mutual* knowledge of harm and vulnerability, then recognition and acknowledgment together form the two moments constituting the Third that holds this knowledge.

If one can admit having denied the other's humanity without the complementary reversal in which now one's self must take up the position of being unworthy to live, the Third has been reached. True remorse takes us to the third position beyond "Only one can live." The splitting has been overcome of the two moments in the dialectic: the double move in which the master acknowledges his vulnerability and the slave asserts the demand to be treated with recognition of dignity. Moving from projection of vulnerability to acknowledgment of what lies within further includes recognition of the other's independent existence and the harm to which projection led. This, in turn, evokes an internal confrontation with the self's own aggrandizement, even monstrousness, and the possibility of remorse rather than further aggression, as Lear reveals. However, rereading the story through Cordelia we might argue that as the other attains agency her emergence as subject is what destabilizes and transforms their relation.[3]

The foregoing analysis of moving out of dissociation into connection with the reality of the other's mind presumes the dual viewpoints of intrapsychic and intersubjective theory. When there is no possibility of intersubjective repair—when the figure of authority refuses acknowledgment or fears loss of power—the self turns to intrapsychic repair of the internal object instead. When mutual dependency cannot be negotiated, the other must be reduced to intrapsychic object of fantasy, onto whom the subject splits off unwanted weakness. Theoretically, the need is to distinguish such objects of projection from the real other. This move, as we have already seen, is central to the survival of destruction and overcoming of doer–done to relations. That is, the denial of humanity to the other is tantamount to the erasure of intersubjectivity, understood here as the ineluctable fact of mutual dependency on equally human others. The inability to embrace recognition within an interactive system of thirdness leaves the subject alone in a monadic world without intersubjective orientation.

The acceptance of vulnerability and wish to be liberated from the suffering of living without a surviving other of recognition assumes an actual, interpersonal

---

3   Writing as feminists in the Second Wave of the 70s primarily white women took up position as the Other of male domination, destabilizing the opposition of immanence and transcendence, the idea of universal subject ala de Beauvoir. But no sooner had they appropriated subjectivity than they switched roles, now in the position of subject obliged to recognize the identity of the racialized Other. These confounding historical positions collided in confusing ways, now taken up in discussions of "intersectionality." Thus we are constantly rereading and indeed rewriting history—the more this is done in the spirit of repair rather than blame, the more victimhood can be replaced by agency.

or at least symbolic process of repair. The shift out of disconnection and dissociation requires acknowledgment by the subject of his *own* suffering incurred by this loss of the other. In turn, this disconnection separates us from a greater source of inspiration and linking—of self with other, mind with heart, shared suffering in the past and compassionate healing in our present action and imagined future. What I have elsewhere referred to as the movement of "many into one" (Benjamin, 2005). As I conclude this book, I will return to reflecting on how this process appears in the analytic relationship and witnessing dialogues in relation to traumatic memory and historical violence; how we move from the position of "failed witness" or bystander to acknowledging witness and how we become able to experience our own vulnerable humanity in a different way when we recognize the other's, through this action coming closer to realizing the sense of our interconnectedness and responsibility for one another.

In closing, let me say that writing these words in early 2017, at a moment when our political and social world is upended, the ability to recognize others and accept our interdependence has become a matter of greater urgency. It is my hope that as we are called upon to actively resist the infliction of harm, indeed resist the attempt to take our whole society into the mode of doer and done to, there will be some good use put to these efforts to grasp how we may step out of that complementarity into the position of the Third, from one living at the expense of the other into shared, responsible living together. At the moment, we are witnessing millions of people joining together with an inspiring will to resist and struggle against lawlessness without being drawn into violence or lapsing into despair. May this will prevail.

Chapter 1

Beyond doer and done to

An intersubjective view of thirdness

Blame partial
Blame yourself
(Thirdness moves beyond

involved in a process bigger than either of us.

This chapter is the second version of a paper originally written for a volume on the concept of the Third for Psychoanalytic Quarterly, *then rewritten for* Relational Psychoanalysis Volume IV *(Aron & Harris, 2011). It emerged from developing an idea I had initially when thinking about Ghent's (1990) concept of surrender, written for a conference honoring his work in 2000. I began originally to think of the Third as related to an original sense of harmony that exists both in the world and self, an idea one might find in neo-Platonic mysticism (see Benjamin, 2005). But I had already begun to consider with Aron (Aron & Benjamin, 1999) how the shared, intersubjective Third could be differentiated from that of more classical theories in which the Third appears as something in the mind of the analyst alone. It represented an effort to think through the idea of recognition from the ground up in terms of an orientation to a principle, a relationship, or even love, which we refer to in order to step out of the doer done to complementarity. I realized, as I wrote in a separate Afterword to the reprinted version, that my thinking about the Third in this way replicated an idea of Kierkegaard, (brought to my attention by Hoffman in her 2010 book): surrender to the Third, which "is love itself" can be maintained even when the other fails, as the one who remains committed can hold onto the Third "and then the break has no power over him" (Kierkgaard cited in Hoffman, 2010, p. 204). The essence of the third position is that we use it to step out of complementary power relations in which we might feel done to by keeping faith with the intention of our connection. In this paper I tried to ground analytic work based on the intersubjective view of two participating subjectivities by understanding the developmental conditions of thirdness, both the early form of thirdness at the implicit level involving union experiences and accommodation, here called the rhythmic Third, as well as later explicit, symbolic forms of thirdness that recognize one's own and others' distinct perceptions, intentions or feelings, the differentiating Third.*[1] *Here, in this first*

---

[1] Because readers found my terminology in previous works confusing, I have adapted this terminology with the help of Aron's elaboration of my work. Previously I referred to *the One in the Third and the Third in the One.* Aron suggested, based on my discussion (Benjamin, 1998) of Sander, using the term *rhythmic Third* for the former, and I have introduced the term *the differentiating Third* to rename the latter.

foray, I tried to show how clinically, the concept of a co-created or shared intersubjective thirdness helps to elucidate the breakdown into the twoness of complementarity in impasses and enactments and suggest how recognition is restored through surrender. This includes accepting moments of disruption and the need to acknowledge them to the patient as a surrender to "what is."

The introduction of the idea of intersubjectivity into psychoanalysis has many important consequences and has been understood in a variety of ways. The position I will develop in this paper defines intersubjectivity in terms of a relationship of mutual recognition—a relation in which each person experiences the other as a "like subject," another mind who can be "felt with" yet has a distinct, separate center of feeling and perception. The antecedents of my perspective on inter-subjectivity lie on the one hand with Hegel (Hegel, 1807; Kojève, 1969), and on the other with the developmentally oriented thinkers Winnicott (1971b) and Stern (1985)—quite different in their own ways—who try to specify the process by which we become able to grasp the other as having a separate yet similar mind.

   In contrast to the notion of the intersubjective as a "system of reciprocal mutual influence"—referring to "any psychological field formed by interacting worlds of experience" (Stolorow & Atwood, 1992, p. 3)—adumbrated by intersubjective systems theorists Stolorow, Atwood, and Orange (Orange, Atwood & Stolorow, 1997),[2] I emphasize, both developmentally and clinically, how we actually come to the felt experience of the other as a separate yet connected being with whom we are acting reciprocally. How do we get a sense that "there are other minds out there" (see Stern, 1985)?

   In highlighting this phenomenological experience of other minds, I—like other intersubjective critics of Freud's Cartesianism—emphasize the reciprocal, mutually influencing quality of interaction between subjects, the confusing traffic of two-way streets (Benjamin, 1977, 1988). But this theoretical recognition of

2   Stolorow and Atwood (1992) point out that they coined the term *intersubjective* indepen-
     dently and do not think of it as presupposing a developmental attainment, as Stern (1985)
     does. I (Benjamin, 1977; 1978) have made use of the term as introduced into philosophy
     by Habermas (1968), and then carried forward into psychology by Trevarthen (1977; 1980),
     in order to focus on the exchange between different minds. Like Stern, I consider the
     recognition of other minds (the other's subjectivity) to be a crucial developmental
     attainment. Unlike Stern, however, I (Benjamin, 1988) have considered all aspects of
     co-creating interaction with the other, from early mutual gazing to conflicts around
     recognition, as part of the trajectory of intersubjective development. The major difference
     between the theorizing of Orange, Atwood and Stolorow (1997) and my own is not, as
     they believe (see Stolorow, Atwood & Orange, 2002; Orange, 2010), that I think the analyst
     should focus clinically on helping the patient to recognize the analyst's (or other's)
     subjectivity at the expense of the patient's own. It is rather that I see such engagement in
     reciprocal recognition of the other as growing naturally out of the experience of being
     recognized by the other, as a crucial component of attachment responses that require mutual
     regulation and attunement, and, therefore, as ultimately a pleasure and not merely a chore
     (Benjamin, 2010).

we want to recognize as naturally as we want to be recognized

intersubjective — two people become a unit - influencing one another

intersubjective influence should not blind us to the power of actual psychic experience, which all too often is that of the one-way street—in which we feel as if one person is the doer, the other done to. One person is subject, the other object— as our theory of object relations all too readily portrays. To recognize that the object of our feelings, needs, actions and thoughts is actually another subject, an equivalent center of being (Benjamin, 1988; 1995b), is the real difficulty.

The place of the Third

To the degree that we ever manage to grasp two-way directionality, we do so only from the place of the *Third*, a vantage point outside the two.[3] However, the inter-subjective position that I refer to as *thirdness* consists of more than this vantage point of observation. The concept of the Third means a wide variety of things to different thinkers, and has been used to refer to the profession, the community, the theory one works with—anything one holds in mind that creates another point of reference outside the dyad (Britton, 1988; Aron, 1999; Crastnopol, 1999). My interest is not in which "thing" we use, but in the process of creating thirdness— that is, in how we build relational systems and how we develop the intersubjective capacities for such co-creation. I think in terms of thirdness as a quality or experi-ence of intersubjective relatedness that has as its correlate a certain kind of internal mental space; it is closely related to Winnicott's idea of potential or transitional space. One of the first relational formulations of thirdness was Pizer's (1998) idea of negotiation, originally formulated in 1990, in which analyst and patient each build, as in a squiggle drawing, a construction of their separate experiences together. Pizer analyzed transference not in terms of static, projective contents, but as an inter-subjective process: "No, you can't make this of me, but you can make that of me."

Thus, I consider it crucial not to reify the Third, but to consider it primarily as a principle, function, or relationship (as in Ogden's (1994) view), rather than as a "thing" in the way that theory or rules of technique are things. My aim is to distinguish it from superego maxims or ideals that the analyst holds onto with her ego, often clutching them as a drowning person clutches a straw. For in the space of thirdness, we are not *holding onto* a Third; we are, in Ghent's (1990) felicitous usage, surrendering to it.[4]

Elaborating this idea, we might say that the Third is that to which we surrender, and thirdness is the intersubjective mental space that facilitates or results from surrender. In my thinking, the term *surrender* refers to a certain letting go of the

---

3   I am greatly indebted to Aron with whom I formulated important portions of this paper and descriptions of the Third in a jointly authored paper (Aron & Benjamin, 1999); Aron emphasizes the observing function, but modified by identification, which he has formulated more recently in Aron (2006).

4   Ghent's work on surrender was the inspiration for my first formulations of some of these thoughts, which were presented at a conference in his honor sponsored by New York University Postdoctoral Psychology Program, May 2000.

Rythmic third — not developmental

self, and thus also implies the ability to take in the other's point of view or reality. Thus, surrender refers us to recognition—being able to sustain connectedness to the other's mind while accepting his separateness and difference. Surrender implies freedom from any intent to control or coerce.

Ghent's essay articulated a distinction between surrender and its ever-ready look-alike, submission. The crucial point was that surrender is not *to someone*. From this point follows a distinction between *giving in* or *over* to someone, an idealized person or thing, and letting go into *being with* them. I take this to mean that surrender requires a Third, that we follow some principle or process that mediates between self and other.

Whereas in Ghent's seminal essay, surrender was considered primarily as something the patient needs to do, my aim is to consider, above all, the analyst's surrender. I wish to see how we facilitate our own and the patient's surrender by consciously working to build a shared Third—or, to put it differently, how our recognition of mutual influence allows us to create thirdness together. Thus, I expand Ghent's contrast between submission and surrender to formulate a distinction between complementarity and thirdness, an orientation to a Third that mediates "I and Thou."

Complementarity: doer and done to

Considering the causes and remedies for the breakdown of recognition (Benjamin, 1988), and the way in which breakdown and renewal alternate in the psychoanalytic process (Benjamin, 1988), led me to formulate the contrast between the twoness of complementarity and the potential space of thirdness. In the complementary structure, dependency becomes coercive; and indeed, coercive dependence that draws each into the orbit of the other's escalating reactivity is a salient characteristic of the impasse (Mendelsohn, 2003). Conflict cannot be processed, observed, held, mediated, or played with. Instead, it emerges at the procedural level as an unresolved opposition between us, even tit for tat, based on each partner's use of splitting.

In my view, theories of splitting—for instance, the idea of the paranoid-schizoid position (Klein, 1946; 1952)—though essential, do not address this intersubjective dynamic of the two-person relationship and its crucial manifestations at the level of procedural interaction. The idea of complementary relations (Benjamin, 1988; 1998) aims to describe those push-me/pull-you, doer/done-to dynamics that we find in most impasses, which generally appear to be one-way—that is, each person feels *done to*, and not like an agent helping to shape a co-created reality. The question of how to get out of complementary twoness, which is the formal or structural pattern of all impasses between two partners, is where intersubjective theory finds its real challenge. Racker (1968) was, I believe, the first to identify this phenomenon as complementarity, formulating it in contrast to concordance in the countertransference. Symington (1983) first described this as an interlocking, dyadic pattern, a corporate entity based on the meeting of analyst's and patient's superegos.

Ogden (1994) developed his own perspective on this structural pattern in the notion of the *subjugating Third*. He used the term *analytic Third* differently than I do, to denote the relationship as that of an other to both selves, an entity created by the two participants in the dyad, a kind of co-created subject-object. This pattern or relational dynamic, which appears to form outside our conscious will, can be experienced either as a vehicle of recognition or something from which we cannot extricate ourselves. Taking on a life of its own, this negative of the Third may be carefully attuned, like the chase-and-dodge pattern between mother and infant. From my point of view, it is somewhat confusing to call this a Third because, rather than creating space, it sucks it up. With this negative of the Third (perhaps it could be called "the negative Third"), there is an erasure of the in-between—an inverse mirror relation, a complementary dyad concealing an unconscious symmetry.

Symmetry is a crucial part of what unites the pair in complementarity, generating the takes-one-to-know-one recognition feature of the doer/done-to relation (Benjamin, 1998). In effect, it builds on the deep structure of mirroring and affective matching that operate—largely procedurally and out of awareness—in any dyad, as when both partners glare at each other or interrupt in unison. As we pay more attention to this procedural level of interaction we come to discern the underlying symmetry that characterizes the apparent opposition of power relations: each feels unable to gain the other's recognition, and each feels in the other's power. Or, as Davies (2004; see also Davies & Frawley, 1994) has powerfully illustrated, each feels the other to be the abuser-seducer; each perceives the other as "doing to me."

It is as if the essence of complementary relations—the relation of twoness—is that there appear to be only two choices: either submission or resistance to the other's demand, as Ogden put it (1994). Characteristically, in complementary relations, each partner feels that her perspective on how this is happening is the only right one (Hoffman, 2002)—or at least that the two are irreconcilable, as in "Either I'm crazy or you are." "If what you say is true, I must be very wrong—perhaps shamefully wrong, in the sense that everyone can see what is wrong with me, and I don't know what it is and can't stop it" (see Russell, 1998).

As clinicians, when we are caught in such interactions, we may tell ourselves that some reciprocal dynamic is at work, although we may actually be full of self-blame. In such cases, our apparent acceptance of responsibility fails to truly help in extricating us from the feeling that the other person is controlling us, or leaving us no option except to be either reactive or impotent. Attributing blame to the self actually weakens one's sense of being a responsible agent.

In the doer/done-to mode, being the one who is actively hurtful feels involuntary, a position of helplessness. In any true sense of the word, our sense of self as subject is eviscerated when we are with our "victim," who is also experienced as a victimizing object. An important relational idea for resolving impasses is that the recovery of subjectivity requires the recognition of our own participation. Crucially, this usually involves surrendering our resistance to responsibility, a resistance arising from reactivity to blame. When we as analysts resist the inevitability of hurting the other—when we dissociate bumping into their bruises or jabbing them while stitching them up, and, of course, when we deny locking into their projective processes with the unfailing accuracy of our own—we are bound to get stuck in complementary twoness.

Once we have deeply accepted our own contribution—and its inevitability—the fact of two-way participation becomes a vivid experience, something we can understand and use to feel less helpless and more effective. In this sense, we surrender to the principle of reciprocal influence in interaction, which makes possible both responsible action and freely given recognition. This action is what allows the outside, different other to come into view (Winnicott, 1971a). It opens the space of thirdness, enabling us to negotiate differences and to connect. The experience of surviving breakdown into complementarity, or twoness, and subsequently of communicating and restoring dialogue—each person (not just the analyst) surviving for the other—is crucial to therapeutic action. This principle of rupture and repair (Tronick, 1989) has become essential to our thinking. From it emerges a more advanced form of thirdness, based on a sense of shared communication about reality that tolerates or embraces difference, one which is interpersonally realized as both partners feel freer to think about and comment on themselves and each other.

The idea of the Third

Initially, the idea of the Third passed in to psychoanalysis through Lacan (1975), whose view of intersubjectivity derived from Hegel's theory of recognition and its popularization by the French Hegelian writer Kojève (1969). Lacan, as can best be seen in Book I of his seminars, saw the Third as that which keeps the relationship between two persons from collapsing. This collapse can take the form of merger (oneness), eliminating difference, or of a twoness that splits the differences—the polarized opposition of the power struggle. Lacan thought that the intersubjective Third was constituted by recognition through speech, which allows a difference of viewpoints and of interests, saving us from the kill-or-be-killed power struggle in which there is only one right way.

In many analytic writings, theory or interpretation is seen as the symbolic father with whom the mother analyst has intercourse (Britton, 1988; Feldman, 1997). Not only in Lacanian theory, but also in Kleinian, this may lead to a privileging of the analyst's relation to the Third as theory and of the analyst's authority as knower (despite Lacan's warning against seeing the analyst as the one supposed to know), as well as to an overemphasis on the oedipal content of the Third. Unfortunately, Lacan's oedipal view equated the Third with the father (Benjamin, 1995c), contending that the father's "no," his prohibition or "castration," constitutes the symbolic Third (Lacan, 1977). Lacan equated the distinction between thirdness and twoness with the division between a paternal *symbolic*, or law, and a maternal *imaginary*. The paternal Third in the mother's mind opens up the sane world of symbolic thirdness (Lacan, 1977).

I agree that in some cases we might speak of someone's letting go and accepting the full blow of the reality that mother has her own desire and has chosen father, and this might indeed constitute one kind of surrender to the Third (Kristeva, 1987). I respect Britton's (1988; 1998) idea, and its adaptation by Aron (1995), that the triangular relation of a child and two others (not necessarily father and mother) organizes the intersubjective position of one subject who observes the other two in interaction. But unless there is already space in the dyad, unless the third person is also dyadically connected to the child, he cannot function as a true Third. He becomes a persecutory invader, rather than a representative of symbolic functioning, as well as a figure of identification and an other whom mother and child both love and share.

The only usable Third, by definition, is one that is **shared**. Thus, I contend that thirdness is not literally instituted by a father (or other) as the third person; it cannot originate in the Freudian oedipal relation in which the father appears as prohibitor and castrator. And, most crucially, the mother or primary parent must create that space by being able to hold in tension her subjectivity/desire/awareness and the needs of the child. I will say more about this form of maternal awareness as a form of subjectivity that helps to create a different relation between two subjects with different needs.

The problem of oneness

The issue of maternal subjectivity, as we have known for some time, is relevant to critiquing developmental theories that postulate an initial state of oneness between mother and baby (Benjamin, 1995c). A fascinating point can be found in Lacan's (1975) critique of object relations theory. Regarding Balint's idea of primary love, Lacan objected that, if the intersubjective Third were not there from the beginning, if the mother-baby couple were simply a relation of oneness, then mother could nurse unstintingly in total identification with baby, but there would then be nothing to stop her, when she was starving, from turning the tables and eating the baby.[5]

Thus, the child is actually safeguarded by the parental ability to maintain aspects of subjectivity, enabling her to suspend her own need in favor of the child's immediate need without obliterating the difference between *I* and *thou* (Buber, 1923). In a related vein, Slochower (1996) argues that we must consciously bear the knowledge of pain in giving over to the patient, who cannot bear our subjectivity.

This ability to maintain internal awareness, to sustain the tension of difference between my needs and yours while still being attuned to you, forms the basis of the *differentiating Third*—the interactive principle that incarnates recognition and respect for the other's common humanity without submission or control. This

---

5   Shockingly for us today, Lacan (1975) alleged that Alice Balint portrayed certain aborigines as doing just that.

differentiating Third is also the basis of the *moral Third*—the principle whereby we create relationships in accord with ethical values—and the *symbolic thirdness* which includes narration, self-reflection and observation of self and other. The *differentiating Third* is analogous to the ability to project the child's future development (in other words, her independence as a separate center of initiative), which Loewald (1951) considers a parental function in his famous paper on therapeutic action. The sustained tension of difference helps create the explicit symbolic level of thirdness in which we recognize others and ourselves as having distinct intentions or feelings, separate centers of initiative and perception. This *differentiating Third* is exemplified by the mother's ability to maintain awareness that the distressed child's pain (e.g., over separation) will pass, alongside her empathy with that pain; that is, she is able to hold the tension between her perspectvive and her child's, her identification with him and the adult's observational function. This mental space of thirdness in the caretaker must, I believe, in some way be palpable to the child. As a function, in both its symbolic and soothing aspects, it can be recognized and identified with, then made use of by the child or patient.

The analyst is only able to soothe—that is, help regulate the patient's arousal level—to the extent that she is maintaining this position of thirdness (not overwhelmed by identification with the patient's state, in the sense understood by the theory of projective identification). In this sense, oneness needs to be modified by thirdness. However, this thirdness needs to be close and accessible enough, conveying a sense of a shared potential to the patient, so that the analyst is not giving empathy from a position of pure complementarity (the one who knows, heals, remains in charge). Otherwise, the patient will feel that because of what the analyst has given him, the analyst owns him; in other words, the analyst can "eat," that is shape, him in return. The patient will feel he must suppress his differences, spare the analyst, participate in pseudomutuality or react with envious defiance of the analyst's power. Lacking the sense of a shared differentiating Third, the patient has nothing to give back, no impact or insight that will change the analyst.

The flip side of this absence of thirdness is that the analyst, like a mother, may feel that her separate aims, her being a person with her own needs, will "kill" the patient. She then cannot distinguish between when she is holding the frame in a way that is conducive to the patient's growth and when she is being hurtful to the patient. How can she then bear in mind the patient's need to safely depend on her, and yet extricate herself from feeling that she must choose between the patient's needs and her own? Such a conflict may occur when an anxious patient repeatedly calls on weekends, or when the analyst goes away.

Clinical vignette I: Rob

Let me illustrate the dynamic that is instituted when the patient's world is organized by the choice between submitting to being eaten by or "killing" the other.

Rob, a patient in his forties, grew up as his mother's favorite, the one who existed to fulfil her expectations, her perfectionist demands, her unfulfilled ambition—in short, to live for her desire. Rob married a woman who is committed to being a perfect, self-sacrificing mother, but who refuses sex; thus, Rob can never fulfil his own desire as a separate person, nor can the couple come together as two bodies in the oneness of attunement.

Rob forms a deeply passionate attachment to a woman at his work, and while considering leaving his wife, takes his own apartment. But his wife demands that he swear on the Bible that he will not contact this woman for 6 weeks while he is considering the situation; otherwise, she will never take him back. Rob has submitted to this demand, but is confused. In effect, he does not know a real Third and cannot distinguish a moral principle from a power move. He feels bound to his promise, but also coerced, and at the same time frightened of losing either his wife or his lover. He tells his analyst he feels suicidal.

At this juncture, Rob's analyst, a candidate in supervision, is gripped with terrible urgency as well, feeling that she must protect and save her patient. But she is about to leave for a long-planned week's vacation and finds herself fearing that her leaving might kill the patient. Separation means murder. She feels divided: coerced, but bound to her patient, deeply concerned and afraid to leave, but aware she is caught in an enactment. She cannot get to that feeling of the mother who knows her baby's distress will pass. She wants to be the good mother, available and healing, but can find no way to do this without complying in some way with Rob's notion that he can only stand alone by abjuring all dependency. She will be coerced by Rob as he is by his wife.

Patient and analyst are thus replaying the relationship in which the child must submit to the mother who devours; yet the mother who leaves destroys the child. The Third here is perverted, turned from a commitment to truth or freely agreed-upon shared principle (*moral Third*) such as "We need to give our marriage a chance," into a promise extracted, "Give in to me or else." The wife threatens the patient that he will go to hell for leaving her, thus giving expression to a moral world in which goodness/God is opposed to freedom, where freedom is only possible in a world of moral chaos ruled by the devil. The perversion of the moral Third accompanies the kill-or-be-killed complementarity and marks the absence of recognition of the other's separateness, the space that permits desire, the acceptance of loss.

In consultation, the analyst realizes she must bear her guilt for wanting to be separate and to have her own life, just as the patient must bear his. She has to find a way to distinguish between her deep empathy with the patient's fear of abandonment, on the one hand, and submission to him in his urgent, extracting behavior, his demand that she give her life, on the other. In the observational position provided by supervision, it becomes clearer how the interaction is informed by the belief that separating and having one's own independent subjectivity and desire are tantamount to killing, while staying means letting oneself be killed.

The analyst is inspired in the following hour to find a way to talk to Rob about how she has to bear the guilt of leaving him, as he must bear his own guilt. This dispels the sense of do-or-die urgency in the session, the intense twoness in which someone must do wrong, or hurt or destroy the other.

The one in the Third

One of the important questions I want to address here is how we think about the way human beings actually develop this differentiating Third. Here I part company with Lacan (1975). The deeper problem with the oedipal view of the father as representative of the Third is that it misses the early origins of the Third in the maternal dyad. Lacan tells us that the thirdness of speech is an antidote to murder, to "your reality" versus "my reality," but his idea of speech misses the first part of the conversation. This is the part that baby watchers have made an indelible part of our thinking. In my view of thirdness, recognition is not first constituted by verbal speech; rather, it begins with the early nonverbal experience of sharing a pattern, a dance, with another person. I (Benjamin, 2002) have therefore proposed a nascent, energetic form of the Third—as distinct from the one in the mother's mind. It is present in the earliest exchange of gestures between mother and child, in the relationship that has been called *oneness*. I consider this early exchange to be a form of thirdness, and suggest that we use the term *rhythmic Third* for the principle of affective attunement and accommodation to share patterning that informs such exchanges. (I previously called "the One in the Third," which meant that part of the Third that is constituted by our felt experience of being one with the other.)

For the observing, critical functions of the differentiating Third to actually work as a true Third—rather than as a set of perverse or persecutory demands, as we saw in the case of Rob—requires integration of the capacity for accommodation/ attunement to a mutually created set of expectations. The primal form this accommodation assumes is the creation of, alignment with, and repair of patterns, the participation in connections based on affect resonance. Sander (2002), in his discussion of infancy research, calls this resonance *rhythmicity*, which he considers one of the two fundamental principles of all human interaction (the other being specificity). Hence the name *rhythmic Third* is inspired by his work. Rhythmic experiences help constitute the capacity for thirdness, and rhythmicity may be seen as a metaphor for the model principle of lawfulness underlying the creation of shared patterns. Rhythm constitutes the basis for coherence in inter-action between persons, as well as coordination between the internal parts of the organism.

Sander (2002) illustrated the value of specific recognition and of accommo-dation by studying how neonates who were fed on demand adapted more rapidly to the circadian rhythm than those fed on schedule. When the significant other is a recognizing one who surrenders to the rhythm of the baby, a co-created rhythm can begin to evolve. As the caregiver accommodates, so does the baby. The basis for this mutual accommodation is probably the inbuilt tendency to respond symmetrically, to match and mirror; in effect, the baby matches the mother's matching, much as one person's letting go releases the other.

This might be seen as the beginning of interaction in accord with the principle of mutual accommodation, which entails not imitation, but a hard-wired pull to get the two organisms into alignment, to mirror, match, or be in sync. Sander's study showed that once such a coherent, dyadic system gets going, it seems to move naturally in the direction of orienting to a deeper law of reality—in this case, the law of night and day. In using this notion of lawfulness, I am trying to capture, at least metaphorically, the harmonic or musical dimension of the Third in its transpersonal or energetic aspect (Knoblauch, 2000). I have also referred to it as the *energetic Third.*

Again, this aspect of lawfulness was missed by oedipal theory, which privileges law as boundary, prohibition and separation, thus frequently missing the element of symmetry or harmony in lawfulness. Such theorizing fails to grasp the origins of the Third in the nascent or primordial experience that has been called oneness, union, resonance—but really consists of two beings aligning to a third pattern. Research on mother—infant face-to-face play (Beebe & Lachmann, 1994) shows how adult and infant align with a third, establishing a co-created rhythm that is not reducible to a model of action-reaction, with one active and the other passive or one leading and the other following. Action-reaction characterizes our experience of complementary twoness, the one-way direction; by contrast, a *shared Third* is experienced as a cooperative endeavour.

As I have stated previously (Benjamin, 1999; 2002), the thirdness of attuned play resembles musical improvisation, in which both partners follow a structure or pattern that both of them simultaneously create and surrender to, a structure enhanced by our capacity to receive and transmit at the same time in nonverbal interaction. The co-created Third has the transitional quality of being both invented and discovered. To the question of "Who created this pattern, you or I?," the paradoxical answer is "Both and neither."

I suggest that, as with early rhythms of sleeping and nursing, it is initially the adult's accommodation that permits the creation of an organized system with a rhythm of its own, marked by a quality of lawfulness and attunement to some deeper structure—"the groove." In "intersubjectivity proper," that is, by the age of ten months, the partners' alignment—as Stern (1985) proposed—becomes a "direct subject in its own right" (Beebe et al., 2003b). In other words the quality of our mutual recognition, our thirdness, becomes the source of pleasure or despair. The basis for appreciating this *intention* to align and to accommodate seems to lie in our "mirror-neurons" (Gallese, 2009; Ammanti & Gallese, 2014). Beebe and Lachmann (1994; 2002) have described how, in performing the actions of the other, we replicate their intentions within ourselves—thus, in the deepest sense, we learn to accommodate to accommodation itself (we fall in love with love).

The *shared Third*

If we grasp the creation of thirdness as an intersubjective process that is constituted in early, presymbolic experiences of accommodation, mutuality, and the
intention to recognize and be recognized by the other, we can understand how
important it is to think in terms of building a shared Third. In shifting to an
intersubjective concept of the Third, we ground a very different view of the clinical
process from the one espoused by those who use the concept of the Third to refer
to observing capacities and the analyst's relation to his own theory or thinking.

Contemporary Kleinians view the Third as an oedipal construct, an observing
function, conceiving the analyst's Third as a relation to theory rather than a shared,
co-created experience with the patient. Britton (1988; 1998) theorized the Third
in terms of the oedipal link between the parents, explaining that the patient has
difficulty tolerating the Third as an observational stance taken by the analyst
because theory represents the father in the analyst's mind. The father, with whom
the analyst is mentally conversing—actually having intercourse—intrudes on an
already shaky mother-child dyad. Indeed, one patient yelled at Britton, "Stop that
fucking thinking!"

In discussing Britton's approach, Aron (Aron & Benjamin, 1999) pointed out
that his description of how he worked with the patient shows a modulation of
responses, an attunement that accords with the notion of creating the identificatory
aspect of the rhythmic Third. The safe shelter that Britton (1998) thinks the patient
must find in the analyst's mind may rely on the analyst's differentiating Third,
the connection to an observing position outside the dyad. But it is experienced by
the patient as the accommodating asymmetry of the mother (who also has a
differentiating Third) with her baby, a point I shall return to when I consider how
the two thirds are interrelated. For now my point is that this accommodation allows
or invites the patient into a shared rhythmic Third based primarily on his need for
affect attunement and recognition.

In seeing the Third as essentially an intersubjective co-creation, the analyst
offers an alternative to the asymmetrical complementarity of knower and known,
giver and given to. *By contrast, when the analyst sees the Third as something the
analyst relates to internally, the central couple may become the one the patient
is excluded from, rather than the one that analyst and patient build together.*
I suggest that there is an iatrogenic component to the view of the Third as
something the patient attacks because she feels excluded. It inheres in the view
of the Third as *the other person or theory*—although I take Britton's point that
because of the lack of a good maternal container, the analyst's relation to an other
may symbolize, or may even feel like, a threat to the patient's connection.

But I think that, most frequently, the other with whom the analyst is conversing
may be another part of the patient, the co-parent or developed aspect of the patient
in contrast to the child part (Pizer, 2002)—the adult part that has often collaborated
and joined the analyst and his thinking. As the more traumatized, abandoned, or
hated parts of the self-arise, this collaborator is experienced by the betrayed child

as a sellout, a "good-girl" or "good-boy" false self, who must be repudiated along with the part of the analyst whom the patient loves. Thus creating a shared Third requires constant attention to the multiplicity of our part selves.

An example from the literature

The effects of the usage of the Third as an observing function from which the patient feels excluded, and therefore attacks, are especially well illustrated in a description of impasse by Feldman (1993). He described a case in which the patient was speaking of an incident from childhood in which he had bought his mother a tub of ice cream for her birthday, choosing his own favorite flavor:

> When he offered it to her, she said she supposed he expected her to give him some of it. He saw it as an example of the way she never wholeheartedly welcomed what he did for her and always distrusted his motives.
>
> (p. 321)

Feldman apparently did not investigate what in that moment might have caused the patient to repeat a story that implied his mother "habitually responded . . . *without thinking, and without giving any space to what he himself was thinking or feeling*" (p. 323, italics in original). Feldman argued that the patient's motive was to regain reassurance, to reestablish his psychic equilibrium—seen as non-analytic needs—and that, when the patient failed to receive reassurance, he needed to emphasize how hurtful the episode had been. Feldman noted that the patient withdrew, feeling hurt and angry. I would speculate that the patient was trying to communicate something (for instance the shame produced by the rejection of his need for soothing) that the analyst had missed in assuming that he already understood.

What the analyst understood and proposed to the patient was that the patient could not tolerate the mother's having her own independent observations (much as he, the analyst, felt not allowed to have them; note the mirror effect here). The mother was instead thinking about her son in her own way by using her connection to an internal Third. Feldman maintained that he neither "fit in with" nor criticized the patient, but rather showed that he had been able to maintain, under pressure, his own capacity for observing and his way of thinking, and this, he believed, was primarily what disturbed the patient. The patient had "sometimes been able to acknowledge he hates being aware that I am thinking for myself" (p. 324). As is symptomatic of complementary breakdown, Feldman found himself unable to maintain his own thinking except by resisting "the pressure to enact a benign tolerant relationship" (p. 325) or to otherwise fit in—in other words, to soothe and regulate the patient.

It is notable that Feldman was insightful in recognizing that insisting on "the version of his own role that the analyst finds reassuring may put pressure on the patient to accept a view of himself that he finds intolerable" (p. 326). Feldman accurately described the impasse in which the patient was "then driven to redress the situation" (p. 326) and assert counterpressure.[6] What he did not recognize was how his view of the Third—in my terms, a *Third without the oneness of rhythmicity*—contributed to this enactment. His case narrative demonstrates that thirdness cannot reside simply in the analyst's independent observation, nor can it be maintained in a posture of resisting the patient's pressure, rather than responding to it: that is, without recognizing and soothing distress related to shame, rejection and so on. In effect, this is an illustration of the complementary situation, in which the analyst's resistance—his effort to maintain internal, theoretically informed observation, as though that were sufficient to make a Third—led to the breakdown of the intersubjective thirdness between analyst and patient.

My way of analyzing this case would be rather different than Feldman's, by which I do not mean that in the live moment, I might not feel something like the pressure and resistance that he felt, but rather, that I would see the situation differently in retrospective self-supervision. The patient, in response to Feldman's prioritization of "observing" or "thinking," insisted that the analyst was behaving like his mother; in other words, he correctly read Feldman's refusal to mold, to accommodate, to show understanding and give space to what he himself was feeling. The ice cream was a metaphor for the intersubjective Third, part of the patient's effort to communicate about what he wanted in treatment—and had wanted in childhood—to share, most likely his perception of emotional reality. The mother (or analyst) was unable to see the ice cream as a shareable entity— in her mental world, everything was either *for her child* or *for herself*; it was not a gift if it was shared, but was so only if it were relinquished.

How might this dynamic have affected the mother's envy and sense of depletion each time she gave to the patient? How much could she have enjoyed sharing anything with her child? In a world without shared Thirds, without a space of collaboration and sharing, everything is mine or yours, including especially the perception of reality. Only one person can eat; only one person can be right.

The analytic task in such a case is to help the patient create (or repair) a system of sharing and mutuality, in which now you have a bite, now I have one, as when you eat a cracker with your toddler. The toddler may have to insist at times on "all mine," but the delight of letting Mommy take a bite, or letting her pretend to, as well as of playfully pulling the cracker away, is often an even greater pleasure. Feldman's patient was trying to tell him that in their co-created system, the Third was a negative one; there was no intersubjective thirdness in which they could both eat, taste and spit out interpretations of what is going on as a shared project. In order to repair ruptures such as Feldman described, the analyst and patient must be able to share their perceptions and observation, rather than simply opposing each other.

6   In a later work, Feldman (1997) discussed how the analyst may unconsciously foster impasse by becoming involved in projection and enactments.

In my understanding of such complementary oppositions, if the analyst feels compelled to protect his internal, observing Third from the patient's reality, this generally is a sign of a breakdown already occurring in the system of collaborative understanding and attunement. The analyst needs the differentiating aspect, but this "independent thinking" cannot be achieved by, in effect, "refusing to fit in," refusing accommodation. In order to receive the patient's intention and to reestablish shared reality, the analyst needs to find a way to fit, to accommodate, that does not feel coerced—bringing together his ability to reflect with the identificatory impulse of the rhythmic Third. The clinical emphasis on building the shared Third is, in my view, a useful antidote to earlier, often persecutory idealizations of interpretation—even those modified ones, such as in Steiner's (1993) position, which recognizes the necessity of the analyst's accommodation to the patient's need to feel understood, yet considers it less contributory to psychic change than acquiring understanding.

Rather than viewing understanding—that is, the Third—as a thing to be acquired, a relational view sees it as an interactive process that creates a dialogic structure: a shared Third, an opportunity to experience mutual recognition. This shared Third, the dialogue, creates mental space for thinking as an internal conversation with the other (Spezzano, 1996).

Integration: differentiation with oneness or the *moral Third*

To construct the idea of the shared, intersubjective Third, I have brought together two experiences of thirdness: the differentiating aspect that needs to inform even the oneness of accommodation, empathy and resonance and the rhythmic aspect that informs shared reflection, negotiating and repair of ruptures. I now want to suggest briefly how we can understand these in terms of what we have observed developmentally in the parent-child relation. We need to distinguish the rhythmic Third in the One, the principle of accommodation, from the Third in the mother's mind, which is more like the principle of differentiation.

I have suggested that, while it is crucial for the mother to identify with the baby's need—for instance, in adjusting the feeding rhythm—there is the inevitable moment when twoness arises in the form of the mother's need for sleep, for the claims of her own separate existence. For many a mother, this is experienced as the moment of truth, rather like Lacan's kill-or-be-killed moment. Here the function of the Third is to help transcend this threatening twoness not by fostering the illusion that mother and baby are one or by self-abnegation; rather, at this point, the principle of asymmetrical accommodation should arise from the sense of surrender to necessity. The mother needs to feel that this is acceptance of the baby's nature, not a submission to a tyrannical demand or an overwhelming task.

If a mother resorts to priding herself on how overworked and self-denying she is, she may undermine knowledge of her own limits and the ability to distinguish necessary asymmetry from masochism. Likewise, the mother needs to hold in mind the knowledge that much infant distress is natural and ephemeral, in order for her to be able to soothe her child's distress without dissolving into anxious oneness with it.

An important contribution of infancy research, as Fonagy et al. (2002) have emphasized, is an explanation of how the mother can demonstrate her empathy for the baby's negative emotion, and yet by a "marker"—exaggerated mirroring—make clear to the baby that it is not her own fear or distress that she is displaying. Fonagy et al. propose that mothers are driven to saliently mark their affect-mirroring displays to differentiate them from realistic emotional expressions. The baby is soothed by the fact that mother is not herself distressed, but is reflecting and understanding *his* feeling. This behavior, the contrast between the mother's gesture and her affective tension level, is perceived by the child. I would suggest that this kind of interaction constitutes a form of protosymbolic communication and thus is an important basis for later symbolic communication about one another's minds (e.g., "I know you are upset by this but I think it will turn out okay.")

The study of marking shows how the feeling about behavior and sharing/communicating about it are not identical. Such an incipient differentiation between the gestural representation and the thing/feeling helps build a shared symbolic Third. It relies on the mother's relation to a differentiating Third—her ability to represent her distress as distinct from her child's, and so as a necessary part of the relationship rather than a disregulating urgency in her mind. It is the place where self-regulation and mutual regulation meet, enabling differentiation with empathy, rather than projective confusion. Thus, we see the synergy of the attunement function, the rhythmic Third, with the containing function of the differentiating Third. I emphasize that this is not only a matter of differentiation because the mother needs the identification of the rhythmic Third, and not merely an abstract idea of what is right. The Third degenerates into mere duty if there is no identificatory oneness of feeling the child's urgency and relief, pleasure and joy in connection.

Let me give an example written by someone who was himself a parent and was writing about a parental experience, which is an important point, but even more important to me personally, it was written by Stephen Mitchell, whose subsequent death was a great loss. It represents a statement by a founding relational theorist about the importance of the principle of accommodation to the other's rhythm in creating a shared Third. Mitchell (1993) underscored the distinction between submission to duty and surrender to the differentiating Third, what I am calling the Third in the One:

> When my older daughter was about two or so, I remember my excitement at the prospect of taking walks with her, given her new ambulatory skills and her intense interest in being outdoors. However, I soon found these walks agonizingly slow. My idea of a walk entailed brisk movement along a road or path. Her idea was quite different. The implications of this difference hit me one day when we encountered a fallen tree on the side of the road. . . .

the rest of the "walk" was spent exploring the fungal and insect life on, under, and around the tree. I remember my sudden realization that these walks would be no fun for me, merely a parental duty, if I held onto my idea of walks. As I was able to give that up and surrender to my daughter's rhythm and focus, a different type of experience opened up to me. . . . If I had simply restrained myself out of duty, I would have experienced the walk as a compliance. But I was able to become my daughter's version of a good companion and to find in that another way for me to be that took on great personal meaning for me.
(p. 147)

The parent thus accepts the principle of necessary asymmetry, accommodating to the other as a way of generating thirdness, and is transformed by the experience of opening to mutual pleasure. Mitchell asked how we distinguish inauthentic submission to another's demand from authentic change, another way of questioning how we distinguish the compliance of twoness from the transformational learning of thirdness. To me, it seems clear that in this case, the internal parental Third, which takes the form of reflections on what will create connection in this relationship, allows surrender and transformation. This intention to connect and the resulting self-observation and acceptance of what is lawful, in accordance with "how it is," produce a sense of the *moral Third:* the orientation to a larger principle of lawfulness, necessity, rightness or goodness.

It would be simple (and not untrue) to say that the space of thirdness opens up through surrender, the acceptance of simply being, stopping to watch the fungi grow. But I have been trying to show how important it is to distinguish this from *submission*—to clear up a common confusion between surrender and an ideal of pure empathy, whereby merger or oneness can tend towards inauthenticity and the denial of self, leading ultimately to the complementary alternative of "eat or be eaten." For instance, some authors have warned against the idea of the analyst's authenticity as if it meant imposing the analyst's view in a reversal of the old reluctance to disclose and impose (see Bromberg's 2006 critique) and a consequent failure of empathy. This opposition of empathy and authenticity splits oneness and thirdness, identification and differentiation, and constitutes the analytic dyad as a complementarity in which there is room for only one subject.

I have found that analysts who have worked deeply with patients in a style that emphasizes empathic attunement frequently come for help with stalemates based on the exclusion of the observing Third, which now appears as a destructive outside force, a killer that threatens the treatment. This issue is crucial because submission to the ideal of being an all-giving, all-understanding mother can gradually shift into a persecutory experience of being depleted, losing empathy, being devoured. As one supervisee put it, she began to feel so immobilized that she imagined herself cocooned in a condom-like sheath, "shrink-wrapped."

The relational perspective is not that the analyst should demand that the patient recognize the analyst's subjectivity—a misunderstanding of the relational position on intersubjectivity by those like Stolorow and Orange (Stolorow, Atwood &

Orange, 2002; Orange, 2010) who emphasize the important part played by decentering from one's own subjectivity. It is rather that the analyst learn to distinguish true thirdness from the self-immolating ideal of oneness that the analyst suffers as a persecutory simulacrum of the Third, blocking real self-observation. The analyst needs to work through her fear of blame, badness, and hurtfulness, which is tying both the patient and herself in knots.

As a supervisor, I often find myself helping the analyst create a space in which it is possible to accept the inevitability of causing or suffering pain, being "bad," without destroying the Third. I observe how both members of the dyad become involved in a symmetrical dance, each trying not to be the bad one, the one who eats rather than being eaten. Yet whichever side the analyst takes in this dance, taking sides itself simply perpetuates complementary relations.

The concept of thirdness formulates an alternative to this dance, by adding the differentiating Third to the rhythmic aspects of accommodation and empathy Third. It aims to distinguish compliance to a needed other from the acceptance of necessary asymmetry (Aron, 1996). However, such necessary asymmetry does not imply a view of the maternal bond as involving only one-way recognition of the child's subjectivity by the parent. Such a view is incompatible with an intersubjective theory of development, which recognizes the joys and the necessity of reaching mutual understanding with the other. One-way recognition misses the mutuality of identification by which an other's intention is known to us. To separate or oppose being understood from self-reflective insight or understanding the other misses the process of creating a shared Third as a vehicle of mutual understanding.

My contention is, then, that we need the differentiating Third even when we aim for oneness, that is, that oneness is dangerous without the Third—but it does not work properly without the flip side, the rhythmic joining in a shared Third. We (Aron & Benjamin, 1999) have talked about the need for a deep identificatory sense of joining the other as a prerequisite for developing the positive aspects of the observing Third. Without this identificatory underpinning, without the nascent thirdness of emotional attunement, the more elaborate forms of self-observation based on triangular relations become mere simulacrum of the Third. In other words, if the patient does not feel safely taken into the analyst's mind, the observing position of the Third is experienced as a barrier to getting in, leading to compliance, hopeless dejection, or hurt anger. As Schore (2003) has proposed, we might think of this in terms of brain hemispheres: the analyst's shutting down the right-brain contact with her own pain also cuts off affective communication with the patient's pain. Moving dissociatively into a left-brain modality of observation and judgement, the analyst "switches off" and is reduced to interpreting "resistance" (Spezzano, 1993).

Typically, observing thirds that lack the music of the rhythmic Third, of reciprocal identification, cannot create enough symmetry or equality to prevent idealization from deteriorating into submission to a person or ideal (Benjamin, 1995d). Such submission may be countered by defiance and self-destructive acts.

Analysts in the past were particularly prone to conflating compliant submission on the patient's part with self-observation or achievement of insight and defiance with resistance. One of the most common difficulties in all psychotherapeutic encounters is that the patient can feel "done to" by the therapist's observation or interpretation; such interventions trigger self-blame and shame, which used to be called by the misnomer "resistance" (although they may indeed reflect intersubjective resistance to the analyst's projection of her shame or guilt at hurting the patient). In other words, without compassionate acceptance, which the patient may have seldom experienced and never have internalized (as opposed to what ought to be), observation becomes judgement.

Analysts, of course, turn this same beam of critical scrutiny on themselves, and what should be a self-reflexive function turns into the self-flagellating, "bad-analyst" feeling. They fantasize, in effect, being shamed and blamed in front of their colleagues; the community and its ideals become persecutory rather than supportive.

Breakdown and repair

There may be no tenet more important to overcoming this shame and blame in analytic work than the idea that recognition continually breaks down, that thirdness always collapses into twoness, that we are always losing and recovering the intersubjective view. We have to keep reminding ourselves that breakdown and repair are part of a larger process, a concomitant of the imperatives of participating in a two-way interaction. This is because, as Mitchell (1997) said, becoming part of the problem is how we become part of the solution. In this sense, the analyst's surrender means a deep acceptance of the necessity of becoming involved in enactments and impasses. This acceptance becomes the basis for a new version of thirdness that encourages us to honestly confront our feelings of shame, inadequacy and guilt, to tolerate the symmetrical relation we may enter into with our patients, without giving up negative capability—in short, a different kind of *moral Third*.

Until the relational turn, it seems, many analysts were content to think of interpretation as the primary means of instituting the Third. The notion of resolving difficulties remained some version of the analyst's holding onto the observing position, supported by theory, and hence formulating and interpreting in the face of impasse. Relational analysts are inclined to see interpretation as action, and to recognize, as Mitchell (1997) pointed out, that holding onto interpretation could perpetuate the very problems the interpretation is designed to address. An example is when an analyst interprets a power struggle, and the patient experiences this, too, as a power move.

Relational analysts have explored a variety of ways to collaborate with the patient in exploring or exchanging perceptions. For instance, the analyst might call for the patient's help in figuring out what is going on, in order to open up the space of thirdness, rather than simply putting forward his own interpretation of what has just gone wrong (Ehrenberg, 1992). The latter can appear to be a defensive insistence on one's own thinking as the necessary version of reality.

Britton (1988; 1998) explicitly considers the way the complementary opposition of my reality and your reality gets activated within the analytic relationship when the presence of an observing Third is felt to be intolerable or persecutory. It feels, Britton remarked, as though there is room for only one psychic reality. I have been trying to highlight the two-way direction of effects in this complementary dynamic, the symmetry wherein both partners experience the impossibility of acknowledging the other's reality without abandoning one's own. The analyst may also be overwhelmed by how destructive the patient's image of her is to her own sense of self. For instance, when the patient's reality is that "You are toxic and have made me ill, mad and unable to function," the analyst will typically find it nearly impossible to take that in without losing her own reality.

I believe that the analyst's feeling of being invaded by the other's malignant emotional reality might mirror the patient's early experiences of having his own feelings denied and supplanted by the parent's reality. The parental response that the child's needs for independence or nurturance are "bad" not only invalidates needs, and not only repels the child from the parent's mind; equally important, as Davies (2004) has shown, the parent is also subjecting the child to an invasion of the parent's shame and badness, which also endangers the child's mind.

Where this kind of malignant complementarity takes hold, the ping-pong of projective identification—the exchange of blame—is often too rapid to halt or even to observe. The analyst cannot function empathically, because attunement to the patient now feels like submission to extortion, and it is partly through this involuntary response on the analyst's part to the patient's dissociated self-experience that trauma is reenacted. Neither patient nor analyst can have a grip on reality at this point—what Russell (1998) called "the crunch," often signalled by the feeling expressed in the question, "Am I crazy or is it you?"

The analyst caught in the crunch feels unable to respond authentically, and against her own will, she feels compelled, unconsciously or consciously, to defend herself against the patient's reality. When the analyst feels, implies or says, "You are doing something to *me*," she involuntarily mirrors the *you* who feels that the other is bad and doing something to you. Therefore, the more each *I* insists that it is *you*, the more each I becomes *you*, and the more our boundaries are blurred. My effort to save my sanity mirrors your effort to save your sanity. Sometimes, this self-protective reaction shows itself in subtle ways: the analyst's refusal to accommodate; the occurrence of a painful silence; a disjunctive comment, conveying the analyst's withdrawal from the rhythm of mutual emotional exchange, from the One in the Third. This reaction is registered in turn by the patient, who thinks, "The analyst has chosen her own sanity over mine. She would rather that I feel crazy than that she be the one who is in the wrong."

This deterioration of the interaction cannot yet be represented or contained in dialogue. The symbolic Third—interpretation—simply appears as the analyst's effort to be the sane one, and so talking about it does not seem to help. Certain kinds of observation seem to amplify the patient's shame at being desperate and guilt over raging at the analyst. As Bromberg (2000) pointed out, the effort to represent verbally what is going on, to engage the symbolic, can further the analyst's dissociative avoidance of the abyss the patient is threatened by. In reviewing such sessions in supervision, we find that it is precisely by "catching" a moment of the analyst's dissociation—visible, perhaps, in a subtly disjunctive focus that shifts the tone or direction of the session—that the character of the enactment comes into relief and can be productively unravelled.

Britton (2000) has described the restoration of thirdness in terms of the analyst's recovery of self-observation, such that "we stop doing something that we are probably not aware of doing in our interaction with the patient." One way to characterize this, in accordance with Schore (2003), is as the analyst's regaining self-regulation and becoming able to move out of dissociation and back into affectively resonant containment. Another way to describe it is that the *analyst needs to change*, as Slavin and Kriegman (1998) put it, and in many cases this is what first leads the patient to believe that change is possible. While there is no recipe for this change, I suggest that the idea of surrendering rather than submitting is a way of evoking and sanctioning this process of letting go of our determination to make our reality operative. To do this—and I think this has been clarified only recently, and insufficiently remarked upon prior to recent relational and intersubjectively informed literature[7]—is to find a different way to regulate ourselves, one in which we accept loss, failure, mistakes, our own vulnerability. And, if not always (as Renik (1998a) contends), we must certainly often feel free to communicate about this to the patient.

Perhaps most crucial to replacing our ideal of the knowing analyst with an intersubjective view of the analyst as responsible participant is the acknowledgment of our own struggles (Mitchell, 1997). The analyst who can acknowledge missing or failing, who can feel and express regret, helps create a system based on acknowledgment of what has been missed, both in the past and the present. There are cases in which the patient's confrontation and the analyst's subsequent acknowledgment of a mistake, a preoccupation, misattunement or an emotion of his own is the crucial turning point (Renik, 1998a; Jacobs, 2001). As Davies (2004) illustrated, the patient may need the analyst to assume the burden of badness, to show her willingness to tolerate it in order to protect the patient. The analyst shoulders responsibility for hurting, even though her action represented an unavoidable piece of enactment. A dyadic system that creates a safe space for such acknowledgment of responsibility provides the basis for a secure attachment in which understanding is no longer persecutory, outside observation, suspected of being in the service of blame. This sense of mutual respect and identification contributes to the development of a differentiating Third.

---

7   See Bromberg, 2000; Davies, 2002, 2003; Renik, 1998a, 1998b; Ringstrom, 1998; Slavin and Kriegman, 1998; Schore, 2003; and Slochower, 1996.

As analysts, we strive to create a dyad that enables both partners to step out of the symmetrical exchange of blame, thus relieving ourselves of the need for self-justification. In effect, we tell ourselves, whatever we have done that has gotten us into the position of being in the wrong is not so horribly shameful that we cannot own it. It stops being submission to the patient's reality because, as we free ourselves from shame and blame, the patient's accusation no longer persecutes us, and hence, we are no longer in the grip of helplessness. If it is no longer a matter of which person is sane, right, healthy, knows best or the like, and if the analyst is able to acknowledge the patient's suffering without stepping into the position of badness, then the intersubjective space of thirdness may be restored. My point is that this step out of helplessness usually involves more than an internal process; it involves direct or transitionally framed communication about one's own reactivity, misattunement or misunderstanding. By making a claim on the potential space of thirdness, we call upon it, and so call it into being.

This ameliorative action may be thought of as a practice that strengthens the differentiating Third—not only the simple, affective resonance of the rhythmic Third, but also the maternal Third in the One, wherein the parent can contain catastrophic feelings because she knows they are not all there is. I also think of this as the *moral Third*—reachable only through this experience of taking responsibility for bearing pain and shame. In taking such responsibility, the analyst is putting an end to the buck passing the patient has always experienced—that is, to the game of ping-pong wherein each member of the dyad tries to put the bad into the other. The analyst says, in effect, "I'll go first."[8] In orienting to the moral Third of responsibility, the analyst is also demonstrating the route out of helplessness.

In calling this the *moral Third*, I am suggesting that clinical practice may ultimately be founded in certain values, such as the acceptance of uncertainty, humility and compassion that form the basis of a democratic or egalitarian view of psychoanalytic process. I am also hoping to correct our understanding of *self-disclosure*, a concept that developed reactively to counter ideas about anonymity. In my view, much of what is misunderstood as disclosure is more properly considered in terms of its function, which is to acknowledge the analyst's contribution (generally sensed by the patient) to the intersubjective process, thus fostering a dyadic system based on taking responsibility, rather than disowning it or evading it under the guise of neutrality.

Let me briefly illustrate with an example presented by Steiner (1993), which touches on the analyst's difficulties with feeling blamed. Steiner cites an interaction in which he "went too far" in his interpretation, adding a comment with a "somewhat critical tone to it which I suspected arose from my difficulty in containing feelings . . . *anxiety about her and possibly my annoyance that she made me feel responsible, guilty, and helpless*" (p. 137, italics added). In supervising and

---

8   Drucilla Cornell (2003) has explicated the principle of *Ubuntu*, crucial in the South African reconciliation process, as meaning "I'll go first."

reading, I have seen numerous examples of this kind of going too far, when the analyst thinks he has managed the discomfort of suppressing his own reality and reacts by dissociatively trying to insert it after all (Ringstrom, 1998). Despite this aside to us, his colleagues, in the actual event, Steiner (1993) dismissed the patient's response to him as projection, because he felt that "I was being made responsible for the patient's problems as well as my own" (p. 144). He does not seem to consider the symmetry between his reaction and her reaction, in which she tended to feel persecuted because she felt that Steiner "implied that she" (that is, she alone) "was responsible for what happened between us" (p. 144). So, rather than "disclosing" that indeed *he was feeling responsible* and that he had gone too far, he rejects the possibility of confirming her observation that "over the question of responsibility, she felt I sometimes adopted a righteous tone which made her feel I was refusing to examine my own contribution . . . to accept responsibility myself" (p. 144).

While Steiner accepts the tendency to be caught in enactment, and the necessity for the analyst to be open minded and inquiring in order to be helped by the patient's feedback, he insists that the analyst must cope by relying on his own understanding, just as he insists that the patient is ultimately helped only by understanding rather than by being understood. Both analyst and patient are held to a standard of relying on individual insight, the Third without the one, rather than making use of mutual, albeit asymmetrical, containment (Cooper, 2000). Steiner's definition of containment excludes the possibility of a shared Third, of creating a dyadic system that contains by virtue of mutual reflection on the interaction. Thus, he rejects use of the intersubjective field to transform the conflict around responsibility into a shared Third, an object of joint reflection. And he dismisses the value of acknowledging his own responsibility because he assumes that the patient will take such openness as a sign of the analyst's inability to contain; the analyst must engage neither in "a confession which simply makes the patient anxious, nor a denial, which the patient sees as defensive and false" (Steiner, 1993, p. 145).

But what is the basis for assuming that the patient would be made anxious or perceive this as weakness rather than as strength (Renik, 1998a)? Why would it not relieve her to know that the analyst is able to contain knowledge of his own weaknesses, and thus strong enough to apologize and recognize his responsibility for her feeling hurt? It seems to me that it is the analytic community that must change its attitude: accepting the analyst's inevitable participation in such enactments, as Steiner seems to do, also implies the need for participatory solutions. The surrender to the inevitable can be the basis of initiating mutual accommodation and a symmetrical relation to the moral Third—in this case, the principle of bearing responsibility ("I'll take the hit if you'll take the hit").

Accommodation, co-creation and repair

I will illustrate this creation of shared responsibility in a case of breakdown into complementarity, a prolonged impasse in which any Third seemed to destroy the life-giving oneness.

Clinical vignette II: Aliza

A patient whose early years in analysis provided an experience of being under-stood and safely held, began to shift into trauma-related states of fearing that any misunderstanding—that is, any interpretation—would be so malignant that it would catapult her into illness, despair and desolation. Aliza, a successful musico-logist, had fled Eastern Europe as a child and had suffered a series of catastrophes with which her family had been nearly unable to cope; among them was Aliza's having been left by her mother with strange relatives who barely spoke her language. After several years on the couch during which Aliza experienced me as deeply holding and musically attuning, a series of misfortunes catalyzed the appearance of catastrophic anxieties, and my presence began to seem unreliable, dangerous and even toxic. Of course any analysis as it deepens will expose areas of shame that are dealt with projectively, dramatize failures by and traumas with early others that must be enacted to be addressed, and thus disrupt the attunement of the rhythmic Third. But in this case, external events added to the frightening quality of these ruptures and posed a greater threat to our jointly constructed container. Aliza needed me more, but thus also feared me more—her disorganized attachment experiences were reenacted such that misattunements on my part destabilized both of us. It was as if I had simply lost the score, our Third, which once guided me.

My efforts to reflect on this turn appeared to Aliza as "thinking," as denial of her desperation, as dangerous self-protection, evasion of blame (in effect, repelling rather than containing her projections). My adherence to the traditional Third, the rules of analytic encounter, began to seem (even to me) a misuse of the profes-sional role to distance myself from her agonies and to withdraw as a person, in effect dissociatively shutting the patient out of my mind. Any effort to explain this awful turn, often when Aliza urgently asked it of me, could turn into a means of shifting the blame onto her, or clumsy intellectualization that broke the symphonic attunement of our early relationship (an example of the right-to-left brain shift described by Schore (2003)). This problem was exacerbated because Aliza often countered her shame by trying to prove she could be an intact adult in talking competently to me about her traumatized child self, but then that self then felt angry and excluded. What had been a subjectively helpful Third now seemed to be a dynamic built on a dissociative or blaming form of observation, rather than on emotional resonance and inclusion.

I began to be overcome by classic feelings of complementary breakdown: feeling helpless, feeling the pull to defend my reality, my own integrity of feeling and thinking, in order to protect myself from shame; in turn, I felt the corres-ponding fear that this shame would lead me to blame and so destroy my patient. When Aliza objected to my formulations as too intellectual, I was reminded of Britton's (1988, 1998) descriptions of how the shaky maternal container is threat-ened by thinking. But it did not seem to me to be the "father" who broke into the previously soothing maternal dyad, but rather a sanity-robbing and terrifying denial that represented the dissociated, disowned, "violent innocence" of Aliza's mother

(Bollas, 1992, p. 165), who responded to any crisis or need with chaos and impermeability. It was this mother whom neither of us could tolerate having to be. Our complementary twoness was a dance in which each of us tried to avoid being her—each feeling done to, each refusing to be the one to blame for hurting the other.

At the same time, from Aliza's point of view, the feeling of blame was *my* issue; her concern was that she literally felt as if she were dying and that I did not care. I began to fear that she would leave and we would thus recapitulate a long history of breaking attachments. In consultation with a colleague, I concluded that I would tell her that what she wanted me to give her was not wrong or demanding, but that I might not be *able* to give it to her. In the event, I surprised myself. I had prepared for the session by trying to accept the loss of Aliza as a person I cared about, as well as my failure as an analyst. I thought that our hopeful beginning, when we had created a deeply attuned dyad, would be at best overshadowed by our ending. I knew we both felt love for each other and that I could identify with the pain she was experiencing—alongside my feelings of frustration, impotence, and failure.

As planned, I began by telling Aliza that her needs were not wrong, yet I might be unable to fulfil them, and I would assist her in seeking help elsewhere if she wished. But I also found myself telling her spontaneously that no matter what she did, she would always have a place in my heart, that she could not break our attachment or destroy my loving feelings. This reassertion of the indestructibility of my love and my willingness to bear responsibility dramatically shifted Aliza's view of me. But it also shifted my receptivity to her because, paradoxically, my acceptance of my inability to find a solution alleviated my sense of helplessness. It enabled me to return to the analytic commitment not to "do" anything, but rather to contact my deep connection to her. She responded by recovering her side of the connection and feeling, with me, the meaning of the shared loss of my value for her. This shift allowed us to open the door to the dissociated states of terror and aloneness that the patient had felt I could not bear with her, and she recovered memories and scenes of childhood we had never reached before. Yet we were still haunted by the specter of the destroying mother, and after a period of this heightened reliving, Aliza said that she would never fully regain her trust in me. She chose to leave in order to protect our relationship, a Third she could not imagine would survive.

Shortly after the terrorist attacks of 11 September 2001, Aliza returned for a number of sessions, having worked in the interim with another therapist. She reported that she had become aware of anger and the feeling of being surrounded by others who refused to acknowledge their own relation to the disaster. Believing that she was commenting on my relation to her and linking this to the way in which she had experienced me in the past, I noted the following:

> Everything I said seemed to be my distancing myself, another experience of the blank faces in your family. When disaster struck, they acted as though

nothing bad had happened at all. Whenever I told you anything I saw, it wasn't my having a subjective reaction to the same disaster as you—it was my seeing something shameful in the intensity of your reaction.

Aliza then spoke of guilt at having "battered" me, and I replied that she was troubled by this at the time, but could not help doing it. She said that she had "tricked" me by eliciting formulations and explanations from me that felt distancing and had so angered her. Likewise, she had often demanded that I tell her what I felt, but had been angry if I did so because then it was "about you."

I acknowledged that in being drawn into these interactions, I often did feel very bad and as though I was failing. I said that in my view, what was important was that, even though she knew this was happening, it felt to her that she had to accept the onus, all the blame, if she let herself acknowledge any responsibility— a "loser-takes-all" situation. This seemed to me related to why she had left when she did. I raised the question of whether she felt that I, too, could not bear the onus, that whatever I would have to admit to for us to continue would be more than I could bear; that I was not willing to take that on in order for her not to be crazy. I suggested, "You couldn't rely on me to care enough about your sanity to bear blame for you."

Aliza replied, "Yes, I saw you as being like the parent who won't do that, would rather sacrifice the child." We considered how every effort I had made to acknowledge my role in our interaction was tainted by Aliza's sense that she was required to reassure the other. She was sure she had to bear the unbearable for her mother (or other), while reassuring her that she was "good" for her. It seemed there had been no way for me to assume responsibility without demanding exoneration— thus, the limits of any form of disclosure or acknowledgment became clear to both of us.

In later sessions, we explicated this impossibility as we arrived at a dramatic picture of Aliza's mother's way of behaving during the horrifying events of the patient's early childhood. I was able to say what could not be said earlier: how impossibly painful it was for Aliza to feel that she, with her own daughter in the present, in some way replicated her mother's actions. But it was likewise impossible for me to bear the burden of being that mother, because then I would pose a terrifying threat to her.

Aliza responded to this description of her dilemma with shocked recognition of how true it felt, and also how it foreclosed any action on my part, any move towards understanding. She was amazed that I had been able to tolerate being in such a frightening situation with her. Again, I was able to reiterate my sadness about having been unable to avoid evoking the feeling of being with a dangerous mother who denies what she is doing. Aliza's response was to spontaneously reach an intense conviction that she must, at all costs, assume the burden of having a sanity-destroying mother inside her. She was aware of a sense of deep sorrow for how difficult it had been for me to stay with her through that time.

Indeed, her response was so intense that I felt a moment of concern—was I forcing something into my patient? However, when she returned after a 2-month summer break and throughout the following year, Aliza spoke of how transformed she felt, so much stronger after that session that she often had to marvel at herself and wonder if she were the same person. Now she had the experience that *her* love survived the destructiveness of our interaction, my mistakes and limitations.

As the process of shared retrospection and reparation continued, Aliza and I re-created an earlier mode of accommodation, which brought into play our previous experiences of being in harmony. She was able to reintegrate experiences of reverence and beauty in which my presence evoked her childhood love of her mother's face, the ecstasy and joy that had confirmed her sense of my and her own inner goodness. We created a thirdness, a symmetrical dialogue, in which each of us responded from a position of forgiveness and generosity, making a safe place between us and in each of our minds for taking responsibility. The transformation of our shared Third had allowed both of us to transcend shame, to walk through disillusion and to accept the limits of my analytic subjectivity.

I hope this vignette is suggestive enough of the complexity of such a process of shared transformation as to make plain the risks as well as the possibilities of this work. I have tried to make clear that disclosure is not a panacea, that the analyst's acknowledgment of responsibility can take place only by working through deep anguish around feelings of destructiveness and loss.

The notion of the moral Third is thus linked to the acceptance of inevitable breakdown and repair, which allows us to situate our responsibility to our patients and the process in the context of a witnessing compassion. This notion seems to me intrinsic to embracing the intersubjective necessity, the relational imperative to participate in a two-way interaction. If involvement in the interaction cannot be avoided, then it is all the more necessary that we be oriented to certain principles of responsibility. This is what I mean by the moral Third: acceptance (hopefully within our community) of certain principles as a foundation for analytic thirdness —an attitude towards interaction in which analysts honestly confront the feelings of shame, inadequacy and guilt that enactments and impasses arouse. In this sense, the analyst's surrender means accepting the necessity of becoming involved in a process that is often outside our control and understanding—thus, there is an intrinsic necessity for this surrender; it does not come from a demand or requirement posed by the other. This principle of necessity becomes our Third in a process that we can actively shape only according to certain "lawful" forms, to the extent that we also align and accommodate ourselves to the other.

In recent decades, the relational or intersubjective approach has moved towards overthrowing the old orthodoxy that opposed efforts to use our own subjectivity with theories of one-way action and encapsulated minds. It is now necessary to focus more on protecting and refining the use of analytic subjectivity by providing outlines in the context of a viable discipline. As Mitchell (1997) contended, transformation occurs when the analyst *stops trying* to live up to a generic, uncontaminated solution, and finds instead the custom-fitted solution for a particular patient. This is the approach that works because, as Goldner (2003) put it, it reveals "the transparency of the analyst's own working process . . . his genuine struggle between the necessity for analytic discipline and need for authenticity" (p. 143). Thus, the patient sees in the analyst a vision of what it means to struggle internally in a therapeutic way. The patient needs to see his own efforts reflected in the analyst's similar but different subjectivity, which, like the cross-modal response to the infant, constitutes a translation or metabolizing digestion. The patient checks out whether the analyst is truly metabolizing or just resting on internalized thirds, superego contents, analytic dictums.

I experienced a particularly dramatic instance of this need to contact and be mirrored by the authentic subjective responses of the analyst with a patient whose highly dissociated experiences of her parents' homicidal attacks materialized as a death threat towards me. After I told her that there were certain things she absolutely could not do for both of us to safely continue the process, she left me a phone message saying that she had actually wanted me to confront her with limits, as she never had been before. In effect, she was searching for the symbolic Third, what Lacan (1975) saw as the speech that keeps us from killing. This Third had to be backed up by a demonstration that I could participate emotionally, that is, could identify with her feeling of sheer terror and survive it.

The patient added in her message that she needed me to do this from my own instincts, not out of adherence to therapeutic rules. I came to realize that she meant that I needed to act as a real person, with my own subjective relationship to rules and limits. And that this had to be demonstrably based on a personal confrontation of the reality of terror and abuse, not on dissociative denial of it. She needed to feel the Third not as emanating from an impersonal, professional identity or a reliance on authority, such as she had felt from the church in which she had been raised, but from my personal relation to the Third, my faith in what is lawful. At the time, I felt how precarious the analyst's endeavour is, the risk of the trust placed in me: could I indeed reach into myself and be truthful enough to be equal to this trust?

All patients, in individual ways, place their hopes for the therapeutic process in us, and for each one, we must use our own subjectivity in a different way to struggle through to a specific solution. But this specificity and the authenticity on which it is based cannot be created in free fall. Analytic work conducted according to the intersubjective view of two participating subjectivities requires a discipline based on orientation to the structural conditions of thirdness. It is my hope that this clinical and developmental perspective on co-created, intersubjective third-ness can help orient us towards responsibility and more rigorous thinking, even as our practice of psychoanalysis becomes more emotionally authentic, more spontaneous and inventive, more compassionate and liberating to both our patients and ourselves.

Chapter 2

Our appointment in Thebes

Acknowledgment, the failed witness and fear of harming

> So in the end we succeed by failing—failing the patient's way.
>
> D. W. Winnicott (1965, p. 258)

My aim in this chapter was to propose a theory of acknowledgment, and further explore the process of creating a Third in relation to failures of witnessing. The struggle to face the analyst's own role in impasses or collisions had been less well-articulated at the time I wrote this. In particular, therefore, I wanted to think out loud about the way in which analysts may free their sense of agency from the shameful, blameful evocation of badness that characterizes impasses and many enactments. This chapter, written in 2005, represented a continuation and development of the themes in Chapter 1, especially developing the idea of the moral Third.

One of the major reasons we are not free to make the best use of analytic agency is that, consciously or unconsciously, we fear doing harm. Since the patient will present to us, in the form of enactment, the very injuries she has come to heal, a dilemma Ferenczi first articulated, we often find ourselves in the position of the "**wounding** healer." Consequently, our task should be to facilitate the creation of a shared Third between therapist and patient that can hold the oscillations between attunement and misattunement, separations and reunion; this Third allows us to work with this paradox: *We may harm to heal.* This effort requires, in turn, that therapists be held by a clinical ethos that allows us to sustain the paradox and recognize that our patients—to reverse Winnicott's dictum—also can and often do survive destruction in the form of our lapses, dissociations and vulnerabilities.

This revision of Winicott's (1971a) idea highlights the need for reciprocal survival in the analytic couple. In turn, this revision corresponds to our awareness that both members—with their projective and dissociated processes—co-create the dialectic of recognition and breakdown.

In my model of intersubjectivity, breakdown is understood as twoness—the complementarity of "doer and done to" with its ball-in-socket interlocking dependency of opposites. Typical of this dyadic structure are rapid oscillations between doing and being done to, a ping-pong (Racker) dynamic, in which reciprocal actions lock in the possible response of the other. In a rigid complementary dyad, movement is generally restricted to reversal—switching to the other side of the polarity—while the two positions remain the same as on a seesaw (Lacan). In my original formulation of "Beyond Doer and Done to" (Benjamin, 2004a/2010; Chapter 1) I tried to clarify that this structure does not allow one to participate as a subject with a sense of authorship and agency. Authorship and agency fail because one feels reactive rather than free to formulate intention, one feels to blame rather than responsible, one feels controlled rather than recognized. Inhabiting a state in which we can express authorship and agency relies on the presence of a recognizing relationship or "Third." I use the term Third to designate a relational position or principle, specifically to mean the representation of a potential relation-ship that we use to break out of the reciprocal lock of complementarity.

As Aron (Aron & Benjamin, 1999) suggested in an early joint formulation of the idea of the Third, we can think of the complementary structure as a straight line, with no room or space to alter the relation of the two positions. Whereas, the Third can be thought of as the point that creates, in a geometrical sense, the opening into space of the triangle or other shape (Aron, 2006). The movement from the locked-in structure of twoness to the spacious opening of thirdness is something we subjectively experience as a freeing of our feelings and minds. This subjective experience of mutual influence as an area of freedom rather than coercion is crucial to the development of responsibility and agency.

The distinction between freedom and coercion in mutual influence is central to my particular construction of intersubjectivity (see Yeatman, 2015). Here the notion is that the other as object of coercion cannot be seen as a subject who partners with us in mutual recognition. The idea of mutual recognition is thus differentiated from reciprocal influence, for it implies this additional axis of freedom versus coercion, in which the other is viewed as partnering subject versus object of control.

Certainly mutual influence and co-construction are a general property of dyadic systems whether we transcend or get stuck in complementarity. But that is pre-cisely why we need to further differentiate the state of thirdness in which partners are aware that each is a subject affecting the other, recognize each other as co-creating a process, from the state of twoness in which one feels unable to affect the other or overly affected by the other, locked into a helpless state, etc. Such states necessarily also occur under conditions of reciprocal influence, yet subjectively the actors do not feel this reciprocity, rather they feel "done to." Meanwhile it is only the outside observer who holds the position of Third that perceives the agency, responsibility and subjectivity of both partners.

I think of the recourse to the Third as relying upon, or shall we say having faith in, certain dynamic principles, especially that of rupture and repair (Tronick, 1989). I think of "thirdness," as the experiential process of realizing the principles in action: for instance, surviving breakdown with mutual recognition. The experience in turn strengthens the Third as a principle of the dyad and the faith of each partner in creating it. In the ongoing struggle with failure and survival, faith grows in the co-created procedural patterns that allows both partners to survive and recognize their contribution to the interaction. In this way we affirm the value of our partner's agency and will, as well as of our own truthful self-acceptance (Safran, 1999).

I will briefly reiterate here what I've previously said about the meaning of the Third and how it functions in analysis. The sense of a lawful world begins with intersubjective co-created patterns: the principle of these patterns being the Third, the experience of interacting according to them, thirdness. When there are violations of those patterns that need to be corrected, a form of acknowledgment is needed to restore the experience of thirdness and thereby establish the Third as a principle that we uphold and that holds us through disruptions—a dynamic Tronick (1989) called rupture and repair, essential in early development (see Beebe & Lachmann, 1994; 2002). Since interactive patterns begin at the procedural level in infancy, creating a rhythm between partners, I refer to the *rhythmic Third*, the mutual accommodation that brings about the sense of union or in-sync-ness. This principle of accommodation sums up the earliest procedural version of lawful relating and mutual regulation or recognition, acts of attunement that contribute to co-creation of expectable patterns.

On this procedural foundation there develops a *differentiated Third* which refers to our ability to express our own intentions and to recognize the other as a like subject deserving respect, on whom ideally we depend without resorting to coercion—with whom we bear the vulnerability of such mutual dependency requisite for realizing our intentions. The differentiating Third becomes the basis for the observing functions we think of as symbolic. In this sense the symbolic relates to differentiation as the procedural relates to attunement or accommodation—it develops through the ability to hold difference in mind, recognize the separate reality of another mind, and thus creates a position in which more than one subjectivity or reality or perspective can co-exist. Because more than one meaning is possible, we can hold the tension of different meanings.

These rhythmic and differentiated experiences of thirdness are continually subject to breakdown, and have to be restored. In other words we have moments of breakdown into complementarity: misattunement or disagreement in which we feel only my way works, only my experience matters, the other is doing something to me and so forth. These moments are overcome when we restore a sense of thirdness, either at the level of rhythmicity or symbolic sharing, or both. The restoration of thirdness through acknowledgment of breakdowns, which can occur at either implicit procedural or explicit (verbal) symbolic level, I see as a crucial part of the dynamic Third: *the moral Third*. The moral Third depends upon acknowledgment of disruptions, disappointments, violations of expectancy, and more broadly upon acknowledgment of injuries and trauma that challenge principles of fairness, and respect for human dignity.

I have come to emphasize this idea of overcoming violations of "lawfulness," expected patterns of attunement, which begins with the level of the rhythmic Third, the implicit procedural communication of pre-symbolic interaction. Thus the term *moral Third* is meant not to suggest a "higher" cognitive function or level of relating, rather, it is a sense of moral order that derives from harmonious or predictable connections at early developmental levels of bodily and emotional interaction. When a caregiver acknowledges an important violation of expectancy, "marks" it (Fonagy et al., 2002), interpersonal safety is restored, and there is a concomitant relaxation which brings the ability to feel and think back on line. In interpersonal relations, we find in response to acknowledgment profound physiological, kinetic, facial shifts may occur that are felt by both partners even without or before words (Bucci, 2003). We have come to understand how the moral Third—upholding the expectation of a lawful caring world through acknowledgment of small disruptions or larger ruptures and recognition of the need to reconnect—is intimately linked to psychosomatic connection and neurophysiology of affective arousal. In turn, this formulation of the idea of rupture and repair (Tronick, 1989) shows how acknowledgment contributes to anchoring the *moral Third* in early forms of intersubjectivity.

Acknowledgment, enactment and the bearing of badness

The developmental principle of rupture and repair corresponds with an essential relational clinical principle, namely the great therapeutic importance we assign to working through enactments. Against this background I will try to make some general comments about the analyst's role in enactments and even more generally about the function of acknowledgment in relation to breakdowns. I wish to specifically address the aspect of breakdown that involves the analyst's subjectivity, her way of registering both the dyadic collapse into complementarity and her own contribution to it. I will stress the analyst's shame at failing and guilt at causing pain or shame as well as how truthful acknowledgment can make an essential contribution to the shared Third and to reciprocal survival. I highlight the effect of the analyst taking responsibility for her contribution, as a way of formulating her insights into the mutual dynamic while simultaneously helping to regulate the affect of both members of the dyad.

I believe the early rejections of disclosure by the psychoanalytic mainstream misidentified the issue by explicitly focusing on what the patient "finds out" about the analyst. Far more important are the explicit parsing of enactment and the implicit regulation and soothing that occur when the analyst confirms what felt wrong by acknowledging the patient's perception. The confirmation, "this did happen," affirms the value of confronting and embracing a consensual reality and bearing together the painful truth (by no means a final or absolute truth)—a vital part of the moral Third.

How the therapist can or should use acknowledgment—whether or not it involves disclosure—relates to the two-person view of ruptures as well as to our understanding of the complementary structure. Complementary relations often lead to impasses based on flooding shame (Bromberg, 2006) in which a struggle is joined around blame: who is bad, crazy, difficult, who will own up (Russell, 1998). In the version of psychoanalysis that stressed the analysis of patient resistance and defense, a good patient's acceptance of responsibility—formerly known as insight—might well involve suppressing protest against bearing alone the feeling of badness. It was thus prone to fostering repetition of early experiences of mystification. These repetitions, as Davies (2004) showed, mobilize the identification of both partners with the child who bears the extruded badness that the shamed parent cannot own. Likewise, each partner is likely to wish to disown the badness which is so unfairly distributed, and feel as Laing (1965) first emphasized a sense of "madness" along with badness.

Laing's work highlighted the problem of mystification, in which parental stability requires the child to assume the mad or bad position, and thus to sacrifice her own sense of reality, in effect, to compromise her mental function. Laing named this "the transpersonal defense," because its point is to regulate the self by stopping the other from taking action on behalf of his own perception of reality. Naturally, when the therapist engages with a patient who has experienced a struggle for sanity with adults who disowned responsibility, the re-enactment of this scenario might lead both to feel as if their minds are in jeopardy. As Russell (1998), who considered such experiences unavoidable and called them "the crunch," first described, each partner is liable to feel "Am I crazy or are you?" In effect, one person's mind has to be sacrificed for the other to live. This struggle corresponds to the complementary structure of "submit or resist," as described by Ogden, which allows for the validation of only one reality, one self. In such enactments the analyst's crisis may take the form of guilty, shameful awareness of being unable to avoid the complementary move of pushing the responsibility, that is blame, back into the patient.

When the patient believes he is always asked to be in the role of the one who is angry or wrongheaded, the therapist's rational calm can appear as an attack on the patient's reality, causing further dysregulation, triggering this struggle for sanity. Equally important, as Bromberg (2006) has noted, attempts at interpretation of what is going—the analyst's effort to reach for the symbolic Third—may appear as a dissociative move on the analyst's part. After all, the patient's conviction that the analyst doesn't want to know his dissociated self-state is based on the lack of access that self-state has to the symbolic, differentiating Third. In other words, unrecognized parts of self don't "expect" to be known or part of a mutually accepting dialogue. They are covered in shame, feel excluded, hiding and alone. The thing the patient is trying to get the analyst to know through enactment—the unconscious communication, as it were—inevitably involves a shameful part of self, or one that is felt to be bad and destructive of the other's love. Exposing this part can be excruciating and so intensifies shame and dysregulates the patient that even the analyst's effort to speak to the more symbolically organized "good patient" may thus appear as a wish not to know.

In this sense, the old psychoanalytic dictum not to reassure is not without sense; however, interpretation of the "darker" side is not necessarily less problematic, rather, it can be felt as distancing and shaming. This is exactly the point at which the analyst is so often tempted to formulate what seems to her organizing or empathic but actually fails to help the patient patient find affective safety. A non-generic reaction that shows impact, that recognizes the feeling of what is being exposed, must be found that is specific to the moment (Bromberg, 2011). If it is not found, the patient may now feel that his effort to signal that something is needed to help him stop fragmenting, and in this sense to repair the relationship, has instead become a form of harming the analyst, plunging both partners into the doer–done to scenario. The fear that an attempt at repair will actually hurt the other is one of the most dire consequences of a parent's fearful reaction to a child's need for a more attuned and regulating response.

What follows from this dilemma, in my view, is that when the shame is great and the analyst is (unavoidably) unable to re-regulate the patient, she experiences her failure as a form of *harming*. The analyst's ensuing shame and guilt, her dysregulation, felt procedurally but left under cover of dissociation, may constitute a crucial element of repetition, of disruption in connection, for the patient. Frightened by our inevitable dissociation and disregulation, we lose our contact with the basic principle of rupture and repair—and thus relive along with the patient the failure to survive breakdown.

In my experience failures in self and other regulation and the reliving of breakdown, which activate the analyst's shame and guilt at harming, need to be countered by full acceptance, by surrender to the Third—here understood as the process of rupture and repair. This might be done by taking to heart Ferenczi's realization that

> it is an unavoidable task of the analyst, although he may behave as he will ... take kindness ... as far as he possibly can ... will have to repeat with his own hands the act of murder previously perpetrated against the patient.
>
> (1932, p. 52)

The analyst's surrender to this inevitability becomes a way of restoring, strengthening, the moral Third. The realization might be phrased thus: the injury we find it unbearable to inflict, the wrong feeling we are pledged to avoid—returns, perhaps in less recognizable form, as enactment. Furthermore, it is often precisely by trying to avoid re-traumatizing the patient that interactive knots are realized because we are then controlled by our fear of harm, failure, shame and guilt. *That fate which we seek to avoid—as the Oedipus myth most importantly illustrates—meets us on the road to Thebes.* Believing he can escape destiny, prevent inflicting the murder predicted by the Delphic oracle, Oedipus rushes to meet it. Expressing a similar notion, the famous parable "Appointment in Samara" tells us how, upon meeting Death in the market, the master informs him that his servant has fled because he feared meeting him here this morning. Death replies he knows this, indeed, he has an appointment with the servant later that day whither he has fled, in Samara.

Ferenczi (1933) not only recognized the analyst's inevitable participation, but the patient's awareness of it (see Aron, 1996)—and hence the potential for mystification. Thus what differentiates the analyst from the original perpetrator is his willingness to acknowledge what was heretofore denied and take responsibility for his own difficulty in tolerating his response to the patient. This "willingness on our part to admit our mistakes and the honest endeavour to avoid them in future, all these go to create in the patient a confidence in the analyst" and allow room for expression of critical feelings, he added. "It is this confidence that establishes the contrast between the present and the unbearable traumatogenic past ... absolutely necessary for the patient ... to re-experience the past no longer as hallucinatory reproduction but as an objective memory." (p. 33) Only in this way can we break through the patient's loss of confidence in "the testimony of his own senses" and counter his identification with the aggressor. And indeed we might consider either of these more likely to sponsor compliance in analysis than real reorganization.

In this view, a significant aspect of retraumatization is constituted by the analyst's failure to acknowledge, which the patient correctly grasps as the *avoidable* failure. It mystifies the patient in precisely the way she has been mystified as a child and perpetuates the doer–done to struggle. One likely outcome of such a failure is that the analyst then feels accused, in effect "done to" by the patient's suffering. When there is an underlying, if dissociated sense that someone must bear the blame, the patient's insight can become a travesty of responsibility. Her self-observation becomes a simulacrum of the Third, for it represents compliance to the other's demand to look only into herself, and thus an unwilling repair of the other. In this way the complementary power struggle around blame may pervert the process of recognizing responsibility and the power to change self and other.

Historically, feelings of shame (by analysts of all persuasions, I suspect) have been sponsored by the long-prevalent ideal of being what I have called a "complete container." As opposed to accepting enactment, this ideal was built on the belief that one could avoid opening the patient's wound in the way Ferenczi saw as inevitable, that one could bring about rebirth without experiencing some form of "death." More concretely, the idea of the analyst's containing through insight and internal conversation the most difficult feelings without "leaking" implied that one could self-regulate in the face of the patient's hyperarousal without showing signs of struggle, without using communication to create mutual containment (see Cooper, 2000).

This expectation of being in control, the healthy curing the sick, so trenchantly critiqued by Racker (1957) seemed to us relational analysts to be more likely to end in dissociation—denial of being affected. The alternative to this view is that the analyst exemplifies the internal struggle (Mitchell, 1997) and models the process of transcending failure, as formulated by Slavin and Kriegman (1998) in their seminal paper "Why the analyst must change." Further, as Safran (1999) points out, the patient's sense of agency and faith in the process, their overcoming of victimization, is thereby furthered. He traces this use of analytic failure back to the work of Winnicott (1965) and on into Kohut (1984), suggesting how this idea has been brought forward by pioneers in clinical theory. Indeed, Winnicott (1965) repeatedly emphasized the use of analytic failures, "In the end the patient uses the analysts' failures, often quite small ones, perhaps manuevered by the patient . . . and we have to put up with being in a limited context misunderstood" and even hated. Despite the analyst's careful adaptation, "it is the failure that at this moment is singled out as important on account of its being a reproduction of the original" and will create new growth (Winnicott, 1965, p. 258).

My argument here is not against the analyst using insight for self-regulation, nor for encouraging the patient to attain it, but for recognizing the intersubjective meaning of offering or accepting insights. The crucial relational theorem could be stated thus: expressing insight to the other is an *action;* it constitutes an acknowledgment of responsibility for one's psychic state; it is not simply a fulcrum for a shift in the patient's self-awareness but for the state of the dyad. When one person accepts responsibility for his actions it changes the other's view of him, and modulates the perception of the hurtful feeling; it creates a shift in self-state for the one who expresses the insight as well as the one who receives the expression. The intention or good will behind the effort—the procedural move— may be more critical than the content. In the therapeutic dyad, insight should have meaning as an intersubjective act of communication, helping to create or reinstitute a shared Third.

In complementary breakdowns the analyst might hold onto the belief that he is maintaining insight into the patient, that this constitutes a Third in his own mind, even though he is no longer in empathic contact (see Feldman, discussed in Benjamin, 2004a, Chapter 1). The analyst is then liable to expect that his insight (reality as he sees it) be accepted, which would mean, in effect, that the patient holds the hot potato of responsibility—*his* illness has caused the rupture. It is precisely in this way that the analyst appears to be reproducing the original injury in the manner Ferenczi noted—for no matter how "kindly" and educative the analyst may appear, he clearly thinks things have gone wrong because there is a wrongness in the patient. This refusal of the attribution or projection by the analyst in order to show the patient its true cause in his past can paradoxically serve to re-enact that past in the present: shaming, stigmatizing. The crucial factor may be that historically, in the original experience of failure, the child's protest of a problem was reacted to not as an effort to repair but as harming. It caused the other to fragment or retaliate. Thus acceptance of the naming of wrongness as a genuine effort to repair constitutes a transformational experience. Of course, insofar as this effort to repair takes place in a context of repetition, the analyst may well miss the repair as he feels pushed to enact the complementary transference of trauma and abuse (Davies & Frawley, 1994).

Thus in moments of opposition the "instinctive" move to tighten and shift into left brain formulation blocks mutual regulation, the shift out of dissociation into connection. What is required on the analyst's part is, actually the opposite: a surrender to the relationship between us at this moment, even if it seems quite uncomfortable and at odds with our ideal of ourselves as analysts, permits a relaxation of the tension—a step into the Third—and thus allows another part of self to come on line. Observation may then feel more genuine and less defensive or persecutory. An invitation to join a shared Third of looking together at "what has happened between us" may be procedurally more liberating than the attempt to figure it out for oneself, as Bromberg (cited in Grief & Livingston, 2013) has noted.

Observation versus acknowledgment

I wish to discuss in somewhat greater detail the case from the accomplished neo-Kleinian analyst John Steiner which shows the difficulty that arises (or used to arise) when the analyst holds to the idea of the Third as observing and figuring it out for himself, the idea of regulating himself through insight and without acknowledging the two-way dynamic to the patient. I see this case vignette as exemplifying the analyst's difficulty in living up to the analytic ideal of a "comlete container." The example, previously discussed in brief (see Chapter 1), comes from Steiner's (1993) much studied article on analyst-centered interpretations, a paper which represented an important contribution to the literature on countertransference at the time. It seems worth reviewing the issue since, in an article published many years later Steiner (2006) gave several similar examples and reiterated his original views. Furthermore, the same position was asserted in objection to my defense of acknowledgment by another British analyst of the same school (Sedlak, 2009). Thus I have reason to believe the issue is still a live one.

Steiner's original article presented the view that the analyst should relieve the patient's anxiety (what we would call regulating affect) by showing understanding, by formulating what the patient must be experiencing as the analyst's action. While such relief through understanding might be necessary, Steiner argued, it was not itself curative; he insisted on the preeminent curative value of the patient attaining insight over being understood.

I think the idea that a patient will be stronger when she can take responsibility and be a contributor to understanding herself in no way contradicts a relational view. However, the vignette Steiner presents to make his case for understanding illustrates the dilemma of separating insight from acknowledgment, observation from intersubjective recognition, the symbolic from the procedural. The relational experience of sharing understanding, intersubjective thirdness, is considered less important than the individual's knowing something—a separation of rhythmic and symbolic thirdness that I discuss elsewhere.

Part of why I chose this illustration was precisely because Steiner was in fact pushing the envelope in this paper, making room for the intersubjective knowing, and recognizing the problem of the analyst's dissociation. He stated, the analyst has a "propensity to be nudged into enactments . . ." and not understand what is taking place at the time, and proposed that the analyst should use the help the patient gives by receiving the patient's communications as corrective criticism of his work (a position also affirmed by Casement, 1991).

In the case vignette, Steiner reports a familiar interaction in which the analyst, who is struggling to contain the patient's projections, ends up pushing back into the patient by adding to his interpretation what he calls a "second critical remark." He says this arose from his "difficulty in containing feelings . . . *anxiety about her and possibly my annoyance that she made me feel responsible, guilty, and helpless.*" Such analytic missteps reflect the common problem mentioned above in which the analyst dissociates in the face of the dysregulation both partners are experiencing. As he becomes reactive and fails to contain he over-interprets, says something that sounds critical and shaming. Steiner is not unaware of his difficulty containing, but what is he supposed to do about it in the moment? Tell her how he is feeling? Note the usage "*she made me feel.*" Whenever we say someone "made me" do something, we are revealing our reactivity, our inability to self-regulate and stay in the space of thirdness where we can take responsibility rather than feeling something has been imposed. However, Steiner at this point does try to figure things out for himself and repair by use of his introspection, telling the patient, who by now has withdrawn, that *she* is afraid he "was too critical and defensive to understand her anger and disappointment . . . to recognize that she also wanted to make contact." To this skillful "analyst-centered" interpretation he even adds that she fears he "couldn't cope with these feelings because they would disturb MY mental equilibrium."

Quite a lot of insight, given how he is feeling, but note that this is presented as what his patient fears, not what he knows he actually was feeling. Steiner did not actually admit to her, as he does to his readers, that he *had* lost his equilibrium or minded having thereby hurt her, and so he goes on to attribute her withdrawal in the moment not to his prior blaming comment but to her inability to reach him the day before. He stops just short of acknowledging that what she fears did come about, or that he is sorry for it.

Why, we might ask, is such a deft containing formulation of the patient's fears not sufficient, why is stopping short of acknowledgment a problem? In part because Steiner's text goes on to detail how there has been a pervasive enactment with this patient, which takes the complementary form where each feels "the other is to blame." In other words, this struggle over blame appears to be the overriding relational dynamic that is unformulated, known but dissociated (Stern, 1997). Steiner reports in one passage that he generally has felt he was being made responsible for the patient's problems as well as his own, and in another reports the patient saying that he makes her alone "responsible for what happened between us," and refuses "to examine his own contribution" (p. 144). He does not note the symmetry—how his feeling about her mirrors hers towards him, and so the two statements about who is making whom responsible remain unlinked.

What seems to be dissociated is the reciprocal nature of the dynamic, the ping-pong of blame, which might be halted by an action he explicitly does not permit himself: acknowledgment of his part. That is, he might break this deadlock by using what could be called—adapting his phrase—an "analyst-centered acknowledgment." In my reading it is significant that at just this point in the narrative he tellingly rejects acknowledgment, inserts an affirmation of his conviction that a "confession" is not advisable because it would only create more anxiety.

From my perspective, Steiner's ideal of "complete container" prohibits him using the insights he shares with us or apologizing to regulate himself and his patient. Indeed, at this point in the text Steiner reiterates the maxim that only patient-centered *insight into self* is mutative. Like him, it seems, the patient must make do with regulating herself through insight—awareness of her fear that he might not be able to contain her anger and disappointment, to recognize her need to connect. In fact, he has just shown us how he himself has actually failed to accomplish the feat of regulating self through insight. He is still worried about who is to blame. Whereupon I wondered: is it a remarkable reversal to demand this feat of the patient? Who will be made anxious, who will experience it as a failure if the analyst acknowledges fault? Is it too wild to ask if the patient's insight is introduced here *in the text where he speaks to us* because this is what re-regulates the analyst, restores his sense of function in role, his confidence in the Third as something existing in his mind? Allows him to feel he can give the patient something and she chooses to make use of it? And by the same token, is it not likely that the patient is restored to regulation because obliquely Steiner has admitted his fault, has acknowledged her fear of his failure to contain her anger? Isn't it the insight and understanding expressed by the other that helps the self to feel safe enough to restore connection and shift self-state? In my view the articulation of the content of the fear, without the confirmation of its intersubjective reality, does go a way towards making the patient feel her mind has been understood. The tacit acceptance of the fact that analysts don't actually admit to anything may be attributed to the frame, and in this sense bracketed, not seen as truly affecting the goodness of the analyst's understanding.

In the best case scenario, then, such a repair of breakdown without full acknowledgment—a tacit procedural acceptance of the rules of the game—benefits the patient because she feels she has been able with her protest to elicit enough understanding that she and the analyst may go on together, until the next time they quarrel over who is responsible. Sadly, however, in many cases patients have been left, defiant or compliant, with bearing the burden of feeling destructive or disappointed, feeling the analyst has withdrawn or retaliated, not survived.

The problem this case exemplifies is not only that the analyst's dissociation will inevitably accompany the patient's but that the analyst's inability to regulate in the face of the patient's helplessness will generally lead him to some subjective experience of being "done to," as in "she made me feel responsible." The patient's implicit or explicit accusation triggers the analyst's shame and thus the patient's shame becomes the problem in the analyst, so to speak.

If, in fact, it is sometimes the patient's insight that restores the equilibrium of both partners, the rhythmic Third, if the analyst implicitly relies upon the patient's contribution to ending the projection-counter projection dynamic, then the question may be: does the analyst elicit that help honestly and show appreciation of the patient's understanding, or, as in Steiner's case, extract it by having the patient take responsibility and survive unspoken the analyst's dysregulation and rupture of thirdness? While the analyst can thus remain "good" and apparently safe, that is not overtly dangerous, the dilemma is that now the patient must be bad (angry, destructive) for the analyst to be good (Davies, 2004). The analyst in such a case may well be "dead," having failed to survive, as Winnicott said, and a semblance of analysis continues to be performed. The danger of destructive fantasies has not been alleviated, only moved to the other side of the seesaw. Analyst and patient can still injure one another. Rather than the safety of bearing this knowledge together they are left with dissociation as the protection against the fear of harming and being injured or damaged.

In practice, in the classically conducted analysis of the past, the way this often manifested was that the "good patient" with her reparative insight had to hold in check the patient who really needed healing, for whose sake she entered treatment: the "bad one" who protested against being unrecognized, the kind of patient a doctor like Ferenczi seemed tuned into but analysts at the time I entered training saw as intransigent. I came to believe that *paradoxically, the stance that was meant to protect the analytic container as a space open to all feelings good and bad— the stance of withholding direct acknowledgment of "what really happened"— might actually destroy the analytic function.* That is, it would preserve the analyst as an ideal object which was in some sense stabilizing for the patient, yet this stability was based on dissociating knowledge of the analyst's vulnerability. At the same time, the complementary relationship arose which embodied the split in which one person is good because the other is bad. The good analyst thus left the patient feeling responsible for his vulnerability as she was for her early objects, now as then bearing the burden of being the destructive one, alone and unrecognized.

Acknowledgment and the failed witness

I would argue that the pressure exerted by an ideal of the analyst as a "complete container"—and by this I mean the unformulated belief that one who is unable to self-regulate without help is failing as an analyst—potentially undermines the moral Third and the analyst's witnessing function. If the analyst imagines he can live up to the ideal of containing, he is liable to fail as a witness when it comes to acknowledging moments when he has exposed his inability to contain. This may lead the patient to confusion and doubt about what is real, what is past, what is present, as Ferenczi warned. We then miss the opportunity to be both witnesser and acknowledger, re-instate the Third by validating that some actions caused pain, felt like a violation of expectancy. We miss the chance to learn from failure, which may be the greatest learning of all (Jaenicke, 2015). This may in turn cause fear that the Third itself—the safety of responsible connection—could be lost.

If the patient feels as though she is responsible for making her analyst lose equanimity, which might for instance manifest as the analyst having nothing helpful to say after the patient has been critical, she is likely to feel she must choose between accepting being destructive or being left alone without the safety of the attachment. In such instances the analyst's own fear of failing or having been in the wrong can become an impediment to recognizing how frightened and destructive the patient might feel at this moment. Fear triggers a dissociation between those two alternating aspects, so that the "I make you feel bad" and "you make me feel bad" are unlinked, not held in a third position that witnesses.

Especially with severely traumatized patients, it is not a simple matter for the analyst to shoulder responsibility for being hurtful or insensitive because the patient's sense of danger and fear of injury may feel overwhelming for both partners. In moments of enactment the symbolic equation can be made between hurt feelings and actually causing damage, even death; the unconscious fantasies of destroying and being destroyed become powerfully active. I believe it is important to attend more fully to a significant feature that appears when such fears of a dangerous object are enacted, especially for patients with a history of trauma or disorganized attachment. *There occurs an elision—a symbolic equation—between the analyst's apparent failure to empathically witness, realize the full extent of the felt danger, and actually harming or abusing.* That is, when the analyst has in some way dissociated the depth of the patient's fear and pain, it is hard for both partners to distinguish the failure in witnessing, from actually being a guilty bystander or perpetrator of the crime. But, as I shall illustrate later, in the hyperaroused self-state this distinction is precisely no longer accesible—for one part of the self, the murder feels like it is happening now, being repeated as one feared it would! Even as another, seemingly helpless, witnessing consciousness, struggles to feel that this is not so.

In such moments, to bear responsibility for the injury that is being re-enacted, can appear both as an intolerable threat to the patient's safety as well as to one's identity as a reliable healer (tolerating threats to one's sense of goodness, as all analysts know, being one of the great challenges of our work). At the same time, this injury cannot be explained away as a repetition because in the self-state of re-experiencing trauma this would appear as a denial of the original harm or abuse. In the moment, this can feel like an unresolvable paradox for the analyst, a damned if you do and damned it you don't situation (see Chapter 6; Ringstrom, 1998).

Yet it becomes all the more critical to find a way to acknowledge the failure in witnessing, that is, the analyst not having fully taken in the depth of pain and terror, and in this way to gradually distinguish between failing to be fully present and actually denying or perpetuating abuse. The analyst needs to show the voice or face of the witness who is moved rather than that of the unmoved bystander upon whom the patient's suffering has no impact. The bystander, after all, is rightly seen as in some sense responsible for abuse or terror, for the breakdown in the moral Third. "How can you stand by and watch me be hurt and frightened?" the victim calls. It is up to the analyst to find a way to answer this call by moving through the position of failed witness, neither denying it nor getting stuck there.

My question has been, "How does the analyst bow gracefully to the inevitability that we must sometimes muddle ungracefully through such moments of breakdown?" To the fact that healing without ever failing is an illusory goal? This returns us to the question of the analyst's surrender. I have suggested that we move beyond Ghent's (1990) powerful analysis of surrender by the patient to a view of the Third as something that requires surrender by both members of the dyad, an asymmetrical but mutual process.

I do not wish to prescribe acknowledgment as a technique, rather show its role in renewing and building the moral Third. I want to clarify that expecting the patient to contain or survive some knowledge of our failures, is not necessarily asking the patient to tolerate failures without protest—it is precisely not asking the patient to hold the hot potato of blame, absorb all the badness in the relationship, not used to exculpate the analyst or to extract forgiveness. It is rather that the notion of the Third means that protest can be given a positive function, that embracing the inevitability of failures prevents bigger failures, and lets the analysis embody the principle of rupture and repair. This experience of thirdness points towards a way of valuing the things that can be learned and revealed by another person querying our behavior or thinking. It offers the patient a different interaction schema at the level of implicit knowing (a form of intersubjective relatedness). It transforms the potentail meaning of such challenges: not a dangerous power struggle but an occasion for mutual exploration and working through together.

The ultimate aim of acknowledgment is therefore, of course, not to relieve the patient of the need for introspection but to remove that process of gaining insight from a framework of blame and shame. Insight must come as an act of freedom, not something extracted or coerced. Arrived at through such a joining of forces, the realizations we attain come to exemplify the perspective of thirdness: recognizing that there are two participants who contributed to the interaction and that the analyst is trying to see both at once as best she can. The analyst's act of acknowledging the failure to hear, witness, or grasp the patient's experience helps to restore the Third procedurally, creating mutual regulation, even as it may also be the first step in symbolically analyzing the meaning of the enactment.

Therapeutic acknowledgment is thus a highly nuanced action, undertaken to transform the complementary see-saw of blame into responsibility, invite the patient into a shared Third, demystify and free each partner to comment on what is happening. It is meant to show that the analyst *can* change (Slavin & Kriegman, 1998). It is an action that develops faith in the *moral Third* because it affirms the lawful ethic of responsibility and counteracts past experiences of denial.

Becoming real through acknowledgment

I want to further illustrate the value of acknowledgment in overcoming the failed witness position by citing a case reported by Slavin (1998; 2010) in which revealing his struggle transforms the process. The case shows what it means to risk truthfulness, to give the patient a chance to become stronger as she, in a situation of relative safety, survives the analyst's dissociation and incomplete witnessing and containing. After many shared experiences of emotional abandonment in which she re-lived the other's unmoved reaction to her suffering, a woman whose predominant memory was that her mother *did not want to hold her*, called out to her analyst. The patient, Emily, exclaimed to Slavin "Can't you see I'm dying a little more each day!?" Slavin reports that he, "with a powerful feeling of resignation," replied that "at moments like this I sometimes feel like all I can do is be here with you in your despair." But he then found himself inspired to acknowledge truthfully to her: "I'm also aware that I'm trying to deal with the part of me that *really doesn't want to feel it*."

Next day Emily reported a strange experience, that Slavin's image as a person enduring the despair had a different feel to it, of "You as a person who's enduring the despair though you don't want to . . . telling me that puts you inside the image rather than outside it." She no longer experiences him as outside her desperation trying to understand it—he is inside it precisely because he does not deny his wish not to witness, to escape it.

Slavin concluded that acknowledging his struggle made visible to her how he replicated inside himself her inner tension, a version of what Stern (2009) and Bromberg (2006) see as the shift from dissociation to holding the conflict. He thus, I believe, models the recognition of Emily's dissociated part alongside the survival of his other mind, which simultaneously feels the wish to not be shut up and trapped inside someone else's despairing mind (the mother's unloving arms), yet knows the pain of being shut out and not held. His admitting a wish to avoid the pain could have been seen simply as a replication of the mother who did not want to hold, simply a repetition of the injury. Why was this not so? By the very admission to her of this aspect of repetition, in a language that showed his awareness of the wrongness of his not-feeling, a violation of what she might well expect from him. What changed things for Emily was the fact of not hiding and denying the problem—acknowledgment as an aspect of the moral Third. She felt this at a physical, procedural level such that he now looked different, three dimensional.

I have been arguing that the fear of doing harm and the guilt that prevents acknowledgment have both caused, and been exacerbated by, the expectation that the analyst cope with all conflict internally. But Slavin shows how the relational paradigm enables the analyst to facilitate the patient contributing actively to a co-created thirdness.

Acknowledging the failed witness part of self that wants to detach, Slavin freed up the other part of himself that empathizes and so allowed a true moment of being with her in pain. It was not necessary to override or conceal the urge to not be with because, as I will elaborate later (Chapter 6) the duality of meanings corresponds to two as yet dissociated needs, to witness and to admit failure of witnessing. In this moment Slavin believes that Emily can bear the truth, his image survives and she survives, survival is reciprocal. Truthful acknowledgment of what had been dissociated breaks through the complementary structure and faces head on the accusation: "You won't hold me," instead of avoidance of blame. So the helpless dance where each partner tries not to step into the bad feeling comes to a full stop.

I take Emily's words to mean: "I don't want to be feeling the feeling that I'm dying, so take it out of me—You hold it!" and the analyst's answer opened up the space of shared thirdness that contained the pain modified by the truthfulness of "I do and I don't want to feel it." Paradoxically, to acknowledge the wounding, the not being with, as Ferenczi advised, is precisely not to repeat the original form of the wound. Slavin's acknowledgment of failed witnessing was at the same time an acknowledgment of her right to want, to claim his recognition for her suffering.

Slavin's ability to maintain the tension of competing impulses to be with and to escape, his belief that she could survive his confirmation of a wish to detach from her pain, gave Emily confidence in her ability to accept his otherness. He became a separate subject, with his own feelings and conflicts. He did not, of course, disclose something particularly personal based on his personhood.

I think what is striking in this description of analytic work is the lack of coercion and omniscience on the analyst's part, and the fact that absent these the patient has room to develop her own subjectivity. Not omniscient or reactive, he is not responding to her coercive demand with coercion. His move is a very skilful reaction to the awareness of dissociation and of different self-parts, one that does not pose a burden for the patient.

Emily now begins to understand that another person can feel with her, be together with her, without having to. It's a moment where she can experience how dialogue between two people works. At a later point Slavin describes for her his conflict about whether or not to push her, and she responds: "This is such a strange relationship. We're here to understand *me*, but we have to understand *you* in order to understand *me*." Knowing and being known go together. The rhythmic Third of playful give and take begins to be assimilated into the symbolizing activity which formerly felt abstract and dead. Thus we see how an analyst's acknowledgment of his uncertainty and struggle posed not a burden but an offer of freedom for the patient. It was an opportunity to manifest the co-creation involved in having a relationship in which recognition is a feature.

In a further sequence, Slavin replied to Emily's persistent questions about how he would react if she committed suicide, saying that despite being terribly grieved he supposed he would go on living. As we discussed this in one of my study groups someone raised the question of envy. How would we think of Emily's obvious feeling that Slavin could go on living outside her despair and possible failure to live? It struck me that failed witnessing generates envy: you feel envy when you are deprived of witnessing and left alone, you envy the other person (like Emily's mother) who can escape into her seemingly intact world and not be present and feel with you, who doesn't have to bear that pain and shame. It seems to me that the envy is not of the analyst's "good milk," his analytic gifts, but envy that he is on the other side of the barbed wire while she is in the death camp; he does not really have to live day and night with this despair.

Perhaps we could also say that this envy functions to help Emily dissociate from her own pain, her wish (modelled on mother who would not hold her pain) to go home with the happy people who don't feel (as Jack Nicholson's character famously put it in *As Good as It Gets*, "the people who have picnics and eat noodle salad by the lake"). This envy seems generated by having been repelled, thrust out of a mind that would not hold her, a maternal body that would not bear pain with her, what Bion (1962a) called the mother's "comfortable state of mind" that does not contain the child. And indeed this not-knowing, not-recognizing is a grievous injury that is immensely difficult to heal. It is no doubt accompanied by a lack of experience with rhythmic thirdness that functions as a deficit, the result of an infancy devoid of affective meaningful recognition of distress.

Slavin holds the part that doesn't want to feel, which belongs to mother, but also which Emily—because of her envy of mother's seeming lack of need and wish to be free of need—couldn't be sure was not actually a part of herself. The multiple selves of can see and can't see, can feel and can't feel, do and don't need, become difficult to disentangle until the moment at which Slavin owns both opposing impulses, brings them together in a containing thirdness, and so, paradoxically makes the opposites distinguishable. The power of acknowledgment is not only the affirmation of truth as bearable but the linking of self-states and emotional positions that in being sundered, dissociated, prevent the wholeness of feeling one with ourselves and the other, even though we are also many.

Dissociation of collective trauma

The moral Third builds on speaking and witnessing and feeling together certain agonies, but survives and shows its mettle from recognizing our failure to do so. I believe there were many historical reasons underlying the psychoanalytic movement's commitment to dissociatively outrunning the analyst's appointment in Thebes, including the belief that only thus could psychoanalysis attain the less vulnerable status of science (Benjamin, 1999). Certainly, to hold the paradox that one both harms and heals requires linking states that inevitably tend to be dissociated. But along with our compassion for the difficulties involved, we might now be able to consider how, by denying their own reactions to trauma, the postwar generation of European analyst in particular blocked the road for the next psychoanalytic generation (my own) to face the knowledge of our history, their agony and the terrible price of survival.

In the last decade since I began work on this essay in 2005 we have seen how reflection on this process has generated a flourishing reflection on the transmission of collective trauma within psychoanalysis as a social group (Aron & Starr, 2013). Taking up the theme the "Wounds of History" (Salberg & Grand, 2017), contemporary analysts have addressed the way that the failure to witness in regard to its own history led psychoanalysis into grave difficulties confronting trauma in individual patients. I shall close with an example of such difficulties facing the past, where the force of intergenerational trauma activated identifications with the aggressor in mystifying ways, triggering dissociation and even a loss of self— one that was not worked out until much later.

Many years ago in Germany I took part in an intense enactment of the failure to witness and acknowledge in the face of transgenerationally transmitted trauma. In this enactment there occurred a symbolic meeting of victim and perpetrator in which the hope of healing foundered on a lack of openness. I had been asked to supervise a case as part of a workshop on intersubjectivity sponsored by a psychoanalytic group. The night before, with an inexplicable urgency, the presenting analyst, a young woman in training, handed me a typescript of two recent dreams of her male patient. The man, in his thirties, had had two dreams: in the first, an innocent victim, an old woman who belonged to a despised and denigrated group was being killed by his family while he looked on horrified; in the second, he himself had been exterminating small animals, invasive rodents, and then trying to hide the evidence of their blood on his bedding. When the analyst presented her case the next day, I asked for details of the patient's associations or session material, but she said she had none. The family history presented was oddly thin.

I soon felt embarrassment for the woman who seemed uncomfortable as well, and so with mindfulness of the topic, intersubjectivity, I asked about her own experience and reactions to the dreams in the session. She said she recollected nothing. As I began to feel increasingly anxious about exposing her to shame I also reviewed my initial speculation—one which I had not immediately assumed due to given the young age of the patient, who was born much after the war— that there were Nazi perpetrators in his family history. (At this time there was very little literature on the transmission of trauma from one generation to the next, and so I did not leap to the idea that it might have been his grandparents, not parents, who were Nazis.) Finally I asked the presenter directly about what the parents had done during the Nazi period and she came forth with facts about the patient's father being in the S.A., his subsequent decompensation after the war, including psychotic ideation about carrying dangerous germs on his work uniform that could harm his children. After further questions she stated laconically that the patient's uncle, the father's brother who was mentally disabled, had been put in the psychiatric clinic and then killed (implied was he had been murdered in the Nazi eugenics program).

As this information was communicated without comment and a notable lack of affect, and as it was ignored by the workshop participants who spoke of every-thing but the patient's father and his history, focusing the discussion on various other theoretical matters, I gradually found myself in an unaccustomed state. I felt myself forcing my mind to work against a thick fog. Even through the fog I registered vaguely a powerful wave of anxiety, an unformulated yet palpable perception of danger. Later, I put this perception into words, when I wrote "Here I am, the only Jew in this room, and I am supposed to be the one who talks about what is going on . . ." After some time I pushed myself to try addressing the issue again, saying that when a person knows that their parent has murdered people, or at least been present during murder or supported it, that is itself a terrible traumatizing thing; that the identification with such a father, which is now pushing its way to the surface in the treatment, has to be horrifying.

It is hard to describe the condition in the room at that moment, the anxiety that gripped everyone, the heaviness of the air. Especially the panic emanating from the therapist who, as I later found out, was indeed very preoccupied with the Nazi references and had already discussed her fear with the supervisor, the one who shepherded me before and after the meeting without speaking a word about it.

Despite my clear statement, there was no further mention by anyone of the problem of dealing with the Nazi past of genocide, murder or violence. I began to have a powerful reaction. I felt increasingly unreal and paralyzed, as in a dream where you try to run but can't move your legs. The audience was asking me theoretical questions about intersubjectivity in the treatment, but I could hardly focus. One part of me, as if from far far away, was thinking about Nazis and Jews; the other, nearby but in a fog, struggled to take in these questions and felt unable to answer them. I even ruminated self-critically afterwards about my inability to speak about the intersubjective, but without realizing why. I could not link the two things that were happening, could not associate this "How" to any reflection on the horrible "*What*" we had been speaking about.

I only came out of this fog many hours later, in another city, where a psycho-analyst friend, by coincidence seemingly, began telling me about a recent meeting where an émigré Jewish analyst spoke about his first return to Germany since he escaped in the thirties. She explained how she herself had been deeply affected and thus more aware of the need to speak about the Holocaust, which she had done at a conference shortly thereafter. As if the elastic band separating me from my experience suddenly snapped, the feeling I had in the meeting that morning re-entered my body. Now, in the presence of a responsive witness, I recognized it: it was terror. I realized that I had felt myself to be not merely a witness to a violence the perception of which was being denied by everyone else around me, but that actually I had felt as though I were in danger in the moment. It was as if the deniers themselves had become the perpetrators.

Denial of violence instigated the reliving of violence. Mystification, the result of what Grand (2002) has called "malignant dissociation," by the participants, had paralyzed my mind, my sense of agency, and left me unable to protect myself from this danger. I realized how exposed I had been. It was this experience that gave rise to my insight that denial, failure of witnessing, becomes elided with committing the injury.

I then began to develop a sense of outrage at having been asked to contain alone the history of violence while they, who suffered the collective trauma of being raised by and identifying with perpetrators, admitted knowing nothing. I recognized that the presenter had tried to evacuate the knowledge into me as symbolic repre-sentative of the survivors, so that I could in turn, break the dissociation, help her make it real. Instead, the denial intensified the projection of unwanted knowledge, the violent dissociation paralyzed me and I reacted as if to "real" danger. Strikingly, this paralysis took the form of a manifest, conscious concern with not hurting or damaging the presenting analyst, as if I were the perpetrator and she my victim. Panicked and uncontained by the group as a witnessing Third, she instigated this reversal. At lunch I uneasily noticed her visible relief at having gotten through the presentation, which later appeared to me as the relief of surviving unharmed, as if she were someone who had received a stay of execution.

I later came to understand more deeply how the accused can be terrified of their victim. I realized that as a representative of the victim group I could become the accuser-destroyer, in addition to which my position as supervisor made me feel responsible not to harm. Like the analyst who in the enactment comes to feel like the abused child while the patient appears to her as the parent, I was challenged to speak the unspeakable, to break the taboo on confronting the abuser. But in doing this, I would become a perpetrator. There was no way out.

In this way, we enacted the deep symmetry that underlies the complementarity of "doer and done to." This mystifying bind combined with the fearful horror all felt at the crime that could not be spoken. My "associated" conscious anxiety, driving my explicit behavior, was to be "good," that is, not injure or humiliate, while my implicit and more powerful dissociated experience held massive fear of being attacked—a replica of the patient's dream in which he watched with horror, alone in his feeling, surrounded by his family, as someone was killed.

I seemingly took in or replicated the patient's experience as if by osmosis; while in the dissociative state produced by intense fear, I felt like both perpetrator and victim, as did this patient. My fear that I would become a murderer by exposing the other—the therapist and the group's association—or perhaps identification with murder left me adrift in a state of knowing and not knowing; in turn, I felt some anxiety at being exposed by the group as unable to think, as if I were now weak. I also experienced firsthand the elision between failed witness and the perpetrator: the failure of witnessing by the large group, the imposition of silence and denial, felt like a real threat, an attack on my mind and my person.

I can say now with some regret that for me the enactment continued even after I wrote to the institute members about this event, expressing as much my outrage as grief. In their expressions of regret I (correctly or not) perceived nothing more than perfunctory concern with their own failure to witness, no reflection on or connection to what the event meant for them personally, or for their cohort who were all second generation Germans (and a few secretly Jews).[1] I reacted to the part of their response that persisted in dissociating themselves from the suffering, acting as though an embarrassing thing had happened only to me, not to them. In a sense, I engaged in a very familiar kind of outrage in which one moves from injury to judgment, missing my chance to witness. This kind of move to political argument or moral judgement might be thought of as a shift away from bearing pain to a protection from pain. While this leap to judgement is a common dissociative move, it is also a not uncommon reaction triggered by the kind of "malignant dissociation" that occurs when there is a social failure to uphold the moral Third, to acknowledge trauma and injury.

1.   I do not wish to leave the impression that denial is the predominant response I encountered in Germany. At the same time in the 1990s, other psychoanalysts in Cologne formed a group of children of Jewish survivors and Nazi perpetrators to open a brave, personal dialogue on the intergenerational effects of the Holocaust that continues to this day (Hammerich et al., 2016).

As I tried to illustrate here, such malignant dissociation can evoke a powerful specter of violence, and in large groups it may feel almost as violent as the acts it serves to deny. I now suspect that the more violent the trauma, the more violent the dissociation feels, the more paralyzing to thought and agency—and so the more violent the analyst feels in bringing it to speech.

In retrospect, with the experience of collective trauma I subsequently acquired, I recognized my own inability to be empathic with the sense of shame that is so paralyzing when one feels that one has been identified with the perpetrator, the destroyer. I also realized that my behavior during the workshop embodied an idea of being solely responsible, of protecting the other, the group from exposure; and that afterwards I just as intensely repudiated this guilty assumption of responsibility with outrage, a familiar dynamic of projection and counter-projection. In truth, though, it was I who had been holding myself responsible, as one might in the therapeutic dyad, for containing the shameful projection without speaking. I had done this because I feared that speaking would cause harm—to them or me—which at that time felt a shockingly real possibility.

That feeling of fear was so intense, it felt like terror in the face of some awful violence I must hold in and not show. I, alone and without a witness, could not encompass the violence of this trauma; believing myself to be the only representative of the victim, the Jews, in the room and yet with no official place as this representative I could not play my appointed role of allowing this trauma to be symbolically expressed in order to heal. It now seems understandable to me that occurring as it did in a large group of second generation perpetrators the enactment unfolded with such intensity, provided such an intense experience of dissociation of trauma.

We are now able to have greater perspective on how the post-war development of psychoanalysis was shaped by the escape from Nazi genocide; by the failure to acknowledge the analyst's inevitable responses to trauma, including guilt at surviving where others died. The psychoanalytic movement's norm of the "complete container" may have mystified and shamed the analyst. But it also defended against knowing about the analyst's powerful subjective feeling states and equally powerful escapes into dissociation, the analyst's own experiences with the world as a failed witness, a Dead Third as Gerson (2009) has called it. In this way the community left each analyst alone and uncontained with the fear of harm, and became instead the enforcer of a persecutory ideal. This ideal was a poor substitute for the moral Third that grows out of faith in acknowledging injury, witnessing trauma: the lawful process of encompassing vulnerability, witnessing pain and catastrophe.

In my view, this failure in the communal process of working through the subjective experiences of the psychoanalysts such as Ferenczi first recommended resulted in the inability to acknowledge and thereby give back to the patient a reflection of his own internal conflicts and the struggle to change—a true failure of recognition. To acknowledge such failure is the essence of the *moral Third* because it involves the lawful act of assuming responsibility rather than passing it off to the other, and at the same time bearing pain and shame in order to witness or recognize the other's feeling. When the analyst goes first, she is giving the patient a chance to assume, without demand or coercion, his own responsibility and thus embrace liberation from victimhood. It is at the same time a way to surrender to the Third, that is, to affirm faith in the necessary rhythm of rupture and repair, in the potential of the analytic dialogue and the pursuit of truth.

Chapter 3

Transformations in thirdness

Mutual recognition, vulnerability and asymmetry

This Chapter is divided into separate parts, the first emphasizing developmental theory in light of the Third and the second the clinical theory that is associated with it. My original reflections for this Chapter, "You've Come a Long Way Baby," given at IARPP in 2011, considered how the study of infancy, in particular the mother-infant relationship, led to an intersubjective psychoanalysis in which mutuality or mutual recognition plays a central role. So it was necessary to return to another point of origin in my theorizing: intersubjectivity as seen from the vantage point of recognizing women's, specifically mother's, subjectivity. This was a perspective that could evolve only through the co-incidence of feminism with intersubjective theory. Originally, I asked: If it is important for a mother to recognize her infant's subjectivity—that is, as another I rather than simply an It—how does anyone develop this capacity?

This question guided the moves I made in The Bonds of Love *(Benjamin, 1988), weaving the problem of recognition of women as subjects together with the evolving theory of intersubjectivity, as grounded in both psychoanalysis and infancy studies. The point of this move was to open psychoanalytic thought to the complexity of how we come to recognize the Other, to grasp the reciprocal action of two subjects knowing and being known, affecting and being affected, and thus to confront the problems attendant upon that bi-directionality.[1]*

The first part of this chapter presents the different ways of thinking about the Third as a position and a function, with its aspects of rhythmicity and differentiation. It is an expansion of Chapter 1, "Beyond Doer and Done To" and attempts to show the relationship between affect regulation and recognition. My original categories "Third in the One" and "One in the Third" are further explained as well as the importance of establishing a sense of the "lawful world,"

---

1   In terms of critical theory, the point was to take intersubjectivity out of the framework of normative model of societal discourse—an ideal—in which it was placed by Habermas and feminist followers like Benhabib (1992); to place it instead in a material developmental process, understood psychoanalytically, that recognizes the dialectic of obstacles in the struggle to recognize the other (see Benjamin, 1998; Allen, 2008).

a metaphor for the moral Third. I also suggest the expression "our Third" as a personal experience of intersubjective connection.

The second part, the discussion of clinical consequences and how we work with our own subjectivity, our vulnerability as analysts, illustrating the way in which we combine our understanding of affect regulation and recognition in our clinical work, use acknowledgment and our own vulnerability to create the moral Third. I also discuss further the idea of surrender in motherhood and in analysis, considering the consequences of elevating responsibility for the Other in Levinas' sense over our need for reciprocity and our desire for mutual recognition.

PART I. YOU'VE COME A LONG WAY BABY

In writing this chapter I wondered what might serve as a metaphor for mutuality that does justice to the concept. I thought of a tiny seedling, something that starts out small, as little more than a germ, needs tender responsiveness, much cultivation before it becomes a complex plant with deep roots, unfurls its leaves, produces flowers and bears fruit. But the limits of the metaphor are obvious—since in the human case the supportive environment and devoted horticulturalist of the sprout engage in a complex non-linear dynamic system that is bi-directional. The sprouting and unfurling and opening are talking back to the cultivator and are necessary to bring out her full capacities, as they are receiving the environmental nurturance they are amplifying and making it more complex. In a sense, it might work better to say the plant is the system of mutuality and two unequal people cultivate it. The plant, their mutual adaptation and recognition, is their Third.

Using the term mutual recognition has been hard for some thinkers to reconcile with the historical understanding of psychoanalyst and patient, the one who gives understanding and the one who receives, the healer and the healed. Not surprisingly, in psychoanalysis the possibilities of mutual recognition have been contested. The question has been raised repeatedly as to why recognition would need to be reciprocated. Isn't the point of psychoanalysis that the analyst recognizes the patient? Recognizes his or her needs, suffering, agency, self-expression? In more recent thinking, the patient who contributes to knowledge and so is not to be simply treated as an object of knowledge, nonetheless has been characterized as "the suffering stranger" whose need calls us to surrender (Orange, 2011). In what sense is it necessary, or desirable, then, that patients should experience mutuality, or in some form, a recognition of the analyst's existence as a separate subjectivity (see Gerhardt et al., 2000)?

Intersubjective vulnerability and the need for recognition

A consideration of recognition in early life takes us immediately to the associated problem of dependency as the organizer of our first relationships. Orange (2010), elucidating the concept of recognition in my work, expressed this idea with the term intersubjective vulnerability.[2] We need the other to recognize us, to be responsive or affirming, confirm the impact of our actions, and we can be hurt or harmed when the other fails or misrecognizes us. Why not see this need as determining a one-way relationship between the one who gives (mother) and the one who receives recognition (child)? Why do we need to think in terms of mutuality? Indeed it is true that for many people mutuality feels much too dangerous; being at the receiving end of recognition has not been a reliable experience, while giving it is often confused with submission to power.

Although it is true that human infants start out very asymmetrically dependent on the powerful caretaker, and that many of our patients have not found a viable way out of that asymmetry, it is a limited way of life and they enter analysis to overcome it. A host of post-Freudian thinkers have formulated the argument that analysis provides an ameliorative experience, asymmetrical in nature, of receiving the recognition—responsiveness, reflection, or mirroring—that was lacking in early life. But what of the ameliorative experience of giving? Paradoxically, it would seem to be a lack of a positive asymmetrical experience that has made them incapable of symmetry. The complicated task is to help them become more capable of mutuality in an asymmetrical relationship. The evolution into mutuality involves asymmetrical vulnerability to injury and thus requires our asymmetrical responsibility for the process (Aron, 1996; Mitchell, 2000), providing an opportunity to recapitulate developmental steps in the course of being safely held and understood in a very asymmetrical way.

However, a more careful consideration might reveal that the historical absence of trustworthy asymmetry already reflects a problem in the area of mutuality, and so some version of mutuality contributes the amelioration. Perhaps this idea can be framed by postulating that even in very asymmetrical relations of infancy there are germs of mutual recognition that need to be recognized and cultivated in analysis. The mirroring mother needs the mirroring baby, as facial mirroring is a bi-directional process in which each follows the others direction of affective change (Beebe & Lachman, 2002; Beebe et al., 2013). The child needs understanding in part so as to be able to understand the other's mind, to not be clueless. To mentalize, grasp the other's mind, is perforce an action in relation to the other and not merely a capacity. Psychoanalysis must be based on understanding the process of development by which human beings become more capable of mutuality, more able to recognize the other. This development ideally is associated with more vitality, agency and ability to balance dependency with independence.

2   In her original commentary on "recognition-as" Orange was critical of my use of the concept of recognition, apparently based on certain misconceptions cleared up in her subsequent reading of my work (Orange, 2010) that I define recognition as a "Must", something the one must give the other. However, Orange's parsing of the concept in terms of "recognition as", which focuses our minds on acknowledgment as a vital form of recognition raised valuable questions which will inform some of what follows.

Oddly, we must take account of just how little attention was given to the development of mutuality before the emergence of relational psychoanalysis and simultaneously the study of infancy (see Benjamin, 1988). The necessary tension between the relationship of mutuality—the connection between the two persons who recognize the other as Thou in Buber's sense of I-Thou rather than I-It—and the asymmetrical responsibility of both mother and analyst was first clarified by Aron (1996). The analyst is responsible for the process of mutual regulation, the safety of the container, the ongoing attunement to the patient's needs and process. As Mitchell (2000) puts it, the most asymmetrical aspect of analysis is constituted by the fact that the patient is meant to abandon and let go of responsibility for all that goes on while the analyst maintains it. Of what then does mutuality consist and why does recognition theory need to shine light on the marbling of its subtler lineaments within the well-known figure of asymmetry?

Through our experience with classical analysis and our critical attention to its problems, relational analysts have come to recognize that this asymmetry expressed in terms of knowing, objectivity and authority (Hoffman, 1998) may also intensify the issues of control attendant upon accepting dependency. The complementarity of giver of attention and given to, knower and known, can devolve so that one person appears to be the knower and director, the other the object. The patient may at one moment relish the freedom of abandon, but at another feel it is offered only as long as he is the one who is powerless, like a child who has no effect on the other. Such feelings, of course, go with the territory of the transference. The point is that asymmetry of responsibility has its shadow side of power, can become sucked into the complementary transferences of doer and done to, and thus present us with the same necessity of working our way out into thirdness as any other form of splitting.

The modification of this complementary breakdown can only occur through awareness of how the analyst's view and style of performing asymmetrical responsibility serves either to impede or facilitate the move into thirdness. The outcome depends on how we use the intersubjective relationship to encourage development of the patient's sense of agency and authorship by recognizing his impact upon us and his contribution to the ongoing work. My way of thinking about this evolution towards a more mutual relationship within the analytic process is expressed in the idea of creating the shared Third.

Bromberg has eloquently described the experience of movement towards mutuality in analytic work from the analyst's perspective. He recounted that as he became able to hold in awareness the separate inner worlds of himself and his patient while yet feeling their connection, his inner world became more available as a source of knowledge about the other. This simultaneous difference and connection made it unnecessary for him to "figure things out on his own" because he and his patient were now felt to be "parts of something larger than either of us alone." Thus, gaining access to unconscious experiences in each partner "became a matter of finding it *together. A give and take that gradually builds a linguistic bridge between the inner and outer worlds of each of us*" (Bromberg in Greif & Livingston, 2013, p. 327). We might say the "larger something" is the Third, which reveals itself through the give and take.

From this perspective, asymmetrical responsibility would not consist of figuring it out alone, but of the charge of keeping the attention on self, other, and the bridge. If the analyst commits to go with the patient to the brink of the abyss (Bromberg, 2006) that looms before her, he can feel himself being in her world with her even as he stays aware of his own inner world: building the bridge (Pizer, 1998). With this, Bromberg is describing the subjective experience of thirdness: being part of something larger with the other person, a shared process of exploration. The felt sense of being in this place together includes each person's respective worlds as well as the symbolic links between them.

Fortunately, not only clinical practice but the rich field of infancy studies has provided ample templates and metaphors for such evolution. In what follows we shall trace how mutuality arises—even under conditions of asymmetry—because analyst and patient are involved in a process I like to think of as "building the Third."[3] Mutuality consists of this ever more *subjectively realized* sense that we are sharing in the doing and feeling: co-creation is felt experience of building together rather than merely posited and perceived as mutual influence from a God's eye view. Mutual influence can exist objectively without our having the slightest sense of having an impact, or receiving one. More important, mutual influence can consist of a tight, reactive feedback loop with negative impact, in which someone consistently avoids connecting when invited and looms or intrudes when not, as in the chase-and-dodge interaction (Beebe & Stern, 1977). Mutual recognition is what happens when we *share and reciprocate knowing*. We know the other is a person who is, or at least could be, connecting, aligning with our intentions, matching, getting it and being gotten.

Symmetry and asymmetry: the rhythmic Third

The study of mother-infant interaction inaugurated a paradigm shift whose revolutionary implications were at first resisted by mainstream psychoanalysis but were eventually accepted in North America. The metaphor of the infant with the breast was upstaged by the social infant who engages in play interaction. The symmetrical aspects of give and take, mutuality and reciprocity were the focal point of the new infancy studies (Tronick et al., 1974; Stern, 1974a/b; 1977; Tronick et al., 1977—cited in Benjamin, 1988; Tronick, Als & Brazelton, 1979; Trevarthen, 1977; 1979). Stern (1985) explicitly contrasted the giver-receiver relation of nursing to the symmetrical, reciprocal relation of face-to-face interaction between mother and baby. Stern's sensibility was based on a deep appreciation of the need to know other minds in order to connect, the intersubjectivity of each

---

3   Thanks to Yitzhak Mendelsohn for the metaphor of building for the process of co-creation. Thanks to Beatrice Beebe for the emphasis on the centrality of sharing.

of us knowing that the other knows that I know (Stern, 2004). That reflexivity of knowing that we know, and hence we are connected from within, as subjects not objects of knowing, is what we might call the Basic Recognition.

For me the idea of mutual recognition versus split complementarity, first developed abstractly and philosophically, assumed more concrete form through the manifest contrast between soothing or satisfaction and knowing or sharing intentions in interpersonal engagement. In *Bonds of Love* (Benjamin, 1988), I used this paradigm shift to articulate the distinction between sharing of states and asymmetrical complementarities such as giver and receiver. I cast identification via state sharing as the opposite to the doer and done to relation, that is, the reversal via projective identification that imbues the other with the power and agency one lacks or the helplessness and passivity one disowns. "Being with"—Stern's formulation which later became an essential part of clinical theory (see, Boston Change Process Study Group, Stern et al., 1998; BCPSG, 2010)—figured as a form of relating that transcends or modifies the dualisms of asymmetrical caregiving. That is to say, we can be giving care in a complementary way or in a way that includes emotional reciprocity and state sharing. Intersubjective relating that transcends dualism is one way of thinking about what I gradually came to understand as functioning in the position of the Third. The Third *as form* operates in all moments in which a tension is held mutually rather than through splitting of opposites in complementary relations.

The Third in this sense presents procedurally in nascent forms of mother-infant relatedness where we see the emergence of recognition. State sharing, attunement, matching specificities, moment to moment alignment of intentions and feelings—all forms of recognition Sander (1991) called "moments of meeting"—comprise a framework of expectancy essential to early development in the dyad. They form the basis of the earliest experiences of thirdness, by which I mean interactive manifestations of the *Third*. As a *function*, we find thirdness in the initial co-created pattern of reliable expectations of alignment and matching or state sharing that mother and baby experience as "our way of being together," patterns which create the dyad's secure attachment (Ainsworth et al., 1969; 1978) but also the intimacy of mutual knowing (Stern, 2004).[4]

If mothers or babies are used such language, they might think of it as "the Third we build together," or "Our Third." The idea is that both partners contribute, neither one alone determining its directions; rather than being engaged in a pattern of simple reactivity—as in the split complementarities of active-passive, doer–done to, giver-receiver, knower-known—both partners are actively creating alignment of direction according to their own abilities (Beebe & Lachmann, 1994; 2002; Beebe, Jaffe & Lachmann, 2013). Understanding how mothers and babies adapt and create mutual regulation, we could infer they are guided by the meta-

4   Of course insecure attachment and non-recognition can also have a reliable pattern, with contingent responses that have a negative emotional valence, such as mother looking away when the baby gazes, and baby in turn looking away when mother touches or seeks contact.

expectation of returning to alignment with "our Third." This relational expectation has been conceptualized by Tronick (1989) in terms of the principle of disruption and repair: disruptions of the interactive patterns are tolerated and repaired in an ongoing process that fosters resilience. As Beebe and Lachman (1994) point out, if the dyad is mutually regulating in such a way that normal violations of expectancy—mismatching or disjunction—are adjusted and the couple returns to matching, then infants contribute as much as mothers do to the process. As mother-infant dyads move through moments of procedural adjustment, that is repair of disjunction, each moment strengthens the infant's resilience, gives the mother confidence in her capacities, and enlarges the space of negotiation and accommodation of difference in their shared thirdness—experienced as "Our Third." This principle of expecting repair of violations is highly significant because our concept of the recognition process involves repeated breakdown, ongoing negotiation and reorganization, enabling higher levels of complexity and resilience.

Negotiating and repairing disruptions illustrates the general proposition that, potentially every time we are changed by the other—every time we shift to match, accommodate, reflect the other's need—that change is registered and produces a corresponding shift in the other's sense of agency, impact and self-cohesion. This inherently satisfying mutuality of impact is the deep structure of recognition without which, I believe, there is a failure of meaning. Without it, there is only the emptiness of being an object for the other rather than an agent in a lawful world. To be sure, the mother's deliberate accommodation is vital, insuring this evolving process. Without her accommodation, the infant is left to regulate on his own without repair and so without faith in the other's recognition of his impact. Conversely, we may imagine that the experience of mutual impact deepens trust in attachment, in the recognition process, in "Our Third."

What distinguishes recognition from regulation or mutual influence is this: gradually the sense of affecting the other to create correspondence of intention and action becomes a distinct and appreciated part of the experience rather than being an unrealized concomitant of our action. Recognition becomes an end in itself: human beings want to *share* attention and intentions (Beebe & Lachmann, 2002) not only for the sake of state regulation and soothing but also, as with more complex contingent responsiveness, for the sake of *sharing* itself (Beebe, in conversation). Recognition involves knowing and being known, as in "moments of meeting," when, as Sander puts it, "one individual comes to savour the wholeness of another" (2008, p. 169).

The Third corresponds to the locus on the axis of intersubjectivity where we recognize others as separate, equivalent centers of being/feeling rather than as objects, as Thou (Buber, 1923). Since I have repeatedly heard that the meaning of the Third is elusive, the term not immediately graspable, in what follows I will outline my usage of the concept, with the caveat that this is still a work in progress. I propose thinking of the Third as a position—a relational psychological position applying to tensions and oppositions within and between selves. Thinking of the Third as a position draws from and bears resemblance to Klein's formulation of the depressive position, in which we can accept within ourselves a host of binaries, including that of doer and done to. But in my usage it is meant to describe the state of the relationship, the stance towards real others, not to representations of internal objects.

As I suggest here, this position may be viewed in terms of both form *and* function in development. As *form*, the third position designates both a kind of relationship and its organizing principle, which transcend splitting or dualism. The *function* of such a relationship or principle is to serve as the basis for lawful relating to other humans, to enable recognition of the other, to move us out of tendencies towards control and submission. Form and function coalesce in various pheno-menal experiences of thirdness or co-creation—sharing of states, harmonizing, recognition of other minds through matching specificity (Sander, 1991), under-standing and negotiating differences. All express the position of differentiating without polarizing, connecting without erasing difference.

We may imagine the psychological position of the Third originating in the mutual accommodation, the system of adaptation and fitting (Sander, 2008) between mother and infant that I now call for simplicity's sake the rhythmic Third (see Chapter 1). Initially (Benjamin, 2004) I tried to conceptualize this position with the phrase "the One in the Third," meaning the kind of joint harmonious creation (Third) based on recognition or being "in tune." We may think of a rhythm developing from the caregiver's recognition of and accommodation to the infant's earliest needs and the evolving mutual adaptation in feeding and holding, sup-porting the emergence of shared intentions (Sander, 1995) and communication. This rhythmic Third also builds upon the sharing of positive affect states or attention as well as the intentional coordination of actions—for example, gazing, head nodding, leaning in or away, vocalizing, movement in general—that support the recognition process in the procedural dimension. It creates a basis for inter-acting in a way that allows the baby to exercise agency through regulation of his own state by affecting the other in a more differentiated way (Sander, 1991). That is, the issue of whether our action has the intended impact and is recognized as intended becomes central.

To the extent that mutual alignment and the development of the rhythmic Third proceed well enough, they also generate stable representations of procedural interactions, that is, patterns of (positively contingent) expectancy: "Our Third." Actions may match or violate those patterns, but significantly smaller violations may be followed by return to the expectable, which itself becomes an expectable pattern; this implies reorganization at a more complex level (Beebe & Lachmann, 1994). Or, as in disruption and repair, the dyad may find a specific form of correc-tion. The relationship of safety in dependency, which has been called attachment (Ainsworth, 1969; Bowlby, 1969)—so vital for our clinical understanding—is shaped by whether such patterns of fitting and coordination can be relied upon, and whether they are constituted by control or responsiveness to needs, broken by exciting novelty or in disruptive ways. All of which, of course, influences the dyad's level of arousal, or mutual affect regulation.

The outcome of such ongoing adjustment contributes to the construction of what I think of as lawfulness in human relating, a rhythm of recognition. Here, try not to think of law as in decree, prohibition, government. By lawfulness I am denoting not prohibitions or decrees, or even explicit rules. I mean the quality of reliable patterning and coherent dyadic organization (Tronick, 2005; 2007) at affective and sensory-motor levels of interaction that might be thought of as a baby's idea of the "natural order of things." Now it is true that the natural order and system to which an infant may become used could be highly depriving of agency or quite painful, an arrangement involving control and pathological accommodation. It would be without the essential element of contingent responsiveness whereby one's intentions are affirmed. So in this usage, lawfulness would signify sharing of intention, the infant equivalent of the aesthetics of harmonious existence, something like the implicit relation to harmony in music or synchrony of motoric movement in dance. The harmonious, coordinated movement is the opposite of both tight control and fragmentation or disintegration; it thus expresses physically what later appears psychically. In this sense, as we coordinate, we are able to savour each other's expressions of intention.

Rhythmic thirdness depends on co-creation, that is continuous mutual adjustment that persists through variation of patterns, which allows for acknowledgment of difference and deviations by both partners. The representation of "the lawful world" thus includes difference as well as harmony in co-creation. I hold this to be a key representation in the infant's mind, the basis, long before speech, before a symbolic order, of a lawful world known through the sensory-affective musical order of coherent mutual relating (see Knoblauch, 2000). Not the paternal "law of separation" (Chasseguet-Smirgel, 1985), the Law of the Father, of do or don't (oedipal law), but the "law of connection."[5] Of course this rhythmic Third will have great consequence for our later relation to the symbolic domain.

Affect regulation and mutuality

The dimension of early mutuality that I refer to as establishing the rhythmic Third, originally understood through infancy studies, has more recently come to be theorized in terms of affect regulation. Some years after infancy research began to revolutionize psychoanalysis, the introduction of neuroscience into the field started to confirm a view of affect regulation (Schore, 1993; 2003; Siegel, 1999; Hill, 2015) that meshed with both recognition and attachment theory. What seems particularly germane is the connection between affect regulation and emotional integration. Affect regulation refers to maintaining a range that is neither over- or under-aroused such that both painful and positive affect can be differentiated

5   In other words, I am sharply distinguishing the idea of "the lawful world" and lawfulness from Lacan's law of the father, the father's No, the prohibition, the taboo, the boundary that comes with the symbolic order.

and shared. Siegel (1999) and Schore's (2003) articulation of the integrating function of emotion (Fosha, Siegel & Solomon, 2012) corroborates Stern's (1985) earlier views, and suggests that self-cohesion (Kohut, 1977) comes from the ability to share and express affect states. The proposition might then be expressed as follows: *recognition of affect by the other*, in communicative action, promotes the integrating function of emotion within the self.

Conversely, and by extension, the integration of discrete, articulated emotions that results from recognition serves to diminish hyperarousal, which is to say, makes the having of feelings less anxiety producing; it thereby expands the "window of affect tolerance" (Siegel, 1999; Schore, 2004). In a recursive move, we can say that the expansion of what can be known, borne, and communicated in turn widens the field of mutual recognition. Conversely, as the recognition process allows more emotions to come into play between two partners, it extends the range of experiences they can share and reflect upon—including those otherwise unbearable experiences that people come to therapy to heal or at least make less disruptive and damaging. Thus recognition and regulation are co-determining.

The proposition that recognition and regulation work in tandem points us towards a further intersubjective issue: that the *sharing* of affect states is complicated not only because affects themselves may exceed the level of our own tolerance. They may also, unfortunately, exceed what the *other person* can tolerate. Once affect has broken the window of tolerance, emotions are no longer recognized (by self or other) as specific feelings; rather, affects take on an aspect of chaotic dysregulation. As they are not contained in articulated form, they become intolerable to the psyche or disruptive to the attachment relationship. They interfere with the mutual coordination of intentions, impede sharing of states, and are liable to cause dissociation and disconnection.

In this incarnation affect can appear dangerous; in common parlance feelings are threatening, even though in actuality the emotions are not being *felt*. It also becomes difficult or impossible to recognize feelings, emotions as such, for as we often note in the clinical situation, what is being transmitted is disorganized, inchoate, sub-symbolic. The transmission is felt to be too uncomfortable or over-stimulating for the receiver who cannot therefore locate them in the containing window, who feels unable to "think." Whereas specific emotions can be identified and shared as a coherent, organized experience, the sharing of hyperarousal is quite a different matter. It is contagious, but not experienced as voluntarily shared. Such experience feels impinging and thus not mutual but asymmetrical: here arises the sense that "something is being *done to* me."

A person holds such dissociated affect in self-states which are experienced as not-me or shameful and thus disruptive to the ongoing "Me" (Bromberg, 2000). I would add, they are also disruptive to the shared "We" that creates meaning together. The pressure of this unformulated experience (Stern, 2009), conveyed in unconscious communication and dissociated enactment calls out for, though it often impedes, recognition by self or other. When the other is able to meet this pressure with understanding of what has been inchoate, overwhelming and isolating, that is contain, there occurs a palpable experience of the value of the other's separate mind—in this sense, recognition of the other.[6]

Thus dissociation and recognition become poles of affect relations—negative and positive poles of connection. Early lack of recognition predicts disorganized attachment and later dissociation (Beebe et al., 2010). The more dysregulated and incoherent the affect, the more experience leans towards dissociation and away from recognition by self and other. The less recognition of affect, the less coherence and containment, the more dysregulation and consequent dissociation. *Hence, recognition and regulation, while not exactly the same, are dynamically linked.* They are both indispensable to connection and, clinically, to repair of what has remained disruptive or traumatic in early relating. When there has been a tilt towards asymmetry without a sense of responsive subjectivity, the attention to affect regulation helps to restore the conditions for recognition. Likewise, the acknowledgment to the patient by the analyst of failures in recognition—a failure that is a violation of expectation for help or understanding—is a form of repair that restores mutual regulation.

Thinking in terms of the synergistic relationship between recognition and regulation enables us to better understand the procedural dimension of two persons gradually building a rythmic Third and to appreciate its therapeutic function. Each therapeutic relationship constructs its own complementary dilemmas reflecting both partners' attachment histories, each must therefore find its own forms of thirdness through which to engage them. The relationship, regardless of content, becomes the medium for changing the internal working model of the individuals' respective attachment paradigms (Ainsworth, 1969; Bowlby, 1969; 1973), which may vary with self-states. When growing trust in the evolving implicit thirdness alleviates mutual dysregulation and creates a zone of affective sharing this can be translated into the patient's internal working model of attachment, their representation of the other. In this way previous unlinked, dissociated experiences can be wired together (Siegel, 1999; Bromberg, 2006; 2011; Schore, 2011) through mutual recognition.

Maternal subjectivity and the differentiating Third

Whereas I formulated the rhythmic Third by looking at the early attuned dyad, the differentiating Third was initially observable to me by focusing on the mother's subjectivity. For this reason I originally described this differentiating position as "the Third in the One" (Benjamin, 2004a), meaning this: if we think of what used to be called "oneness" as an experience of a harmonizing pattern that feels like union, this Third differentiates between the two partners that harmonize to create that pattern. This view of the Third incorporates the recognition of different parts, different needs, different feelings that go into the way mother and baby create

6   McKay in conversation.

their mutually regulating pattern. Eventually, this difference becomes the basis for recognition of the other as a person with their own mind and perspective.

Mother, of course, ideally holds this awareness in mind from the beginning. But as time goes on each does something different to make it work. Mother is primarily responsible for making it work, for scaffolding the baby's action, while baby "plays along." The differentiating Third refers to an awareness of the distinct part played by other required for the coordination and resonance to work, the "something more" than just us two matching even while we are feeling "at one." This surplus attention to the other's regulation based on recognition of difference characterizes the mother's asymmetrical responsibility.

While developmental theory takes for granted this asymmetrical awareness in considering the needs of the baby, we are here considering its emergence in the mother. For the mother, her position in the shared Third which she and baby are building derives from the representation in her mind of the relationship, what it is and how it should be, her fantasies and her ideals. And as we shall discuss shortly, it matters a great deal whether this vision expresses the third position or the dynamic position defining alternatives as being either "for you or for me," control or submit and sacrifice; whether from a vision of differentiating thirdness or complementary twoness. It matters whether the mother can have an experience of mutuality in which she appreciates baby's part, recognizes his sprouting version of subjectivity; whether she can recognize his responses even though necessarily less defined and contingent than hers, and so encourages baby's agency and co-creation—as opposed to simply trying to manage the baby as object to fit her need for order or reactively accommodating to the point of behavioral unpredictability, internal chaos and depletion.

The ability to provide recognition depends not only on empathy or attunement, her ability to connect with what she can identify as "the same," but also upon her ability to do this while distinguishing their very different bodily states and capacities for self-regulation and soothing, to name only one category. Without this distinction, the mother's identification with a distressed baby (stiffening, howling, grimacing) can be overwhelming to her; her anxieties about consoling and being consoled may interfere with recognizing the difference. She may respond by fragmenting or becoming rigid, hyperaroused or shut down and manifestly dissociated. There is a synergistic relation between maintaining her own self-regulation and learning to read and respond to the communication of her particular baby's movements and sounds in order to help regulate his states. On this vital though usually ignored capacity for knowing the difference depends the quality of a mother's mirroring, her attuning, and hence the mutual recognition or Third.

We (including the mothers among us) expect good mothers to be not merely dutiful, submissive, sacrificing but also able to support the mutuality of play, as well as the differentiated affective connection that allows each person some agency. Furthermore, the mother is supposed to be able to divide herself and present to the baby the facet of herself that matches his need. She should be able to focus her attention and join with the baby's excitement even when she has been sleepless all night, in other words, when she is aware of her different need. How does she do this? How does a mother divide herself in the way that Slochower (1996) called holding, create mental space for conflicting desires, and move between multiple self-states so that this responsibility does not vitiate her own vitality and empathy? We shall delve into the problematic realm of such expectations shortly.

For now, let us acknowledge that the asymmetrical responsibility for soothing, for scaffolding the baby's actions so the couple can co-create a rhythm, poses a challenge for the mother of managing her *own anxieties and conflict*. Meeting this demand further illuminates the function of the differentiating Third, that is, appreciating the existence of more than one mind, set of needs or point of view. The mother must be able to relate to more than one thing or person, for instance to more than one child at a time. Recognizing both her own need and the baby's need as legitimate, but knowing whose need comes first, allows the mother to relate to the baby's cry in the middle of the night not as a persecutory experience of being "done to," submitting to the tyrant baby, but as a necessary condition. This is just how babies are, this is "How it is," rather than how she would wish when she is deprived of sleep.[7]

How she maintains a sense of her own goodness and her self-regulation is intertwined with tolerating the difference between her ideals and What Is. But let us note how such acceptance of necessity and difference, the holding of multiplicity, in short, the relation to the Third depends upon self-regulation and the ability to facilitate a satisfying pattern of mutual regulation (Beebe & Lachmann, 2002; Sander, 2002). In other words, she has to get her baby organized enough to feel some sense of effectance: I can soothe and calm this baby's distress. Of course her ability to do that vital thing (which sometimes feels like a dire necessity, for instance, if there's a needy toddler nearby) depends upon being able to regulate her own anxiety when something has gone wrong. As we shall see, this depends on a number of things, but here I emphasize her relationship with her ideals— being able to tolerate her own imperfection and that of her child. So conversely, her regulation depends on what we think of as dynamic and characterological psychic attributes, which may or may not enable her to accept conflict, multiplicity and disappointment. These affect how tightly or loosely she holds her ideals, her

---

7   This idea grew out of a commentary on Sander's ideas about the maternal dyad as a system of mutual adaptation. His perspective inspired me to formulate this idea of the Third as dually aspected, both accommodating and differentiating. Sander's study demonstrated how babies adapt to sleeping through the night precisely because mother accommodates them by feeding on demand. I used it to theorize the rhythmic Third, in which one accommodation elicits another (Benjamin, 2002; 2004a). However, as my own taxing experience of night feeding a newborn whose circadian rhythm was thrown off by an extra week in the hospital nursery under bilirubin lights made clear to me, establishing this rhythmic Third is supported by a mother's own relationship to the differentiating Third.

personal "religion" of good mothering, and whether she dissociates or collapses when she does not live up to them. Her idea of goodness can guide her to balance her identification with the baby's emotional states with the ability to keep her own mind; but it can also dictate stringent requirements, make her more unresponsive and anxious. Some maternal "religions" polarize good and bad, deny the conflict between mothers and their babies, while others are more compassionate and flexible and yes, joyful. All of the above constitutes a mother's relationship to the differentiating Third.

Thus we can see how maternal self-regulation is informed by differentiating capacities even as it correlates with accomodation to the other's rhythm to create mutual regulation. Rhythmic and differentiating thirdness contribute equally to support negotiating the conflict between how things are and how we wished them to be: another way to express the relation of disruption and repair. Further, capacity for holding difference helps to resolve moments of dysregulation and prevent full on ruptures. For instance, in early face-to-face interactions, attunement and adaptation depend on the mother's acceptance of difference. She is able to back off and cease to stimulate when baby gazes or leans away to down-regulate, tolerating the difference between her initial intention and baby's response. She can interpret her baby's glancing away not as a rejection but as the baby's own need to lower stimulation; when she accommodates his personal pacing, this then becomes his contribution to their joint rhythm. Later, he does not have to respond exactly as she would like in order to reassure her, nor she to him. Both work within the usual optimal range of one Third matching (Beebe & Lachmann, 2013). Building the rhythmic Third thus depends upon the mother's differentiating Third, even as differentiation depends upon the regulating function of rhythmic coordination. The "reward" of accommodating to the needs of her little partner is that the mother can share in states of high affective intensity, joyfulness, play as well as feel able to comfort and soothe.

The differentiating Third is a position that contributes to capacities for reflective awareness, observation and thinking about difference, all of which can be more or less symbolically mediated (see Aron, 2006). This position has often been understood as symbolic functioning, and sometimes it has seemed to me more appropriate to call this the symbolic Third. I believe, however, that differentiation is the overarching feature, that it is a thread running through the recognition we create both in pre-verbal, proto-symbolic and in verbal, symbolic communication. While there are many ways to slice this pie, the cut I am making is not primarily between sub-symbolic procedural and symbolic relations, between implicit relational knowing and explicit verbal communication. Rather, I am suggesting a categorical distinction between two crucial elements that constitute the position of the Third: the creation of harmony, fittedness, joining and the acceptance of difference, division, opposition. Writ large, recognition of the other subject in the psychological domain contains these two elements, regards him or her as a feeling agentic being like the self and yet different, not-self.

Separate subjects, shared reality

What allows the position of shared reality, being with the other yet having one's own separate experience of that togetherness? In Winnicott's theory (Winnicott, 1971a), which has strongly shaped my thinking, it is the mother's "survival of destruction": her ability to persist without collapsing or retaliating in the face of the child's assertion of his fantasy of control or absolute independence. This is what creates the sense of a shared, external reality distinguished from the inner world of objects under one's fantasied control. This, Winnicott maintains, is directly related to the child's developing the capacity to "use the object" as an outside other. This capacity depends upon recognition of the loved object *"as an entity in its own right"* (Winnicott, 1971a, p. 105). This means the object (other) "is objectively perceived, has autonomy, and belongs to 'shared reality' . . . the subject is *creating* the object in the sense of finding externality itself" (my italics, Winnicott, 1971a, p. 105).

This experience of being able to effect change in the mother as an outside other was meant to be sharply distinguished from the fantasy of a good object, especially when deployed to offset a lack of confirming responsiveness for autonomy. It goes beyond mirroring as it implies conflict or challenge that is negotiated by recognizing two separate minds (see Pizer, 1998). Thus it is an essential experience of differentiation as part of connection.

This Winnicottian view of recognition is what primarily distinguished my take on intersubjectivity from the intersubjective systems theorists, for whom the concept pointed not to the potential for mutual recognition but the fact of mutual influence (Stolorow & Atwood, 1992). Recognition of the other's separate center of agency and authorship was conflated with mirroring, and the idea of the child's recognizing the mother as a separate center of mind taken to mean the child provides symmetrical mirroring to mother (see Orange, 2010). Actually the point, following my reading of the Hegelian idea of recognition, was that realizing mother's separateness gives a whole new meaning to his agency and her responsiveness to him, as in, "Your recognition now has value for me, because your independence confirms my independence." The mother (or analyst) remains particularly responsible when she survives destruction by the child's (or patient's) pushing the limits and negating her separate existence. In this context, the mutuality of recognition—understood as each partner's survival of the impact of the other and being changed by the other without collapsing or having one's subjectivity erased—is quite different from simple mirroring, mutual or otherwise.

In analysis, when the analyst gives *acknowledgment*, admits fallibility in the way Orange (1995; 2011) advocates, this action constitutes a form of survival, *an avowal of one's separate intact subjectivity that can be apprehended as such.* Survival means the analyst has not been coerced, her acknowledgment has not been extracted, but has been given freely. Consequently the patient can feel her fantasy of destruction has clashed with reality, separating projection and fears of retaliation from the other's real actions. This is what it means for the patient to recognize the analyst's separate existence *outside* her mind.

In this iteration, recognition of the analyst (or anyone) is not a demand that can be directed at another, but something that emerges freely. Of course, any stance of demand by the analyst would present the opposite of thirdness. This might occur in moments of complementary breakdown to be sure, when the analyst might seem to pressure the patient to accept her view of reality. But as we have seen, the recognition that follows upon survival of destruction was intended by Winnicott to denote precisely the opposite of having to comply with or repair the other. When the child or patient discovers that the mother/analyst can survive opposition, she becomes a person from whom something real can be received without a price, without sacrificing what feels real to self. Two different realities can thus exist; both minds can live. When the other/analyst is able to avoid submission without retaliation, can think for and regulate herself, and so be responsive from her own center of initiative, she is neither controlling nor enveloping with weakness, neither a burden nor a puppet.

Acknowledgment, marking and containing

The mother-child relation is also asymmetrical regarding how mothers come to recognize their children's subjectivity. This occurs primarily through the mother's relation to the differentiating Third. It is another point at which the mother's aware-ness of separateness can actually enhance her responsibility for inflicting dis-appointment or the pain of separation. This awareness of responsibility can be held even as she respectfully, empathically recognizes her child's distress. I suggest that the mother's relation to the Third informs the behavior called *marking*—the way an attuned mother will add a differentiating gesture that enables her in painful moments of pain or frustration to both emphasize and soothe baby's distress, indicating she is not dysregulated herself. Gergely's (Gergely cited in Fonagy & Target, 1996a & b; Fonagy et al., 2002) concept of marking, based on the study of mothers' actions with distressed babies, articulates the importance of how the mother communicates gesturally to the baby that she recognizes his pain, she may even feel pain, but she is not dysregulated. She does this by exaggerating her mirroring of baby's distress. "Ooh," says Mother grimacing, "that really is a nasty scratch, that hurts!" This mirroring may take place in an easier context for mother, as in *"The big dog is scary, but, Look—Mommy is not frightened."* Or a mother might use it in a moment of differentiation when the baby protests upon her return from work, and she is able to contain that feeling: to offer reassurance and soothing by calibrating her expression even though she herself is somewhat jangled.

This form of differentiating acknowledgment conveys a positive double message and thus embodies the third position. It not only soothes the baby, but it also constitutes an early form of proto-symbolic communication at the procedural level. Significantly, the differentiating aspect is as important here in early procedural interaction as it is to later symbolization. The baby begins to learn that different minds see things differently, and indeed, she learns how other minds work: what Fonagy and Target have advanced as the idea of mentalization

(Fonagy et al., 2002). Understanding other minds as separate, different, yet able to be trusted because they can recognize my mind, constitutes an essential part of the differentiating Third.

It would seem that acknowledgment that involves the mother's marking or differentiating denotes the same, or similar, phenomenon as containing in Bion's (Bion, 1962a; 1962b) language: a process in which the infant's pain and frustration, what Bion called raw beta elements, are transformed by the mother's reverie into symbolized emotions, alpha elements (see also Ferro, 2009; Brown, 2011). The acknowledgment of a painful feeling, provided inside the range of affect tolerance, can become the basis for eventual symbolization or alpha function, the naming of what is missing or feels wrong. Common to both the concepts of marking and containment is the importance of the differentiating element alongside the rhythmic.

We may begin to see the congruence here between various conceptualizations of maternal function and its effects on the relational interaction: marking, containing, recognition through matching specificities (Sander, 1991), and the integrating of emotions (Fosha, Siegel & Solomon, 2012). Though the differentiating gesture of recognition—in particular, the acknowledgment of what has just happened at the feeling level—begins with marking procedurally, it also prepares the way for commentary and thus for symbolic articulation of emotional events. The child becomes able to use this experience of mother marking and narrating to identify his own emotions and to communicate in a more differentiated way.

When, on the other hand, marking is lacking and the mother is too dysregulated by the infant's distress to respond, or when she experiences herself as failing, we infer that an infant feels a wrongness. The mother's dysregulation translates into the child's fantasy of his mother being "destroyed" by his distress, by his need for loving responsiveness. "Mother disappears behind closed doors whenever I cry or fuss." In this way the feeling of being destructive arises, of having reduced mother to "a state of dissolution," as described by Klein (1952), who of course attributed much of this to the infant's aggression but also noted that the external object's condition played a role. The sense of the other collapsing leads to the feeling of a broken or fragmented self, but not only: it also manifests in a vision of the world as collapsed, ruined or broken. The world appears incoherent, its sense or meaning is precarious. This is to say, it is not simply the "object," mother who has been destroyed or made bad, for whose sake the self feels destructive and guilty. The world itself has become unreckonable, its goodness spoiled, its territory treacherous with pitfalls, as with the feeling that "people are crazy, life is dangerous."

True repair of violations cannot be made simply internally, as in the desperate effort to repair the object when as Klein put it, the ego feels horror at the damage it has done. So long as there is not a relational repair—an experience of healing the broken Third with mother, or later, with the analyst—the world itself does not appear intact or lawful, it is a broken world. The needed repair of self, mother, relationship and world requires *acknowledgment* from the other. Herein lies another form of dependency on the other's recognition in action.

The moral Third

Let us consider further: what do we mean by relational repair and how does recognition play a role in creating a coherent, lawful world? Empathically modulated acknowledgment, marking of pain and disruptions—the violations of expectancy, the many small insults infant flesh is prey to—gives rise to what I call the moral Third. The moral Third, relying on both rhythmic and differentiating aspects, embodies recognition of the discrepancy between what is and what ought to be; it grows out of the correction of violations of the child's sense of the natural order of things, restoring the sense of a lawful world. The moral Third develops through acknowledgment, which later becomes so crucial in regard to empathic failures and trauma.

The mother's marking, which contributes to this formation, can also be observed as a feature of her ongoing narration to her preverbal baby. For instance, when there is a jostling, jangling, or other unexpected disruption and mother's accompanying voiceover goes, "Ugh, that was bumpy!" or "Ooh, that's too cold!" The mother's sense of there being rightfully shared expectations is conveyed as she recognizes violations of expectancy not only in moments of distress but as part of scaffolding the uneven flow of lived interaction. Thus the moral Third is shaped not merely by what is predictably anticipated but by what has been ratified by repair and correction as "made right."

From the baby's point of view (and the patient's), acknowledgment confirms that something was indeed wrong, out of alignment or unharmonious, and that it warrants remediation—even if not such a big deal. Putting things right is itself a motive, like creating beauty or harmony. Implicitly, the mother's affirmations of expectancy and violation demonstrates faith in the possibility of putting things right, of harmonizing what was out of sync or at least sharing in the sense of loss and disappointment. This sort of recognition of disruption, of lapses in attention and responsiveness, or of larger dissociations and missed meeting, is needed as well and even more explicitly in analysis.

The moral Third builds upon both early experiences of a harmonious responsive relatedness as well as a reliable acknowledgment and repair of disruption. As I said, harmony may be viewed as a rhythmic instantiation of lawfulness. The psychological construct of a lawful world is a notion closely related to the idea of the Third growing out of rupture and repair, the procedural action that becomes the basis for explicit, symbolic repair and recognition of different points of view. This construct grows from the responsiveness and self-correction of the one we depend upon, not the fulfillment of imaginary demands for a completely predictable controllable universe.

Here is where mutuality enters the picture: a vital outcome of interactive repair is the infant's own emergent sense of agency and impact on the mother. Her response to her child's impact in turn confirms the experience of mutuality: Baby appears to be *causing* mother to change and adjust with each change in baby. Mother is not the only mover. Further, mother needs this reciprocity to confirm her adjustments. Developmentally, this impact amplifies the sense of trust and safety that begins with mother's recognition of baby's cry. Recall that the mother's responsiveness to a baby's distress (Beebe et al., 2010), a predictor of secure attachment, both expresses and transmits in practice the principle of a lawful, caring world. In a lawful world where the self has agency and impact, the I is *recognized* by the Thou in a way that confirms that the Thou has a sentience and mind like one's own.

Furthermore, the acknowledgment of the infant's discomfort or suffering implicitly communicates the mother's respect for her child as a separate body worthy of care. Thus the correlate of the lawful world, wherein you can trust the other's protection, is recognition of the worthiness or, in general human terms, the dignity of the child's person (Bernstein, 2015). This dignity is linked to the sense of self-cohesion (Kohut, 1971), which depends on such recognition. Having had such experience of the moral Third allows a person to gauge her own and the other's behaviors well enough to have an existential platform for action in the world. The sense of self-cohesion (being), the worthiness of self and other, and the experience of agency are united through the reliability of caring others.

Where does mutuality come in? If the mother's responsiveness is too asymmetrical, feels forced, or unwilling, or her responses are too reactive, too tightly matched and rigid, the complementarity of giver and given to leaves no room for the baby's responses and agency. The mother's accommodation only serves the creation of the Third when it moves out of the complementary position of submission or control, when it is not conveyed as anxious perfectionism, duty or sacrifice, but her genuine experience of her child as a sentient being with whose needs she identifies and whose feelings she attunes to. This recognition is what makes her acceptance of the Third a profound experience of surrender rather than submission. As in erotic life, surrender to the Third involves giving up some control over the self in exchange for enjoying the transformational effects of our mutual impact on each other, the intersubjective thirdness, of "*you change me, I change you.*" Surrender creates the space for mutuality even with asymmetry.

In order for the asymmetrical responsibility of soothing and regulating to be more than following rules, more than duty, depletion, and management of an object, more than "*I do this for you*," maternal practice must draw vitality from the pleasure of holding her baby's body, looking into his eyes, matching his smiles and laughter. Otherwise, bodily care and responsibility are dissociated from recognition of the other's felt experience of being an agent, a creator, a responder. Thus, the position of the moral Third, however abstract it sounds, is not a function of mere "reason" but founded in the embodied connection of two minds.

Shifting contexts for a moment to psychoanalytic and social healing of trauma, the vision of the moral Third is invoked in the context of witnessing violations as well as restoring some lawfulness to a broken world, which begins with acknowledgment. In general, the recognition of each individual's humanity—as opposed to dehumanization—is the ethical underpinning of the position from which we provide acknowledgment of suffering. In witnessing and confirming what has taken place, again, we affirm that the victim is worthy of being heard, deserving of dignity, of recognition for suffering and caring protection by the lawful world (Gerson, 2009).

While I go into the matter of such "world recognition" elsewhere (Chapter 7), in what follows I want to describe some clinical implications of the developmental view of the Third for psychoanalytic practice. I will therefore return to the subject of mutuality in relation to clinical acknowledgment, our way of recognizing the pain, distress, trauma and violations of lawfulness to which our patients have been subjected. I make the assumption that the developmental model of recognition as constitutive of the psychological repair of violations between self and other has some bearing, despite important differences, on suffering in later life.

PART II. RESPONSIBILITY, VULNERABILITY AND THE ANALYST'S SURRENDER TO CHANGE

How to change a lightbulb: clinical implications

Old joke: How many analysts does it take to change a light bulb? Answer: One, but the light bulb has to want to change. New Answer: One, but the analyst has to change first.

As we have learned in relational practice, the "analyst needs to change," as Slavin radically formulated two decades ago (Slavin & Kriegman, 1998; see also Slavin, 2010); this is the difference the other can make (Benjamin, 1988). "Going first," surrendering first—giving up our own self-protective stance to hear the other's expressions of pain or fear from their point of view—manifests the analyst's assumption of asymmetrical responsibility (Benjamin, 2004a). However, some patients like to beat us to it, changing before we realize; we then try to catch up and recognize their contribution to altering our shared dynamic. And of course, sometimes it seems we just move in tandem, going together.

Significantly, the relational turn has shown how the importance of being changed by the other (Slavin & Kriegman, 1998) complicates Winnicott's picture of surviving destruction; revising Winnicott, we affirm how important it is for the analyst to change "in quality" as McKay (2015) has pointed out. Survival requires that the analyst *is* changed, making palpable the patient's impact on her and her accommodation to it. Further we emphasize that the analyst may often fail before succeeding at responding in a way that allows the patient to come to see us as existing independently of his projections. So on one hand, we stress the analyst being changed in the sense of fitting in and adjusting, acknowledging and repairing ruptures. But on the other, we take heed of how the analyst's failures and misrecognitions will challenge the patient, who must be able to endure disruptions, sometimes ruptures, in order to be able to make better use of intersubjective relatedness. Thus we add to Kohut's original understanding of repair empathic failures the notion that in such moments the analyst's subjectivity comes into play and is recognized as such (Magid & Shane, 2017). As we recognize how both partners are challenged to change in appropriate ways, our theory holds the tension between asymmetrical responsibility for the other and the mutuality of co-creating "our Third" together.

Nonetheless, the analyst is the watchful tender of the process. Like the mother who recognizes distress or protest with both empathy and marking, when tension rises the analyst provides acknowledgment by working with the mix of rhythmic and differentiating aspects. In determining whether rhythmic joining or differentiated marking needs to be more prominent, we are of course making use of different parts of our own subjectivity. How we respond varies with what and whom we are interacting, differing self-states and different individuals. But this is also a process of procedural trial and error, based on implicit knowing as well as on our reflection. This process of adaptation involves what Ipp and Slavin call achieved empathy (Ipp, 2016), which goes beyond attunement, and evolves over time, "contingent upon certain psychic work . . . deep processing together that enables the varying self states of analyst and patient to be held in tension simultaneously." In this vision, relationally achieved empathy depends upon the patient's participation that enables a different kind of knowing. Together we begin to feel and name what felt wrong in their early relationships.

At first, with my patient Wendy, I notice that my expression of empathy with her suffering seems not to be calming; I have to find a way to engage her in telling me what feels wrong or unhelpful. After some time, Wendy is able to tell me that she becomes frightened when I, thinking to witness and validate her suffering, actually seem to confirm that something is wrong. And further, "wrong" means she is damaged, irremediably. This means that she will never find her way out of pain. In the eternal present of fear, my expression of empathy feels insufficiently marked; a mirror of her own fear. And since she cannot receive protection from me, she seeks it by being dismissive of her feelings as well as my responses. I have to keep tacking between trying to tune in to her and regulating myself when she scornfully pushes me away. I speculate, based on stories as well as our interaction, that Wendy's mother was highly anxious and dysregulated, unable to console her and frightened of taking care of a baby. In our reconstruction her mother appears to have oscillated between dismissive reactions to her child's feelings and making her own needy demands for attention.

At first it seems as if Wendy's criticisms are, procedurally, simply the equivalent of the baby leaning as far away as possible from mother, crying and pushing away. But gradually, as I invite her feedback, she begins to tutor me in what she feels I *should* be doing to give her what she really wants: performing an exaggerated and encouraging response appropriate for showing a preschooler that everything is alright. More marking, less soothing. Increasingly creative, she creates a narrative solution for me, she demonstrates the persona she calls "Tough Mama," probably derivative of some television character, who is sympathetic, but practical and humorous, affirming that "life is rough, girl, but you know everyone's got their shit to deal with." The ironic tone alludes to "Mama's" own experience surviving life's inevitable woes, a kind of symmetry that reduces her shame; at the same time, it confirms that the coherent world is still intact. My use of irony would show the frightened child part of her that I am neither collapsed nor retaliating.

Once I have procedurally shown my understanding, and done my best to sound like "Tough Mama," Wendy can articulate her fears in a way that enables us to experience together her fear that something is terribly wrong. We come to see that my response needs to gesturally embody my sense of differentiation because she fears that I (as mother) will merge with her fear, fragment with anxiety, and become disorganized. This in turn will cause her to lose self-cohesion— and besides, if she is to be safe, I should already know that. Gradually, then, we become able to see how much any sign of not already knowing frightens her and triggers a response of mistrust and critique.

Often hard to bear with, Wendy's early demands for correspondence with her idea of a marking mother with no dangerous emotions of her own is like matching a child's stick figure drawing, black and white. There are only small openings for expansion of her inner world to give us room for play. But as I accept her suggestions as a form of agency and a genuine contribution, as I play along with a little humorous marking that reassures her I won't be angry about her critical form of protest when I haven't done it right, I begin to survive her pressured angry state intact. We find a name for this little "mean girl" who is so critical of herself and everyone else, whose expectation of my either fragmenting or becoming angry is reactive to a mother who has left Wendy feeling destructive and alone. At moments, she surrenders, expressing her hope that I will survive in a different way, her gratitude when I do.

A very different dilemma affects Gina, whose mother was retaliatory, controlling, sometimes violently abusive or triumphant; and otherwise, simply unresponsive and neglectful. Gina wants me to show the frightened child self-state that I am authentically moved by her pain, and she is scanning my face to see my emotions. She searches for signs of my identification with her. My matching her level of emotional distress with my face and voice as well as my words dramatizes the fact that I am not unmoved, not distant from her pain, not shutting her out of my mind. If exaggeration is needed in the response Gina seeks, it is not to differentiate, it is to confirm with palpable emotion that I know her suffering is real, that the bad thing really did happen. My acknowledgment of the many violations and pain she has suffered will be soothing to her.

Gina repeatedly affirms that she wants to be tightly held, yet what makes her anxious is the element of asymmetry between us, which might mean that I am merely observing, distant and clinical. Rhythmicity, not differentiation, is what she craves. Ideally, for her, the feeling should be mutual: I should want to console as much as she wants to be consoled. Insofar as our roles are asymmetrical, our goal should be to harmonize and feel of one mind regarding her pain and her need. Paradoxically, being allowed to make this demand (which I cannot always meet) assuages her anxiety that I might see her urgency as tyrannical and demanding, which might lead me to self-protectively close myself to her desperation, refusing all care and concern. My expression of empathy and explicit acknowledgment reassures her that her need has not been apprehended as something destructive that will evoke hostility, even if I only sometimes meet it with spontaneous protective feelings. As Gina trusts my willingness to "change" for her, it becomes increasingly possible for her to articulate and take into account her fear of being punished for being too much, too demanding.

However, there is a need for me to survive as a separate person that eventually sets a limit. The growing edge of responding to her need to shape our process must be balanced with my ability to distinguish it from fearful control. This is not easy, and when surrender drifts towards complementary acquiescence, I find myself feeling pressured by her urgency. I am also aware that if I am reacting ambivalently to the pressure to fully and authentically mirror her feeling exactly, keeping all difference out of the picture, this represents my way of holding her own doubts and fears. So when this complementary reaction intensifies, when accommoda-tion turns towards submission, I sense that a disruption is unavoidable. Guilt arises in me, the fear of frightening her, and I struggle to metabolize the dissociated pressure coming from the part of her that is vigilant, not actually feeling the pain she demands I feel with her, rather fiercely wary of betrayal. And when this strain shows on my face, in my voice, or my words, Gina demands to know what is wrong, my true feelings, preferring the truth to being left in the dark, alone, with the feeling of a hidden threat, that the bottom may fall out. In such moments of collision it becomes possible to explore the feelings behind the demands, the unspoken or unarticulated anxiety that was causing me to chafe and react (see Slochower, 2006; Stern, 2009), because part of Gina knows that only if she recognizes my reactions, and her part in them, will I honestly be able to continue recognizing hers.

The backdrop for both Wendy and Gina is helplessness and a pervasive lack of safety, which makes for a particularly mistrustful form of the need to influence my behavior. The question for them is whether trying to elicit soothing or responsiveness will backfire, cause more disruption (see Schore, 2003). The more I can respond to that activity not as an attempt to control me but a complex mixture of fear, need for acknowledgment of what caused the fear, and need to have their agency recognized, the less we fall into complementarity. But there are many moments of enactment in which some simulation of the original complementary dilemmas with mother occurs, when their anxiety or my reactivity requires us to negotiate a repair of rupture. As this proceeds, as I continue to elicit their commu-nications in the enactment rather than expect to "figure it out on my own," so that their efforts more effectively contribute to the building of "our Third." It is in this repair of rupture, through my recognition of the desire or intent behind the vigil-ance, that the asymmetry of my responsibility for the moral Third and the mutuality of their contribution can be joined.

Surrender and the Third, again

My theory of the Third developed in response to reflecting on such breakdowns and impasses (Benjamin, 2004a; Aron, 2006). So far in this chapter I have said a great deal about how the Third works and relatively little about its collapse, about the accompanying fears of abandonment and injury, of being shut out or closed in. I have not yet spoken of the analyst's fear of finding demons in her own cabinet, a fear with some important parallels to the frightening side of motherhood, when darkness falls in the nursery (Kraemer, 2006). Here surrender to the longing for recognition meets the reality of anxiety aroused by the responsibility of caring for a helpless infant or fragile patient. With deeply injured patients, the analytic process of disruption and repair may confront an analyst with her lack of goodness and parallel maternal confrontations with fears of inadequacy and destructiveness (Kraemer, 1996). When that darkness falls in the consulting room and the shadow of past objects falls upon all those present, we find ourselves facing the specter of our own historic experiences in which repair failed.

The form of acknowledgment that constitutes witnessing of past injuries, letting ourselves be guided at the procedural level by the patient's responses, may well depend on bearing such feelings of harming or failure. The idea of surrendering to the Third as an act of acceptance, giving up our own self-protection in favor of hearing the pain of the other, appears helpful in such moments. But surrender rather than submission (Ghent, 1990) as a connection to the Third—as an act of facilitation that potentiates the thirdness between us (Benjamin, 2004a)—is a complex matter for the analyst. Those who would translate Ghent's idea into a practice where the analyst goes first and thereby facilitates the patient's surrender (Benjamin, 2004a; Orange, 2011) would do well to recall that Ghent's idea was that the individual wants to "come clean," let go of defenses in order to expose the vulnerable true self, to be known as well as to know the other. Precisely because this wish to be known as well as to know the other cannot be expressed, it manifests as masochism. Essentially, then, he associated mutual recognition with the outcome of surrender, but knew how easily it could manifest as submission, even in the analyst. Indeed, beginning with Ferenczi and later Racker, the analyst's quandary of avoiding the reversal from sadism into submission has shaded with ambivalence our experience with mutuality. In impasses and enactments, finding a way to negotiate surrender without submission to the other's demand to replace your reality with theirs can be quite elusive for the analyst (Pizer, 2003).

It was actually towards this end—finding a position of surrender in relation to impasses and complementary oppositions involving submission and dissociation that I initially reflected upon Lacan's (1975) idea of the Third (Benjamin, 2004a). The Third was conceived as that which differentiates us from the imaginary relationship of kill or be killed, presented by Hegel as a struggle in which the weaker party substitutes slavery for death, while the victor gains freedom and dominion. More recently, I suggested the formulation of this complementary opposition, in which each person struggles for recognition by imposing or defending their own version of reality without recognizing the other, as corresponding to the fantasy of *"Only one can live"* (see Chapter 7). Part of the project of recognition theory is to articulate both the dynamic forces behind this breakdown as well as those that create the material, psychological conditions for the third position in which this complementarity can be overcome.

Relevant to our understanding of both mothers and analysts is that the unconsciously held imaginary of a world in which *Only one can live* can become the shadow side of asymmetry. It may be associated with the tendency whereby surrender turns into submission, which is either embraced or defended against in reactive self-protection. The fantasy *Only one can live* may be unconsciously attached to notions of maternal sacrifice and goodness, and by extension to the maternal position in analysis. In that constellation, it appears that the child or fragile patient can only live at the expense of the mother or analyst. The question of how to preserve or save the life of the fragile, vulnerable other without sacrificing the life of the self is vexed in theory, and at times agonizing in practice.

Facing a psychic world—which has its real counterpart in cruelty and suffering —in which the absolute self establishes itself at the expense of the other has led some theorists to embrace Levinas' idea of asymmetrical responsibility for the Other as a kind of antidote (to what, we must consider further). His philosophy constitutes the ethical subject in the act of accepting the essential, absolute and asymmetrical responsibility for the Other's suffering. This has been posed as an alternative to the idea of recognition as a solution to the self's problematic relation to the Other (see Oliver, 2001; Butler, 2004; Orange, 2011). However, I will argue that theorizing responsibility in opposition to reciprocity of recognition and mutual knowing ultimately contradicts the practical experience that a loop of reciprocity is necessary to sustain thirdness, which in turn helps contain some of the complex feelings we have in the face of the other's need.

Let me briefly suggest how I think this problem plays out. Orange (2011), inspired by Levinas, has adumbrated an ethic for analysts in which the suffering of the Other takes precedence over self, contravening the classical subject of analysis. When the self is imagined as the isolate Cartesian mind he is actor, not acted upon, knower not known, and resists the impact of the other. By contrast, when the self surrenders as, in Levinas' formulation of the "Me" (accusative) who allows the other's pain to overtake him, to accept the impact of the other's suffering, he gives up the classical "I" (nominative) who knows, categorizes, objectifies the Other. This reversal is a vital move, fundamental to intersubjectivity and to all critiques of objectification and instrumental reason that challenge knowing as domination (Benjamin, 1988; 1997). In this way Levinas and relational psychoanalysis meet (Rozmarin, 2007).

However, the idea of elevating the Other and his suffering in order to ground ethical subjectivity in responsibility begins to contradict the purposes of relational psychoanalysis and our current view of mother-infant relations when it eliminates the dynamic force of reciprocity and recognition. As Orange concedes, there is a virtual erasure of subjectivity in the face of the Other and in "Levinasian therapeutics asymmetry outranks mutuality [and] . . . responsibility often overwhelms the also indispensable reciprocity . . ." (Orange, 2011, p. 57). What this would imply for us is that the healer or maternal figure should not need the other's reciprocity to fulfil her role. The result is a complementary relation of giver and given to—rather than a dialectical relationship of support between responsibility and reciprocity—thereby foreclosing the surrender and mutual vulnerability Orange herself expounds as a relational position. Orange's advocacy of fallibility, listening to the other's version of reality, with the position that only we are responsible for doing the right thing? Surely if we are going to learn from the patient (Casement, 1991), be humble in the face of their criticisms (Ferenczi, 1933) we are in some sense part of a system of mutual correction and repair. As we are not engaged in abstract thought but (hopefully) practicing healers, at times our ability to stay firm and survive destruction so that we can be recognized as different, vital subjects in our own right will be more helpful than bowing down to the other's suffering. How else will the patient get a taste of the mutuality (perhaps unknown heretofore) now consider vital in both therapy and in early mother-infant interaction?

As the appeal to certain crucial passages in Levinas implies (Baraitser, 2008, p. 103), an image of the sacrificial mother who takes on the pain or suffering of her child subtends this therapeutic ideal. As we know, however, there is an important element of mutuality in our developmental theory of subjectivity and thirdness in the mother-infant dyad, which is at odds with the foreclosure of mutuality in this ideal. Baraitser (2008), who has contended for adopting the Levinasian ethic as a basis for constituting maternal subjectivity, illustrates this problematic opposition. In her view, a maternal subjectivity based on a Levinasian idea of responsibility for the stranger Other is necessitated by the loss attendant on the mother's encounter with the baby as Other, and the "relentless attacks" on her psyche by the demands of her infant. Baraitser's useful admission of the degree to which mothers (isolated, Western mothers who have not been surrounded by babies throughout their girlhoods) experience self-loss and fear of destructiveness with their infants poses the dilemma for us.

This dark side of maternal experience was discussed by Parker (1995) who, in the tradition of Klein and Bion, contended that mothers's ambivalence—being torn between love and hate—could lead to a subjectivity based on self-reflection and holding the tension of opposites. For Baraitser, destructiveness is not opposed by love, as in Klein, but by responsibility. But what psychic force or feeling makes us responsible? Baraitser explicitly follows Butler (2000), who rejects the form of recognition that follows from shared survival of breakdown. Seemingly, her argument is that this understanding of how analysts or mothers survive their negation does not to take destructiveness seriously, would reduce its role in the psychic world to "a lamentable occurrence." Butler contends that destruction is destructive when it is practiced as such. But this view conflates the psychoanalytic meaning of a patient's frightened fantasies of damaging the internal object with her negation, or the child's defiant testing of a parent, with real harming. Here,

I believe lies a crucial misunderstanding. We analysts are called upon to acknowledge "real" destructiveness and abuse that our patients have suffered, but we are called more generally to recognize the pain that is felt when they or we ourselves face fear of our own hatred, guilty self-reproach, knowledge that we may hurt those we love, including our children. Our commitment is to recognition of those parts of self that feel monstrous, and the shame this induces. In particular, the mother must survive her own knowledge of rejecting or hateful feelings.

For Baraitser, there is no way for the mother to establish her child's survival as the child does hers, no means of reassurance that her destructive fantasies are not real, that bring the other into focus as an external being who can be loved. The mother becomes a subject for him, but not for herself. The mother apparently cannot actually tolerate "destroying the object in fantasy"—that is, hold the ambivalence of love and hate. Nor can she fight for recognition as she would with an equal, opening herself to a Winnicottian dialectic of destruction and recognition. Therefore Baraitser turns away from recognition theory and proposes the mother become an ethical subject in the Levinasian version of responsibility for the stranger Other, her child.

The language of the infant's "relentless attacks" in this text suggests that encountering otherness in the form of a helpless infant reactivates in the mother the psychological possibility of a world in which the infant really could devour her or she really could murder him: Lacan's kill or be killed world in which "Only one can live." It evokes a kind of primal scene experience, as fantasy and reality merge in the feeling "I alone am responsible in this life and death situation, I must keep this infant alive," or mushrooms into "The choice is either I let you devour me or I am responsible for your death." I speculate that for Baraitser this fear is meant to be metabolized and contained by the ideal of responsibility, formulated as, "This Other calls me to rescue her/him from death." That appeal resonates with Levinas' expression of how the face of the Other commands "Do not kill me!" The mother's ethical subjectivity of Thou shalt not kill is a psychically powerful solution to the imagined attacks and counter-attacks, a fearful cycle that can now be checked by the ideal of her responsibility for the Other.

However, I believe there is in fact another solution to this problem, involving a different analytic take on the mother's reactivity. When the responsibility for another vulnerable being cracks the mirror in which a mother hoped to see her control reflected (Lacan notwithstanding, it is mother not baby who requires that mirror) she is forced to recognize a helpless/fragmented or raging/exasperated version of *herself who is not in control*. This is not her baby's attack, but her own. In a confrontation with a wailing, inconsolable infant whom she cannot soothe, the problem is not encountering the Other without but inability to recognize and acknowledge the "other within." As one mother put it, the problem is not surviving destruction by and for the child but surviving knowing she is feeling "I hate you." One survives accepting such hatred by reclaiming the capacity for love and growing into a more reflective subject through embrace of ambivalence, says Parker (1995).

Confronting the raw and extreme ambivalence of mothers towards helpless, vulnerable infants—Can a mother hate her baby?!—Kraemer (2006) eloquently declared, has caused most writers and thinkers, including psychoanalysts, to become faint-hearted, even those brave ones like Winnicott (1947), who famously described mothers' hateful feelings in "Hate in the Countertransference." The mother's state of mind can and does often replicate the intense complementarity of "Only one can live," feeling that one must choose being either destroyed or destroyer, lacking the moral Third. Where the ethic of responsibility aims to counter the reality of fear, the psychoanalytic question is, What helps mothers to bear and surrender to this knowledge of self? The idea of mother's surrender to encountering this strange, other version of herself, could be taken not simply as ethical responsibility but as self-knowledge, in Parker's sense. The Third of maternal surrender would then be: this is my helplessness, this is my rage and anxiety, this is my imperfection, all of this *is me* (Magid, 2008). But then these would also be contained within a tension that has on its other side love and learning with the newly forming other.

Baraitser's proposed ethic of responsibility is ambiguous regarding how the mother's encounter with the infant stranger changes her, silent about love, emphasizing only that mother is transformed by meeting alterity. This seems to exclude the mother's identification with baby, the satisfactions or raw expressions of need, as well as with the developing child. This more expansive possibility is introduced instead by referring to Levinas' narrative about the father—not mother—in regard to (no surprise) the son. There is a possibility for a parenthood that does more than encounter strangeness, for getting to know the other in a way that does not control or objectify—though not yet attributed to mothers.

But this move seems to open up the question, why does the mother not have access to the other's survival of destruction, to a degree of distinction between fantasies of destroying and actual harm that is vital for stepping out of the doer–done to complementarity. Is this reciprocity truly absent from the mother-infant relationship? As I originally contended, a mother's sense of power to harm, the fearful fantasy of primal destructiveness, can be profoundly affected by her baby's flourishing, by her moment-to-moment pleasure in engagement (Benjamin, 1988). Survival of destruction can, as with analyst and patient, even under these very asymmetrical conditions, be mutual. Within limits, there is a parallel between infant and mother each experiencing the other's survival; for although mother has to contain the fearful feeling that her baby may not survive, in reality she may then discover that he has done so (Kraemer, 2006). Even though she may have been filled with self-hate, despair and resentment, wanting only to be left alone in peace, when her baby greets her smiling and cooing, completely unaffected by her internal process, this reciprocating recognition of her does modify her sense of destructiveness. As one mother proudly reported, when she was impatiently and irritably diapering her toddler after a long day he looked up at her and said, "Mommy sometimes good, sometimes bad." The mother has the opportunity to overcome her destructive fantasies through building the Third with her infant, especially the moral Third of disruption and repair.

Perhaps this need for reciprocity and recognition from the child—well accepted by infancy researchers—is the sticking point in the devaluation of reciprocity. Mothers may recoil, Kraemer (2006) suggests, at recognizing their need to use the baby as a love object, an object of desire. This fear of exploitation naturally underlies psychoanalytic suspicions of reciprocity by both children and patients. However, it has also been difficult to theoretically recognize the mother's need for her baby's responsiveness: "Fully acknowledging the critical ways in which the mother is nourished by her baby's confirmation of her usefulness" (p. 780) is part of recognizing the mother's subjectivity, Kraemer asserts. The fact that mothers depend upon this reciprocity of the baby's responsiveness is exactly the acknowledgment of her subjectivity denied by the ethic of responsibility.

Mothers do need, are dependent upon, this confirmation, Kraemer suggests, in a way that parallels what analysts may feel some more courageous ones have also been willing to admit, like Searles who said that with one patient "My life depended upon her being able to accept something from me" (cited in Kraemer, 2006, p. 781). When guilt and shame are associated with accepting need and desire as the possible antidote to destructive feelings, some may find a safer antidote in the elevation of renunciation and loss as the ethical point of maternal subjectivity. Attaching need and desire to our ethical position, not to mention pleasure, seems virtually unthinkable—presumably because it is associated with using and assimilating the baby to the needs of the self. And yet, how is it possible for the mother not to identify with all the sucking and slurping and squeezing, and yes biting, without erasing her bodily presence? What if the mother does admit her erotic pleasure in her baby, asks Taniguchi (2012), what if we have not forgotten the erotic desire attached to the mother who finds "delicious . . . her baby's soft, plump flesh," and what if the erotic horror and delight of such fantasy is not dead or closed off to psychoanalytic consciousness as so many continually assert, but is alive and well (Wrye & Welles, 1994)? Going further, what if the point of psychoanalysis is that there is no purified subjectivity, no intersubjectivity without the intrapsychic fantasy world, no mothering without the enigmatic transmission of desire, of the message (Laplanche, 1997; see Chapter 4)? And what if there is no true love without acknowledging the truth lovers feel, "I want it, take advantage of me . . . use me up!" (Amichai cited in Atlas, 2013).

The idea that the mother, or the analyst, needs nothing back, not even the recipro-city of responsiveness, protects us from that fantasy of devouring, lusty or fearful. The fantasy of the mother who needs nothing is more than a denial of practical reality, it is a way of reintroducing through the back door an idea of a subject who is independent of the object, is not shaped by the other; a translation from the omnipotently knowing masculine subject into the serving, all-giving subject who as one mother proudly asserted to me needs no one because "I am the mother!" (Benjamin, 1988). Perhaps where the ideal of the self-contained individual sub-ject manifested for women as mothers was in the idea of not needing anything. Taylor (2007), the Hegel scholar, critiques the individualist position of altruistic unilateralism, maintaining that the parental fostering of the child's growth only succeeds "where a bond of love arises . . . where each is a gift to the other, where each gives and receives ... the line between giving and receiving is blurred."

The satisfaction of imagining oneself fulfilling this role, even sacrificing for it, might be likened to the alienated form of recognition, a "look-alike," in which the sense of power or control substitutes for the engagement with another subject. Whereas the baby's needs and vulnerability in conjunction with the mother's power to harm seem to affirm this view of maternal subjectivity, the baby's active responsiveness and the mother's capacity to feel the goodness of connection are linked in the alternate constellation. The two positions, existing in most of us, are then dissociated. We might see surrender to the Third as the ability to stand in the spaces of knowing we contain all these parts of self.

The denial of the need for a reciprocal response overlooks the way that from the moment of the baby latching on the mother feels she is being validated in her need to be a source of goodness. "Fully acknowledging the critical ways in which the mother is nourished by her baby's confirmation of her usefulness" (p. 780) is part of recognizing the mother's subjectivity, Kraemer asserts. The fact that mothers depend upon this reciprocity of the baby's responsiveness is exactly the acknowledgment of her subjectivity denied by the ethic of responsibility. In those moments where her baby cannot provide that affirmation, when her baby is unconsolable and unsoothed, the mother (often unconsciously) identifies with his suffering in a somewhat undifferentiated way as a version of her own unmothered, unresponded-to needy self: this now appears as the needy demand she hates in her baby and herself. As she fails to calm her baby she herself feels more chaotic and unsoothed.

The analyst who projects his own need onto the patient is likewise inclined to feel more hatred of the unconsoled, dysregulated part of the patient, who is preventing him from being the all-good and giving power, a guise for his own unmet needs. Accepting the part of self that does not want to be responsible for an other human being's fragility, does not want to be exposed in our own suffering because we are too depleted or our own needs are unmet becomes a great challenge for many analysts. In this sense the moral Third becomes vital to differentiating moralizing from acceptance, bearing the unknown, the "not-me" the "ungood," that emerges (Mark, 2015) in facing our own suffering in the context of our ongoing relationship to the other.

This might be one way to read Freud's (1923) experience when he said that the rules of analysis forbade us using our personality, even though it might be helpful, in the face of the patient's "negative therapeutic reaction" because we would then fall prey to the temptation to play savior or redeemer. Unfortunately, Freud did not address the fact that we might be seduced by the power to heal because it is so much more comfortable to see the other as the vulnerable, needy one. The projection of those unmet needs and vulnerability can re-emerge in seduction or idealization of the analyst's all-giving quality (see Celenza, 2007). However, feeling helpless to ameliorate the other's pain is also a genuine source of suffering. And further, at the unconscious level, the baby and the mother are each parts of one self, the needs and the suffering move in underground tides of identification between us, not nearly as distinct as a non-psychoanalytic ethic of the Other imagines. Insofar as unconscious symmetry and identification always operates between analyst and patient, even when we play complementary opposite parts, we cannot wholly take our roles at face value.

The need for reciprocal recognition does not arise because we push the patient to recognize our independent subjectivity, but rather because we cannot deny him the experience at some point. It will arise either because of our misattunements, or the need to overcome joint dissociation, or because the patient herself is pushing to know where the analyst really stands, as when Slavin's patient Emily who comes to realize that in this peculiar process it is sometimes only by understanding you that we can understand me (Slavin, 2010). Or it may be that the patient is wanting precisely the experience of "recognizing that we recognize each" other that comes with shared transformation. Or, it may be that recognizing the other within, confronting one's own demons called up by the patient, is what will enable the analyst to meet the patient in the ways she most desperately needs (McKay, 2016).

One demon the analyst must confront is that of identifying (projectively) his own need to be saved with the patient and the role of savior with self, a form of complementarity that can easily be masked by a notion of asymmetrical responsibility. It is always necessary to be aware of how the psychic aspiration to realize an absolute form of responsibility for the Other might hinder us from the awareness of our own needs to affirm goodness and avoid the sense of badness—which if we think as Racker (1957; 1968) does, has probably led us to become healers in the first place. The reciprocity of needing the other's reflection to correct our own tendency to be unaware (dissociated), also informs our symmetrical vulnerability to each other.

This realization returns us to the analytic position of recognizing the fears of both desire and destruction that make the idea of asymmetrical responsibility appear so reassuring. At the same time, it may help us to liberate the deeper longings for recognition (knowing and being known) that constitute our most potent allies in letting go of self-protectiveness and accepting what we need to learn from or with the other. This movement of recognition can then inform both our sense of responsibility and our surrender to the shifts between hope and dread, leading us to openness to the other.

Interestingly, the practical conclusions we reach by assuming that each partner, in very different ways, survives for the other and reciprocally enables recognition is consonant with Orange's actual clinical theory and hermeneutics of trust. She accepts that the analyst should be changed by confronting her own reactions to the patient, however humbling and shaming, and it is her responsibility to "go first" in surrendering to that reality. Seconding Jaenicke (2011), who in declaring "To change we have to let ourselves be changed" (p. 14) makes a case for the analyst's vulnerability that suggests how true responsibility also requires mutual exposure (see also Jaenicke, 2015).

Orange (2011) recognizes in Ferenczi's original efforts to create a relation-ship of trust and honesty, his acknowledgment of failures to heed and be present with his patients, how the pressure of a complementary breakdown, often brought about by the analyst's dissociation regarding the patient's trauma, requires the analyst to risk her own vulnerability and openness. "When he felt his own com-passion breaking down, or worse yet, when his patients felt it breaking down, the two grown-ups had to explore together what kinds of evasions or dissociations on both parts might be interfering with healing the completely devastated child/adult who had entrusted a raped and shattered soul to this analyst."

Since we do need this action by the other, since we are not all-knowing but fallible and vulnerable to the other, how can we conceptualize this process with-out positing the other's reciprocal role in relation to our acknowledgment and shared exploration? In my view, the practice of confronting such dissociation together—especially disavowed negative feelings, or efforts to sidestep them through avowed goodness and compassion—alters the ideal of one-sided responsi-bility and calls for the balancing idea of recognition. When the analyst faces that she cannot repair the breakdown alone, admits her failure as Ferenczi (1933) suggested, and invites the patient to be honest in her perceptions; when the patient is relieved by the analyst's acknowledgment and willingness to change and so gains the sense of his own impact—he may then recognize the analyst as an external other who is trying to understand him even if "doing a bad job at the moment" (Bromberg, 2011). This sequence does not simply reverse who plays Subject and who Other, who is giver or given to, knower or known; it does create an experience of seeing one another, differently. We now become two subjects—both an I—who recognize how we each are affecting the other Me in creating a pattern of interaction. We step into the thirdness of this mutual recognition, surrender together to our vulnerable self.

The analyst thus, by exposing herself, becoming vulnerable, practices relinquish-ing the aspiration to knowing and certainty, while at the same time enabling her patient to recognize her as a fallible Other. The analyst's surrender, which indeed bears resemblance to the Me who welcomes and hosts the full impact of the Other's suffering, also critically requires an I who hosts her own otherness and vulner-ability as psychoanalysis uniquely comprehends and makes possible. The move of placing recognition of the other at the center of our struggle to transcend objectification means letting ourselves be vulnerable to the other's impact, and this vulnerability *to* the Other must be held in tension with our responsibility *for* the Other, recognizing him in his suffering, his difference. The analytic I attends closely and takes responsibility for the symmetry of intersubjective vulnerability.

At this juncture I believe we can formulate the difficulty in using, as Orange does, a Levinasian ethics of responsibility that rejects reciprocity as a ground for making the relational move towards an analyst who accepts vulnerability, fallibility and the need to change for the other. In order to open ourselves to the suffering of the Other as stranger, as Orange proposes (Orange, 2011), responsibil-ity must be imbricated with a form of analytic mutuality in which both partners survive for the other (see Aron, 1996). The essential relational move of accepting the analyst's vulnerability creates a sense of mutuality within the frame of asymmetrical responsibility. But, I would stress, it is achieving this mutual recognition—this shared thirdness with its rhythmic, reparative and difference-accepting aspects—that is transformational. Asymmetrical responsibility contributes the sense of containing and framework that is essential to achieving this end; we count on it as an expression of caring. But the caring itself lies in the recognition and responsiveness to the other's pain, aliveness, need to know and be known. The process is one in which the analyst's witnessing and recognition can be continually expanded as the patient assumes the subjectivity of the one who changes us and becomes a partner in dialogue. This movement invokes the difference between complementarity and the thirdness in which two separate minds can live (Rozmarin, 2007).

Mutual vulnerability in the psychoanalytic relationship

The idea that we have impact on, change one another is the ultimate implication of mutuality within asymmetrical, unequal relations. But what guides us in embodying mutuality as we try to suspend our awareness between the requirement that our separate minds live and that we attune to the other? Contending with the various interpretations of maternal subjectivity is part of what informs the differing ideas of the ethical basis for care, an issue I will take up in Part III on the ethics of motherhood.

As the bi-directional nature of rupture and repair has become increasingly clear in practice, analysts have been freed to acknowledge the cooperative aspects of working through disruptions or violations of expectancy in enactments. That is, we have come to see how much the patient contributes to the process of recreating the space of thirdness after breakdown. Among other things, this means (see Chapter 2), that from an intersubjective viewpoint, when the patient expresses insight into his own or the analyst's mind, this action relieves and frees up the mind of the analyst—a point that was obscured as long as the process was being described solely from the standpoint of curing the patient of his illness (see Hoffman, 1983; Aron, 1991; 1996). To my mind such practical experience confirms the theory of therapeutic mutuality and points towards viewing survival of destruction as an achievement of the couple. That is, we may think in terms of the Third itself surviving after breakdown into complementarity. The analyst's asymmetrical responsibility consists of explicit tending to this process of restoration of mutual recognition after breakdown.

Let us recall that responsibility is not really the opposite of mutuality—equals can be responsible for each other—but it is limited by all that we can't know, control or feel with certainty. The idea of mutual recognition can become troublesome if it is conflated with cognition, with the knowing of self or other as an "object of knowledge" rather than in relation to shared experience of apprehension, perhaps of the other's difference, perhaps of "this is how it feels to be with each other" (Stern et al., 1998; Lyons-Ruth, 1999; Boston Change, 2010). Even in such a loosely held notion of making meaning together we expect that we will not fully contain without dysregulation or some measure of dissociation all that the patient needs to bring forth so that we can recognize vital parts of him and his inner world; that there is no way for him to manifest it without interacting with our inner world. The sometimes minute, sometimes drastic shifts in self states that express the mix of past and present, dread and hope are simply too complex, sub-symbolic, or enigmatic to be tracked and charted in medias res by one person's skilled analytic mind (Bucci, 2008). We must negotiate a two-way street, in which the analyst's subjectivity is exposed in some measure to the patient as well as, hopefully, to herself. Like the mother dysregulated by her infant's crying, the analyst may become a stranger to herself, may have to recognize parts of herself she does not want to see. Thus we meet the other within and without—for Dissociation is also Us.

But even if, or more precisely when, we accept as unavoidable reality the downside of mutuality, that dysregulation and vulnerability is present in both partners, responsibility sets the boundaries of mutuality. Since some kinds of mutual knowing are not optional but also frightening, part of analytic tact is knowing when not to mess with the self-protective lines of dissociation that people draw, allowing them to know and not know at the same time—and having a sense of when crossing or pushing the line will be fruitful rather than disastrous. Thus even when mutuality is not optional, the discipline of asymmetry, embodied in our rituals, is all the more important (Hoffman, 1998). Whether foreground or background in our awareness, we accept the role of reflecting on the interaction of both partners' experience, aiming to communicate something that is regulating and absorbable for the patient.

Mutuality and asymmetry are co-determinants of the acknowledgment that I (Benjamin, 2009) have been stressing as reflecting the essential responsibility for demystifying one's own contributions to ruptures. This may not include all we know at the time, rather what encourages the patient in expressing what she knows. The symbolic explication of what has happened in disruptions may lean on correction through rhythmic marking or procedural adjustment, but can go further by creating shared understanding of what had been dissociated. Responsibility includes determining when and how we proceed in this way to learn from our patients while furthering the mutuality of knowing each other as "the one who did or said, who felt or thought This."

It bears repeating that the obstacle to acknowledgment is often the analyst's own vulnerability to shame regarding her own dissociation or guilt at being hurtful. The effect of these reactions on the patient, who often saw them clearly, was historically denied, leading to the splitting off of vital parts of each person's experience. Awareness of these feelings, often the obstacle to becoming more regulated and available to the patient, as well as mutual regulation, is a crucial component of the recognition process. From this angle, we grasp mutuality as *mutual vulnerability to each other*. Mutual vulnerability is often our key to doors that were locked in fear and pain.

Mutual vulnerability in practice

The vignette that follows illustrates the movement from dysregulation to acknowledgment of self-protection and mutual recognition of vulnerability (Cooper, 2016) as well as our impact on the other. It also shows how such recognition results in the dissolution of complementarity and opening up to a more resilient thirdness. I am proposing here that the asymmetry of responsibility encompasses the acknowledgment of shared dysregulation—going first—which helps to contain the volatility of shared affect and unlinked self states. At a heightened moment of collision, when the patient may fear being actually destructive and the analyst may fear not surviving, the analyst's acknowledgment facilitates the couple's survival together as more differentiated partners in a renewed moral Third.

My patient Wendy, the one who would like me to strongly mark my affirmation of her pain and simultaneously encourage and reassure her, has often expressed her great fear of being "too big," of being out of control and dangerous, as she felt with her mother. Her need of the other is bad, destructive and a manifestation of her damage. This sense of destructiveness is not surprisingly evoked by any sign of my being less than perfectly powerful and invulnerable. Unfortunately, perfect equanimity is not my response to her in moments of high dysregulation and concreteness, when Wendy asserts that I am not soothing her, I am "making it worse." One Friday, though, we found a place of shared understanding and warm connection, which met her hopes for being soothed regarding her anxiety about separating and being able to take care of herself by getting her work done. She was able to think about how her anxious anticipation of the weekend was linked to a previously unspoken conviction that I would find her bothersome or needing too much.

On Monday following, Wendy returned in an agitated state, unable to finish her work assignment on time, stressed because it was "too much" to get to my office, fearful that she would never get her need for soothing met, that I would fail to make things better. My reaction to her state of fear did not seem reassuring, did not signal a maternal calm unruffled by her agitation. We were now relating in that familiar complementarity where I would be unable to give her that "just right" combination of mirroring and marking, and she would be both deprived and accusing. Knowing that this "right thing" I was supposed to give her was not what was needed, I still could not marshal a non-judgemental way of cutting through. I could feel how the part of me that is organized around trying to be different from my angry, dismissive mother was activated, my need to repair and make things good again. However, my inclination was not to realize but to tamp down my own hostile reaction to her accusation, my own worry about inability to contain her aggression. It seemed I needed to fail in a way that would let us meet, differently.

The following session Wendy marched in determined to deal with our messy encounter and make repair. Now she was going to take charge and be the one who does the thinking no matter how her fragmented mother frustrated her. In a different spirit, I felt a similar determination. She opened with the assertion that

I am unable to soothe her when she is upset, that she has to turn to others who are more encouraging, give her a sense of reality and remind her that she can get her work done. Dramatically, she added (and unfortunately I must alter the phrase to protect her privacy): "I'm in a *whirlpool*, and I need you to come pull me out." "Whirl-Pool!" I repeated, struck by the resemblance between the word and her father's name, Warren Poole, the angry, agitated, chaotic giant of her family.

When I drew her attention to the name she agreed, but used the metaphor to press her advantage: "When I'm flooded, you get flooded," she asserted confidently. I readily acknowledged that this does happen sometimes, I myself knew I had indeed not been containing or thinking as I would have liked. But I added that I felt it wasn't only her flooding, that I felt as if *she* had pulled away from *me* on Monday, and wondered if it was because she had felt dropped on the weekend, afraid to need me again after losing the connection we had had on Friday. I said it was hard to hold on to the part of her that connected, and asked, "What do you think happened to Friday Wendy?"

Wendy was dismissive. There was nothing to think about because a weekend is so obviously more frustration than she can bear, she is alone, has no partner, is pressured by the impossible demands of her job. We might have been enacting a scene in which I was expecting her to be a big grown-up girl even though I had left her alone and never helped her, and she was protesting, refusing to be satisfied with this miserable excuse for mothering. Once again she was *too big*, too destructive for this weak mother so easily reduced to bits. How could she be cohesive and contained when mother could not? As in her childhood, she addressed the problem vigorously, by pumping mother up with instruction on what to do: *if* at such moments I would contain her anxiety by presenting her with reality, *if* I would organize and create a mental structure for her, *then* I could help her as I should, make things less scary. The problem that these efforts to repair the rupture would more likely make the mother-me become more anxious and dangerous was being enacted once again.

"Besides," she added, fixing me with a keen look and imitating my tone of voice, "I would ask you, Why didn't *you* hold on to 'Friday Wendy'? Maybe *you* weren't holding on to her when you couldn't soothe me on Monday. And then you felt bad because you weren't being a good therapist, you were doing a lousy job."

"Touché. You got me there," I replied without hesitation, a little pleased with her openly sparring, putting the issue of who would be to blame for failure of holding on to our connection on the table. I asked her if she wanted to hear how I saw it. With her assent, I felt safe enough to be vulnerable and admit the part that felt shameful to me. So I acknowledged having indeed felt I was not doing a good enough job; actually, I continued, it is a feeling I know quite well. Still, I gently pushed back. I said, I sensed that something more was going on. Yes, she needed someone who had faith in her strength to pull together her work for the meeting, but hadn't I actually said something about . . . Here Wendy interrupted me to launch into rebuttal, when suddenly in mid-sentence she stopped herself and said in a very different voice, one of beginning realization:

Um, Right then, uh, you know when you tried to say that? You know what I was feeling? I felt you hated me, you must hate me for being a mess . . . so immediately I hated *you!* And I started telling you how badly *you* were doing your job.

I was surprised by the sudden shift in Wendy's self-state, it felt like a quite remarkable move from complementary accusation to trust. Something had opened her mind to the way she hated herself and tried to project her state of shame. But was she trying to project her shame? Or was she trying to discover if I knew that shame from inside myself, because I felt it too? I did not analyze that at the moment. Rather, I responded with direct appreciation of the new feeling she expressed. Showing my surprise, I said that it really was about time for us to welcome in her hate, where had it been all this time? My confirmation of how real and true the hate felt in turn took Wendy by surprise. As we went forward I humorously pursued the tack of performative recognition: "Hate must out, it must be known!" Wendy looked pleased, surprised, as well as a little disconcerted by turns, as she became reflective. She hadn't realized how much she was holding on to that hate, how much she felt hated. She was a little frightened that she admitted hating me . . . and a little happy and relieved.

In this moment of recognition our ability to surprise each other brought us closer, both surviving destruction in knowing about the part of ourselves that frightened us, the part that could hurt another person. Our complementary interaction of accuser and accused had barely masked that symmetry. Now, in a position of the Third, her lived experience became organized as if on film: having been left alone, unsoothed and ashamed of her neediness as a young child; boiling with her help-less feeling of hate; trying to be good, helpful and show her mother what to do; when this failed, dealing with frustration by becoming by turns bossy and enraged with her mother, hating herself. We had arrived at a differentiated articulation of a previously formless and overwhelming movement: hated for being shameful and unsoothable, hating for being unsoothed, and in despair, pushing me away in dismissive anger because ashamed at calling and hoping for help.

Wendy and I had often spoken "about" hate, her fatalistic assurance that she would never get what she needs or be soothed, and she had realized how mean she could be with her constant criticisms of herself and others. But now this abstract knowledge was saturated with emotional meaning. My willingness to be vulnerable in front of her (and only a bit retaliatory) convinced her that I was not afraid of her hate, indeed, that her efforts to repair and correct me, make a better mother of me, might not even be seen as hateful by me. Further, I could hold my own vulnerability and keep my mind intact. I could acknowledge my own tendencies to dysregulation and shame, not so different from her own, while remaining willing to hear how angry she had been with me. My risking her knowing about my badness, my failure, opened her to a similar but different risk of intersubjective vulnerability. This meant that feelings good and bad were not "unthinkable." All her life Wendy had imagined that happy people in safe homes didn't even have such vulnerability let alone speak about feelings. It had not been possible to communicate these feelings to her parents no matter how many efforts she made. It was essential, even at the expense of her own sanity, to normalize and conceal the intense despair, the chaos and rage of her unhappy home. Now she was finding out that being safe actually meant having a home in which to be vulnerable, in which pain could be known and thought. I was not pretending to be simply strong, the Tough Mama who would be the complementary opposite to her needy child. I was also vulnerable, and I did not have to match her image to help her find her own feelings. The liberation of this discovery was to reverberate in her more than either of us knew.

In the moment of rupture, when Wendy enacted her shame and fear, she had been convinced that it had destroyed me for good, that it was a truly dangerous whirlpool. My failure would recreate the dangerous, unlawful world of her childhood; she would be plunged into its chaos and left alone. Her anger would be as destructive to me as hers and her father's had been to her mother; she would really be too big for me, so that I could not contain and survive her rage as she had desperately wished her mother had been able to do.

Although this was only one of many fraught moments on our bumpy route of negotiation and repair, Wendy was truly surprised that I not only survived destruction but recognized her need to be held by someone who *knew* her disorganization, accepted her hatred and could acknowledge my own wrongness. I did not have to always get it right the first time, nor did she. The shameful "not-me" girl whom she had so often violently repudiated, could now be seen as a someone that another someone wants to know. Appreciating each other's honesty, we both survived being known differently than before, having in asymmetrical ways our own respective experiences of hostility. I was finding a way to enlarge myself to contain it so that what might have seemed a flood became a newly articulated emotional experience.

This was a particular version of the moral Third, in which we were both suffering exposure. Its rhythmic side was re-established as we joined together in rescuing ourselves from the flood, in welcoming the little girl who was too much, too angry, too mean. By the end of the session the Third felt renewed and vital, rhythmic and differentiated, a co-created process that had room for two subjects, each the other's other, as we laughed together. In this lawful world violations could be corrected—for Wendy, this meant a sane world.

Indeed, the following session Wendy, arriving in high spirits, announced: "Today, for the first time *ever*, I came here without worrying about how the session might be going to damage my mental health. That you might do something wrong which would make me lose my sanity." Wendy continued to elucidate, with humor and feeling, this painful possibility of being damaged, changed by me in the "wrong way." In the months following this moment of recognition, Wendy became noticeably less judgemental and dysregulated, less fearful in general. Her life changed dramatically. Her ability to think in the face of frustration was markedly greater, and her dismissiveness abated, so that she could actually share with me her feelings about losing connection over the weekend or with my absence.

She could say out loud those "crazy" thoughts, like the one that I might ruin her sanity, or that my ideas about people having feelings could not possibly be true. Wendy actually came to trust that I would carry out my responsibility for her, play my role without instruction, value our co-created thirdness and her part in shaping it. Her thinking process accordingly became more creative and less concrete as she found new metaphors of water: surrendering to the beautiful waves in the ocean, rather than drowning in the whirlpool, the flood.

Conclusion

In my discussion of the development of thirdness I tried to evoke and think about the shared movement of intentions and feelings that is mutual influence which can further develop into mutual recognition. Here, in this part, I am highlighting how the analyst changes in response to the patient, which in turn allows the patient to have more impact and therefore experience themselves as an active contributor to the process. As McKay has written, more than simply being understood or given empathy, "recognition is characterized by the experience of being seen by and being allowed access to the mind of another, as elements of the unformulated (Stern, 1997) in one person call forth something unformulated in the other, enabling affective coherence to emerge in a new way for both partners." As part of this process we invite patients to activate us, move us, which entails the challenge to reflect and re-connect with the exposed parts of ourselves rather than engage in self-protective dissociation. Still, surrender to the Third means accepting the inevitability that he will sometimse lapse into self-protective detachment or dissociation of our own limits, especially in the face of a patient's traumatic reactivity and the analyst's responsibility to protect him from the impingement of our subjective response.

The analyst's asymmetrical responsibility in many instances consists of "going first": acknowledging, surrendering, grasping her own part in the interaction. This can give rise to a reciprocal action in which each person changes for and with the other, gradually recognizing one another more fully, encompassing what is hardest to face and bear. In this sense I have stressed how mutual recognition includes *both* partners' vulnerability, an intimate connection in which each person knows the other knows something about her, not all of it matching up with her ideal. There are parallels to and differences from how a new mother tries to bear what she uncovers in herself as she meets the challenge of caring for a newborn. For the analyst, this surrender to exposure constitutes the edgy side of mutual recognition; then again, it's not so easy for the patient either.

Seen in this way, the analytic relationship has more dimensions than the expected complementarity of a protected partner (the analyst who understands) with a vulnerable partner (the patient who is understood). In this view, the patient comes increasingly to what we can call the "use of a *subject*," one whose vulnerability is no longer associated with threatening fragmentation, collapse or impingement. This vulnerability must no longer appear to be caused by the patient's own destructiveness, too-muchness or self-hatred, which changes the status of vulnerability so that it can become an aspect of mutual recognition. This acceptance of the analyst's exposure does not represent an abdication of taking responsibility but adds another dimension to it—honest accountability. It is not an unspoken, unacknowledged demand upon the patient to carry by herself the burden of unspoken knowledge of the other's struggles and susceptibilities by herself. In this way mutuality and responsibility are actually joined in the recognition process through acknowledged and shared awareness of our vulnerability. This can now become a source of engaged connection as we move through cycles of disruption and repair, aiming to strengthen the moral Third.

Things change, as relational analysis has discovered, when we acknowledge that privileging the protective barrier around our subjectivity may also have drawbacks. As an interactive position that re-establishes complementarity and opposes mutuality that barrier can be problematic. Not because we deny the responsibility for realizing our limits, holding and analyzing our complex subjectivity; but rather, because the barrier needs to have enough permeability to let us directly recognize the patient's emotional effect or the impact of his action. In addition, the patient can make use of our vulnerability if we can help him to his own way of making use of the mutuality of shared vulnerability. This use of us and our mutuality means we are creating a dyadic system, a moral Third, based on lawful accountability and protection of insight.

That our vulnerability as analysts will inevitably exceed what we can hold without dissociation and self-protection is the very problem that leads us back into the process of acknowledgment, into repair and recognition. Viewed in this way, the conflict between mutuality and asymmetry is not something to be solved but is instead a recursive paradox within intersubjectivity, one we try to hold in the tension of thirdness. Developmentally, the asymmetry in which mother recognizes child makes mutuality possible; evolving mutuality between the two keeps asymmetrical relations from degrading into controlling the object, non-recognition of subjectivity. This accords with the principle, not always realizable: recognizing the other is requisite to feeling recognized by an equivalent subject.

As we work and move deeply into the recursive paradox of mutuality and responsibility, it can enliven us in the reciprocity of using our subjectivity and being used as a *subject*. So it is not merely the analyst's subjectivity that is finally irreducible (Renik, 1993); it is the fact of mutuality, which must be embraced in all its complexity and vitality or avoided at peril of both partners losing their subjectivity. Knowing that once our subjectivity is freely acknowledged, we must face our own demons and assume responsibility for them, we are poised on the shore of a new continent, and now, together, must all pay close attention to what happens next.

Chapter 4

An Other take on the riddle of sex

Excess, affect and gender complementarity

The road of excess leads to the palace of wisdom.
William Blake, *The Marriage of Heaven and Hell*

This chapter represents the history of my efforts to analyze the tension of bearing the tension of sexuality in light of affect regulation and recognition theory. I do this by locating the origins of our stance towards sexual excitement in experiences in the early mother-infant dyad and continue by following the trail of this pattern into gender complementarity. The crux of this work was an effort to establish a place in intersubjective, relational thought for sexuality, and to further integrate, as in "Sympathy for the Devil," (Benjamin, 1995e), Laplanche's idea of the fantasmatic sexual with relational intersubjectivity. I first gave a version of this paper as a keynote at Division 39, "How Intersubjective Is Sex?" (also called "The Marriage of Heaven and Hell") which formulated the basic proposition that excess arises as that which cannot be symbolized or held in dialogic mental space. I was also aiming to further develop Eigen's early (1981) insight that our psyches can generate so much more than they are equipped to handle.

Excess could be seen as a link to Freud's view of the psyche as grounded in an energetic economy—but without the drive. These ideas were finally published in the paper "Revisiting the Riddle of Sex" (Benjamin, 2004b). However, some years later I took another shot at the project and collaborated with Galit Atlas, in our paper "The Too-Muchness of Excitement," first presented in 2010 and published in 2015 (Benjamin & Atlas, 2015). As Atlas and I continued to work on the clinical theory of how early dyadic interactions can result in later difficulty with arousal and excitement within the sphere of sexuality—"too-muchness"— many of my earlier theoretical speculations were elaborated and concretized. I am grateful for her collaboration, as well as her own contributions to my thinking (see Atlas, 2015, especially Chapters 2 and 3).

Both phases of work on this subject began with reflection on Laplanche's ideas about seduction and the enigmatic message, but the further elaboration of excess by Stein (2008) plays a greater role in my formulations here. Whereas my earlier work emphasized the way the constellation of passivity as femininity was constructed to hold excess by Freud (and the patriarchal culture he embodied), my later work with Atlas emphasized the clinical sequelae of early dysregulation: the effects of unrecognized distress, abandonment and overstimulation during infancy on adult sexuality. We explored how inability to tolerate sexual arousal and the excitement affect, "too-muchness," these early problems with recognition and regulation that later appear in clinical enactments, transference-countertransference.

Both works emphasized the constant tension between intrapsychic fantasy and the intersubjective relationship in practice and theory, a tension corresponding to what Atlas (2015) calls the Enigmatic and the Pragmatic. The interweaving of these two layers can be seen in the fantasies that both mask and reveal intersubjective failures in regulation and recognition. These fantasies are shaped by the meta-phors of gender that are used to process the enigmatic message. In this way I try to integrate a view of sexual fantasy with my earlier critique (Benjamin, 1998; Benjamin, 2004b) of Freud's formulation of the active–passive split in the Oedipus complex: masculine "activity" is seen as an attempt to solve the problem of excess. At the end, I return to the theme that underlay my discussion of Story of O *in* Bonds of Love *(Benjamin, 1988), the search for a form of surrender, a form of thirdness that takes us beyond the complementarity of sado-masochism into shared holding of the excess that is sexuality.*

The problem of excess—theoretical perspective

Freud's notion of sexual pleasure and pain emphasized how we seek mastery over tension; he conceived of a one-person economy in which pain is defined as too much tension (Freud, 1915). The roots of the idea of excess or "too-muchness" (Atlas & Benjamin, 2010) can indeed be found in Freud, so much so that Stein (2008) contended that "in fact the notion of excess serves Freud as a regulative idea indicating the perennial striving of the organism to rid itself of excess stimuli" (p. 50). She expounded on the way that "Freud's early writings are suffused with notions of excess, excess of stimuli causing trauma, dangerously accumulated psychic energy, unbearable drive charge manifested in symptoms." She points out how in Freud's earliest thinking: "When physical tension cannot be transmuted into affect, it becomes anxiety" (Stein, 2008, p. 50; Breuer & Freud, 1895). We may note that this formulation suggests an important link between Freud's view of tension and contemporary affect regulation theories.

But this idea of tension raises the question regarding excess: "What is it that makes for too much?" From an intersubjective point of view, pleasure and pain occur within a two-person relationship; they are psychic experiences having to do with how we register the responses of another and how the other registers us. Psychic pain in its intersubjective aspect may be intrinsically linked to failures of recognition and regulation, to arousal caused by inadequate or overwhelming responses, and this failure of the other is registered and pre-symbolically represented (Stern, 1985) by infants in their internal working model of attachment (Bowlby, 1969; see Fonagy & Target, 1996a & b).

It is important to recognize not only the failure of the other to regulate but also the overwhelming of the psyche (see Eigen, 1993; Benjamin, 1995a) by the other, or more precisely the psyche's response to the other's stimulation, in our understanding of excess. If we consider this overwhelming of the immature psyche as another take on Freud's (1926) idea of original helplessness, we can see how we are still working to grasp a primary experience and identify a through line in our intellectual history related to excess. This perspective on "too-muchness" recognizes the original helplessness and anxiety Freud first identified, as well as the implicit role of excess in his thinking but, as we shall eventually see, the translation of this helplessness into the feminine position of passivity in Freud's oedipal model served to obscure many of the primary causes of this state.

Understanding excess in the context of the need for a maternal figure to respond to and hold both excitement/desire and affect within a secure attachment based on affect regulation (see Schore, 1993; 2003; Fonagy et al., 2002) means grasping how the arousal associated with desire can become overwhelming to the immature psyche. Without the outside other, the originally helpless self cannot process arousal associated with internal tension or external stimulation. Without the mother's containment of pain and excitement, the baby cannot self-regulate. But this is a two-way process: recognition theory considers an individual's state of internal tension to be inextricably tied to the intersubjective sharing that is the basic recognition between self and other (Benjamin, 1988). There is also the matter of the mother's own ability to regulate her excitement and anxiety, and how she may communicate or make demands upon her child's ill-equipped and immature psyche for regulation and containment. To sum up: once we regard maternal responsiveness as not only satisfying needs or soothing anxiety but also sharing affect states, giving meaning to emotion, to intentions and acts, and conveying mother's own subjective states, we can formulate a more complex understanding of how failures of recognition and problems in affect regulation (Schore, 1993, 2003; Fonagy et al., 2002) relate to the generation of excess.

In this regard the "generalized theory of seduction" introduced by Laplanche both complicated and expanded the intersubjective perspective on excess. Laplanche's (1987; 1992; 1997; 2011) work on sexuality constituted an important effort to renew, in a sense to rescue from backsliding, Freud's original "Copernican" move: a decentering from the ego of self-contained mastery, founded on the idea of the unconscious as alien. Laplanche's mission was to argue for recognizing the internal otherness of the unconscious to be founded upon external otherness (Laplanche, 1997, p. 654). Part of this project entailed the recasting of seduction in terms of the intersubjective concept of the message, what the adult communicates. This is not exactly unconscious (Laplanche, 2011) but pre-conscious, perhaps best thought of as something in the adult pre-verbal transmission, requiring a work of translation by the child. The "enigmatic message" conceptualized the overwhelming of the child's immature psyche by communications from the Other, the adult's psyche: thus an implantation of something other and too much (Laplanche, 1992; 1997). Once this otherness is now implanted within the self, the question of the Other as external is always preceded by the Other within. This idea of otherness ultimately will be seen as implicating the social ordering of sexuality and interpersonal relations (Laplanche, 2011).

In Laplanche's revised general seduction theory, the excess that is sexuality for all human infants begins with an enigmatic or compromised communication from the Other in the course of real interaction involving the child's care: the mother's sexuality experienced as something too big and not yet comprehended or metabolized by the child. Excess thus derives from the general fact of seduction: the surplus transmission, the implanting of elements of the mother's own not conscious not transparent meanings, that go along with the implicit bodily care. Laplanche contends that Freud was too concrete in thinking seduction must either be real or imagined, and missed the category of the message. Insofar as the sexuality of the mother, or other unconscious components of adult mind (hate or love one might suppose) are conveyed along with care of the child, these necessarily enigmatic transmissions stamp human sexuality with excess (Laplanche, 1987).

The formation of the sexual through alien implantation functions both as a kind of general trauma and the source of psychic structure (Scarfone, 2015). Because the child cannot translate the adult's message into a meaningful pre-conscious/conscious representation, and indeed the mother herself is not aware of her message, it functions as a demand for mental differentiation (Scarfone, 2015) and generates the part of the psyche that evolves as unconscious. In Laplanche's view, the enigmatic message, with its demand for "translation," some form of symbolic work, is constitutive of the child's unconscious in the broadest sense. Uninvited and psychically unassimilable, the excessive, enigmatic message constitutes a bridge between actual (specific) seduction and fantasy. It is not that a literal seduction becomes fantastical, but that an implicit and not directly sexual enigmatic message, perhaps carrying the "noise" of the adult's unconscious sexuality (Laplanche, 2011), takes shape within the self as a question—"what does the Other want of me"—which must be translated and processed through fantasmatic activity. In this sense the general intersubjective condition of seduction is universal and is distinguished from specific, actual seduction.

Stein's many contributions (1998a; 1998b; 2008) have suggested multiple meanings of the excessive, its relation to the enigmatic message, but also the poignancy of sex, its transits beyond representation into an experience of otherness and mystery. The mysterious and asocial effect of the sexual—its otherness—was explored by both Bataille (1986) and Bersani (1977) and associated with the loss of individuation, the experience of merger and continuity (Bataille, 1986) and shattering of the ego (Bersani, 1985; see also Saketopoulis, 2014). Both because of the obstacles to recognizing sexuality in its primal form, incestuous desire, and the potential for violating the borders of the ego, sexuality has been set apart in a separate realm of either transcendence or debasement (Stein, 2008; Rundel, 2015). The incommensurability of sexuality with other modes of social interaction marks it and makes it at best only partially assimilable—necessarily excessive (see Bataille, 1986; Laplanche, 1987; 1992; 1997; Benjamin, 1995a; 2004b; Stein, 1998a; 2008;

Fonagy, 2008), and this in turn contributes to unavoidable transmission of the message as enigmatic and alien. In other words, to grasp the alien, foreign quality of implantation requires continuous decentering work—while it might appear simply a matter of going into another room and pointing a finger at a person who did something, such thinking will never grasp the *excessiveness* of such an alien force within.

Thus in multiple senses the sexual, understood as an effect of the Other and of otherness, is *bound to be excessive, to exceed what the relational dimension can help the immature psyche contain and regulate* (Benjamin, 2004b). Consequently, the psychic demands of the excessive are ordinarily met through a form of splitting that separates the fantasmatic process of the sexual from other forms of using the object. *The enigmatic message itself, opaque and not conscious , because not symbolized*, is inevitably dissociated from other psychic processes.

If, then, we begin with the proposition that sexuality is bound to exceed what the relational dimension can contain (Benjamin, 2004b), it is nonetheless evident that the capacity to hold and process this excess through mental and physical action varies considerably. We must still track the intersubjective vicissitudes of bearing excess, which generally *derive from the uncontained and unsymbolized excitement originating in the child or the mother's reaction to the child.* My contention is that such processing of the enigmatic message and associated excess depends on the individual's early development of the overall capacity for holding excitement. This capacity begins quite early with interactive experiences of affect arousal in the attachment to mother or other caregivers.

Therefore, an abstract conception of parental sexuality, a "generalized other" who transmits an enigmatic message, is practically insufficient for psychoanalysis, as Stein (1998a) pointed out. We also must identify how that transmission is elaborated in conjunction with specific patterns of attachment and recognition. These patterns may not be universal structures as figured in the Oedipus complex. Other dimensions of affective experience that are subsequently translated into the sexual are liable to be riven with the same faults.

The excessive aspect of sexuality is thus inseparable from lack of emotional containment or affect regulation, which prevents absorption of this "alien body" (Fonagy, 2008) in the individual's psyche. As Fonagy states, "sexual arousal can never truly be experienced as owned. It will always be an imposed burden . . . unless we find someone to share it with" (p. 22). He continues: "The enigmatic dimension of sexuality creates an invitation that calls out to be elaborated, normally by another" (Fonagy, 2008, p. 22). I am proposing that the offering and acceptance of this invitation to the other is precisely what is blocked by the experience that all affective and bodily arousal is dangerous—dangerous not merely because it is inherently enigmatic, but also because it makes a real demand upon the other for recognition and regulation. At the intersubjective level of "pragmatic" (Atlas, 2015) interaction, there is a faulty connection. This fault leaves the subject unable to rise to the demands of the sexual, with its inherent challenges and aspects of otherness. The ensuing fear of the sexual and sense of too-muchness stimulates efforts at mastery, frightening fantasies, dissociation: the cure becomes its own problem.

The dilemma of rising to the demands of the sexual—the matrix of fantasies and desire—shapes the relationship of intrapsychic and intersubjective. Stein, following an early line of thought by Laplanche, argues that when the maternal object is lost the autoerotic object substitutes for the lost object that can never be refound. The idea is that the original nourishing, functional object that provides the "milk" is lost and must be replaced by a fantasmatic sexual object, the "breast." Stein declares that emergence of excess in sexuality, its driven and peremptory qualities, is "powerfully influenced by the pursuit of a lost object that has become fantasmatic and displaced"[1] (Stein, 1998a, p. 262). We notice that Stein here introduces another meaning of excess, independent of the one that arises from the greater power and maturity of the mother or the opaqueness and unconsciousness of her desires.

The idea that the needed object of attachment is lost and transformed into the autoerotic sexual object seems to me, however, to conflate fantasy with theory, positing a generalized loss of the attachment figure. It tries to explain the traumatic aspect of the sexual in terms of an intrapsychic, one-person, view of an original lost object. But this idea of a lost maternal object appears in light of the intersubjective idea of seduction to be a re-inscription of the intrapsychic idea of the drive, as in lost gratification, and of the oedipal renunciation—not accidentally the wheel on which the gendering of excess in Freud's thinking turns, as we shall see. Further, it is as if the lost object replaces the intersubjective mother of attachment, who in our theory is conceived to be a figure of continuity and ongoing relatedness, even while she is a source of surplus, enigmatic transmission. The idea of a lost maternal object would make sense to me as a specific, possibly traumatic experience, as insecure attachment; but this would be in contrast to the idea of an ongoing intersubjective maternal relationship in which excitement can, potentially, be recognized and contained.

Intersubjective theory conceives the connection to the mother as an external other as one involving multiple functions and interactions that correspond to the infant's many states, including excited arousal, dysregulation, being soothed, playful and curious, while gazing, cuddling and so on. In this sense the infant does not necessarily "lose" the breast mother when he ceases to suckle, or substitute the fantasmatic for the pleasure of nursing. Rather, the experience of nursing is diffused into diverse forms, other forms of painful urgency or distress that can be soothed, but also the sense of being held and recognized by the other through mutual gaze, playing and smiling. As excited and aroused as the infant may be by the breast in the state of hunger, when the satisfaction of hunger is secure, he should be able to integrate the self-state of joyful arousal in association with agency and enjoyment of play. Initially, the action changes not from need satisfaction to autoerotic fantasy but to other forms of soothing and play with mother.

---

1   "The sexual object is thus not identical with the object of the function . . . [and] the object one seeks to re-find in sexuality is . . . displaced. . . . It is therefore impossible ultimately ever to rediscover the [original] object." (Laplanche cited in Stein, 2007, p. 186)

Perhaps it is only when this double process of regulation and recognition fails that a premature process of self-soothing occurs, which prefigures and evolves into fantasmatic auto-eroticism. This prematurity, substituting for the regulation in nursing experience and the recognition of affect states of distress or play-ful connection, may then organize a specific way of coping with excess. In this way developmental trauma, like abuse, would arise from particular conditions of transmission, inflecting the general seduction of the enigmatic message. Laplanche accounts for such forms with the idea of "*intromission*, a violent variant of implan-tation that relates to the bodily interior . . . an intrusion, the emergence of the sexual in a non-metabolizable way that precludes the differentiation of psychic agencies" (Scarfone, 2001, p. 62).

In clinical work with developmental trauma, it becomes evident how the unreliability of primal satisfaction and soothing, of the functional object of need, leads to a basic template of "seduced and abandoned," or "excited and then dropped," quite apart from the enigmatic message. However, when this template of insecurity, abandonment, and lack of soothing dominates, it obstructs rather than initiates the process by which psychic structure develops in the effort to translate and assimilate the enigmatic message. In this case, the transmission of something unconscious from the mother that is unassimilable and excessive *cannot even be allowed to form sexual subjectivity as an exciting otherness*—with all the usual attendant conflicts and frustrations psychoanalysis has recognized. When affective arousal, in all and any forms not only sexual excitement, is felt to endanger the attachment and be uncontainable by the other, even within a protective "preserve" of dissociation or splitting, such excitement is not tolerable.[2] Or, autoerotic and transgressive activities do preserve excitement, but only within a sphere of dissociation which feels literally alien, abject, other, "perverse," or a threat to self-cohesion. As when direct sexual trauma has been experienced, arousal and safety of attachment are more drastically split apart than in the "ordinary" forms of tolerated dissociation and otherness we know as sexual. In other words, the inability to *tolerate* the otherness of the sexual and its inevitably high level of arousal manifests as the fear of "too-muchness," both in intimate relations and the transference. Clinically, this fear appears accompanied by a concomitant experience of shame (Stein, 1998b, 2008), a sense of inadequacy related to the inability to bear excess, that is, to experience desire without fragmenting, which in turn affects an individual's sense of being adequate, a "real" man or woman.

If for everyone sexuality poses a burden that requires an other to lighten it, as Fonagy (2008) contends, then how can it be borne by individuals who cannot use the other, for whom "excess" cannot be contained in any relationship? For such persons, the other with her own potential arousal and fantasies poses only a threat.

---

2 From a relational perspective the sense of an alien, other self would be understood in terms of dissociation of self states, but the ability to negotiate the transition from one self state to another depends upon attachment and affect regulation, mediated by recognition (Bromberg, 1998; 2011).

The experience can be that of impingement, engulfment, flooding and invasion; given the overstimulation, excitement and anxiety become indistinguishable. The need for the other to contain excitement through recognition in this way leads to a further intersubjective dilemma: intense anxiety about the other's presence as a subject with her own affect, which has been experienced as dangerous rather than a source of resonance and pleasure.

Accordingly, the basic issue around dependency—needing an other who is outside one's control or influence (Benjamin, 1988)—becomes intensified. It then translates as a fantasmatic relation to an other who becomes *more* dangerous outside. This is the consequence of a primary object relation in which affect regulation fails, in which the other cannot be relied upon to be attuned, accommodating, engaged in a way that recognizes and creates mental space for excitement. The other cannot be relied upon to be responsive and recognizing of the child's communications in a way that allows the (smaller, younger) self to have agency and internal control. This other cannot therefore serve as a container for projections—as enjoying sexuality requires (Stein, 1998a; Fonagy, 2008)—but is, rather, liable to overpower the child with her dysregulated affect, with her messages, her projections. This fantasy of the unreliable maternal container, I will suggest, is what was confusingly carried into the notion "feminine passivity."

The demands posed in general by the sexual must be worked out specifically in each pair, in the intersubjectively regulated arena of affective and bodily care with its management of arousal, intensity and proximity. The maternal message conveyed in this arena consists not only of her unconscious sexuality, but involves such content as anxieties about injury, fragmentation, depletion or over-stimulation by the infant, thus influencing the realm of the sexual. And, conversely, the skin and body eroticism of the mother, her gaze and connection with her infant, "cradle" the message and calm it down. Hence the production of excess is located within a complex configuration of relational experience. On one side, the mother's contribution, on the other, the infant's efforts: not only to manage his own affect but to influence mother so as to regulate his own anxiety and stimulation as well. These efforts to have an impact on mother's behavior, to affect the recognition process, may be seen as inversely linked to fantasmatic activity—the more effective I am the less I need to resort to fantasy to manage the arousal and frustration linked to faulty recognition. Complex, sub-symbolic representations of both the mother's and the infant's actions and affects all influence the way that messages are translated and excess is metabolized.

Mysterious and mystifying

If the excessive and mysterious aspects of sexuality derive from more than one source, still all of them center on the experience of otherness, the dependency on the other to contain, recognize and thus organize the infant's bodily experience. Patterns of misrecognition—for instance maternal intolerance of baby's eagerness and excitement that stimulate sexualization and misreading on her part—contribute to the difficulties in translation and the sense of the sexual as "alien" (Fonagy, 2004; Stein, 2008). In my reading, the inevitable excess of the adult's messages, the "general seduction," can be intensified by specific relational instances of misrecognition and failure of containment (Benjamin, 2004; Benjamin & Atlas, 2015). I have therefore tried to distinguish the otherness that is mysterious and psychically productive from that which is mystifying. In other words, the sexual that is mysterious, incommensurable and therefore generally uncontained by adults should not be conflated with that which is mystifying due to an insecure attachment riddled with hyperarousal and misreading of basic needs and subsymbolic bodily signals.

My aim here is to contrast and yet hold the tension that is often lost between two different perspectives, what we might call general and specific: the *intrapsychically mysterious*—the residue of the enigmatic (Atlas, 2015) that is necessarily seductive and opaque, stimulating fantasy and creating a space for the symbolic that is universal, luring us to contact a forever elusive ideal—and the *intersubjectively mystifying*. Part of the mystification process consists of the way that failures in interpersonal regulation and containment lead to withdrawal into more extreme forms of fantasy. In the mystifying aspect, affective tension that could not be understood by the child, represented, or "bound" in dialogic exchange may later appear as though self-originating, a one-person process of fantasy creation (Benjamin, 1995a; 2004b). Of course this may be seen as a general feature of fantasmatic activity, as Laplanche (1997) seemed to suggest when he wrote "the otherness of the other person is blurred, re-absorbed in the form of *my* fantasy of the other, *my* seduction fantasy, and the otherness of the unconscious is put at risk . . ." (p. 659). But I believe this general condition takes on a further quality of alienation when the outside other is perceived as truly dangerous.

Thus, for instance, the position of passivity, which Freud associated with feminine masochism insofar as it involves being subject to the other's drive, is only threatening or excessive because of this relation to the other. If passivity assumes such a frightening appearance this might be seen as an effect of a particular relation to an other—one that involves projection, power, degradation, thus resulting in an alienation from self, not due to something essential in the position of the drive. The adoption of a form of passivity may be seen as both a generalized culturally mandated template of gender and a specific feature of the collision between adult action or messaging and childhood sexuality, for instance when a child is forced into the position of container for the unregulating and dysregulated parent. I consider how such passivity may be an experience of having to bear unwanted levels of stimulation or excitement that an uncontained other is expressing in a dissociated way: traumatic rather than ordinary excess.

A patient, Isabelle, whom I (see Benjamin, 1995a) have previously discussed, is confused about whose excitement she is reacting to, Mother's or her own. The mystified experience is improperly attributed and in this sense mentalization is interfered with. Excitement then becomes dangerous and threatens to disrupt psychic regulation. Transgressive elements mixed with autoerotic soothing and containing have enabled her a partial way out, a kind of manic defense. The vicissitudes of excitement and the ability to contain arousal are linked in complex ways to the consciously known but frightening communication with her mother.

Isabelle, whose mother would dance around the room in excitement during her piano lessons, was confused about whose excitement was being expressed at any given time. Additionally, in adolescence Isabelle's mother would verbally attack Isabelle after she revealed herself in confessions that Mother had extracted from her. Mother appeared to be trying this way to extrude her sense of badness and too-muchness into her daughter. The confusion between badness in the self and the object, which protectively serves to regulate the more powerful parent, is a relational aspect that resurfaces, confused, in the child's fantasy (see Fairbairn, 1952; Davies, 2004).

In Isabelle's case, she presented with many compulsive sexual fantasies and activities, which seemed to function both to self-soothe and to imaginatively engage a powerful, protective other to whom she would submit. She was fearful that her compulsive activities had damaged her insides or exposed her to disease. Her expressed wish was that the other, whose excitement she would open herself to contain, would in turn supply her with a sense of being structured, controlled, managed—in other words, take over the regulating function her mother lacked. Unlike those patients who inhibit desire and fear excitement, Isabelle reacts to an impinging, dysregulated object by adopting the passive "feminine" position to absorb helplessness. She submits to sexual excitement with the express wish to be controlled and protected, perhaps from her own fantasied destructiveness.

Isabelle's wish was for the analyst to contain her excess, though she believed this would be impossible. Even as she felt forced to be her mother's container and failed, so would the analyst fail to process her mother-like manic reactions to anxiety, which now had assumed the form of an Other within Isabelle and were associated with the invasion of dangerous objects. As a daughter who overtly rejected this passive position with mother, she nonetheless later assumed it repeatedly with men, incurring her mother's wrath, a condemnation she now expects from me as well. She was the girl who chooses the route of concealing her loss and longing for mother as well as her need to please her father by creating a transgressive version of the role he wanted her to take: containing the difficult mother. She incorporated this action even as she sought release from it by becoming a precociously sexualized feminine object, accommodating and pleasing men.

As Isabelle began to reject this compliant role, and yet was unable to contain the vast amount of tension within, she sought analysis. She recognized herself in formulaic versions of "feminine masochism," in which she allowed herself to be a slave to master, held but controlled. Adding to the confusion was a barely recognized link between her unmothered baby self and her longing to be known by her father, as they were allied in their task of holding the spilling-over fragile mother. This connection to father gradually became visible as part of her efforts to create a repaired, loving mother–baby couple with men.

The realization of her need for something other than sadomasochistic satisfaction to relieve the too-muchness was slow in coming to Isabelle because of her anxiety at needing or depending on a dangerous mother, and because she felt dangerous herself. She was sure she was too much, too powerful for any analyst, her excessive desires too wild to be understood or contained. She had come to see herself as shameful and dangerous, mystified as she was by having absorbed all the aspects of aggression, helplessness and dysregulation that both parents evacuated into her. Making the distinction between her own overstimulation and that of her mother was not possible in real interaction—she had to push out her mother aggressively even as she yearned to be held and contained by her.

In encountering such forms of desire, we might indeed question whether such experience of excess should be understood in its sexual manifestation alone, or rather seen as a more complex configuration of many relational issues that include efforts to regulate anxiety and stimulation, to manage interpersonal aggression linked to her maternal attachment. Isabelle's reconstructions of history reveals a mother–child dyad in which excess (a fusion of excitement and aggression) is processed through sexualization. Her initial preoccupations exemplify the way in which fantasy explicitly takes the body as a container for the unbearable. In the absence of a transforming, regulating other, failures in affective containment coupled with overstimulation can be reworked and translated into sexual tension, and thus discharged. They may or may not reflect some explicitly sexual trans-mission from the other. As Stein (1998b) has put it, "it seems that the human organism has the capacity to [use sexualization] to deal with the excess . . . in other words, sexualization is a capacity, a positive achievement . . ." (p. 266). Sexual fantasy thus substitutes for the affect regulating function of the outside other; another dimension of the Other within.

In dealing with bodily excitement and regulation, then, we are always liable to touch upon the paradox of sexual excess: sexuality itself is potentially excessive and creates experiences of stimulation and tension even as it serves as a method of regulating self and other, not only through discharge but also through the con-tainment of otherwise unrepresented, unmentalized experiences with significant others (Benjamin, 2004a; Atlas, 2015). I consider many forms of sexuality to be actions the individual takes to soothe or regulate the self, rather than primarily to engage or elicit responses from an other person. In this context, sexual discharge means using the body to solve the problem of mental excess, that is, emotional content which cannot be held in the dialogically created mental space is transposed into the register of physiological arousal and resolved at that level.

Sexuality not only originates in the opaque and unsymbolized form; conversely, it functions to contain otherwise unrepresented, unmentalized experiences with significant others. Bodily contact can be metaphorically equated in fantasy with the entry into the other's mind, the experience of being recognized or held, invaded or excluded. We may consider the gradations of the desire to reach the other, the frustrated desperation to get in accompanied by urgent need to discharge, as well as the different inflections of the wish to enter or be entered: from the wish to be held safely to the urge to break in forcibly, from the wish to be known to the wish to be cracked open. We may think of sexuality as a means of expressing the need to get me into you, or get you into me; but conversely, we may think that the experience of excitement generates or intensifies the need to get in, as in, "Help me contain this tension; let me put this tension into you."

Thus we have a whole lexicon of experiences involving the causes and effects of uncontained sexual excitement and unmanageable arousal, in which we alternately see sexuality as an Lengine ("drive") motive and as a vehicle of expression. As Stein (1998a) concluded: "Sexuality [is] suitable to serve as one of the most powerful coins in the mental trade between different levels and contents" (p. 254). Analysts now work in both directions, not only "discovering sexual themes and motivations behind the ostensibly non-sexual" (p. 254), but also finding other motives in the sexual.

Excess and the mind-body split

If sexuality provides an alternate register for processing tension and managing excess, when it functions in lieu of the outside other or substitutes for communicative and symbolic processes, this can only work by dint of a split in the self. Above all, by splitting mind and body, the self can play two parts, with the body as container for experience that the mind cannot process symbolically. The body can be employed as an alternate part-self to hold and discharge the tension of split off experience with important others. Painful affect and overwhelming excitement that are left unprocessed and unrepresented in communicative dialogue can be represented in sexual fantasy and then discharged physically.

Transgressive sexuality can also be a form of encompassing pain and vulnerability, creating a scene of witnessing and containing. Thus for Isabelle, whose autoerotic activities and fantasies were initially used to process her mother's enigmatic message, the orgasm became a place to hold and have witnessed the too-muchness inside her. Feeling shut out of her mother's mind early on, Isabelle tried to get back in, seeking attention; thus she explicitly associated her fantasies of master and slave with her mother's abusive response to her confidences. She described her adolescent autoerotic habits of bringing herself to unbearable states of excitement and orgasm in which the Master's voice said, "You've got to take it"— and she did. She used the container of her own body to create a replica of the too-muchness, a positive version of shattering the ego (Bersani, 1985; Botticelli, 2010; Saketopoulis, 2014), which demonstrated her ability to survive (Benjamin, 1988). She used her physical body's submission to create a surrender in which pleasure and pain became indistinguishable.

But Isabelle also spoke of how she fell in love with her lover, the one she shared all these feelings, fantasies and excitement with in young adulthood, because before she met him she had seen a work of art in which he portrayed a cactus on which, mysteriously, snow was falling: peaceful soothing white snow. She said, this is "what did it," what let her know that he could recognize and contain what was inside her, calm her. His physical strength signified his ability to hold all the excitement and pain. His recognition of both the overstimulation and the soothing

—as symbolically represented in his art—would bring her home to the part of herself that needed to be found and held (Benjamin, 1995a; Rundel, 2015).

In the absence of intersubjective regulation by the other, the excited sexual body became a split off container for unrepresentable pain and for aggression. Both her mother's aggression and her own—as well as the rage she experienced in early adolescence that she was prevented from turning back against her mother. Only later does Isabelle imagine being held safely in an other's mind, without penetrating or being penetrated, in such a way that her internal tension is regulated. Isabelle experienced the coming together of the mysterious excess and the suffering of passion with the witnessing of her psychic pain, restoring her to a home in her own mind in which otherness could dwell without consuming her.

Isabelle's story illustrates how excess is processed through sexualisation, through fantasy that explicitly takes the body as a container for the unbearable. This sexualisation takes the form of complementarity between doer and done to, enacted in the intrapsychic fantasy world, within what we might call the monadic sexual economy. This complementarity, unrelieved by the thirdness of recognition, has already marked the interactions in the mother-child dyad in significant ways. The principle movement in the monadic sexual economy is not the exchange of recognition, the communication of affect between subjects, but rather a fantasmatic seesaw of activity and passivity. There is no mutual penetration of minds, but rather a fantasy of a powerful doer and, as Isabelle put it, "the one who submits."

The monadic economy

The regulation of tension in the monadic economy takes place through bodily discharge of tension—sometimes compulsively, as for Isabelle. Dimen (2003) has proposed that discharge befits a one-person model. Freud's economy of libido, as opposed to the idea of pleasure (Lust), Dimen suggests, is associated with a kind of sexual hygiene in which discharge is "the bridge between sexuality and sanity." I would distinguish discharge from the two-person economy insofar as the point is only to regulate one's own tension, not to enjoy the other or to contact another mind. Discharge, when it is detached from those purposes, means the use of the body to solve the problem of mental excess, that which cannot be held in the dialogically created mental space.

In the dialectic of intersubjective and intrapsychic, which includes the relational reversal according to which sexuality expresses relational configurations (Mitchell, 1988), there is a place for thinking of the use of sexuality to process shared somatic/affective tension. Physiological arousal can become sexual, can be represented in fantasy, in order to facilitate transmission of tension and its regulation or recognition via communication between subjects. If we follow the infancy researcher Sander's logic, according to which greater specificity of recognition allows the dyad to contain more complexity (Sander, 1991; 2002), we might conclude that fantasy elaboration also allows more tension to be contained and processed. This can occur through the satisfaction of shared fantasies of desire, of healing, of reparation. We need not view the intrapsychic creations of fantasy as exclusively part of a one-person discharge economy. Shared intrapsychic fantasies can rather serve as the basis for shared affect and mutual regulation or sexual pleasure.

Thus, we can think in terms of dyadic systems based on interacting intrapsychic and intersubjective economies, which simultaneously make use of both enigmatic and pragmatic aspects, as Atlas (2015) has argued. In other words, a co-created fantasy in which I do something to you, or you to me, can be the basis for intersubjective state sharing. "I get into you, you get into me" can be exciting and connecting, transforming the pain of excess into pleasure. The mutual enjoyment of fantasy is predicated on *owning* of desire, holding excitement inside the body— a capacity often debased precisely by its conflation with the feminine passive receptacle. To own one's own feelings while *receiving* an other is possible simultaneously.

But my argument is that excessive phenomena that appear as *solely* intrapsychic productions in the individual should also be imagined in conjunction with features of the original intersubjective dyadic systems that result in experiences of too-muchness. In particular, we could say that some failure in the intersubjective economy of recognition and mutual regulation leads to the need to discharge tension (to evacuate contents symbolized through the body) into the other who is unconsciously perceived purely as object-container. For instance, when the other is absent or mentally missing, this may result in excess of pain, loss or flooding, and lead to the fantasy of raping the impermeable other, as in Atlas' patient Leo (Atlas, 2015; Benjamin & Atlas, 2015). Sometimes the maternal or paternal action directed towards discharge of her or his own excess transmits a message that cannot be contained through fantasmatic sexuality alone. It readily devolves into looking towards the child as a holding Other reduced to the position of passive container. Such actions represent a version of discharge whether or not they are overtly sexual. Thus, there are ways in which adults conscript children into containing sexual energy or tension, distinguishable from concrete seduction, that nonetheless constitute in Laplanche's sense a compromising of the enigmatic message—its turn towards violation, an excess that the other produces but does not help one to bear.

Re-visioning gender, reformulating passivity

One aim in formulating the problem of excess and affective regulation within an intersubjective framework of unconscious transmission was to take another look at the historical association between passivity and femininity. In this formulation we think of the polar complementarity of active-passive as a structure that belongs to the intrapsychic economy of discharge and its fantasmatic representation: either you put the excess into me, or I put it into you. I will suggest that, accordingly, the psycho-cultural templates heretofore defining masculine and feminine in terms of activity or passivity may be traced back to the transmission and the processing of excess. Activity and passivity as opposing stances in the realm of sexual excess can generate a destructive cycle in which the one is experienced as invasive, grabby, controlling, while the other is perceived as shutting out, excluding, uncontaining, which in turn provokes invasion, and so on—an endless cycle. Traditional gender solutions, in which the feminine passive side is viewed as the container for excess, can be seen as part of the sexual mythology given theoretical form by Freud.[3]

If deconstructing these gender positions reveals their origins in an attempt to solve the problem of excess, then to challenge these positions means to contest the idea that human beings cannot otherwise manage tension. So on the one hand we could say that the masculine-feminine polarity has served important functions in managing excess, while on the other, say that psychoanalysis is continually exposing how this objectifying technique falls apart: how it arises through splitting, how much suffering and pain and internal contradiction it generates. When we consider the management of tension and individual self-regulation of arousal and affect to depend on the intersubjective context of mutual regulation and recognition, we no longer take this splitting for granted.

In this light, seduction might broadly be understood as one take on the traumatic experience of helplessness in the face of over-stimulation or being left alone with dysregulated affect—Freud (1920) having suspected the relation between trauma and break in the stimulus barrier, as we shall see. I have suggested that the experience of excess can lead to a splitting between an active part-self (phallic, mental) and a passive part-self (container, bodily), as when the phallic master discharges into the feminine container that is seemingly meant, as Isabelle saw it, to bear that very over-excitement in her sexual body. The body, in this view, is not simply a literal container for discharge, but rather is symbolically, fantasmatically constructed to serve in this way. This construction of femininity or the feminine body can be analyzed as the solution to the problem of excess for the male-identified subject, who retains the active position, repudiating passivity.

I (Benjamin, 1998, following Christiansen, 1996) have related this construction of the masculine position to Freud's (1896) observation that the obsessional position of defensive activity is the characteristically masculine way of dealing with overstimulation. In other words, it rescues the child from the position of passivity, helpless subjection to stimulation. Indeed, Christiansen (1996) proposed we read this to say that masculinity does not *result* in repudiation of passivity, but rather is first constituted by that move, replacing helplessness with defensive activity.

---

3   Viewing Bernini's extraordinary sculpture portraying Apollo and Daphne I was struck by the powerlessness and desperation of both male and female figures locked in an eternal vicious cycle. The male god enacts a violent grabbiness, as the violated young woman evades him by hardening her body into bark, her arms reaching away and upward as they transform into branches. How deeply are our past and present sexual mythologies, our templates of masculine and feminine, shaped by this dynamic of invasion and shutting out, shutting out and struggle to get in?

In the same act of splitting, the male psyche expels that passivity into what is called femininity, a projected object that absorbs what it extrudes.

I have argued that understanding this move is a key to decoding the core fantasy that organizes gendered sexuality in Freud's theorizing of the Oedipus complex (1924; 1926). Reading Freud's texts in this way, it appears that the oedipal boy, overstimulated by the maternal message and unable to regulate his as yet unsymbolized response, strives to master it actively. He is unable to turn back to mother for containment because he fears it would restimulate his wrongful desire, or because he must identify with father. He faces the father's double injunction "You *cannot* be like me; you *must* be like me" (Freud, 1923). It has often been observed that shame and humiliation by the father are often the lot of boys who wish to hang on to their mother's soothing in a pre-oedipal way. The more impossible it is to turn back to mother, the more dangerous-seeming is this arousal, and the object who evokes it. Hence, the more fantasmatic (intrapsychic) activity, which includes alien and frightening images of the maternal, must be called upon to replace mutual regulation. Excess and the oedipal go hand in hand.

The experience of being passively overwhelmed and abandoned is meant to be overcome, Freud suggests, by using the identification with the active father to organize the ego. The sense of loss, but also impotence, shame, and confusion are meant to be soothed by this identification rather than a live maternal presence. Again, through this move, the position of being soothed is further repudiated, creating the split complementarity between active and passive as if this opposition were unavoidable, the only move there is. We might also speculate that the more intense the experience of excess—loss, dysregulation, seduction followed by abandonment—the more the themes of repudiating weakness or passivity, equated with femininity, become a feature, and dangerously associated with the longing to be soothed by mother.

Consider Freud's (1909) early exemplar for Oedipus, Little Hans. Corbet's (2009) critical discussion of Little Hans argues that Freud's emphasis on the boy's narcissistic use of the phallus as an ideal helped to dissociate and bypass the actual relational constellation in the family: the boy's fraught relationship to a scarily uncontrolled mother who beat his little sister (more likely the source of his fantasies than castration anxiety). The mother is not generic, not a symbolic object of desire, a lost object of adoration, a conveyer of generalized seduction, but a real figure. Her unreliability and aggression impair attachment and stimulate violent fantasies that likely did not originate, but do culminate in, the boy's preoccupation with his penis. In an extraordinary fantasmatic move, Freud transforms this traumatic constellation into the theory of Oedipus. He seeks to persuade us that it has to be the penis that symbolically contains Hans' arousal and then discharges the aggression and excitement (just as the horse's penis symbolizes only the father's power, not some combination with the mother's violence). This is what the phallus is for.

In a parallel move, Freud takes the feminine role of passivity to serve as embodiment of containing excess—the unwanted, primitively feared experience of helpless overstimulation—and this passive container becomes an exciting invitation which the phallus can act upon, control, and structure.[4] Or so it would seem to be, to the relief of those who embrace oedipal gender roles. While phallic control is meant to have the function of managing excess, this phallic role carries its own contradictions. Discharge of excess tension into the other, though ostensibly active, also becomes reactive. For instance, early ejaculation expresses the fear of being overwhelmed by excess tension, personified as performance anxiety in the face of the feared/desired object. Containing one's own excitement through phallic control can be difficult, and lacking such control the act of discharge signifies feminine weakness. It is a leakage in the container-self of the little boy who cannot attain the phallic control of the father. The catastrophe of being uncontained and over-excited becomes gendered: It signifies emasculation.

Despite the availability of women to play the passive part, masculinity shaped around repudiation of dependency and fear of passivity is thus always precarious. And while the objectified body of the girl can take up the experience of help-lessness and so become passivized, as Brennan (1992) has added, Daddy's boy can also figure as passive container for excess, being fixed in the position of mirroring and providing attention to stabilize the father. Mother as well as father can occupy the dominance position, using the child of either sex in this way. Isabelle became a container for her mother's excess, and it was her voice she was able to identify as the master. The boy may become the projective container for father's shame, a despised weakling subject to father's contempt. Freud himself continually reminded us to regard masculinity and femininity as positions that can be assumed or fled by men or women.

Still, the identity known as masculinity is meant to be associated with the position of defensive activity, dumping anxiety (Brennan, 1992), mastering stimuli by creating the abjected, containing other; as a symmetrical counterpart, the identity of femininity is to be that accommodating, receiving, and mirroring other. And containing excess is supposed to work through gendered signifiers—markers

---

4   As I have argued previously, this view of the feminine corresponds to the classic image of daughter, the one who Freud insists must switch to the father. Here we see the logic of Freud's (1931; 1933) insistence that this switch defines femininity. Of course, Horney (1926) had already pointed out how Freud's theory of penis envy and the girl's sense of inferiority reproduced exactly the thinking of the oedipal boy. This thinking performs a double move: the daughter as passive feminine object now becomes, via a symbolic equation, a receptacle for the self's active discharge; also (via projective identification) she now stands in as the sacrificial masochistic self whose sexual impulse is turned inward. She will take on the role of accommodating and absorbing unmanageable tension, like a containing mother only more controllable. Another feature of this move is that the mother is split, so that her accommodating aspect is attributed to the girl and her active organizing aspect of "anal control" is reformulated as male, fatherly, and, often called phallic. This maternal side is what the boy identifies with and recodes as masculine while he abjects her sexuality, her organs: hence the disavowal of the vagina Freud took to be normal (Benjamin, 1998).

of culturally intelligible, recognizable identities organized as a binary, which is then subject to reification (Benjamin, 1995a; Celenza, 2014). We could then say that through this reification excess becomes a problem of masculine and feminine identifications and organs. When this fantasmatically based processing of excess through identity fails, shame ensues. But as with Little Hans, the assumptions around these recognized gender meanings make it possible to overlook how these signifiers and the associated fantasies are always embedded in interactions and fantasies that bear traces of crucial early attachment failures. And thus what appears as an inevitable course of development may be seen as an intrapsychic production rooted in the vicissitudes of intersubjective breakdowns in regulation and recognition.

A vivid analysis of the gendered fantasies of a boy who has been conscripted to be a container for excess is presented in David Grossman's (2001) epistolary novel, *Be My Knife*, in which the writings of his adult male character Yair exemplify this dilemma. Yair, in letters that read like monologues on the couch, tells of his desperate desire to be understood, regulated by recognition, especially because of his fear that he is nothing but a screaming baby, a braying donkey foal, an "infantile weirdo." He warns his epistolary lover Miriam to stay back because (note the female body imagery) "disgusting rivers are flowing out of all his orifices . . . the shedding layers of his slightly overexcited soul . . ." Then again he writes, "I have been the hole, how unmasculine." When he speaks of his longing to just once "touch the target, touch, touch one alien soul," he sees himself becoming the screamer, who "screams in his breaking, reedy voice, which continues to change throughout his life." Tellingly, his invocation of feminine hysteria includes identifying himself as the container, the one who has understood this scream "not with my ears but with my stomach, my pulse, my womb . . ." It is almost as if he is forced to be a container, who understands others, but experiences this as emasculation. The oedipal gender binary is clear to him, but he just can't get on the right side of it.

Yair knows the solution to this problem of excess, but he just can't perform it. It is to contain himself phallically: "My father would say to me, the whole body wants to pee, but you know what to take out to do the job." At the book's climax, in a power struggle with his little son, Yair tries to claim the position of that phallic father whose voice appeared earlier: "You will return to me, crawling, as usual, says he dryly." He shuts his little son—his little boy self—out of the house (the maternal container) until he gives in. Yair finally does require the understanding and calming intervention of Miriam, the mother, to rescue him from the tormenting alternatives of emasculated boy impotence or punitive paternal control. Only she can actually soothe the original problem, the overexcitement and dysregulation which has caused such shame and rage.

Grossman's story suggests how a boy's sense of need, shame and loss in relation to the mother is expressed as hyperarousal, overstimulation, excess. But also, how the boy hates the position in which he identifies with both the helpless baby who cries out as well as with being a substitute for the maternal womb, which hears and enfolds. It is a mark of weakness to identify with the womb that hears and recognizes the cry of the child for its mother, the scream of not being heard. Dis-identification is necessitated by the threat of being belittled, "castrated," or seen as the crying, leaky baby by the father. The belittling of the need for maternal regulation can further impair the already shaky container function (see Britton, 1988)—receptivity, holding and responsibility for one's own regulation—thus leaving the little boy uncontained, overexcited and leaky.

This passive relation to excess can seemingly only be counteracted, as Yair's father says, by letting the penis do the job, making it the sole and powerful container, not a receptive one but one that can discharge outward. Accepting this unattainable phallic ideal as a signifier of his own lack, Yair feels himself humiliated, effeminized. He is cut off by his shame from the maternal regulation he still needs—thrown into catastrophic isolation, longing but unable to touch even one other. Thus the problem of being heard and held, the need to have one's excess contained—while struggling to escape being rendered instead a passive container—being rendered instead a passive container creates a locked in complementarity. This doer–done to relation is expressed through gender signifiers, through designated masculine and feminine identifications. I have been suggesting that the notion of the feminine is constructed to hold (both as content and container) these unwanted experiences of vulnerability and helplessness. The failure of the male oedipal position to contain excess through the defensive splitting of activity and passivity in Grossman's story implicates the pre-oedipal, a faultline in the intersubjective experience of early maternal attachment. Excess has been fantasmatically organized, but it alone cannot provide a safe basis for desire.

While the oedipal positions of masculinity and femininity are not unambivalently embraced by Freud as the whole story about activity and passivity, too often Freud did seem to take defensive activity and helpless passivity as the necessary forms of those trends. His conceptualization of passivity, as I (Benjamin, 1998) have said elsewhere, misses the dimension of pleasurable receptivity and makes it seem that the position of receiving stimulation, holding tension or directing it inward is necessarily unpleasure. That the pleasurable thing is to expel tension, evacuate through discharge, rather than take it in. But what about the pleasure Isabelle expressed, of being the one who holds and absorbs the strength of the one who can penetrate her or him? What about the active side of containging? Freud's point of view, always from the side of the (heterosexual) patriarch, sees the passive object as container, occluding the homoerotic identicatory desire to be *like* the powerful father, or to fuse with the idealized figure and be contained through his strength (Benjamin, 1995a).

Furthermore, this view of passivity based on the hetero-oedipal binary does not visualize a third possible position regarding the tension of opposites: one in which the capacity to bear excess pleasurably in a mutually created space of excitement and recognition depends on the intersubjective relation of recognition. This lack of imagining a third position, I suspect, correlates with the traumatic experience of passivity Freud depicted, as the condition of helplessness in the face of impingement, seduction or abandonment. Bearing tension with the other, inter-subjectively, was not conceptualized. This makes discharge necessary to avoid the ego-shattering, traumatic aspects of bearing excess. Attachment trauma, pain, shame and vulnerability are the unrecognized features of the masculine fear of passivity. Alternatively, they are expressed in a fantasmatic register of excitement that converts trauma into sexual excitement.

I have previously suggested (Benjamin, 1988) that the intersubjective economy requires a concept of ownership—a desire of one's own—which we arrive at through a self-conscious reversal that reclaims the feminine or maternal functions of containing and having an inside. Holding, traditionally ascribed to maternal or feminine selves, and *ownership* must be recuperated and taken into our psycho-analytic notion of the sexual subject. A subject who owns passivity, with its pleasure and vulnerability, need not *passivize the other* in the form of domination. Such a subject can have desire for another subject without reducing them to a will-less or overwhelming object who, in turn, renders him helpless before his own impulses. Insofar as being a subject is conflated with the grabby, defensively active Apollonian sexuality, it is no subject at all. [5]

As we have seen, the common flip side of phallic control is a version of male sexuality as uncontained, controlled by the object, lacking ownership of desire. In one such version, sexual excitement takes on a dissociative cast, as the subject declares that the object is so compelling and tantalizing that he cannot be responsible for his action. Agency, or activity, dissolves as the object becomes the doer/actor, the subject the done to/acted upon. The experience "I desire you," in which the subject owns desire must be distinguished from "you are so desirable," and certainly from being overpowered by the object of compulsion. This is not to say that preserved in the form of fantasy the experience "You are so attractive and so overpowering that I cannot contain myself, just the sight of you can drive me wild" cannot be enjoyable within a mutual relationship. But the mutual enjoyment of fantasy is predicated on owning of desire, holding excitement inside the body rather than projecting it into a debased feminine, passive other. To own one's own feelings while *receiving* an other is possible simultaneously.

Ownership implies a notion of sustaining tension rather than eliminating it —holding over discharge, surrender rather than mastery. It is not necessarily the same as "containing" a feeling *for* (on behalf of) the other, which one may do without owning it in oneself. It develops within an energetic economy in which self-regulating action and mutual regulation are synchronized in a matrix of recognition. It is, of course, possible to play with complementarity and discharge without holding to rigidly fixed gender positions. It is possible to bear excitement

---

5   How ironic that this version of male sexuality should have been made iconic by the 45th president of the U.S. who openly spoke of "grabbing pussy." How extraordinary that as I write this, it has been met with a massive opposition—the largest demonstration of women in history and a defiant reversal in which "Pussy" speaks up, "grabs back," and declares women's rights to be human rights.

and feeling in the sense of receiving, witnessing, and holding without "doing" anything—a different experience of passivity. In the experience of sexual union, both partners are able to receive as well as transmit to each other, alternately or simultaneously.

"Perversion" and the abandoned child

My patient James, a film instructor and director, begins the session declaiming confidently his views of the film *American Beauty*, which he has watched with his class. He tells me that he now truly understands how perverted the protagonist Lester is, because he can identify with him. He worries that I don't really understand him, James, and don't realize how much he feels like Lester in his marriage. I have my own take on this film, and he is right in assuming that I won't be agreeing fully with him.

As I recall the film in my mind, I reject simplifying Lester's identification with and overstimulation by the passive, tantalizing friend of his teenage daughter in terms of the usual meaning of "perverse." Lester's wife is impermeable and sealed like the shining veneer in her perfect house, symbolizing impenetrability. He cannot get in to her mind or her body and his wish to enter her can only appear as attacking or messy, invasive and disgusting. Throughout the film Lester fantasizes compulsively about the daughter's cheerleader friend, an intentionally tantalizing nymph. But this irresistible stimulation shifts dramatically in the moment when she reveals to him that she is actually a virgin and a neglected child whose parents pay no attention to her. Suddenly, as if waking from the dream, Lester recognizes that this un-parented girl is a person with her own center of feeling. He finds himself needing to feed and take care of her, as if she were the little child and he the mother, giving her a bowl of breakfast cereal. The bright lights of overstimulation are shut off, and feelings of abandonment and grief bring about an identificatory connection to the girl as his abandoned child-self. I think my patient is warding off the same identification.

James now rebukes me that I do not not sufficiently recognize his aggressive and perverse character or the destructiveness of his fantasies about women. He reacts strongly against my interpretation, which takes the form of a response to his comments on the film, along the lines of what I have just stated: that in the end Lester actually uncovers his identification with the abandoned baby part of the girl. James objects strenuously, telling me I am a "sucker" for Hollywood endings, calling me naïve and gullible. He (defender of Freud, Lacan, and critical of my American style relational analysis) is far more capable than I of taking a hard look at Lester's character. Indeed, I now find myself feeling doubt, wondering if I am really "soft" on aggression, afraid to confront him or myself with destructiveness. Maybe I am, as he says, "gullible," ready to be gulled.

However, as I listened to the contempt infusing James' assertions, I sense intuitively that there is more than defensiveness in my urge to argue. I feel that tell-tale sign that my patient is trying to pin something on me that is shameful and it represents an important part of the enactment between us. I remind myself that this session falls only a week before a scheduled absence on my part, and I begin to think about the word "sucker": who is the "sucker," who is the needy baby missing the breast? We are seemingly in a reversible complementarity where he is struggling to feel like the powerful one and make me the naïve helpless one, an obvious gender binary. I wonder if it is I who cannot face my fear of the dangerous man, in this case, my patient's extremely contemptuous father who used to deride men who were dependent upon women as suckers for a warm body.

I suggest to James that in this debate we are enacting the very matter at hand: perhaps it would feel more masculine and powerful for him to be the one who can tolerate the "hard" truth of Lester's depravity. I am thinking that as he persists in identifying with a powerful though perverse father who despises the baby in himself and others, he needs to have me hold the position of that baby. So I describe my own self-questioning: was I the one who was in the position of the baby, the "sucker" who still needs a mother, who is dependent and gullible? This would mean that he, with his hard clarity, surely did not need me to be his mother, did not feel abandoned; instead, he could impress me with his masculinity. He could keep at bay his feelings of helplessness when I am the one leaving him, he could protect himself with his "bad boy" aspects of independence and trans-gression (I do not think or say at this time: am I incapable of being a *hard enough* self-contained father to make his wishes for passivity feel safe and exciting (see Grand, 2009)? Can I be the idealized father he could never have, not in identificatory love, not even in erotic fantasy?).

James seems to be momentarily taken aback by my clarity, my turning of the tables. The power position, the protective self-state he assumes must lie in repudiating the needy baby self has been destabilized. As this self-state gives way to openness, he seems affected by my thinking about him and surviving his attack. He considers whether he is afraid to face the contempt of his father and his fear that he can't deal with being and wanting too-much, the problem he shares with Lester. The despised neediness, the longing for someone to soothe him, becomes less shameful as he experiences me as a thinking mother/father who is not destroyed and can hold his anxiety. Yes, he agrees, he is enacting something familiar, something that reminds him of his father which he had thought he had seen through, but now seems still to be very compelling.

James and I were familiar with the feeling that his father shamed him for being close to his mother, but this moment had revived in the enactment a fear of being overwhelmed and ashamed connected to his mother's frequent absences and her anxious response to his father's overbearing behavior. As part of the story we could begin to recognize how much his father's need for soothing—a need he turned to drinking alcohol to fill—was part of his own experience of excess, how much James had to contain for his father's sake. It became palpable how he sought to keep from being overwhelmed by his shameful need and potential abandonment at the beginning of the session, taking safety in a boisterous and defiant declaration of his identity with the "pervert." The part where Lester is murdered by the man in whom he evokes an eroticized little boy's need for a father is still lurking in the background, an unsymbolized fusion of trauma and excess in homosexual desire (Botticelli, 2015)—one that forms as a fantasmatic wish to actually be the passive boy (girl) with the penetrating, exciting father—to be like the passive girl who tantalized him.

Over time James becomes able to acknowledge his fear of being humiliated if he acknowledges the baby part of himself that has at times been so urgently, desperately needy that he imagines "break and entry" into the female body, so that he has only just avoided sexual trouble with his students. He can see that for him masculinity is a congelation of aggression and power, dangerous and per-verse. To embody it is to be excited and in control—phallic, potent—and protects him from feeling weak and vulnerable. He can be what he would never want to have, and have what he would "rather die" than be (Butler, 1997). We can begin together to understand the part of himself that continues to attack and block with shame what we have long known of his pain around the missing mother of attach-ment and holding, the desire for tenderness from his father.

The experience in the early attachment relationship becomes especially rele-vant in relation to clinical treatment of patients whose sexuality developed in response to maternal unpredictability, overstimulation and abandonment. Later oedipal templates of dominance and submission, seduction and betrayal are super-imposed upon an earlier experience (an example of *nachtraeglichkeit*)—one of being left alone to deal with internal and external stimuli. In some cases, the analyst is paradoxically asked to hold within her mind a child who is frightened that being taken back into a maternal mind from which he has been ejected will be over-whelming. The difficulty in the enactment—as with James—is that the analyst becomes derogated as she holds the self-state that needs connection and unconsciously makes demands on behalf of that part.

Further, if the analyst is not tuned into the primal level at which fear of arousal is embodied, her empathy in any area can become an enactment of the feared overstimulation. The analytic situation will then not only expose the patient to the risk of being attached and then dropped, but will also awaken the shameful need that the patient originally tried to get rid of. Thus Atlas (2015) in her work on too-muchness describes a patient who, fearing her affective response, apparent in her voice, face, and bodily state, to his story, scolds her: "Stop that fucking feeling!" He adds, "I can't stand it when you suddenly sound moved. Don't be offended, it has a physical effect on me; it's uncomfortable, even disgusting."

Fear and loathing in the consulting room

Atlas and I have discussed in greater detail (Atlas, 2015; Benjamin & Atlas, 2015) her work with Leo, whose analysis brings together the ruptures of early attachment and the preoccupation with sexuality and masculinity. Leo might well be reading from Yair's playbook. Pushed aside by a younger brother born soon after him, with no safe attachment as baby, no ability to defend his masculinity by being the mother's boy (and lacking a supportive father), Leo relinquished his desire. He has repeated dreams of a woman who beckons, then leaves, which he takes to mean that he once had a chance but "screwed up," losing his love object. Leo says: You have to be careful, because if you just make one wrong move, you've lost her, the one you love is gone.

Leo talks about the impossibility of relaxing and enjoying the breast (maternal and sexual) because he must always be ready for the moment when the breast arrives, he must be active and gratify *it* by suckling from it. "I have to be in a constant state of hunger, ready for action." This active function, we note, is a kind of premature renunciation of the part that comes first—being soothed and satisfied—a passive baby position, which would displease the mother who has patience only for the active male. In effect, Leo must tolerate being constantly dysregulated, must bear without help the state of constant hunger, his own internal tension. But in his mind this state explicitly represents the essence of masculinity: "If I'm not hungry, that means I'm not a man, because men are hungry all the time, and any real man would have had sex with her by now." He expresses the fear that the woman will find out that he *needs* her breast, that he wants to suckle and play with the breast, and that he will lie back like a paralyzed baby in the face of this longing. "It is so unmasculine." The assumption is that a real man is not supposed to need the breast, but rather to control it.

Thus Leo shapes as a gender struggle the traumatic experience of having to manage his own excitement without holding, of being first offered the breast then denied it, seduced and abandoned. The problem of surrendering to sexual excitement is linked with anxiety about needing the other to make the bearing of excess possible, the imperative to avoid shame by self-regulating. As Atlas notes, Leo's ruminations on sex are suggestive of the humiliation that the fervent, excited infant experienced when the breast was suddenly taken away from him.

Of course we would expect that this threat of being dropped at the drop of a hat turns into an attempt to control the analyst, to manage her as a source of stimulation, which in turn is felt by her as an invasion. This kind of complementarity can easily lead to impasse, and the therapeutic couple does seem to hover on the verge of one at many a moment. Leo is anguished that he will never be loved by his analyst, that she will be repulsed by his excessive sexual preoccupations. At the beginning of the analysis he announces that he is disturbed by her breathing, especially when she breathes deeply. "You're breathing," he reprimands Atlas occasionally. "That means you're preoccupied with yourself." And he adds: "Maybe your breathing shows that you're having a hard time, that you need air." Later he says it points to the fact that he is "too much" for her and she will try to escape shortly. Atlas reported that initially, although understanding his fear of being abandoned and his own wish to escape and need for air, she was quite dysregulated by what felt like an intrusion, leaving her no space to breathe; and so at times she did indeed imagine getting rid of him.

In this oblique way Leo expresses a stifled longing for a feminine container that is strong enough, a wish in the form of a reproach: someone should be able to hold him without needing to escape. Yet he also believes the lonely baby's longing for connection is too intense, too dysregulating and dangerous for the mother, and so he must find some other form of discharge. Faced with this absence of intersubjective regulation, he turns to the fantasmatic, autoerotic position of discharge: he can calm the overstimulated excited self through a representation of the little boy in homosexual erotic pornographic fantasy, escape from the tantalizing object in being the one who controls the satisfaction.

A significant turning point in the treatment occurs towards the end of the first year, when Leo accuses Atlas of trying to prove to him that she is "worth something." He says she has a father complex exactly like his older sisters do, that she is trying to show that she is as good as a man, can think like a man. Listening to him it dawns on Atlas that although his observations obviously contain many projections and rest on stereotypical notions of masculine and feminine, there is something true in what he says. Her relationship with him is defensive, devoid of feelings; she is hard and constricted when she is with him, not soft and tender. She realizes that she uses her mind constantly, making a point of displaying that she is the one who knows. "I suppose my behavior, which he experiences as masculine, was one of the ways for me to survive with him, not to be too 'feminine', not passive, not needy, not someone that can be penetrated and attacked." Atlas tells him that she would like to explore why her feminine parts do not emerge in their relationship, and as she says this begins to grasp in her own mind that this must be the way she avoids being afraid of him. At some point she shares this thought with him as well and asks if it is possible that he, too, is afraid she might attack and hurt him.

Leo responds, Yes, he is fearful of exactly the same things. She allows as how they are both afraid, and that her way of protecting herself is not very effective, because "just like the other women in your life I, too, transmit to you that I might humiliate you at any given moment, and the only way not to get hurt is to be what you call 'a man'." When Atlas says: "We are both vigilant because the two of us believe we can hurt each other," she hears him sigh in relief. For the first time both analyst and patient have room to breathe.

In other words, the helpless needy position, the vulnerable feminine position, is one Leo believes each partner must try to avoid, as whoever occupies it is shameful, destabilized and going to be hurt. Like James, he pushes back when he feels his analyst might put him into that position, trying to escape this hated vulnerable baby self he cannot rid himself of. But it is also threatening, when his analyst occupied the vulnerable position and he plays the destructive part. As we see, a complementarity can develop around dominance and powerlessness, leading to an impasse in which each partner feels frightened of being wounded, subject to being dropped, in danger of being invaded or controlled. Each partner is trying not to be too "feminine," passive, or vulnerable, as the therapist recognizes when she reviews her own behavior. The underlying need for soothing and understanding might have been missed had the therapist not opened up this impasse by acknowledging her own fear and reflecting on her own defensive efforts to be the controlling subject in the masculine position—a revelation made possible by the patient's efforts to think about his own experience of the analyst, to risk challenging her aggressively, and her ability to absorb the impact while still thinking.

Initially Leo rued the fact that he could not imagine compensating for the maternal absence by using the phallic ideal as a container, by being a man who can potentially control any love object by dint of masculine power. This ideal figures in his fantasy when he imagines how a real man would take charge. The idea of being always ready and in control, always ready for the breast, seemed like the only way to have a woman without feeling too needy, too babyish, too repulsive and humiliated—the only release from too-muchness.

Eventually, though, Leo comes to believe he need not live up to this idea of control, that he may in fact do the wrong thing, "miss his chance to catch the ball," and still be a man—challenging the internal assumption that there is only one chance before something or someone will be taken away. And the therapist is allowed to breathe and miss her chances to "get it."

Leo's treatment also exemplifies the need to work with the problem of excess through the articulation of attachment trauma, the intersubjective failure in the early dyad. This failure in turn relates to the language of gender signifiers: what it means to be a man or have a woman express the dilemmas of containing excess. Leo is eventually able to tolerate seeing his analyst as a woman, and experience himself as a subject of sexual desire without being overwhelmed and so fearing the activation of the abandoned, emasculated boy. He becomes able to bear sexual tension without fantasizing that the woman, who is both the projected image of that helpless boy and the unresponsive mother, has to be taken, submissive and under his power.

Excess in the analytic relationship

As we have seen, the effort to counter the shame of being overwhelmed and dysregulated, expressed as emasculation, takes the form of striving for phallic control. The fantasy of masculinity masks a lack of self-regulation and holding, a grasping in the face of feeling flooded by too much stimuli with no secure attachment to modulate tension. The turning of tables and self-protection through intellectual superiority represent a kind of "masculinity as masquerade" that both partners are tempted by. Leo's efforts to symbolize his plight using metaphors of sexuality and gender, are of course the kind of symbolic work psychoanalysis was originally designed to make use of, and with his proficient use of this language analysis progresses. But this should not obscure for us how these symbols foster an escape into the cultural binary of active-passive that also works to mask the origins of excess in early maternal failure. This, I would argue, is exactly the occlusion that was fostered by the psychoanalytic adherence to the oedipal model as the only meaningful basis for analysis.

My suggestion is that we understand the sexual anxieties expressed by Leo in terms of intersubjective failures in the original dyadic systems that resulted in the inability to hold the excess that is sexuality. These failures must be re-enacted as ruptures and repaired in the treatment. The experience that the other is absent or mentally missing, which results in too much pain, loss, or flooding, is actively countered by the experience that the analyst survives and contains the excess with her thinking, feeling subjectivity. Excess contained is not the same excess. We can distinguish between the enigmatic message delivered alongside adequate care from the compromised message full of "noise" (Laplanche, 2011) in the context of being uncontained.

Insofar as the lack of early mutual regulation has created this dilemma of being unable to self-regulate, the patient feels shame at his inability to contain himself. The shame of excess is about the exposure of weakness involved in identifying with the baby parts that need maternal care. The working-through of this shame in the clinical relationship requires the reliving of the painful self-states and analyst bearing it with the patient—that may involve allowing potentially shameful aspects of desire to be attributed to her with the inevitable impairment of affect regulation that shame involves. The fears that ricochet between patient and analyst take a complementary form—being too much, abandoned and shamed, or being the one who shames and abandons—and so are unformulated and dissociated. The analyst must watch for signs of her own self-protection and shame as signals of the emergence of excess.

Both Leo and James enact with their analysts the shame of revealing their dysregulation, their fear of excess, perceived as the passive feminine position which each partner would try to avoid. In a typical reversal, the female analyst came to embody the position the patient feared—the position of being exposed and holding the extruded baby longings—unless she defended herself with the (masculine) activity of thinking. In Leo's case this thinking, at first a mark of the danger in the mother-baby couple, was transformed by both partners thinking and reflecting on the enactment together. In James' case, the mother assuming the role of thinking felt protective of the couple, and likewise enabled the move into shared thirdness. In both cases, working through this enactment, the couple could together transform the feminine position into the active part of maternal holding by articulating what had been repudiated, the excessive.

Freeing the feminine position from debasement went hand in hand with alleviating the pressure to contain the shame with a phallic defense. In this way the analytic couple is able to move out of the complementarity—reinforced by gender—in which someone has to hold the shamed position. The movement into a position of thirdness in which fear is recognized allows the analytic couple to confront the problem of excess and the attendant longings for a soothing, reliable maternal figure.

We can see clinically how helpful it is to theorize the fault lines in early affect regulation that shape our ability to bear the excess and otherness of sexuality, and the perpetuation of these faults in the efforts to repair them through gender fantasies. In a rereading of Freud's theory, I have reintroduced the intersubjective context of early attachment, tracing the reified gender positions to efforts at mastering otherwise unmanageable excess. With this in mind, we can anchor clinical analysis in an intersubjective framework that focuses on the way in which excess has not been contained relationally, as well as revealing how gender fantasies strive to compensate for such relational failure. By adding to our general understanding of attachment and affect regulation the role played by gender signifiers in shared fantasies of repairing the self we may clarify an important dimension of how the enigmatic message is processed. In the analytic relationship we can try to move through the complementary oppositions organized by these fantasies (see Celenza, 2014) into a thirdness of mutual regulation and recognition that contains the too-muchness.

We can trace that movement in my work with Isabelle, who, like Leo, could not imagine that I would be able to "take it." This was her version of destroying the object; that is, in her mind the conviction held sway that I was too weak to ever handle her intensity, her too-muchness. I had to survive her dismissive attachment, her dissociation of any need for me, which in her mind was a protection against being helplessly subjected to the noise of her mother's messages of a weak mother figure. In her state of suspicion, she perceived even affective resonance on my part as a sign of this boundary dissolution, activating the fear that I would be unable to hold her dangerous impulses and feelings. And, indeed, this suspiciousness was often painful for me to contend with. The enactment around her fears could be seen as a reaction to the mother evacuating her rage, anxiety and shame into her. But rather than being in touch with her fear of the other's discharge, as Leo was when he feared the breath, Isabelle protected herself by defiantly asserting her sexual power. For although she rejected and rebelled against her mother overtly, her defense, perhaps syntonic with her role as feminine daughter, had consisted of her ability to *be* the container, to bear any pain, any penetration or invasion. Hence she challenged me to be as strong as her masculine ideal, strong enough to penetrate her.

In one early session Isabelle complained about my way of responding and refering to a consultant who had been "penetrating," she demanded that I finally "say one thing that touches me, that hits the mark." As I demonstrably remained cool and verbalized my sense of her fear, that no one would ever be strong enough to hold her, Isabelle became visibly calmer. It was then that she was inspired to reflect aloud on the link between her mother's verbal assaults, which she had to endure for whole nights at a time, and her fantasies of taking an extreme amount of pain and stimulation in sex, of submitting to the master. Somewhat soothed by my recognition she began to grasp that the pain she was asking me to hold for her was linked to what she had to hold for her mother. She was then able to recount her fantasies of submitting, of "taking" whatever was given, of letting herself be shattered (Bersani, 1985), replicating the traumatic assaults with the aim of repairing them in the sexual interaction. Her move into a space of shared thirdness allowed me to reflect along with her, beginning to understand how her sexuality had been shaped both by the need to hold the excess, to creatively imagine a way to repair and heal the self that was overwhelmed by it.

When she returned after this session, Isabelle remarked for the first time on the peaceful quality of the space in my office. She was able to experience this containing space around her, not impinging or abandoning, and be silent for a moment. She then began to associate:

> That little patch of light . . . As a kid I would go to a special spot by the river, walk though those trees alone . . . find some peace . . . My mother had no peace, ever. It was a long walk to get to that spot . . . or going to all kinds of extremes with myself . . ., it was my private escape where I didn't have to mirror or reflect the ones around me, a peaceful place equivalent to the place of orgasm.

It was these associations that led her to recall the peaceful snow on the cactus of her boyfriend's painting.

A short time later she reiterated this view of safety, escape, orgasm, and peace:

> Paradise is a place where I wouldn't be invaded . . . like in the most ultimate climax sexually, I lose myself. It can also be self-destructive, like when speed hits your bloodstream, escape. I am so far outside and within myself, I can't be invaded.

The association between the excess of orgasm and the peace of solitude in nature at first seems paradoxical, and yet losing her mind seems to correlate with freedom from invasion, and thus with finally calming the affect storm of overstimulation and dysregulation. Perhaps moving from her use of dissociation, the "escape when there is no escape," into something more like real safety.

Orgasm functions not only as discharge of excess but as a means to be at one with the self, not divided by the need to protect oneself from or reflect the other, a letting go into dedifferentiation, a place of creative regeneration of self (Rundel, 2015). We might also see it as a means of moving from submission to surrender. Isabelle's experience is reflective of Ghent's (1990) usage of the term surrender, which denotes a form of letting go of mastery and control that allows us to transcend the terms of dominance and submission, a letting go in which the person does not give over *to* the other—although perhaps *with* the other.

Having allowed me to recognize the yearnings for home and healing in her fantasies of submission facilitated for Isabelle a surrender to the space of aloneness in the presence of the other. In this intersubjective holding space the excess was transformed, translated into a desire for an experience of the self at peace, at one, with the outside and the inside. In this version of thirdness the other does not have to be excluded nor is invasion feared, there is no master, no one who submits and takes it. Ghent suggested that submission was a look-alike, a perverse form of surrender. We might imagine that giving over to the other is the form taken by longing for giving over to the rythmic Third in the presence of the other (see also Benjamin, 1988).

In my understanding, surrender relies on the space of thirdness, going beyond complementarity to encompass and perhaps reflect on the fear of excess together. With Isabelle and Leo we see a congruence between the affective calming—the exhale, the experience of space—and the symbolic formulation of the fear involved. Keeping in mind the two aspects, rhythmic and symbolic, we create a space of thirdness in which we connect to the painful reality. Uncovering the traumatic failure of mutual regulation, we gradually modulate the pattern in which the too-muchness of excess takes the form of dominance and submission. This complementarity in turn is enacted in the analytic relationship. As the couple becomes able to work through the enactment of this complementarity, the space of thirdness gradually develops.

Trauma, surrender and the Third

I will suggest that in the space of thirdness, when excess is differently held and processed, what has appeared as passivity can be refigured as surrender. In the reappropriation of passivity, the internal experience of submitting to the complementary active partner is transformed into surrender; to a process of exploration and recognition. When we are able to alternate freely between complementary positions such as activity and passivity, when we can move in and out of symmetrical positions, we are relying on an orientation to a shared Third, to a dance jointly created and recognized as belongs to both of us (Benjamin, 1999; 2002). This orientation to the Third changes the relational pattern. Surrender is also one way of formulating this third position in relation to activity and passivity. How would the renewed integration of what we have called passivity change our imagining of sexual subjectivity? I have suggested that there is a space in which the reversal of the active-passive complementarity takes us out of the power relation and into a form of thirdness, the surrender to a process of mutual recognition.

What happens when the potentially traumatic experience of passivity is held, enjoyed, represented because it is felt as surrender, not to the other but to a shared process. Surrender can be distinguished from what appears or is labelled as passivity but is actually a feature of traumatic experience with isolation or excessive stimulation. I have suggested through my reading of Freud and Grossman that the attempt to bind, master, and represent such traumatic experiences has shaped our images of masculinity and femininity. Clinical work supports the need to explore the experiences underlying these gendered sexual signifiers that have structured yet limited previous theoretical understanding.

In erotic life as in analysis, when we open ourselves to the sexual fantasies associated with the gender complementarity we uncover their traumatic or shame-filled origins. It becomes possible to experience the thirdness of mutual recognition not as the erasure of these parts of our mental life but the possibility of their expression and communication. Seeking this form of repairing the self. Grossman's Yair reveals his screams, cracks and holes, reaching for an other who will help him overcome the damage of shame that has left the self in desperate isolation.

His dramatic imagery of sexual wrongness already incorporates abraded, alienated longings for recognition to calm the excess, as his epistolary love-letter "therapy" seeks to use the erotic as a site of sexual healing.

Returning to the analysis of excess and its relation to passivity, we can see how the erotic can become therapeutic when trauma, passivity and psychic pain are integrated in the relation between self and other. The film theorist Kaja Silverman (1990) has offered an interesting illustration of this issue. She was pursuing the question, what happens when defenses are stripped by trauma, when phallic masculinity fails to protect men and women from the insinuation of death. Silverman, trained in literary criticism, takes up the notion of trauma as it appears in *Beyond the Pleasure Principle* (Freud, 1920) and uses it to discuss the collapse of phallic masculinity in films about World War II, as exemplified by "The Best Years of Our Lives." As you recall, Freud (1920) portrays the protection from trauma as provided by an internal shield, a psycho-physiological barrier, rather than by another person(s). For Silverman, the idea of this protective shield becomes a metaphor associated with masculine armor and phallic self-holding. She compares its breakdown with the breakdown of the organizing gender constructs, the dominant fictions. The film portrays a double trauma: the individual men returning from the war have suffered trauma or shock, and the cultural schema of masculinity did not protect them. The fabric of the "phallic fiction" was torn, failed them. They lack any collective representation of suffering to enfold them.

The film shows how their wounding and symbolic castration results in a kind of gender reversal, in which women now gaze upon the spectacle of male lack. This spectacle is erotized, but not as humiliation or fetishistic denial. Without a fetish to embody and displace the wounding, the film nonetheless depicts the sexual excitement of this role reversal. As the woman undresses the veteran Harold Russell who actually lost his arms, his hooks now removed, she is aroused and will make love to him. The ex-pilot who suffers flashbacks and nightmares exchanges a gaze of mutual recognition with the woman who gazes on the scene of his social displacement.

We might consider how the scene of gender reversal seems to derive its erotic charge from an intersubjective process. The recognition of pain and vulnerability, the wound to the phallic version of masculinity offers a release: a letting go of the destructive illusion of the phallic contract, which prescribes stoic loneliness and denial. In the film, the couple faces the abyss of breakdown together—as described by Bataille (1986), the breakdown is like the vertiginous experience of death in a different form, one which allows us to share its dizziness together. With this acknowledgment of the reality of loss and breakdown, the lovers in the film interrupt the circuit of defensive activity and perverse passivity. The sign of the wound functions as the opposite of a fetish, it signifies the possibility of overcoming disavowal, representing vulnerability, witnessing pain and suffering—the intersubjective moment of surrender.

The film suggests a vision of trauma transformed into a therapeutic erotics of recognition, whose energy derives not merely from reversing the old gender opposition, but from reclaiming what it sacrificed. Eros in this version begins with mourning the loss of the intact body and the ideal of manhood, to which so much has been sacrificed. It is mourning in the presence of an other, a depressive solution, accepting passivity, loss and death. Breakdown of the phallic fiction opens fissures in what would otherwise remain the seamless wall of repetition. It becomes possible to witness suffering and thereby bear mourning, to own desire and enjoy passivity.

In this way a relationship is formed that absorbs the too-muchness of pain and longing: there is a chorus of "voices"—different self-states joining each other—that becomes a rhythmic Third as well as an acknowledgment of loss to which the couple surrender. And in this surrender they find a transcendence of suffering. This surrender involves using the erotic to bear passivity, helplessness and vulnerability.[6] The distinction between passivity and surrender becomes possible as fear of passivity gives way to the joint creation of interpersonal safety, each person's gift to the other of a holding presence and an understanding witness. The witness who bears it with us ensures that vulnerability will not plunge us back into traumatic excess. But this can only occur through a depressive awareness that strength derives not from denial but from acknowledging helplessness, damage, and the overwhelming of the psyche by suffering.

This vision is significant for our larger understanding of what is therapeutic and transformational in erotic life. The integration of passivity and bearing of excess in surrender to an erotic Third—the dance of love—allows us to metaphorize psychic pain rather than act it out through a sadomasochistic complementarity. When erotic partners can transcend the fixed complementary positions of active v. passive, the helplessness of excess and the holding of the enigmatic message can be borne and integrated by both sexes, by any version of sexual identity, straight or queer; gender conventions no longer need be used defensively. Rather they can become conventions of play, forms of expression, available for use in our fantasy elaboration of the inevitable enigmatic and excessive elements that mark sexual life.

6   I notice there is a formal parallel here to the idea I (Benjamin, 1995e) formulated regarding Eros, where I suggested that in light of Freud and Bataille we might imagine destruction as helping to cross the sea of death that separates us. That is, the erotic is a form in which we can sustain the paradoxical tension of the Third, where recognition takes up what is otherwise felt to be too painful or destructive for the self.

Chapter 5

Paradox and play

The uses of enactment

I originally intended to write one chapter on play and ended up with two, one emphasizing the shifts and overlaps between enactment and play, the other (Chapter 6) the role of negation. In this chapter I tried to play with and put into the pot ideas cultivated in quite different theoretical territories. It was mostly written from a place of uncertainty and questions and this makes for some unclarity that may be unavoidable. This chapter is divided into three sections. Part I introduces the idea of accepting paradox, and makes use of Bateson's idea of the double bind, as interpreted for analytic purposes by Ringstrom (1998) who has contributed greatly to thinking about play and improvisation. I discuss how recognition occurs in action through enactment and play, and how we might use the idea of paradox to reconsider the relation of the two. I am thinking here about the movement between enactment and play as parallel to the shifts between complementarity and thirdness. While enactment is known to present dissociated experience in unlinked form, play can allow opposing experience to be accepted in the paradoxical form of thirdness. I consider the developmental origins of the capacity for play and how clinical work addresses deficits in that development. Part II presents a lengthy clinical illustration of some of these ideas; Part III aims to differentiate relational clinical theory from those contemporary theories that emphasize either symbolic or procedural-implicit modes of inter-action, by recoupling them. I outline how relational thinking pays attention to dissociation and the forms of intersubjective relating, which in turn informs how we put this recoupling into practice.

PART I. THE PARADOX IS THE THING

My contribution is to ask for a *paradox* to be accepted and tolerated and respected, and for it not to be resolved. By *flight* to split-off intellectual functioning it is possible to resolve the *paradox*, but the price of this is the loss of the value of the *paradox* itself.

(Winnicott, 1971b, xii)

[T]he paradoxes of play are characteristic of an evolutionary step . . . similar paradoxes are a necessary ingredient in that process of change which we call psychotherapy. The resemblance between the process of therapy and the phenomenon of play is in fact, profound. Both occur within a delimited psychological frame, a spatial and temporary bounding of a set of interactive messages. In both play and therapy, the messages have a special and peculiar relationship to a more concrete or basic reality. . . . the pseudocombat of play is not real combat.[1]

(Bateson, 1972, p. 191)

I will begin these reflections on fostering the movement from enactment to play by turning to the meaning of play in psychoanalysis. Thinking about movement itself is important. Borrowing from Gadamer's (1989) reflections on play as any movement of To and Fro, we might view play as an action that creates a Third by containing the Either/Or poles within a larger movement: tacking Back and Forth to encompass both or multiple sides. The idea of play as "any movement" between opposites, by contrast with being stuck on one side, or locked into a repetitive back and forth between two sides, approaches the heart of the matter. Play is not necessarily jocular or humorous. In psychoanalysis, it above all implies dramatically acting or trying on a feeling or idea rather than being subjected, taken over, in the grip of it.

Ringstrom (2001; 2007), in his seminal work on improvisation and play, elaborated the essence of improvisation in terms of the key improvisational phrase "Yes, And!" which replaces the "No, But." The improvisational method of responding with "Yes, And" puts into practice the idea "Both, And," a version of the Third. The third position being the one that, again, allows movement—in this case, beyond the rigid opposition of "Either/Or" of "My Way or Your Way." The Third of Yes/And suggests a kind of movement that releases us from the impasse that is generated with the action of complementary twoness: the struggle for control of "My Way or the Highway," in which there can be only one reality, one right interpretation. Metaphorically, that phrase symbolizes the idea that there can only be one direction of movement, and by extension, there is only enough space for one mind to live. The Third refers to a movement in which both directions contribute, so that there must be, if not harmony, then at least a coordination of traffic. Play implies freedom of movement between the two.

Enactments in the dyad take on the complementary structure of doer and done to in which each motion is so tightly coordinated that each person's move is predetermined and controlled by the other. There is no give or (yet another meaning) "play" in the system, no alternation, and no coordinated realignment to adjust to the other.

---

1   Bateson goes on to say that "pseudolove and pseudohate" in the transference are not real, a statement we might have to modify to make paradoxical: real and not real. Exactly this sense of play as involving the paradox that something is both real and not real was an important effort to formulate the resemblance between play and psychoanalysis.

Here we come to thinking about process, about how the dyadic shift from complementarity into thirdness is paralleled by the transition, gradual or sudden, from enactment into play, with its Both/And cooperative structure. In this transition, the acceptance of paradox plays a great role, for paradox is a form of relationship that does not resolve the opposition by denying one side, or by simply synthesizing. Paradox means entertaining incompatible versions of what is going on, the two directions on our mental highway, each of which seems "true" on its own (Pizer, 1998). As Winnicott (1971b) articulated, to resolve paradox through "split-off intellectual functioning" is to forfeit its value, which is maintaining both sides of what seeks expression.

From this vantage point, we recognize that enactments themselves are paradoxical. They both hinder and further our work, depending upon how we engage them. At the beginning of the relational turn some 25 years ago, an important development was the move into reconsideration of enactments—regarding them not as missteps but as both inevitable and opportune. In this move, as formulated by Ghent (1992) early on, enactments were a kind of live theatre, where the goal is to recognize the meaning of the scenario in order to "demystify some earlier traumatic set of experiences that could never be integrated" (Ghent, 1992, p. 151). It took some work to realize that enactments were hard to recognize precisely because these unintegrated experiences were obscured by the shadow of dissociation which, fell upon the analyst as well (Bromberg, 1998; 2006; 2011; Bass, 2003; Black, 2003). Enactments came to be seen as a dramatization of dissociated self-states, revealing unformulated experience that require us—in the midst of confusion, shame or guilt—to reflect on our own participation, often aloud with the patient (Maroda, 1999; Renik, 1998b).

And here we may accept the crucial paradox that by making dissociation *communicative*, the very enactment that conceals also serves to reveal. As Bromberg put it:

> A dissociative mental structure is designed to prevent cognitive representation of what may be too much for the mind to bear, but it also has the effect of *enabling* dissociatively enacted *communication* of the unsymbolized affective experience. Through enactment, the *dissociated affective experience is communicated from within a shared "not-me" cocoon.*
>
> (Bromberg, 2011, p. 21, my emphasis)

Or as Ghent (1992) put it, what is calling for recognition is masked by something that closely resembles itself. "Need masquerades as neediness," (p. 152). The need for a witness to one's pain may appear as the plaint that no one sees or understands what has been suffered. Or the need to assert a truth that was denied and mystified may appear as a conviction that it is being denied once again. In this way the analyst, too, would often be drawn into the dissociation of the "blackwashed" need.

The paradox of enactment: concealing and revealing

Notice the dialectic here: even as it prevents symbolic play of the kind psycho-analysis historically privileged, enactment can enable communication by "playing something out." In this sense, enactment itself presents a paradox: it is only a misstep because (parallel to Winnicott's point about destruction) it is liable to be missed—if we fail to recognize it, to work within the drama, to eventually grasp its generative potential (Aron & Atlas, 2015). Despite Freud's early recognition of "acting" he opposed it to the use of language: the metaphor of textual inter-pretation rather than theatrical participation dominated psychoanalysis (Benjamin, 1998).

Essentially, through dramatization or performance of what cannot be spoken the concealing/revealing action of the shared not-me can be understood to work like dreams. But rather than looking at them from the outside in and decoding, as in original dream interpretation, enactment demands that the analyst work as a participant from the inside out. We must lend ourselves, let ourselves "play a part" as Freud (1905) notoriously refused to do with Dora. The "shared dissociative cocoon" (Bromberg, 2006) incubates the not-me experience—until it bursts its confines so that meanings can be negotiated and symbolized. Play, then, might be seen as a way of making a transition from dissociated to expressive awareness by lending ourselves—"playing along"—without yet knowing its meaning but aware that something more than meets the eye is unfolding.

The tension of paradox is essential to psychoanalysis, indeed a formal condition of its way of working between illusion and reality. Paradox is the invisible under-girding of our method, the condition for using transference. Indeed, it is far more essential to the idea of transference than has been recognized. To be able to play, or learn to play, as Winnicott famously declared what we analysts and patients must do, is to make use of the paradoxical space of analysis. The most obvious paradox we require is the one that permits play by simultaneously engaging in a way that feels real and not-real, though very consequential: emotionally what happens between us serious make-believe.

And yet such paradoxical positions are also inherently unstable; they tend to break down into one side or the other when the affective arousal becomes too pain-ful or frightening. The contradiction between their realities can become too intense, no longer make-believe. We might say that this instability makes for the inevit-ability of enactments, in which the wish to escape the tension of opposing realities which has become too painful drives the effort to resolve paradox. For instance, "You are my mother; you are not really my mother," either of which could become too painful. Here is where we see the splitting to resolve the tension by restoring or perpetuating dissociation.

As Ringstrom (1998) has shown, the theory of the double bind can help us to better understand breakdowns of paradoxical tension. A key paradox is that while the patient is enacting past injuries she must also hold some sense of the analyst as the safe person who will help repair them. These two visions can easily become incompatible realities. As long as the dyad can negotiate the tension between the pull to repeat and the push to repair—living within the paradox—things look "good." But when the two sides split apart thirdness devolves into complimentary twoness. The analyst then finds herself unable to respond to both demands, to embody the role of both/and, healer and harmer. When the repetitive dimension takes the lead, it can be frightening to both participants and stymying for the analyst, especially when she is invested in being the healer, the "good one."

While enactments bring dissociated self-states into play at the stress point where the repeating versus repairing sides of this paradox break into Either/ Or, this breakdown can be vital to articulate the patient's dissociated fear and mistrust: "If you are the one who hurt me as I was hurt in the past, how can I trust you and see you as the one to witness or understand me." For instance, the dissociated unlovable state emerges that feels rejection is too real a possibility to engage in play with the feeling of being loved and accepted by the analyst. If both positions—trusting and not trusting—seem crazy or threatening to the attachment, then acknowledging or escaping the danger or disappointment may seem equally impossible moves. Here we may find ourselves in the double bind, the "crunch" (Russel in Pizer, 1998).

If the analyst tries to resolve paradox by moving to the side of realism, telling herself that this enactment of injury is "not real" and "just transference," her denial of danger may intensify the patient's anxiety and struggle. Here, acceptance of paradox may mean accepting the apparent failure. Because, to paraphrase Winnicott's formulation about the usable object surviving destruction, *the person who fails is paradoxically the one whom you desperately need to witness how she failed, to receive the communication.* That is, when the analyst can bear her own realization that she has played the role of harming, she can step back into the role of the one who acknowledges and thus offer something new. This then restores a more complex version of the paradoxical relation between playing out the Both/And of repetition and repair. The paradoxical form of repairing by acknowledging the failure can be seen as a form of meta-communication, a term introduced by Bateson.

In whatever version we enact the repetition of an original failure our (however tenuously maintained) analytic vision of paradox tells us we are trying to facilitate the dramatic emergence of new experience. We allow ourselves to become part of a complementary opposition that serves to expose the "truth" of a hidden self— perhaps in us. We have found that the collaborative effort to unpack the dramatic meaning is part of the process of restoring the paradoxical space of thirdness that holds the old and the new. In the intense collaboration of unpacking enactments, a new space opens for self-states and their accompanying "truths" that have felt irreconcilable to share the stage.

Enactments can be potentiating, in the sense that one agent in a chemical interaction helps potentiate another, by calling forth a part of self into collision with a corresponding part embodied in the other. The enactment may allow both partners to become more aware of what was dissociated, to recognize the affectively charged experience of the patient—and at times that of the analyst as well—that had been incoherent, disorganized, and even disruptive to a person's sense of self. The effort to restore regulation and coherence by articulating this emotional content is one in which part of the incommunicable "not-me" becomes communicable. The not-me who is hurt, injured by non-recognition, is not identical to the not-me who holds unrecognized needs and desires, however. The reason for dramatizing both the failure *and* the needed recognition is to bring these two not-me experiences or associated states together—loss and desire, disappointment and relief, repetitive and generative dramatizations.

Meta-communication: the nip and the bite

Seeking more insight into how we release enactment binds, I turned back to Bateson's ideas about meta-communication and its connection to the development of the capacity for play. Both play and meta-communication involve the mental holding of more than one truth or view of reality. There is an aspect of differentiation involved in play in addition to the obvious rhythmic thirdness of joining and harmonizing, as seen in early face-to-face play or improvisation. The differentiating aspect has important consequences for the ability to use meta-communication—commenting upon or signalling the intention of the communication. Meta-communication also helps to creates space for play: "Let's pretend that . . ."

Bateson's (1972) work made the link between meta-communication and play, showing how both rely on transmitting two different meanings in which one meaning modulates and inflects how the other should be received. He provided a new emphasis on the non-verbal, proto-symbolic communication that categorizes the message. Both animals and humans play by signalling that the thing normally denoted by this particular behavior is precisely now not being denoted: This nip is not a bite. That is, it is not an act of hostility but of affection or invitation to play. The idea of psychoanalysis, Bateson thought, is to set up a space for play in which a "pseudo-form" of the action is communicated, not merely symbolically represented. This allows us to nip or love to our heart's content, as it were.

However, Bateson (1972) added, in play combat when people get too aroused they might accidentally lunge at their partner or strike too hard. Bites happen. Excitement and aggression mix and so may get mixed up. Extrapolating, we could say that heightened affect arousal can destabilize the paradoxical holding of something as both in the past and not the past, as when the past is too frightening or painful, and so the play gets mixed up with the real. The nip no longer serves as a signal of not biting, but rather feels too much like the bite it is denoting. In fooling around, teasing hits a sore spot and someone's feelings get hurt. Sameness and difference collapse in certain states. The experience becomes not just "like" the past, it *is* the past. Paradox collapses when too much arousal breaks down the categorical difference between symbol and symbolized, nip and bite. We may think we are nipping and the other may feel bitten—or we may be so fearful of biting that we can't properly engage the other's nip.

Bateson, having moved from anthropology and animal studies into collaboration with family therapists and systems theorists, famously noticed how schizophrenic communication reflected the inability to frame any message or understand in what sense it should be received, to categorize the relationship between speakers and receivers (see Ringstrom, 1998). The ability to grasp, signal and denote in this way is part of applying necessary distinctions between the category of the frame and the category of what takes place inside the frame: the rules versus the content of the "game" (Bateson, 1972). Without such discrimination of categories, this ability to differentiate, for instance between play and reality, the transitional area within the frame is not protected and the content can become threatening. The ability to read categories may fail entirely. What if this were a clue about what causes breakdown in paradox and play?

We see this collapse in patients who, in certain self-states, assure us that we cannot care about them because we are merely professionals, not persons, but in other states behave as if they expect us to *really* care. This "categorical" collapse likewise means there is no *inside* separate from the outside, that is, no protected area for exploring the internal world so that everything can be played with as illusion or pretend (Milner, 1987).

Marking and meta-communication

How play is developed and relates to our capacity to understand our own minds and others'—mentalization—was the concern of Fonagy and Target (1996a; 1996b; 2000), coming from an entirely different background than Bateson, that of developmental and psychoanalytic child psychology. Fonagy and Target analyzed the development of the capacity for differentiating beliefs or thoughts from reality, which prevents thoughts and feelings from being frighteningly real. They (Fonagy & Target, 2000) associated this capacity for differentiation with the use of the procedural communication we have considered, called "*marking*" or markedness (Fonagy et al., 2002). Recall that in marking her responses to the baby, the mother simultaneously exaggerates and mirrors the baby's reaction to show she understands the fear or pain but does not think the situation is serious—as in, the falling down has not hurt you. As Fonagy and Target (2000) describe it, mother mirrors the baby's affect with a slight difference, so that it is apparent she understands the baby's distress but is not herself upset which conveys "that there is nothing 'truly' to worry about, but more importantly the parent's reaction, which is *the same yet not the same as the baby's experience*, creates the possibility of generating a second order (symbolic) representation of the anxiety. *This is the beginning of symbolization . . .* [emphasis added]" (p. 856). I would also see it as the beginning of meta-communication, as I will discuss in a moment.

This idea of the origins of symbolic capacities in a differentiating thirdness that distinguishes feeling from reality, relates to our understanding of reflexivity as well as the ability to hold two meanings at once: this nip stands for a bite, but means something less frightening. This relates to our use of metaphor, which was central to the classical definition of play, as reverie in pschoanalysis. However,

Fonagy and Target expand our grasp of the importance of relating two different meanings to different minds, or mind and reality. The symbolic function that later crystallizes in metaphor is broader and begins earlier in proto-symbolic, gestural marking of same but different. Importantly, that this differentiating function also underpins dramatic *action*, simulating affects or attitudes in exaggerated or ironic ways that provide a commentary on how a given communication is being received or communicated. That is, we meta-communicate through action. Meta-communication through play makes use of symbolization, but as we see is rooted in the implicit domain of pre-symbolic, procedural action.

The most important aspect of differentiation for both play and mentalization, in Fonagy and Target's (1996a; 1996b; 2000) theory, is the separation of thoughts/feelings from reality. Initially children hold a view of pretend as a separate domain in which things are not frightening but separated. However, they also operate mentally in the mode of "psychic equivalence," in which thoughts and reality are not separated but congruent. If I think it, it must be true and generated by the "outside." The child cannot safely play until he separates pretend from the mode of psychic equivalence. We can see how this separation is what underlies the ability to distinguish the nip from the bite.

To generalize, enactment occurs in the mode of psychic equivalence—"you are that thing I fear" and implies the use of dissociation to substitute for differentiation of real and not real. Play is a mode based in the ability to differentiate, where pretend can be retained as a domain of emotional expression because it does not seem equivalent to reality. It is not what it is. Sometimes the play is a very serious drama, not a comedy, but it is still held in mind as feels real but is not real. The movement from enactment to play roughly corresponds to the move from psychic equivalence into differentiation: differentiation of real and pretend, of my mind and the other's mind, of multiple meanings. Fantasy and pretend can now be used to process emotions, "rewrite" negative emotions, and so regulate one's own affect while communicating with the other (Fonagy et al., 2002).

Fonagy and Target's theory, like Bateson's thought, pays attention to the *form* of thinking, and therefore the development of capacities that are intersubjectively mediated. Rather than merely addressing frightening or painful psychic *content*, for example, oedipal rivalry, fear of dependency, we are theorizing the *form* that holds content. With this more elaborated sense of what functions contribute to play, we might better follow Winnicott's (1971a) famous directive that the therapeutic work is "directed towards bringing the patient from a state of not being able to play into a state of being able to play" (p. 44). An important effect of using an analytic version of meta-communication or markedness is to introduce the capacity to play with reality, to interact in a way that helps to develop the missing structures of differentiation and attunement.

The double bind

We might see Bateson's (Bateson, 1956; 1972) theory of the double bind as representing what happens when the difference between the procedural and the symbolic levels is not marked but takes the form of an unremarked, mystifying contradiction. Originally, Bateson's theory of the double bind (Bateson, 1956) described a set up in which the person is subject to two mutually exclusive demands, so that to fulfil one would violate the other. Resolving the contradiction would require stepping outside the frame, but any outside perspective is prohibited or reabsorbed as part of the original demand inside the bind.

Ringstrom (1998) points out that "Historically, the resolution to the double bind has been in some form of meta-communication, that is, news of a difference . . . a spontaneous and unpredictable level of language about the confounding paradox" (p. 302). But how can this occur? Traditionally, analysts tried to interpret enactments by referring to the repetition of the patient's past, and the analyst's response would then procedurally be felt as "more of the same," a perpetuation of the power struggle or posing the threat of having one's own mind disrespected or negated (Mitchell, 1997). In other words, it did not serve as a viable form of thirdness but as the pseudo-Third of detached observation, the look-alike for meta-communication. Conversely, though, once the bind is in effect, empathic understanding can be felt as undifferentiated mirroring, a sign that the other is not able to think her own thoughts. Differentiating and joining are opposed and split into complementary roles, either one of which is threatening.

The contribution of Ringstrom's (1998) discussion of double bind theory was to show how enactments of this kind are organized around the mutually exclusive injunctions to repeat and to repair, the vectors of old and new experience (Stern, 1994). The bind leads the clinician especially to feel "damned if you do and damned if you don't" (Ringstrom, 1998, p. 299). Instead of paradox, the contradictory demands to be the repeating and the needed object—or the one defeated and the one who survives—are presented in such a way that they cannot both be fulfilled at once. The demands ought to be paradoxical insofar as we can only repair by repeating, as when the analyst can only survive if he is tested by being "destroyed." But in the impasse the analyst is experienced in the mode of psychic equivalence, where thoughts are too real, so the patient's belief is simply true, she *is* either the injurer or *is* destroyed. How do we release ourselves and our patients from such binds? This question vexes at least some clinicians some of the time.

When a person is able to at least partially be in touch with the space of paradox, they might be enacting in the spirit of *"This looks like the past, but this time it will turn out differently, I will get what I need,"* or even, *"This time I will 'win'"* (This is probably the spirit in which the analyst should take it). Because of dissociation, at least one self-state is in the psychic equivalence mode and experiences this staging as real—not "pretend," not a nip but a bite. Yet another self-state may be backstage, sometimes observing or even making sidebars in the wings, knowing it is meant as a nip. The dissociation is partial, perhaps in both partners, and the analyst, it is hoped, can see the leading edge possibility of a way to engage both states at once. Here is where play comes in—because it is a way to bring in the other less frightened self-state without negating what the injured one feels.

Meta-communication from within the drama can sometimes speak to both the injury of repetition and the hope of repair together. What I mean by meta-communication is this: a form of reflecting or creating difference without disrupting rhythmicity, staying inside the flow rather than stepping outside to comment, performing recognition in action.

Performing recognition, meta-communication in action

The question of how we meta-communicate without appearing to invalidate one side of the paradox is related to how we play by affirming with marking, by finding the Yes/And improvisational position. Play describes one method of keeping a foot in the Third space of paradox, acknowledging what feels real to the patient, while speaking from a place of difference. At times, of course, this occurs first by enacting the collision, putting the other foot in our mouth—but at least this gets the feared repetition out in the open. At other moments, through play we more gradually move the enactment into a space of collaboration without collision. We try to reshape the impasse by speaking from "inside" the play, as we lend ourselves and become the part we are asked to play. We *perform* recognition rather than merely verbalize it, using our rhythmic capacities, thereby marking it and creating a degree of difference. This is what it means to use our subjective expression to improvise, to introduce play within the enactment, to shift self-state so as to repair disruption or open up to emergent meanings of what is going on.

For instance: a patient expresses exasperation that the analyst is not advising her as to how to solve a predicament she can't solve. She begins in a state of concreteness, without reflection: "I know you aren't supposed to tell me what to do, but why can't you help me figure it out? Aren't you supposed to know?" she demands. The analyst replies with a Yes/And move that recognizes the patient's fear: "Uh Oh. You're right, I guess I should know what to do—but what if I don't?" The patient challenges: "Are you saying you are just like me, you know as little as I do? That's my point, how can *you* help *me*?" The analyst replies: "It really would be a disaster to be up shit creek without a paddle and have an analyst with no paddle. You're right, you need someone who has a paddle or knows how to get one" (Again Yes/And, adding to the improvisational tone, with a meaning to the meta-communication: your need for help, for a grown up to be in charge is not wrong). Patient, shifting state, speaking metaphorically and reflectively, somewhat rueful in tone: "Yeah. I guess that would be my luck, I get the analyst with no paddle. Like having a Mom who never tells you it's bedtime, so the kids are up until all hours eating cookies and watching TV." Analyst: "Yes. You get the useless Mom instead of the one who tucks you in, reads you a story, and tells you there are no monsters behind the closet door. *And when you don't have that, it's hard to calm down enough to figure out what to do.*" The analyst is confirming that she is both the useless one (destroyed) and also the one who knows what it is to have a useless mother (surviving). Patient: "Yeah, I probably could figure things out if I weren't so pissed off about having to do it all by myself. I just had to take charge of the kids when Mom was out of it, I didn't want to know I was scared. I don't want you to be scared either." Analyst: "It is frustrating and scary to have to be big when really you're just a little girl. You don't want to have to tell me what to do, but it's kind of irresistible unless I give you what you need: bath, bedtime, healthy snack, colored bins to sort all the toys." These previously shared metaphors of an intact mother are now used to recognize and differentiate the "blackwashed" need from the appearance of controlling behavior, the masking in which the wish to have a parent reverses into acting like the child's imitation, bossy and angry—a repetition of complementarity that has been enacted many times. While playing with the metaphors the analyst's tone, the procedural music, suggests not interpretation but affirmation of the patient's feeling, pointing towards the leading edge.

Communicating from *within* the action, playfully or ironically, can shift from blocking and defending into more marked forms of thrusting and parrying; sometimes a good catch and throwing back a "zinger" or curve ball can make movement possible (see Ringstrom, 2007). These procedurally recognizable actions communicate by using marking behavior. Such *commentary-in-action*, or meta-communication as performance, takes us back, so to speak, to the early developmental stage where marking creates safety, thus supplying the needed relationship, the building blocks of later symbolization and differentiation. The therapeutic effect is to sponsor intersubjective development, the missing capacities that make meta-communication, use of metaphor and dramatic play possible.

Acknowledgment, sometimes sober and serious, is of course a crucial form of meta-communicative action. Not only when there are collisions, but also in the course of dialogue. The sense in which acknowledgment remains an action inside the play is that we do it as actors rather than observers, perhaps because we have actually bitten and we don't deny it, even if we meant it as a nip . When the analyst finds herself playing two opposing parts at once—causing injury and recognizing the feelings of unsafety, confusion or hurt, acknowledges at the implicit meta-level, that we are open to the other's perspective and feeling. We might later play with what just happened, meaning will be created together. We reinstate the paradox that we are simultaneously vulnerable participants and responsible observers, both repeating and repairing as we rebuild the Third.

Acknowledgment in this way gives permission for the patient to likewise meta-communicate. In the patient's case, the freedom to comment on what the analyst is doing or saying is a way out of the bind, and restoring the paradox that the analyst is both the one who repeats the old and creates the new. In facilitating this shared thirdness we are trying to offer an experience, to repair a basic, original fault in which play—trying on feelings and beliefs in the mode of pretend, fantasy, or symbolization—did not develop in relation to emotional life. This experience of co-created thirdness is itself the repair. Such relational repair of disruption is qualitatively different from the simple satisfaction of sharing a "reparative" fantasy of goodness that seemingly restores the dyad's regulation. The patient is becoming able to actively use the contrasting modes of joining and difference to express his own emotional experience. Repair by the analyst through acknowledgment is now distinguishable from complementary demands associated with one person "winning," and the other "losing," or submitting—it is not more of the same zero-sum game (Ringstrom, 2015; 2016). The forward motion of our back and forth, give and take, liberates the capacity to think because thinking something is not felt to be equivalent to making it so . . . or not forever.

PART II. ENACTMENT, PLAY AND THE WORK

I have been trying to make a framework for thinking about play and paradox as form, considering dramatic interaction, meta-communication and the performance of recognition. My clinical theory of the Third is an attempt to formulate a process that embraces and ultimately requires binocular vision of both the rhythmic and the differentiating or symbolic principles of interaction. The Third grows through actions that consist of fitting/accommodating/joining and differentiating/articulating.

Play relies on the same principles as the action of marking, in which the coordination of implicit and verbal meanings creates attunement with a difference.[2] The differentiating moment of marking should be embedded within the attunement to the other's inner experience—otherwise marking turns into dissociative distance. We grasp the other's anxiety but we are containing and relativizing it. In this way rhythmicity and differentiation in thirdness work together. Differentiation of meanings or the other's perspective is not dependent on symbolic function, rather it contributes to the emergence of the symbolic. Differentiation begins procedurally, with gestures that frame and inflect the meaning of communications, which in turn establishes the basis for meta-communication and the ability to use symbols and metaphors.

The use of symbolic capacities to represent affectively saturated rests on pre-symbolic experience with both differentiating and rhythmic thirdness. Otherwise, words will be divorced, split off from, and at odds with the procedural. This decoupling of the implicit and symbolic often evolves into a detached or disso-ciated form of observation, a simulacrum of the Third—the split off intellectual functioning that cannot hold paradox. Whereas play, with metaphor or dramatic interaction relies on integrating implicit, procedural with symbolic communication, inability to play is characterized by decoupling, characteristic of dissociation.

Clinically, we are tuned into this decoupling: to failures in integration, or moments when the clash or incongruence between these domains strikes us. As our process of coming to recognize the unformulated intentions of both partners

---

2　Consider the parallel with Stern's (1985) point that when the mother recognizes the baby's excitement she expresses it cross-modally, that is, in a different form: if the baby crows the mother shimmies, thus mirroring with a difference.

necessitates using our own reactions, we are aware of disjunction between the two channels, of chafing or constriction of our movement (Stern, 2009; 2016), the signs of dissociation. This takes place not simply in the patient, but in ourselves and in relation to our shared rhythm. Dissociation presents frequently as failure to coordinate the implicit or affective with the symbolic. Relational analysis has a developed clinical lore of attention to dissociation based on our affective-somatic reception of both channels of intersubjective action. It seems to me that we often struggle with coordinating symbolic understanding with attention to the implicit movements in the couple. We are aware of when our attention is freer to notice disruptions, obstructions, the feeling of being able or unable to move and so hold both avenues of communication in mind. Play, after all, procedurally implies freedom of movement not just within the mind but between us. In the double bind, for instance, we can't move.

Increasingly, as such attention to movement and implicit sub-symbolic action has increased, we are better able to focus on the How and not merely the What of intersubjective relatedness: implicit relational knowing, the quality of "being with" the other (Stern et al., 1998; Stern, 2004), but also contradictions between procedural signals of the other's self-state and the words that metaphorically and symbolically create pictures and narratives concerned with those states. We are interested in whether images and words have resonance and impact or function in dissociation. We are aware that the use of reflexive function can become detached observation and so perpetuate dissociation.

The development of the capacity for play involves integrating procedural and symbolic channels and thus countering dissociation. The expanding ability to use different channels to modify and inflect meaning makes meta-communication possible. In working our way out of enactments we usually need to meta-communicate, and this helps to initiate or further expand the individual's capacity for play. The meta-communication from "inside" the interaction becomes part of a shared process with the patient, who is also struggling to say the "unthought known" (Bollas, 1987). The emergent shared affect, metaphor or meaning is then experienced as a shared Third; the intersubjective process of creating thirdness along with the recoupling of affect and symbol may then be more important than the content.

This process is so important because the decoupling of symbolic thinking and implicit action often accompanies or underlies the contradictory demands encountered in enactment, especially the double bind. Decoupling may occur only in some self-states or be pervasive, it may have accompanied the developmental trauma or damage patients come to heal. Recoupling is part of what is involved in creating or restoring the space of paradox, in which two different levels of meaning, procedural and symbolic, work in tandem. Thus I am proposing that we grasp meta-communication as more than a form of explicit commentary on what's going on, and view it as a form of recoupling thought and feeling dramatically or in fantasy. I would contend that even when meta-communication involves the analyst formulating what is happening in the relationship, this implies an intersubjective process with sub-symbolic procedural dimensions. Recoupling addresses not only a specific moment of dissociation in enactment but a developmental need to experience the Third in action.

I will accordingly describe my work with a patient, Hannah, whose symbolic capacities were detached from affect, whose sense of the rhythmicity of attunement was so constricted that her mode of reflection was largely persecutory or negative of the Third. Such individuals can symbolize, be humorous and self-ironizing, yet their most painful experiences drop into the mode of psychic equivalence because they have known neither reliable attunement with states of distress nor marking of difference. The observing function and, indeed, analysis itself are consequently identified with a shaming scrutiny, split off from the emotional connection of compassion—have become a simulacrum of the Third.

In Hannah's case, this decoupling of the rhythmic and the symbolic appeared to be the effect of a failure of both attunement and differentiation. The lack of maternal marking of her anxieties led to a detachment of the heavily relied upon symbolic thinking from connection to affect, so that Hannah seldom experienced a defined emotion in a way that fostered coherence. Thinking was not genuinely containing and ineffectual against the shame of dysregulation. Thus despite her seeming capacity to produce reverie and make use of metaphor, something was missing that makes for the ability to play with reality. Any problem Hannah experienced appeared to be "Real."

I should note that I originally used this piece in a presentation in front of the British Psychoanalytic Society, where my assertions about enactment and acknowledgment were considered quite controversial—so much so that a brief version of my presentation (Benjamin, 2009) was published along with a reply by a member of their society (Sedlak, 2009) in the "Controversies" section of the *International Journal of Psychoanalysis*.[3] Originally, however, the paper aimed to illustrate improvisation and show how the symbolic work of analysis depends upon the rhythmic Third as well as acknowledgment.

In this writing I will illustrate the bind between the repeated and needed relationship, the use of meta-communication and the recoupling of rhythmic and symbolic. In this instance, recoupling is part of creating a third position, moving into play with the paradoxical tension between the forward and trailing edge, the needed and repeated relationship. Together we succeed in creating a dramatization of past injury with a "new" reparative outcome that involves the recognition of past vulnerability and the need for a moral Third.

In a synthetic formulation, Aron and Atlas (2015) have suggested how we might view this reparative outcome as foreshadowed in the work. They adapted Jung's

---

3   Interested readers may note how thoroughly different and incompatible are the views of psychoanalysis taken by Sedlak and myself in this debate. In my reply to him (Benjamin, 2009b) I addressed the fundamental difference in assumptions: how from my perspective the analyst's subjectivity is not a lamentably necessary means of knowing the other but an offering of something needed, related to our developmental need for connection with the other, and thus intrinsically healing.

idea of the prospective function to theorize how enactments are generative, bringing the future into the present: with the prospective function, often operative in dreams, the mind looks forward; it "exercises or rehearses, it anticipates, prepares, shapes, and constructs" (p. 310). Aron and Atlas (2015) suggest that we think not merely in terms of what is reparative but what is generative—thinking not in terms of how collisions simply repeat the past but also create the new, bringing hidden potential to the fore. This transformative potential, the generative element, lies not only in working through the enactment but in emphasizing the tendrils of development it evinces, what Tolpin (2002) called the "forward edge."[4] This formulation has also been related to the "leading edge," the reparative aspect of the analytic work (Kohut, 1977).

"I do schtick"

Hannah began her treatment in a state of continual psychic pain, a kind of pervasive unhappiness that seemed without cause—it simply was what she had always felt. Her pain was most readily associated with feelings of immense shame, now lived daily but dating from childhood, when she had felt isolated, outcast, Other—unable to grasp and mesh with the implicit rules of relating to her peers. This state in turn seemed to represent something like the forced introjection of her mother's despair and self-hatred linked to the absence of any consoling, containing maternal presence. Family life was overshadowed by the mother's depression, anger and social alienation. Hannah in young adulthood had used her intelligence to learn how to function in the normal world, but she suffered continually from excruciating feelings of failure triggered by any moment of social anxiety, which brought on lamentations of ruin and disgrace.

Hannah strove for insight but could not believe in comfort or consolation. My appointed role in her drama seemed to be that of joining her attacks on herself, to be her critic or at best a stern mentor; her role was to struggle against failure to be a good enough patient or student of analysis. In this way we were meant to enact her existing "self-cure." In the early days I often found the combination of self-beratement and assumption of my superiority quite painful to listen to. For Hannah initially psychoanalysis was idealized, associated with a persecutory ideal of knowing everything. It had little to do with empathy and much with judgement—while her feelings remained raw, uncontained.

Hannah described how her mother had always responded to accounts of being excluded and ridiculed in childhood with anxious despair, unable to comfort or encourage her. The experience was one of distorted mirroring by a parent who was entirely one with her anxiety and despair—reflecting back only the same,

---

4.   Apparently there is a difference to be made between "leading v. trailing edge" interpretations, first suggested by Kohut and developed by Lachmann and Tolpin's developmental
"forward edge." (Lachmann, commenting on Tolpin, IAPSS Keynote 2014)

"echoing the child's state without modulation, as in the mode of psychic equivalence, concretizing or panicking" as Fonagy and Target (1996a) put it.[5] As we reflected together, Hannah could think about her mother's lack of attunement to emotional cues or a baby's need for regulation as well as her impaired ability to differentiate between herself and her children. It seemed that mother had never been able to soothe and match, to create a rhythmic Third with her as a small child. There truly *was* "something to worry about."

Thus Hannah's precocious intellectual and verbal development gave her an apparent access to mentalization and insight into others, but barely masked her profound aloneness, emptiness and fear of being poisoned by the other's toxic anxiety or deadness. Even while Hannah sought in me an antidote—a more powerful, more perfect and satisfying mother, attuned and empathic, an idealized object with whom she could aspire to identify—at any moment of vulnerability when she actually felt need she was liable to be overwhelmed by shame. She strove to protect herself by convincing me that all was lost, inviting me to join the self-beratement, obscuring her longing for consolation, so that I had to resist the contradictory injunction to repair by repeating. I often found myself in the position of a helpless bystander, as if she were forcing me to witness to her attacks on her shameful, "monstrous" self (see Benjamin, 2009). My empathic formulations at any rate failed to reach the shamed, urgent part of her that needed yet refused a witness and a consoler, one who could contain and respond to her pain while marking it as not her own.

The other side of the ongoing enactment expressed the danger that I as bystander might view her positively and so fail to witness her distress, to contain her anguish, hold the injured self-state. In taking up the leading edge, keeping in mind her functioning, presentable self, or allying my ideal self with her need to be connected and "good," I would be denying her pain, rejecting her suffering monstrous self. If I tried to mark the difference, rather than reflect exactly the same despair, it seemed I was shutting out the frightened part, which would find no home in my arms or mind. The affective experience of different with same had no inner template. My empathic reverie had to fail.

Reading Ringstrom's translation of the double bind retrospectively made clear the structure of this enactment: if I did not join Hanna's despair I would be denying and refusing to contain her pain; but if I did join it, I would be missing her need for both soothing and hope, a leading edge pointing the way out. Meta-communication in the form of commentary, while not forbidden, seemed unable to touch the part of her that was dwelling in psychic equivalence. There was as yet no space for it. I tended to think of her traumatized self-state as one in which her mother's anxiety had become her own, rather than her separate reality being

5   Alternatively, say Fonagy and Target (1996), the mother may avoid reflection on the child's affect through a process akin to dissociation, which effectively places the mother in a pretend mode, unrelated to the external reality of the infant—the child's genuine feelings or intentions.

confirmed by mother. We thought in intergenerational terms: this powerful sense of catastrophe might reflect her mother's immigrant trauma of being alien and endangered (Faimberg, 2005). Yet, even as we spoke of it, her wound was mixed with such deep shame that it had to remain hidden—and paradoxically it also had to be known and healed.

At the time I could not so precisely formulate this bind, and I often struggled to maintain contact with Hannah's need for a vital, soothing mother, to not drift off into dissociative space when she self-protectively shifted into "insight," her substitute for the missing rhythmic thirdness and soothing she had missed. In retrospect, it seemed that the more one part of Hannah craved soothing, the more her vigilant self felt with traumatic certainty that the mother figure would collapse, would fail to survive her bid for regulation and so would retaliate in some shaming way. This mother in turn would be crushed by Hannah's destructive disappointment, and must be protected by Hannah demonstrating her own unworthiness. The she who needed and she who repeated dimensions could not come together.

However, as many small disruptions were survived, Hannah and I attained some rhythmicity that allowed us to play with the negativity that shadowed her every move. Hannah could recognize her identification with the "one who was doing the beating," as Guntrip's (1961) patient famously put it and her expectation that I, as the powerful one, would join the beating. Hannah had a dream that her whole family was having a picnic and Adolph Hitler was joining them. In the dream, as she reported humorously, she told herself that Hitler really didn't seem like such a bad guy after all. I expressed my appreciation for her audacity in inviting "Hitler" in and she acknowledged her hatred of her family, giving playful expression to her identification with the evil-doer: at the end of that session she quipped, paraphrasing Flaubert on Madame Bovary, "Hitler c'est moi."

At about the same time Hannah began to express her intense wish for solace, her identification with the fearful and injured animals she rescued, and her wish to become the kind of mother she could be with her animals. In turn, her longing evoked anguish over the part of herself who hated her mother, even wished she were dead in order to escape the sense of being infected and poisoned by the dead food of her mother's body/spirit. These feelings were associated with the dream as she flipped into the horrible thought that she might wish to exterminate the animals, just as she wished she could expunge her shameful self or her reviled mother. A confusing fantasy of infanticide-matricide afflicted her, a sense of being the hated mother. The emergence of both the longings and terrors suggested an implicit belief that I could contain such dangerous emotions, that we, in our shared space of thirdness, could contain them.

With this greater safety, Hannah and I were finally able to revisit her interpersonal trauma and dramatize a different outcome, a release from her painful self-cure. Hannah returned from a weekend in the country with some other young people, relating a familiar tale of woe. Unable to engage in witty banter, she had become withdrawn and grew excruciatingly uncomfortable, as she felt observed scornfully by her friends. Hannah believed that as she had become progressively anxious, they had made fun of her all the more. In this instance I did not question in my own mind her extravagant conviction of failure and shame. But even while I was empathic to her fear, I challenged her conviction of ruin and catastrophe. I let myself speak from "inside" the drama, but with my own subjective perception, which contained alongside empathy an element of difference: a kind of protective indignation. I had a barely formulated thought, as if she really were my own child: "There is nothing wrong with Hannah. She is at least a match for her friends in integrity, personal insight, and intelligence. Why should she be shamed?" I also spoke from my sense of the moral Third, which led me to formulate my indignant response as a question: why didn't she deserve the understanding and compassion from her friends, which she would surely have given had the situation been reversed? I warmed to my topic and continued asking: "Why were these feelings not a part of imperfect but acceptable humanness?"

To my great surprise, Hannah began the next session with an unusual response, saying how surprised and gratified she was by my "staunch defense." Hannah now went on to reflect that in her mind she had thought accepting her friends' making fun of her was the right thing to do, that she had been trying to take responsibility for her problems by identifying with her friends' judgment. I said rather with emphasis to mark it, "Indeed, you do identify with this kind of judgment! You might even have elicited their contempt because you actually feel it yourself." She readily agreed: "Yes, I do shtick, I make a shtick out of vulnerability when I'm anxious." I said, "Yes! It really is a *stick*—you punish yourself with it and invite people to join you. What you have to be responsible for is not your vulnerability—that's just human—but for your punishing and beating yourself, for your lack of compassion towards *you*."

I waited while Hannah took this in, wanting her to take the lead as we were now improvising from the same script. She allowed as how her self-beratement proceeded from thinking this was a way of facing reality (a form of self-protection), but it suddenly occurred to her that there was a different way to listen and respond to the other. What she was able to hear from me this time was not a refusal to bear her despair or witness her demise, but rather my presence at her side defending her vulnerability as well as a way of connecting, my defense of a principle of empathy for vulnerability. This is an idea about behavior she herself believes in. Suddenly, this principle, embodied by me, became a felt conviction about herself—"I don't deserve to be treated badly when I am frightened and need soothing." This constituted a recasting of the original scene of distress, in which relief is provided rather than catastrophically absent, an absence that led her to self-regulate by telling herself what a bad girl she was.

Further work revealed the generative function of my willingness to enact the role of a protective mother who stands up for her child, rather than a collapsed and deflated mother, one who can mark the pain as real, but not her own and not catastrophic. I could recognize how much this was a reflection of my identification with Hannah, based on my own struggles with shame and social non-conformity, my own hard won solution of placing compassion and kindness over superiority and invulnerability. I admit that this value system, highly reflected and intellectually worked out but still rooted in my own personal pain, is not neutral, it is deeply personal and specific. However, it also seemed to resonate specifically with Hannah. My indignant reaction to the pain visited upon Hannah by her protector self did accord with my ideas about compassion, my sense of the moral Third. My response came from a conviction that it was possible to accord dignity and respect to the fragile, frightened Hannah while simultaneously holding in mind her strength, not least as a person struggling to understand her own pain. She could shift from enacting a masochistic submission to a look-alike Third of punitive scrutiny into a shared thirdness, which combined the rhythmic oneness of empathy with a narrative of compassion and respect for human vulnerability. My ability to see a Hannah who is more than her "weakness" was like the position of the mother who sees beyond her baby's pain to a coherent self who will be free of it. In this way both soothing and differentiating were shaped via the maternal function of imagining the child's future function (Loewald, 1960). What Hannah was able to identify with in me was the strength that comes not from hating the shame-filled parts of self, but accepting psychic pain as a position of the moral Third: accepting What Is.

What fostered the movement towards accepting the reparative protection and soothing, which in turn allowed her to relinquish shame and have insight into her self-cure, her preference to hurt herself before the other could hurt her? A form of meta-communication from "inside" the drama in which I incarnated (Hoffman, 2010), a version of my protective self being called upon by her frightened self, lent myself to the enactment. I was not commenting from outside, rather I was responding personally to her pain. In this sense our "moment of meeting" was deeply personal, as my response deviated from the script, introducing an element of difference that came from my personal style of thinking and marking. I did this, spontaneously and implicitly, by playing the part inside her story of a witness who identifies with the suffering but also uses her indignation to be protective.

Hannah had idealized me and wished to identify with me; but now this ideal persona turned out to be radically different from her previous idea of strength— one that dissociated from pain and suffering. Instead she discovered a version of the moral Third that lifts dissociation by according safety and respect to the fragile, frightened self-state, affirming the dignity to be gained from struggling to understand one's own pain and that of others. No longer dissociated, both self-states, the weak and the strong, converged in a generative moment, a dramatic shifting from blame and shame to understanding and acceptance.

Hannah explicitly articulated this meaning in her own language sometime later when she said that what I had given her was a moral universe. She reflected on the impact of experiencing me as a protective mother who stands up for her child but also believes in her child's resilience. This offered a version of anger that came neither from the place of helpless victimization nor from a simulacrum of insight that was conflated with a fantasy of acting like a normal person, who has no shameful fears, who needs no recognition of distress. In accepting my

marked recognition of how painful that was, she was able to give up her dissociative aspiration to a fantasized normality in favor of a different experience of
being with the other. The implicit experience was that she could be lovable as
a vulnerable being, one whose anxiety is visible but can be borne by the intact
other.

With the establishment of this greater sense of safety, Hannah spontaneously
brought up her "secret life," the hiding place of her real anger, her worst feelings
of rage and loneliness associated with adolescence, when she was desperate and
promiscuous, and ran away from home. All her rageful self-affliction was really
aimed at her mother, whom she hated beyond reason, not least because she still
needed her to provide the missing experience of home. As she contemplated my
leaving for the summer, Hannah was able to speak for the first time of the feared,
shameful, hated image of her own need: a stalker. A vision of the girl who had
killed her college roommate because at first they had been close, but then she
suffered a stinging rejection when the roommate felt suffocated. The appearance
of the stalker girl deepened our sense of the fear and destruction that had haunted
her during our first summer separation. This time she was able to imagine my
accepting and embracing the girl, her abandoned self. A nascent version of sustaining the paradox of repetition and repair was being constructed: the girl would
be too much for me—and, the girl was just a needy child and I could hold her.
We then were able to take in and give a name to this "not me" figure of shameful
rejection, which she had tried to ward off and had enacted with her friends; it
became a more metaphorical character with which Hannah could play.

Finding a dance partner, the rhythmic Third

As I have said, my sense of what Winnicott meant by playing was the use of fantasy and metaphor—alone or with the other—that is now usually referred to as
reverie and associated with transformations into articulated emotions. Theorizing
of reverie has become a defined perspective, influenced by Bion's idea of thinking
and alpha function. Ferro (2009), one of the main proponents of working with
reverie, has suggested we think of the metaphorical figures that appear in the field
as "characters." We can let these characters (like the stalker girl, but also objects
representing an emotion or impulse, like a bomb, a plant, a wall) play in the room,
without always specifying which real person they are currently attached to or their
transference meaning. In translation to relational analysis, we might think these
characters represent aspects of previously dissociated self-states or feelings.
However, I believe that play with the other also involves the real relationship, it
creates a real shift in the relations between self-states and self and other (Peltz &
Goldberg, 2013).

My thesis is that in analysis learning to play is a process that includes not only
use of metaphors but also incremental moments of marking and meta-communication in action informed by the rhythmicity and differentiation originally
lacking. This involves dialogic play with the other on the stage of enactment where

dissociated characters first appear. Gradually, these characters can be owned and become more obviously parts of self rather than not-me, and so attached to the other in less restricted ways. Thus Hannah's repudiated needy self that originally came into the relationship through enactment gradually evolved into a character in our emergent play with the same material.

Here I will illustrate with a moment of spontaneous shared reverie, the kind in which unconscious communication creates a synchrony of rhythmic and symbolic, form and content. Play occurs as a back and forth movement. Hannah began a session speaking about a man she had begun dating, somewhat older, very admired and liked, whom she found to be amazingly solid, compassionate and understanding. She said he was able to call up the best in people, in her. Perhaps, because Jane Austen was an author we had often referred to, my reverie turned to the character of Knightly in the film *Emma*, which I had recently viewed. Knightly, though obviously in love with Emma, is older and wiser. Emma has taken in an orphaned young woman, Harriet, a farm girl, whom she now tries, against Knightly's advice, to pair with a higher born man who considers himself too good for Harriet. In the scene at the ball, this man publicly spurns Harriet, leaving her to stand embarrassed, without a partner, as everyone looks on. Knightly, who of course is going to marry Emma, comes to Harriet's rescue, dancing with her and saving her from humiliation. It is after Knightly has thus restored Harriet's dignity that he and Emma finally dance together, achieving a compelling erotic synchrony of gaze and movement. I recalled now their dance, a beautiful representation of the rhythmic Third.

I decided to share the story and the dual image of Emma/Harriet with Hannah, formulating how touching it was that Knightly first accepted the more ashamed and socially awkward "part" of the character. From there we entered into a surprising moment of meeting. Recalling the film, Hannah burst out: "I love you, I really love you!" She paused, then explained: "I can't believe you would compare me to Emma or someone I fall in love with to characters in a Jane Austen novel. I have always wished I could aspire to the dignity and self-knowledge of Austen's characters." It was as if in this moment I had rescued Hannah's Harriet self, and she felt it.

Now we see one of those coincidences born of unconscious mental sharing that sometimes occur as minds meet. Hannah added: "The odd thing is, this morning, as I was taking the train in from the Island, I saw these fat suburban matrons, and I was feeling a kind of scorn for them, but then I caught myself, and I said to myself, *What would Jane Austen say about that attitude?* And then as I continued listening to them, I heard that they had lovely voices. And I thought, *they really are lovely women*". Hannah here has her chance to play the daughter who repairs the worthiness of the maternal other even as she directly recognized her loving feelings with me/Knightly. She also partners with me in a shared reverie that transforms her default rejection of the mother/fat women into a fantasy of creating the good: it is her prospective vision of being a loving woman, as well as her own embodiment of a moral Third.

Austen's voice, like the voices of the matron-mothers, represents a maternal Third with which it is possible for her to identify, and it is notably parallel to the one I associated with Knightly. The voice of the moral mother and the music of the rhythmic Third create a space in which it is possible to contain multiples voices; at the same time, it is the maternal version of lawfulness, a symbolic Third, which says: "All my children are worthy of love"—Harriet and Emma, the fragile and the strong. As we went on to explore in subsequent sessions, there is the Emma in the Harriet, whose beauty can be recognized, and the Harriet in the Emma, whose pain can be accepted. In this and subsequent sessions, Hannah and I continued to play with the metaphors of Emma and Harriet, as we moved through the feelings of what it means to accept Harriet while finding new potential in the role of Emma, a rehearsal for a relationship (Aron & Atlas, 2015) in which desire and safety both feel possible. The story became a representation of the moral Third, allowing us to understand more of Hannah's struggle to embrace the Harriet in herself while finding new possibilities as Emma. There is room for both selves to live.

Knightly, Austen, the man Hannah was dating (whom she in reality would later go on to marry), and I all became characters on the stage (Ferro, 2009) and took turns in the dance of thirdness. The part of Hannah that once appeared as the stalker became a more lovable character, Harriet, who could be integrated into herself, whom I could accept and dance with, not leave alone to become destructive. This particular movement had many emergent facets, procedural and symbolic, implicit and explicit: our exchange itself became a rhythmic experience of fittedness and harmonizing of different voices, infusing the symbolic elements of the shared reverie with vitality. Form and content synchronized, as Hannah and I created a new metaphor in action, describing a dance and doing a dance. This coordinated movement suggested a harmony consonant with the content of our play, deepening the issue of—Hannah as Emma needing the lawful world of the moral Third in which vulnerable, potentially shamed characters like Harriet would be safe.

My play with Hannah around *Emma* might be seen as an example of the rehearsal and preparation described by Aron and Atlas (2015): a generative shared reverie, with the prospective function of anticipating her life-changing bond with this man. And the leading edge was in this case expressed through the character of the man who can "call out the best," who represented one part of the analyst as well. The aim in working with the enactment, then, becomes not only to identify the pathogenic past (Aron & Atlas, 2015, p. 312) and bring out dissociated self-states linked with trauma, injury, loss, pain and shame—the trailing edge—but also to recognize the hidden hopeful, the desires. Not only the not-me of loss or pain but also the not-me of desire and expansion.

However, the integration of the not-me part of Hannah that still felt connected to her damaged and damaging relationship to mother not through shameful vulnerability but defiant, rageful adolescent rebellion remained in the wings. She was not going to stay off-stage forever. As we shall see, her appearance in a collision became part of a generative enactment of a very different kind.

Vicissitudes of stage combat, or, a slip and a nip

As Bateson (1979) said, playful rituals can sometimes get out of hand, participants in the game can get too excited or reactive and forget they were supposed to be "only playing." What was supposed to be only a representative nip becomes a bite. In stage combat, actors often slip and jab too hard; there may be bruises by curtain time. Slips, Freudian and otherwise, are meant to give us pause. So the power of unprocessed emotions in the analytic dyad—in the field of interaction—may lead to the analyst's reactivity, exceeding what she can contain. But such loss of containing in analysis can indeed be thought of as part of the field, "an accident, sustained en route which will therefore, within limits, be thought of as *inevitable and indeed necessary*," as Ferro and Civitarese (2013) assert, but a process that can be reflected and ultimately used to enlarge and potentiate the interaction. In English, the word "accident" is an especially good metaphor for failure to contain, since it is what we call a child's inability to hold it in until he reaches the bathroom. And, insofar as we think in terms of unconscious communication or joint dissociation of that which slips past the analyst's initial awareness, they are part of the "royal road." Do we differ about the degree to which we can fathom the mystery through our own reverie, and how much it is the patient's work in the enactment, which we (sometimes unwillingly) co-sponsor, that moves us both forward? I suspect this might be where the ideas of play in the mode of reverie versus play with interaction may lead to different outcomes (see Stern, 2013; 2015).

I will, in the interest of describing working with enactment, relate a moment where the ongoing movement between enactment and play shifts into an out-right collision. This can certainly be described as an "accident" on my part; my disso-ciated wish for a certain kind of analytic goodness helped drive the interaction, thereby becoming dramatized and eventually understood. This moment illustrates how the not-me as painful repetition that needs to be dramatically portrayed shows up together with the unrecognized not-me that needs to find authentic expression in an intersubjective context: they meet first in a confusing mix, then become more clearly distinguishable as we unpack. Initially, it may be the analyst's outburst, the effort to escape from a bind (see Mitchell, 1993), that creates the accident. In this case the reaction that broke up our joint dissociation was triggered wholly outside my awareness of the repetition of an old pattern.

Originally (Benjamin, 2009), I discussed this collision in terms of how the inter-action of different selves and their dissociation often require an acknowledgment of our part. Here, I am emphasizing as well the potentiating, generative side of enactment: the revelation of new feelings and the expression of the patient's agency, the leading edge of analyzing collision (see Slochower, 2006; Bromberg, 2011), with its production of emergent meaning (Stern, 2015). This collision brought forth a part of self, the defiant adolescent, crucial to Hannah's sense of agency. That agency first took the form of Hannah protesting my reactivity, then collaborating in the process of thinking, unpacking and creating meaning out of disruption. This sharing and collaboration is part of what is potentiating in enactments, making them generative, giving us the sense that, as Atlas put it, the patient comes in to the "kitchen" and we "are cooking together" rather than merely having the analyst adjust their cooking to the patient's reception (Aron & Atlas, 2015).

In a session shortly after Hannah had become a mother and confirmed her capacity to soothe, comfort and love her baby, she began to revisit an old scene of self-criticism. Or so I thought. I heard her berating herself for being too unread in the classics (a patently false representation of herself) to answer her teen-age stepdaughter's homework questions the night before. Perhaps I was frustrated by this lapse, but I found myself unusually permeable to the anger in Hannah's reproaches. I wondered aloud if Hannah was going to carry this propensity to denigrate herself into the relationship with her own children. Immediately, giving the lie to her own self-portrait, Hannah, in quite a different tone, exclaimed, "*That* was draconian!" She then tried to backpedal, to spare me being put in the wrong, as she herself had always been, explaining in an especially insightful tone that I *must* have intended something with this remark since I am a relational analyst. I was upset with myself, but not so dysregulated that I could not immediately acknowledge having said something hurtful. Stating clearly that it was not a strategy but an emotional reaction, I apologized for the harsh remark, and suggested she ought to not let me off the hook so readily.

As we reflected together in the next session, Hannah was now confidently able to express in a more forceful way her sense of being unfairly scolded by me, demonstrating her capacity for self-protection and tolerating what she knew about me without denial. But she then began to reflect on her own action and what was being dramatized in this scene: "Maybe you were reacting to something," she said, "Because actually I wasn't feeling like the mother right then, I felt like I was identified with Lucy, I was the teenager looking down on my stupid mother!" Well, I reflected aloud, if she was actually identifying with the teenage daughter, the one who despises the mother and sees her as pathetically inadequate, then maybe *I* was identifying with the mother. In the moment where Hannah identified her part, I was able to recognize and admit my unformulated counter-identification with the mother who was being despised and discarded. This was a dyad I remem-bered all too well from my own adolescence.

When I acknowledged how I assumed the counterpart role in the complementary relation, that of the attacked and retaliating mother, a different meaning emerged. Ironically—as is common in enactment, the hidden symmetry of dissociated identifications generates the reverse of what one intends. Wishing to rid myself of my assigned role in the drama, I stepped right into it. I became the mother I was trying to protect, because I was also dissociatively resisting being her (albeit in the form of a helpless analyst). In retrospect, I could see the way in which I felt my own need for affirmation of maternal goodness was frustrated by Hannah's story of the attacking daughter and the failed mother. I was not reflecting on my need to see Hannah be healed by absorbing my goodness, and so my conscious disappointment that Hannah was shaming herself masked my own feeling of failure.[6] However, our role-switching revealed that the distinction between attacking herself and attacking me was, in a sense, fictitious. Our iso-morphic identifications with the need not to be put in the wrong, and not to put the other in the wrong, were too symmetrical. Her move actually did express a dissociative attack on the mother's supposed goodness; my retaliation a disso-ciative defense of goodness. Being forever put in the wrong by a mother who was herself far from "good" reenacted the core of Hannah's disastrous fight to the death with her mother in adolescence—one which had condemned her to be the one who is crazy.

Our longstanding work and our experience recognizing the feelings of shame and disappointment allowed us to move easily into the activity of unpacking. I acknowledged to Hannah the way I had inadvertently become the very thing I was trying not to be. Once I acknowledged the part I played, the rejected mother to her defiant contemptuous daughter, Hannah could speak more of her anger at her mother's weakness. To both our surprise, then, she shifted self-states dramatic-ally. A new unexpected character came leaping onto the stage, as she spoke in the voice of the protective daughter who identifies with mother, exclaiming how sorry she was for this poor mother who couldn't soothe anyone: "You don't love her, no one could love her, *she is so unlovable!*"

We paused to absorb this surprise, the forcible impact of Hannah's pity for this shameful person she nonetheless loved and identified with—the one I had for a moment become. I could now acknowledge my shame at my outburst and formulate Hannah's need to protect *me*, as the unlovable mother in the moment I had shown myself to be uncontained and critical. This mother, the one she found it so painful to identify with, was the last piece to emerge in analyzing the enactment. As our unpacking proceeded to this point, we slowed down, allowing us to stay together in feeling sorrow for the poor mother. As this feeling emerged, it seemed that we could listen together to the presence of opposing voices and reversible positions, containing and surviving their conflict with one another in that scene. The space of thirdness, thinking and feeling together, was palpable, open and mutual.

What emerged, "unbidden" as Stern (2009) calls it, Hannah's surprising turn after my acknowledgment of reactivity, seemed to be a revelation of the self-states involved in the earlier phase of her confusion over who was the one doing the beating: identifying as her mother's killer or the unlovable victim; either way, she had been put in the wrong. In our interaction, my recognition of the injury interrupted the switching off between doer and done to and opened up an avenue for agency as well as expression of the self-protective anger that had been miss-ing in our earlier enactment where I was the one expressing indignation on her behalf. This time she was defending herself from my criticism even as she was

6   Rachel McKay, in discussion, clarified this idea of the enactment being driven in part by the analyst's dissociated need for affirmation of goodness by the patient's healing (see Mark, 2015).

unconsciously attacking her own mother. Recognition of the leading edge of protest transformed it into an active assertion, revealed its underbelly of anger, liberated the ability to think and engage in meta-commentary, and to contact the mourning about a connection never made and fulfilled. Thus moving from repetition to something new, our dialogue enable the space of paradox, the relation of real and not real, to be restored.

The collaborative unpacking, creating a mutual container, combines new and old in the process of moving out of enactment. We begin a dialogue of meta-communication that differentiates between old and new, no longer mutually exclusive pulls but part of the thirdness opened up by acknowledgment. This helped to restore the paradox of my playing the part of the rejected, critical mother and the analyst who was present to analyze and hear how she felt about it, differentiating my contradictory roles.

As the meta-communication differentiates between the need to be right and the need to put things right, feelings move from the place of psychic equivalence. The analyst no longer *is* the destroyed, retaliatory mother for the patient, and the patient no longer *is* the destroyed object for the analyst. The meta-communication about the process takes the form of play in which Hannah, as an assertive actor, could react to a bite with a nip: "That was draconian!" The nip, commenting on my bite, reflected the fact that commenting on my behavior was not destructive, and indeed paved the way for a symbolic explication of our roles. The analyst is there to receive the communication, and the patient is permitted to communicate. In this sense both partners survive destruction, that is to say, putting or being put in the wrong. Survival reinstates the paradoxical reality of analysis. What felt forbidden, inaccessible, not possible to speak becomes speakable now in the thirdness of play, made safer by acknowledgment of the violation.

As many relational thinkers have shown, collision may not only be unavoidable but potentiating (Davies, 2004; Bromberg, 2006; 2011; Slochower, 2006; Stern, 2009). Paradoxically, the concealing-revealing function of dissociated action made it possible to "play out" the meaning of the story more fully than my offering a containing formulation would have done: moving from failure to contain, repetition, acknowledgment, repair, new exploration and connection. Hannah's first anxious reaction, aiming to repair my ideal image, might be seen as reflecting a fear that through her anger all goodness would be destroyed and she would be to blame. However, with my acknowledgment we were able together to hold and survive the moment of fearing destruction, and so restore the tension of Is and Ought in the moral Third. We took another step towards replacing her old ideal of invulnerability, the longing for which had protected her against shameful need and fear of the unpredictable, damaging responses such needs might elicit while protecting her object from being "reduced to bits" as Klein (1952) put it.

We are able to move beyond this fear of damage when we create the moral Third, in this case through taking responsibility for hurt feelings. Hannah and I were able to move into a space in which both of us could feel the pain of this mother–daughter story: Mother's sense of being unlovable, unable to be soothed, her daughter's identification with her, but also her deeper pain that mother had never been able to soothe her. Then, with me, the wish to transform that pain into a form that can be recognized and soothed by me in the part of mother, no longer reduced to bits but her surviving witness.

Dramatic enactment of jointly dissociated, powerful feelings can open the way for previously unrecognized self-states to step into the lights. But this use of the collision requires the analyst's acknowledgment and demystification, an invitation to the patient to join in sharing perception, formulating and analyzing, creating metaphors—ways of acting as a co-creator of the analytic process who can share the Third, rhythmic and differentiating. What appears in the guise of analyzing "what happened" might well be seen as constructing a narrative that can sustain the ambiguous relationship between Now and Then. We do not begin by knowing, nor even end by knowing, rather we lend ourselves to a movement from unformulated action to performance that creates meaning. Procedure matches content, as the movement of shared reflection and feeling elicits other self-states who enter the play. In this way a form of mutual recognition evolves with appreciation of one another's experience, separate and together (McKay, 2015).

PART III. PUTTING MUSIC AND LYRICS TOGETHER

I have tried to formulate an idea of meta-communication as part of what we do when there has been a rupture, by making use of enactments, that expose the complementary relationship or the uncoupling of feeling and thought or the shared dissociation. The effort to find our way into a felt connection then arises from within the action, and usually perforce embodies and encourages this recoupling of rhythmic and symbolic. Meta-communication that begins implicitly as performance during enactment can unfold in surprising ways, as if the script were writing itself (Ringstrom, 2007). Once we have performed the content and now the script contains a shared narrative action of the play, we may feel as if we, as partners, have become recoupled. The intersubjective process and psychic content work together.

My clinical illustration aimed to show the process of recoupling, between words and feelings, implicit and symbolic. With Hannah we saw how in the beginning, when symbolic representation is not anchored in the experience of attunement, it is not connected with knowing and being known by an other mind. Emotions first enter the field in dissociated actions that conceal and reveal. Performance of recognition within the dramatic action effects a transition to emotional expression, which then opens the experience to sharing of affect attunement, and thus to play with usable metaphors or characters. This process moves from Hannah enacting her outcast self to using the metaphor of the stalker to our enlivened exchange around Austen's Harriet. In this way we begin to generate symbolic thirdness in areas that were initially too shameful and anxiety-ridden to access. The dramatic interaction of repairing rupture moves from adversarial to collaborative and inquiring, with surprising guest appearances.

My contention has been that without having developed out of attunement and differentiation, a simulacrum of the symbolic Third arises that mimics reflection but is detached. As we work through enactments, moments of recognizing action can occur that link words and thoughts with feelings; implicit action and symbolic expression begin to match up.

I have highlighted how developmentally the same marking process that creates coupling of symbol with feeling gives rise to differentiating thoughts from reality, thus modifying psychic equivalence, making play with reality possible, as Fonagy and Target (1996a) theorized. Playing with the other, recognition, thus involves not only connecting through the rhythmic Third, but also differentiating feeling/ belief from reality. This differentiation in turn results in ability to hold the paradox of analysis, the opposing needs for repetition and repair.

In analysis, recoupling the procedural action and the symbolic is what makes performed recognition distinct; it enacts or dramatizes rather than merely states or formulates. Of course much of what we do involves understanding, formulating, empathizing, reflecting. But the meta-communicating we aim for when we are stuck in enactment binds, or that comes more naturally when we are playing, can— like song or improvisational drama—help to form missing links between implicit and symbolic, words and music. In fact, what characterizes play is the congruence between action and words, or placing them in opposition so as to deliberately produce incongruence. Play requires the ability to use congruence and incongruence to shape new meanings and connection, often surprising and uncalculated.

Conversely, unintended incongruence and decoupling of these channels points us towards dissociation. I would contend that despite our greater attention to interaction and affect regulation, implicit sub-symbolic communication, the rhythm rather than words (Bucci, 2008; Knoblauch, 2000; 2005), the common pull to dissociation tends to uncouple the symbolic and rhythmic, that is, cause us to focus more upon the words or on the music alone, sometimes in alternation. Clinically, we may notice how this decoupling signals dissociation, especially the analyst's.

Decoupling, dissociation and play

> It is part of play that the movement is not only without goal or purpose, but also without effort. It happens, as it were, by itself. The ease of play . . . is experienced subjectively as relaxation. The structure of play absorbs the player into itself and thus frees him from the burden of taking the initiative, which constituted the actual strain of existence. The actual subject of the play is obviously not the subjectivity of the individual . . . but is instead the play itself.
>
> (Gadamer, 1989, p. 109)

Gadamer's insightful description of play might be seen as one version of surrender to the Third—giving over to a co-created structure that transcends and absorbs the individuals so that they attain a freedom from self-consciousness, effort, or strain. Such release into play implies feeling at ease in the paradoxical space of analysis as real/not real, because the boundary is clear and secures the space. But for many individuals, this space of immersion can only be sustained in certain states while in other states the tension of opposites breaks apart. Because play is self-state dependent, we can notice the appearance of strain, which signals that paradox is becoming untenable as dissociated areas are uncovered. Here, as we conclude our discussion of paradox and play, I reiterate that even fruitful clinical work involves dyadic alternations between genuine play and strain, like that between thirdness and complementarity or breakdown. Thus the clinical question becomes how we identify disruptions, how we theorize breakdown, how we envision restoring thirdness and reopening the potential space of surrender to paradox and play.

Civitarese (2008) has proposed thinking about play in the space of thirdness as immersion in flow. He conceives of an oscillation in psychoanalytic process between immersion in the flow and interruption that take us outside the flow: in his terms, interaction or interpretation cause such breaks. He appears to me to be describing symbolic interaction that is decoupled from the rhythmic, which occurs because of some dysregulation in analyst or patient. In other words, play with metaphor and imagery can be interrupted by a kind of thinking "about" rather than with the flow (Winnicott's split off intellectual functioning). Interestingly, psychoanalysts who have emphasized "being with," and the importance of implicit relational knowing have also been concerned that formulating or reflecting on the process would interrupt the rhythmic flow of empathic immersion. It might seem as if the question of how we can avoid disrupting immersion or the rhythmic Third of accommodation and attunement, though differently articulated, is nonetheless common to the clinical theories of empathic knowing and containment through reverie. The sticking point, which has moved relational analysis to focus on enactment, is that repeatedly we find that the analyst becomes increasingly unable to maintain the empathic or containing stance under the pressure of dissociated states or dysregulation. The affect expressed in the mode of psychic equivalence, which cannot be put into play, often pushes towards complementary twoness, rupture or stalemate. This cannot occur without the analyst's identifications with the patient and her objects, but these identifications are usually at least partly dissociated. The aim of my discussion of meta-communication is to suggest that there is a way to move through these obstructions in the flow that plays with and acknowledges them, at times explicitly, when they take the form of enactment or collision. At the same time, the analyst may try to maintain a vision of the Third: meaning, that we are paddling down the stream together and so—regardless of which kind of stream we choose—when we must sometimes get out and lift the canoe over a rock we view lifting together as part of creating a shared Third.

Thus even when the interruptions or collisions generated by the concealing/revealing dissociated action become our focus, the question of how we procedurally use the experience of repair to acknowledge and witness is crucial. We are, after all, often playing with very dangerous and painful elements, such that the word play may give us pause. On the one hand, in working with patients with developmental trauma there is a need to stay empathically attuned to affect regulation, aim for "concor-dance" and a sense of interpersonal safety. But since witnessing and empathy are challenged by the (variously understood) powerful projections or dissociated threats and self-states, this rhythmicity is often disrupted and the analyst's acknowledgment becomes necessary. Even in the best of conditions, the "core consciousness," the state that occurs when we are immersed in reverie or in interactive improvisation can never be wholly sustained (Ringstrom, 2016).

Despite doubts about when and whether I have only myself to blame for disruptions, I conclude that I must see to it that this crisis becomes opportunity. If others succeed at avoiding such crises, I will happily learn from them. If, however, as it seems to me and I shall now contend, in many cases useful opportunities for acknowledgment are being smoothed over—an action I am all too familiar with myself—then I believe that I and most of my colleagues will do better as Ferenczi advised to humbly analyze our own vulnerabilities and support each other in doing so.

For my part, I am interested in what causes these interruptions in play or immersion—assuming we have even gotten it going. I suspect that one-sided focus on either symbolic narrative or intersubjective process may be more likely to cause us to ignore the pressure put on us by contradictory injunctions on different channels. We may be reactive, dissociatively, to the fragmentation of experience this produces. This can cause us to smooth over breakdowns in the tension of paradox, muddle through the complementarity of less visible enactments by returning to what we analysts are comfortable with, our default metaphors, formulations or empathic stance. It is when we are at home with our own comfortable flow that we are apt to be surprised by the unexpected enactment. Especially if up to this point both partners have seemingly ajusted to familiar patterns of reactivity, our reciprocal expectations and reactions are by now on quite cozy and intimate terms, even if sometimes abrasive, like an old married couple. Our dissociative cocoon, with its familiar complementary structure, must now be unwrapped, exposed to the cold air to be seen; jostled and destabilized in order to create movement (the baby parts of us are not happy with this and need some marked reassurance!). For all these reasons enactment and subsequent destabilization may necessarily take the form of interrupting our immersion, perhaps a collision.

An unfortunate illustration of the problems attendant on rejecting the function of enactment may be found in Boston Change Process Study Group, despite their recognition of the generativity of "sloppiness" (Nahum, 2002) that might have seemed to gesture in the direction of exploring our missteps. Instead, a one-sided advocacy for implicit relational knowing and "being with," a hugely useful contribution on their part (Stern et al., 1998; Lyons-Ruth, 1999; Stern, 2004; BCPSG, 2005), has been set up in opposition to examining the dynamic origins of sloppy moments and hence the symbolic side of our work. Despite noting the disjunction between implicit and reflective-verbal domains (Nahum, 2008), they have explicitly rejected examining the dynamic motivation for this decoupling, specifically dissociation (Knoblauch, 2008). Recently, BCPSG (2013) has directly argued against the relational theorizing of enactment and dissociation (especially the analyst's) in favor of repairing disruptions implicitly through "realigning with intention"—without talking about it. So here arises the problem of interrupting the flow. I question this assertion that we must choose between symbolically reflecting on repetition and generating new experiences of "being with" (implicit knowing) rather than being able to recouple them through play. I am not convinced by the categorical assertion that only change at the level of implicit relational knowing is mutative (BCPSG, 2013); exploring the uncoupling of that domain from reflexive-verbal knowing would than appear to be unnecessary.[7]

In countering the idea of dissociation, BCPSG define enactments—without regard to narrative content—as interruptions, mismatches or ruptures in the flow of fitting and joining which ought to be smoothed, not highlighted. These ruptures would then need only be repaired via affect regulation and restoring fittedness at the procedural level rather than unpacking the meaning of the action or self-states involved. BCPSG dispute the necessary emergence of dissociated parts or self-states that need to be addressed, that is, the symbolic meaning of the interruption is irrelevant. The erasure of the category of symbolic repetition flattens out the paradox of repairing by repeating, real but not real, that is essential to the psycho-analytic method.

One might think that maintaining the rhythm of mutual regulation by smoothing disruptions at the level of the implicit would actually serve to further dissociation and obscure the narrative content of dramatic ruptures. It would seem that the patient might be mystified and encouraged to accommodate rather than protest against injury or articulate what feels like repetition of injury. How is this problem addressed? By defining disruptive emotional events as "local" to the dyadic system, BCPSG's proposal decouples the perturbing or painful event from narrative historical meaning. It is hard to imagine that the emergence of historical traumata and emotions related to it would not be blocked by this stance (see Bohleber, 2010); that concentrating solely on restoring harmony via attunement and fittedness would adequately constitute recognition of complex injuries and failures of witnessing.

The problem of dissociation underlies both the erasure of repetition and the patient's historical trauma as well as the unwillingness to analyze the meaning of the analyst's reactivity and participation in enactment. BCPSG explicitly advocate for restoring mutual regulation and moving back into alignment with the patient and counsel against analyzing our own reactions. Since joint rhythmicity

---

7   Ellman and Moskowitz (2008) make the point that once having left the sensory-motor world for the symbolic realm the dyadic experiences of recognition and regulation are symbolically mediated, the implicit experiences are recursively ("nachtraeglich") reformulated and occur at a higher level of differentiation and representation; these are shaped by and contribute to multi-level, and sometimes multi-self narrative dramas. Thus reducing the experience to the implicit and bypasses all subsequent symbolic reworkings.

is considered paramount, the symbolic meaning of our "slippage" becomes unimportant. This position is the more striking because the case vignettes they used to demonstrate their argument entailed complex enactments involving dissociation of different self-states in both analyst and patient. In both cases discussed (Black, 2003; Stern, 2009) the analysts analyzed their own contribution and dissociative moments extensively, with reference to the patients' traumas. Yet their self-reflective analysis is explicitly rejected by BCPSG who reduce it to the implicit domain of failing to fit in or align with the patient's affect.

For instance, BCPSG defend their point with a case presented by Black (2003) in which the enactment involves a moment of laughter by the analyst that seems to evoke repetition of historical injuries, both participants' experiences with humiliation in relation to their fathers. Black shows how the collision encouraged the patient's expression of anger that was new for her. BCPSG focus solely on the transformational potential of the emergent anger and the "vitality" of the exchange as a property of the dyad, while reducing the complex narrative to a moment in which an analyst takes time out from her depressed patient "to enjoy a moment of laughter" (2013, p. 231). It is unnecessary and "shame-inducing" for analysts to consider their own dissociation, they declare. Analysts would do better to simply "regard their behavior as filling important needs of their own, needs that exist side by side with those of the patient . . ." (p. 231). As the analyst's dissociation, reactivity and vulnerability are off limits, Black's laughter is reduced to a "slippage" that can be adjusted (a non-Freudian slip?). Since it is a mistake, not a repetition of our histories nor expression of the not-me experience, there is no need to repair through acknowledgment or unpack the enactment.

The logic behind this clinical perspective is that only the new experience of "being with" is healing. The differentiation between the really real and the not real is denied, and so the mentalizing activity, based on sameness and difference between our experiences is also disregarded. The implicit experience trumps the symbolic. In effect, the analytic relation exists only in its rhythmic dimension, becoming then a real relationship between persons, one of whom (like Mom) sometimes needs a break. The paradoxical tension of the analyst as the one who repeats and the one who receives the communication is lost.

As McKay (2016) has pointed out, the clinical ideal of BCPSG contrasts sharply with the relational one, in which otherness is seen as vitalizing and verbal nego-tiation of the enactment can lead to a new quality of intimate relatedness. We partake in a moment of recognition by the sharing of inner states that have been exposed. The intimacy of such potential recognition is discarded along with the unmanageable, shameful dissociation. By contrast, the relational perspective holds that such recognition might actually heal shame and lead to greater tolerance of vulnerability; the aim of learning something new about ourselves and our patients functions as part of our collective Third. In this sense, permitting the ongoing enactment to evolve into disruption or collision, or even recognizing our own dissociation, can be liberating and generative, as both partners create symbolic as well as implicit knowing.

In recognizing the value of dramatic enactments in analysis, however, we do not therefore reject the effort to realign with the patient's intentions, to create affect regulation. We attend to containing the enactment, hoping it will be safe-enough. But we accept the dialectical movement of exposing the concealing/revealing action of dissociation to create the new, so that enactment morphs into play and we restore the paradox of repetition and repair. Black (2003) argues, and relational analysts concur, that enactments disrupt the rigid dissociative structure of the patient and not merely the dyadic regulation; they grow within but then break open the dissociative cocoon. From this point of view, disruption can be vital in loosening the grip of dissociative order, to perturb the system (Bromberg cited in Greif & Livingstone, 2013). And part of this tightly controlled order consists in the decoupling of affect from thought, procedural from symbolic.

Moments of rupture can create movement in static, stuck complementary relations, and through this motion expose in action the paradoxical pulls of fear and desire that need to be explored. Indeed, the movement between intersubjective positions—between complementarity and thirdness, stasis and disruption, enactment and play—is often foregrounded content rather than background in the analyst's awareness of whether there is space for thinking, freedom to move and be, for both participants.

The process of using enactment and joint dissociation as opportune moments for differentiation and recognition, highlighting disruption and repair, likewise punctuates the relation of immersion and interruption differently than Bionian Field Theory (BFT) (Ferro & Civitarese, 2013), which nonetheless has much in common with relational thought (Stern, 2013; 2015). Turning to that perspective—in effect the opposite of implicit relational knowing—we find a clinical theory that emphasizes the development of imagery in "pictographing" activity, expanding the capacity for thinking feelings, thus a version of recoupling. Influenced by Bion's emphasis on enabling the patient to develop his own capacity to contain and metabolize emotions (Ogden, 1997; Ferro, 2009; 2011; Brown, 2011), the dialogic reverie is infused with new life.

We might say this is a version of what Winnicott saw as the analyst "bringing the patient into the state of being able to play" (p. 44). In fostering the creativity of what Ferro (2009) calls "wakeful dreaming," imagining the sessions as a dream, the analyst facilitates the use of shared metaphors, and thus enables the metabolizing of raw affect (Bion's beta elements) into more articulated emotions (alpha elements), "alphabetization," and "pictographs" (Ferro, 2009; see also Brown, 2011).

As described compellingly by Ferro (2005; 2009; 2011; Ferro & Civitarese, 2013) the process of containing projective identifications and transforming proto-emotions that originate in the mode of psychic equivalence contributes to the growth of the part of the personality that is "constantly working to find, or rediscover, a basic psycho-somatic integration" (2009, p. 219). Despite his emphatic concentration on the field within the session, interpreting all outside material as characters and metaphors meeting inside, Ferro (2005) respects and identifies the repetition of micro-traumas of the patient's history "in the presence of someone who can 'see' and 'repair' the primal damage . . . which has affected the apparatus of thinking"; (p. 6) there is recognition then that patients use enactment to repeat and heal such trauma, by ignoring the real intersubjective process, there is a likelihood of ignoring the way trauma is repeated relationally, procedurally, and not just through symbolic content.

The movement I have described from enactment to play, creating metaphors and bringing new characters on the stage, can be usefully brought together with BFT's method of playing, as Stern (2013; 2015) has shown.[8] Like Ghent, Ferro emphasizes that the pressure of uncontained emotions and needs can be black-washed as aggression. Wary of split off intellectual formulations of paradox or use of interpretation to decode rather than expand the dreaming, the aim is to foster the patient's own development of thinking, and the analyst learning from what the patient says.

I am most appreciative of the way that symbolic thinking is broadened in this method to embrace the use of image-making and narrative to metabolize affect, a medium for recoupling the words and the music. But, despite the opening that allows for movement between enactment and play, there are some important differences worth highlighting in our respective views of analytic methods and goals, as noted by Stern (2013; 2015; also Peltz & Goldberg, 2013) especially in terms of how we view disruptions in the field. Ferro (2007) gives welcome attention to failures of containment and has stated that "microfractures in com-munication" give rise to cracks through which "undigested facts can burst in," becoming the "engine of analysis," (p. 34) a position indeed closely akin to relational theory of dissociation and enactment.

However a crucial point of contention between relational theory and BFT emerges regarding what is happening to us when we fail to contain, and what to do about it (Ferro & Civitarese, 2013). What clinical response is called for when, to use Ferro and Civitarese's (2013) terms, the field, as it must, "also contract[s] the analyst's illness," and the inevitable "accidents" occur (p. 647)? Ferro (2005) has already argued that the analyst should monitor the patient's narrative responses to his interpretations, modify them accordingly, but only seldom interpret them; rather the "person at the helm" uses them as "guidelines . . . to stay on course."

8   Stern's discussion of this issue resonates with me in many respects but I have a problem with his nomenclature: because he refers to the Bionian field theorists, BFT, he gives relatio-nal analysis the name IRP, Interpersonal Relational Psychoanalysis. In my view relational analysis has been eclectically and significantly influenced by Object Relations Theory and Self Psychology, at least as much as by the Interpersonal School. So I stick with "relational theory." Stern raised the interesting question as to how and if my idea of the Third can be assimilated to the Bionian idea of the field. The Third in Ogden's theory is closer to the field, the relational matrix that we create and exist in together. For me, as I said in the introduction, the position of the Third is one crucial movement or position within the field.

Ferro and Civitarese (2013) assume that when the inevitable "accident" occurs, the analyst "given appropriate functioning" in the setting should simply "regain an ideal position for containing the patient's anxieties." Even if the analyst does acknowledge the lapse in containment, for example, let the patient know he is aware of his somewhat critical interpretation (Ferro, 2009) in the previous session, and modifies his "cooking" accordingly, he tells the patient that the dish was too spicy and he hopes the cook will be more careful in the future (Ferro, 2009). We note that in giving examples of acknowledgment, Ferro, who identifies as film director, does not call "Cut!" and review the scene with the actor. The break in our rhythmic Third is repaired implicitly, the immersive flow is not really interrupted, as the director continues to roll the camera. But the patient's confusion or anxiety is not directly addressed, his observations of his analyst not elicited.

If relational analysis has focused on revealing some of our process along with the source of our dissociation, as well as how we made use of this reaction to unpack the enactment, it may be because we are not so sure that, especially in painful accidents, we will regain an "ideal position" without talking through what caused the disruption. Inviting the patient to cook in the kitchen together so that she has a say in spicing the dish (Aron & Atlas, 2015) might appeal to us because, as Stern (2013; 2015) explains, we don't trust the analyst to reflect alone on where the ship went wrong or why he put too much pepper in yesterday's stew. We may be surprised. Failures are used to enlarge the patient's participation.

The exchange of the unspeakable known has implications for how minds meet, how truth can be spoken, and how the container becomes more mutual (Cooper, 2000). But of equal importance is the fact that in the face of injury or rupture, the analyst's acknowledgment becomes an opportunity for repair of the Third, for a new quality of relatedness that emerges as we shift self-states from complementarity to mutual knowing. The transition from complementarity to thirdness, from enactment to acknowledgment reinstates paradox, making play possible. This process of shifting is part of what is mutative in analysis, what intersubjectively anchors the new ability to integrate thought and emotion.

Of course, most analysts agree that if we can maintain the rhythm, recover an empathic stance and contain the "micro-fracture" through understanding, we may still find out something about our own reactivity. But some fractures are larger, more painful, originate in real trauma for which the patient seeks, yearns, for witnessing and acknowledgment as such. Some not-me states are calling to us through the pressure of such reality, unmetabolized and intensified by the fearful equation of inner and outer, then and now. Insofar as this pressure may activate the analyst, we will learn from reconstructing the analyst's part in the enactment. We will think in terms of the uncontained projections or dissociated self-state expressed in the complementary oppositions that tend to either freeze the action or lead to rupture. From the standpoint of intersubjective recognition, the characters of self-states that emerge in enactment are viewed as parts "belonging" not only to the field but to the analyst and patient as respective individuals, (Bernstein, in conversation), all the more stuck to us when we do not own and take responsibility for them. In this sense, the analyst and patient remain separate subjects, who are aware of the painful or positive impact of their actions upon each other—blaming, criticizing, rejecting, joining or withdrawing from shared affect—which is part of what feels "real" in analysis as does the repair through shared knowing of one another. Such reality of feeling can co-exist with reverie and metaphor that contribute to the make-believe of affecting each other in quite "unreal" ways. Working through enactment ideally involves some version of reinstating or accepting the paradox that the relationship is both real and unreal, but only if the reality of what happened between us is not mystified. Then the analyst can be the one who both nips you and aids you in healing from the bites you have suffered.

This form of repair engenders as well a powerful experience of the moral Third, of lawful responsiveness: the patient has the experience that the analyst is aware that she will feel put in the wrong, and that the analyst puts her sanity and safety above his need to be right. The analyst is resisting the pull to be "good" at all costs which might extrude the badness into the patient (Davies, 2004) while making it into a disowned, not-me state for himself (Mark, 2015). The procedural action of co-creating the understanding as a form of thirdness figures in our theory of intersubjectivity as an added dimension; the analyst is able to reflect on one's own accidents—those that trigger shame or self-reproach especially.

The procedural meaning of reconstructing our action together or co-creating a metaphor to express our understanding is that we create a container together, a form of thirdness. This idea of a third space that holds both partners emotions suggests that dialogic engagement fosters a form of mutual containing in which emotions become communication that moves the other. In this movement, epitomized by interactive play, symbolization manifests as an intersubjective process, a form of recognition between self and other. Procedure matches content. The movement of shared reflection and feeling elicits other self-states who enter the play.

The shared activity of reflection is a process in its own right, a form of knowing each other that is transformative: mutual recognition. As Bromberg (2011) put it "mutual knowing or 'state sharing' that not only is therapeutic in its own right but deepens and enriches the opportunity for symbolic processing . . . of each partner's not me experience . . ." (p. 13). Note that Bromberg's description of intersubjective recognition attends to both sharing of states and symbolic processing of the separate experience of each partner. Where the sense of recognizing one another's experience may be "too real" for field theory, it seems that different self-states and meanings interfere with the unison of "being with" in the BCPSG version of implicit knowing. On the one side, the symbolic and symbolizing action seems to outweigh the implicit meaning of how it feels to be knowing each other's minds, on the other side implicit knowing sidelines the symbolic. Intersubjective recognition theory envisions the recoupling, however loose, between interactional and symbolic knowing. The transformations in intersubjective relatedness provide early developmetal experiences that have been missed, even as they create the conditions for analytic play, interactive and symbolic. The intersubjective recoupling that I am proposing is thus about regenerating the rhythmic thirdness of mutual knowing that underlies all trustworthy connection, but this depends upon a vital form of differentiation. It is about restoring the paradoxical relationship to reality and pretend in psychoanalysis, repetition in repair of the really real from the pretend real—the ability to play in the paradoxical space of the analytic field.

From an intersubjective perspective, analysts can accept the ways we do not always know ourselves or the other, but rather surrender to the process of discovery by accepting the limits of our abilities to know ahead of the process itself (McKay, 2015). In this way we open ourselves to emergent meaning (Stern, 2015). We may, of course, become more familiar with the vicissitudes of dissociation and enactment, the nip and the bite; with the paradoxical dynamics of rupture and repair, repetition and reparation; the paradox of expressing pain, disappointment, betrayal even while being heard and received. We accept paradox in order to lend ourselves, including our most vulnerable states and feelings, to a movement toward the improvisational play where shared meaning emerges through our recognition of the other. The analyst's invitation to surrender to this open-ended process is intended to facilitate the restoration of thirdness as play—the state of absorption and participation in something larger. This something comes from the place of the Third, which beckons us from beyond our clinging to the familiar Me. This place, in which the news of difference is enlivening and "safe enough" we find some freedom from the ordinary strain of recognizing otherness. In shared surrender to this Third, we are able to appreciate yet again the rhythmic flow of recognition, as if the improvisation of Yes/And were effortless, as if feelings and symbols were part of our playthings. This is the "real" relationality of the analysis, in which we play with reality and the other, learning how to do it together.

Chapter 6

Playing at the edge
Negation, recognition and the lawful world

My personal relation to play was formed in the context of being with babies and children, especially my own. The idea of play was appealing to me in the abstract as an undergraduate reading the radical Freudians (Marcuse, Brown), Nietzsche, and Schiller, and later when I read Winnicott and Milner, but I was not yet sure what play could mean in adult analysis. Play as a developmentally crucial part of infancy I encountered when I discovered infancy research and the studies of face-to-face interaction in the work of Stern & Beebe (Stern, 1974a & b; Beebe & Stern, 1977). But my felt sense was of having rediscovered the ability to play, as if my experience of play with my own parents came back to me when I had a baby of my own.

In particular, there were songs. My father sang, finding an appropriately themed song for every possible occasion, and so I found myself inventing songs for my child as a way to soothe and comfort, but also to narrate and enliven our shared daily life. One of the songs I made up for my rapprochement toddler son was the song to thematize the "No!" (see Spitz, 1957). The tune of the theme of the Lone Ranger (otherwise known as the William Tell Overture), also beloved in childhood, fit my intentions and it went something like this: "A No and a No and a Yes Yes Yes; a No and a No and a Yes Yes Yes! No and No, Yes and Yes, NOOOO . . . and YES YES YES! No and No and No and No, and Yes and Yes and Yes Yes Yes . . ." And so on. This song expresses best the spirit of this paper, which celebrates the joy of No when Yes is its background—and vice versa.

For this chapter, the Both/And and the Yes/And discussed in Chapter 6 needed to be sublated (aufgehoben—modified and integrated) with the equally import-ant and sometimes paradoxical relation of Yes-And-No. In Part I of the chapter I propose the importance of embracing the No as part of the movement already highlighted from enactment to play. The recuperating of the No, using it to amplify rather than foreclose meaning, restores the tension between the two sides of the opposition, thus creating the Third. In Part II, the clinical discussion, I consider a treatment involving much negation and intolerance of being with the Other. It also illustrates the war between dissociated selves, in which at first it seems that Only one can live. This then necessitates a dramatic enactment in relation to the patient's history of violent trauma in which the moral Third could be encountered and the experience of a lawful world could be authenticated. I am deeply grateful to "Jeannette" for sharing her story and her words, for teaching me.

PART I. BEGINNING WITH NO . . . AND YES

Just as paradox should not be resolved through split off intellectual functioning, so the paradoxical uses of No in early forms of self-assertion should not be reduced through mere understanding. There is need for a space in which to play with the No, recognize it, and allow it to be a defining moment in the improvisational movement of Yes/And. I am using the No and Yes to think through a dialectical movement that may exemplify the relationship of negation and recognition: a relationship in which Yes cannot defeat or subsume No, even though it must find a way to recognize it and the self-expression it embodies: To embrace it without crushing or suffocating it.

The key to creating this recognition without reducing the negation may be found in the idea we explored previously of meta-communication, which makes simultaneous use of both rhythmic and symbolic levels. For instance, when we recognize a symbolic statement of negation, disagreement or separation by using an implicit, procedural gesture like nodding or appreciative uhuh! to affirm that negative. This creates a Third that holds both meanings through rhythmic matching and congruence juxtaposed to incongruence of differentiated/symbolic channels.

To illustrate: in a case presented by the Boston Change Process Study Group (Nahum, 2002), a little girl starts out her play session by saying emphatically that she is blocking the entrance to her doll house and "That's so no one can get in!" (p. 1054). She is keeping the therapist out; she doesn't have to let the other into her mind. It is a powerful statement of No. She is able to push away, but she also needs a recognizing response. It is a good example of how the negative can be brought into make-believe play without disrupting the flow, leaving room for the analyst to meta-communicate from inside the action. The analyst does indeed find a way to affirm her No, joining her *affectively* (procedurally) by saying equally emphatically: "Yeah, that's a good idea! How about giving me something to do . . ." (p. 1054). This is a paradoxical communication: Yes–*No one can get in! I hear your No. You are keeping everyone (me) out, but I will match your rhythm to maintain the Yes of togetherness.* Joining rhythmically, the therapist *recognizes* the symbolic statement of separation, self-protection, closing. Paradox is maintained; the antithetical meanings are held in the Third: the Yes includes the No without denying or evading it. The No dictates the terms of the Yes, and the improvisational move of Yes/And accepts the No.

This view of the dialectic of Yes and No, recognition and negation, seems to resonate with McGilchrist's contention (2009) that in mental life the principle of union outranks division. I am aware that such an idea might be construed to underestimate the importance of difference, but in this case it is tendered as a correction to the over-emphasis on reason. McGilchrist maintains that the right hemisphere of the human brain—which includes metaphor, implicit knowing, and affect—gives us the principle of union, while the left divides, separates, distinguishes. In McGilchrist's formulation, the left hemisphere may be seen as occupying the negative role in the dialectic, breaking up wholeness and union, making distinctions.

In my understanding of the dialectic, such splitting into opposing moments is always necessary in order to create more complex and inclusive forms of union, in the same way that disruption allows more complex forms and processes of repair. McGilchrist writes:

> Yet there is an asymmetry between the principles of division (left hemisphere) and unification (right hemisphere), ultimately in favour of union. Heidegger was not alone in seeing that beauty lies in the coming to rest of opposites that have been sharply distinguished in the connectedness of a harmonious unity. The need for ultimate unification of *division with union* is an important principle . . . it reflects the need not just for two opposing principles but for their opposition ultimately to be harmonized. The relation between union and division is not in this sense, once again, equal or symmetrical.
>
> (p. 200)

As Hegel thought, union and division must "themselves be unified," thus affirming the principle of unification even while accepting division. In light of the philosophical critique of identity (see Adorno, 1966), it is fortunate that McGilchrist immediately modifies his point by asserting that this unification of union and division, in order not to dissolve its other, must sustain paradox: as the Romantic critics of Cartesian reason proclaimed, paradox is not a "sign of error but . . . a sign of the necessary limitation of our customary modes of language and thought to be welcomed . . . on the path towards truth. 'Paradox is everything simultaneously good and great' wrote Friedrich Schlegel" (McGilchrist, 2009, p. 200). In dialectical theory, passing through division creates a mediated union that is not identical with the original union, hence a third position of oneness (Benjamin, 2005).

This view of dialectic and paradox, though posited in abstract form, corresponds to our practical clinical intuition that one tries to be open to both closing and opening: Being open, or surrendered, to both is the third position. We can observe the moves of this dialectic of opening in Nebbiosi's (2016) article "The Smell of Paper." Here the author provides a clinical example with a formulation of the dialectic that speaks directly to the Yes and No, union and division. This is the dialectic in which recognition and thirdness take shape in an effort to encompass both sides of the opposition. Nebbiosi describes tuning in to a kind of non-verbal consciousness associated with music[1]—the right hemisphere functions McGilchrist describes—from which he was able to generate a meta-communication (see Chapter 6) that made use of the opposing positions to create movement. This movement through the enactment of a stand-off, a potential double bind where Yes and No would become hardened, took the action into a space of paradox and play. Nebbiosi was able to present his patient with a form of paradox, a version of the Third that opened up the stuck complementarity of their positions by accepting both sides.

Nebbiosi describes his patient Teresa as a formidable, highly rational and logical, dismissively attached professional woman who had escaped the misery of rural poverty in which she grew up by her intellectual prowess and success in school. It appeared to Nebbiosi that books had become for her not just a better world in which to live but also an extension of her body. She even loved the smell of paper. However, Nebbiosi came to realize his identification with the "closed and haughty Teresa," who reminded him of his lonely adolescence, and so make contact with the heretofore dissociated pain of that loneliness. He could recall how he hid behind his sense of superiority, and in this way develop a more complex empathy for Teresa (Ipp, 2016). This narrative, autobiographical consciousness was mediated through his musical consciousness, his bodily spontaneous reaction to his patient.

The crucial intervention occurred when Nebbiosi reacted one day to Teresa's defiant enactment of a negation, one whose meaning was not at once obvious. She began by denouncing the avant garde, a hyperbolic and impassioned declamation occasioned by the fact that her boyfriend had invited her to a theatre production; she declared all such art to be meaningless, absurd, detestable, worthless. Nebbiosi felt personally affected by Teresa's negativity, not so much its symbolic content, but the procedural sense of her action which seemed to say, "no one and nothing could change her mind!" He felt sad, deflated. Despite her fervour, Teresa noticed the effect she had and inquired about her analyst's sad response, which seemed to convey his feeling that he could have no impact on her. He responded: "Yes, maybe, I feel that we're both alone," and explained:

> At moments like this you want to end the conversation, no matter what I think; and I want to keep the conversation going, no matter what you think. We're alone because in these moments we're shut off, we're both convinced we're right. But I'd like to keep talking to you and I think you'd like to keep talking to me too.

> (Nebbiosi, 2016, p. 7)

---

1   Ringstrom (2016) refers to this by adapting the term "core consciousness" from Blank in order to describe the kind of unselfconscious absorption of immersive flow, which corresponds to the rhythmic Third, in contrast to the biographical narrative of symbolic consciousness.

In this way Nebbiosi encompassed Teresa's negation within a recognition of their shared dilemma—each person thinking s/he is right, creating the classic complementarity of "My way or the highway." However, this meta-communication was not delivered observationally from outside the immersive experience of enactment, but procedurally from inside the emotional experience. Significantly, he says "*We*" are both alone and shut off. Because of this affective joining, Nebbiosi's recognition of his patient's symbolic statement of negation and the difference between them also paradoxically affirmed a symmetry between his Yes and her No.

Normally this kind of symmetry, experienced during a complementary opposition, is missed. But by focusing on the procedure, on the music, the way the opposing themes echoed each other, resolving the chord produced by their opposing notes and thereby affirming their relationship, Nebbiosi was able to find a Third. A To and Fro movement, as in Gadamer's (1960) sense of play, opened their opposition into the third position of *Aufhebung* (dialectical transformation): the possibility of continuing conversation, further movement. In this way, as Nebbiosi articulates, the musical resolution of the dialectic between opposing themes opened immediately to a new possibility. As theorized in the last chapter, a direct meta-communication from inside the drama that addresses the partners' emotional states and their complementary face-off unsticks the action. It moves the relationship back onto the axis of the rhythmic Third and shifts the self-states of both partners, so they can engage in the space of play where access to reverie is possible.

This opening seemed to make way for a flash of intuition, which led Nebbiosi to inquire seemingly out of the blue about his patient's memory of her first trip to an amusement park. Notably, the recollection was of a moment when Teresa had allowed something *new* to perturb her closed system; it was a roller-coaster ride that she had very much relished, shared with the boyfriend with whom she intended to lose her virginity that very night. Nebbiosi affirms that her memory is wonderful, but that he also understands her shame. He waits for her to express curiosity and explains: "Because it was fun to be scared. Because experiencing fear was making you feel open to life." In this moment, procedure mimics symbolic content, the two are coupled as the mood shifts towards openness. The roller-coaster memory in turn engenders a significant metaphor: Teresa goes on to admit to her love of frightening horror movies, the thrill she enjoys. The acceptance of the No opened the way to a metaphor that revealed a previously dissociated connection between fear, surprise, and the new—a self-state that finds pleasure in loss of control. In this way, a wholly unexplicated mutation of "avant-garde" emerges and together with the metaphor of the roller-coaster expresses both the fear and joy, the negative and generative sides of the couple's intersubjective process. As Teresa leaves, she invites Nebbiosi to join in play: "Yeah, but avantgarde theatre . . . what a bore!" and both laugh, closer than they have ever been.

As I emphasized in the previous chapter, the dramatic art of psychoanalysis requires narrative and symbols, the creation of metaphor, even though it also builds upon the implicit, procedural and proto-symbolic inflection by which we mark difference. The transformation of inchoate feeling into metaphor is part of the process of transforming enactment into play insofar as metaphors do not simply reflect thought, are not pre-digested material. Rather they are "cognitively active," generating "truly new" links between formerly disconnected material in the implicit domain, says McGilchrist (2009, p. 179). As we have seen, play with metaphors is a way to express psychic creativity and create "emotional literacy," richly explored in the field theory of reverie (Ferro, 2005; 2009; 2011; Civitarese, 2008). However, in that school of thought the narrative meaning of the "characters" introduced into the imaginary field takes precedence over attention to implicit intersubjective interaction. Relational analysis adds attention to the intersubjective procedure, the music as we see in Nebbiosi's vignette. Attention is paid not simply to the flow of metaphor but the direct recognition of the impasse that triggers a movement of self states, the intersubjective dynamic that opens and closes to metaphor.

In art we expect a dramatic performance to incorporate both rhythmic (procedural) and symbolic (narrative) levels, to integrate music, gesture, and story. If we conceive of psychoanalytic enactment in terms of recoupling procedural and symbolic domains, we see how metaphors can emerge not simply as a representation but also as a manifestation of implicit opening towards the new emergent meaning (Stern, 2015). But metaphors also reflect the paradoxical nature of such experiences in which negatives are transformed: the scary roller-coaster becomes the embodiment of exciting vitality; the closed door of the dollhouse becomes a symbol for the right to determine who and what goes inside and out. Thus metaphor, the mind's play, can contain the history of the negating element as well as link seeming polarities or opposing desires in a form that opens towards recognition (see Samuels, 1985).

We recall the opposing themes of the paradox that may become split in the double bind: I want to repeat and repair; I want to push you away or feel pushed away but also have you receive the communication. This doubleness of meaning can erupt into a potentiating conflict (Benjamin, 2015) or be generative when the analyst is able to recognize its leading edge (Aron & Atlas, 2015). In this sense the truth of the whole transcends the real appearance of the opposing parts. As we have seen what allows us to access this whole is the acceptance of paradox, living within oppositions and difference. We can do this when we trust the possibility of returning to resonance or fittedness (BCPSG, 2002) with the other, a complex oneness in which we *harmonize* difference. In harmonizing difference is not denied; the different sounds or colors should retain their integrity. But harmony, which may include resolution of a prior dissonance, does ultimately serve to intensify the expression of order and union. Calming and connecting while letting difference be. Challenging harmony by moving into dissonance or variation on the theme, swinging as far out as possible while retaining the elastic connection that permits return from the manifold to the One, allows movement and complexity —the To and Fro of play (Benjamin, 2005).

Differentiation and recognition

Playing relies on and furthers a differentiating-while-joining movement of recognition. As I see it, the dialectic of harmony and dissonance, recognizing and negating, matching and marketing, embodies the same principle of the differentiating Third that underlies the magic of intersubjective attunement as Stern first revealed it: through cross-modal responses the resonance and participation in the other's mind is demonstrated (Stern, 1985; 2004). It becomes clear that this Other Mind can know/feel as I do, that my inner feeling states are being read (Stern, 2004), even in the negative. "I know, and we can join in knowing, that you don't want to open." Not simply mirroring (Stern, 1985; Benjamin, 1988; Beebe, 2002) but embracing difference. Stern (2004) distinguishes intersubjective relating from the bonding of attachment. Intersubjective relatedness—recognition in my terms— involves psychological intimacy, protection from psychic aloneness. Thus reading the intention of the other's negative is a vital part of relieving their aloneness. Recognizing the negation is an important moment in the dialectical movement of opening and closing, the use of play and paradox. It is often key to the art of opening the closed communication of complimentary oppositions into the space of thirdness and play.

Differentiation is important in that the child needs to occupy her own position as the subject of symbolic thinking, which means knowing that her thoughts need neither exactly reflect reality nor the view of the other. We could say, then, that I can only feel that my mental experience is knowable by another mind and corresponds to reality if I can also feel that my mental experience is different from the other mind, is my own mind (see Fonagy & Target, 1996). It can (and is allowed to) diverge from reality or the other's view of it, can be part of the motion of dividing and uniting that makes the Third.

When dramatizing, fantasizing or symbolizing in the arena of play, the child or patient implicitly believes that she is (1) being known and received by another mind, and (2) is doing so without the condition of perfect identity between the thing and the communication, without a singular and absolute reality. A recognition of the other mind—inherent in the anticipating and/or wondering how the other will receive this—undergirds the process and contributes to the satisfying communication it intends. Like the imprecision of the analogue as opposed to digital sound, the slight difference is a sign of something real, not mechanical.

Developmentally, we might say that play progresses from procedural interactions working with matching—mismatching, with expectancy and surprise (as with the peek-a-boo game), to verbal expressions that represent more complex feelings symbolically. From the beginning, differentiation—that is, recognition of the other mind—is always part of the function of play as a two-person activity. Here an example comes to my mind from my greatest teachers in the area of play, my children. When my younger son was a bit older than two, not too far along in speech and still very fond of saying No to everything, his 6-year-elder brother was playing with him at the dinner table by setting up a series of questions all of which the younger with great glee could answer "No!" Finally, thinking to trick him, my older son asked him, "Can Jonah say anything besides NO?" We observing assumed immediately that this language construction would be too complex, but Jonah, waiting just a beat, and with a sly grin, answered an emphatic "YES!" Then, following the surprise effect he had achieved, with perfect timing, he crowed, "Busted!"—delivering an expression he must have heard his brother and other 8-year-olds use. Had he declared outright what he had implicitly demonstrated—"I am not as easily fooled as you imagine, I think for myself, and I can fool you!"—we could not have been more shocked. Showing that he knew his brother was operating on the belief that Jonah would not understand, whereas in the important sense he did get it. What he got presumably being the procedural marking, the violation of the pattern of expectancy by his older brother, perhaps cued by a change in rhythm—this was most likely the giveaway and not the fairly complicated syntax of "besides."

Playing with surprise, with rhythmic breaks in expectancy, is a very early feature of face-to-face play, as in "Gotcha!". This play, which turns on implicit relational knowing, presages the recognition that the other has a perspective different from one's own, that they have a perception one does not hold oneself, and hence they can be fooled (Reddy, 1991; Fonagy & Target, 1996a). This capacity to differentiate one's own mind from an other is part of what we usually denote with the idea of reflective function and what makes meta-communicating possible.

We note that in this play space of thirdness the deliberate violation of a shared expectancy implicitly relies upon and so *confirms* what was anticipated rather than merely breaking it, as a true violation would. And this returns us, recursively, to the general theorem that recognition can use—sustain while sublimating—negation. The little brother's ability to defy the expectation that he would be the one "gotten," to subvert the power relation, to make Yes mean No, all demonstrates how reversal, an intersubjective capacity, could be used to further assert differentiation. It exemplifies how disruption of patterns can serve to perturb the system and create differentiation while enhancing mutual recognition. Clinically, analysts can use play to encourage the assertion of me-against-you and its reversals to find the forward edge of developing agency, the potentiating power of the negative. That is the generative force of the No, the power of the negative that can be harnessed as a marking of difference.

If in play the negative serves not only to break but also to accentuate the lawful pattern being violated, we might say that it functions similarly to Goethe's notion, expressed by Mephisto in Faust, asserting he is the "power that negates," the "force that constantly intends the bad but instead always creates the good." Violations in the realm of play, which contribute to building a co-created Third, are thus the very antithesis of real violation or violence. We shall come back to this difference between violence that negates the law and negation that upholds it.

Playing with the other: intersubjectivity for beginners

Playful relating is a primary way such intimacy and recognition are learned and fostered, knowing and being known. In intersubjective terms, play is something we do together, analyst and patient interacting, in an ongoing dyadic *movement*. In its broadest sense, play is movement, a back and forth between us, that has its own direction or contour which both partners shape and surrender to. This form of rhythmicity, the early pre-verbal forms of thirdness, determines later symbolic and narrative capacities for playing with an other. Beginning in infancy the expectation of coordination, co-creation and having one's own intentions recognized in general, also sets the stage for playing with the other; conversely, having to depend upon disjunctive, unpredictable and inappropriate responses will interfere with the development of play. Unable to safely rely upon the other's knowing and responding to one's own states interferes with the coordination of intentions and directions (Beebe & Lachmann, 2013).

In distinguishing between play as an experience of shared intersubjective reality versus enactment we are referring to the ability to participate in a rhythmic Third. The inability to play with reality, to make the distinction we previously noted between psychic equivalence and pretend (Fonagy & Target, 1996a) stems from damage in the formation of the Third as joint alignment and patterning. Thus operating in the mode of psychic equivalence not only means that the subject tries to enforce a correspondence between "my view" and "reality," but operates with fearful expectations of being unrecognized or subject to coercion that jam the works. Forcing the idea of what is happening into a template that fits one's own feelings through exclusion of those bits that would disrupt or challenge the static view is what "feels right."

From this point of view, when there is deep developmental trauma, enactment can be understood not only in terms of dissociated states or feelings that push for expression in enactment; rather enactment is simply a term for the ongoing mode of complementary interaction that results when the accommodation, responsiveness and attunement of the other to one's own state is not the template for most interaction. The non-coercive, open mode of playing with the other is not yet integrated and the missing, formative templates of experience with recognition of distress and anxiety are needed yet hard to take in. In what sense can we even speak of play when complementarity and coercion are as natural to someone as the air they breathe?

But even here, the analyst, in order to create experiences of the rhythmic Third, strives to find a way of recognizing what it feels like to be in the patient's mind, a way to play together as an equivalent to play therapy. In particular, working to articlate what Ogden called autistic-contiguous experience in the form of playful metaphors can help adults to articulate the residues of infancy: the distress of the baby whose life was shaped by the developmental trauma of non-recognition. Physical correlates of unempathic relatedness such as looming, invading, withdrawing, jostling, sudden movements, loudness, can be expressed in a way that allows for joint play. For instance: "If someone comes too close or seems too demanding it feels like a truck is bearing down on you on the highway. You have to get ahead of that truck, you need to switch lanes, but you can't because you are hemmed in. I feel like you need a sports car with an extra powerful engine to outrun that truck, you need your own lane, maybe some high octane fuel. What kind of car do you think?"

For patients who can shift out of psychic equivalence when they feel safely recognized, shifts from enactment to play can occur through the analyst's ongoing containing and playing with feelings to give form to the formless pain of life without another mind. I see this action as augmenting the metabolizing or of raw emotions through alphabetization (Ferro, 2009), by emphasizing the primal pre verbal experience in the medium of play. The aim is for the patient to learn to play with an other mind, becoming able to mentalize (Fonagy et al., 2002), as part of a recapitulation of the developmental process of recognition. This occurs not only through what is commonly understood as empathy for suffering but through play with awareness of sensation, such as the attention to affect regulation and somatic experience that has been pioneered by work with sensory-motor therapy (Ogden, Pain, & Minton, 2006; Eldredge & Cole, 2008; Rappaport, 2012). Rappoport (2012) describes creating a playful thirdness with her patient around the action and imaging of using her hands to grasp. Therapeutic work with traumatic experience through such somatic work can be related to our metaphors of basic embodied states, movement and sensations that speak to our right-brain differently (Knoblauch, 2000; 2005). These are important efforts to recouple the verbal domain with the physical, pre-verbal domain in order to create the conditions for emotional expression.

The possibility for recognizing emotions of distress in a way that feels "real" to the patient may therefore depend upon a rhythmic thirdness of trust and predictability built through elemental responsiveness to negative affect expressed in relation to apparent trivia. Brown (2011) describes a patient with whom he made better contact after he found a way to understand her complaints about the sun coming in her window which eventually linked up with interpersonal intrusion but initially represented a pre-verbal experience of invasion. Using less "grown up" language (Bromberg, 2011), understanding the process of symbolization more broadly, there are many ways to respond to the experience of being invaded, overheated, sticky, unable to get away from something. I often suggested to patients that if they liked something I said and disliked another, they could spit out the part they didn't like, like the mushy peas in the baby food. Or that, thanks to a favorite cartoon, I suggested the image that we needed to avoid the childhood nightmare of foods touching each other on the plate. In this way we use playful interaction around negative affect to join in and open constricted narrative meaning, facilitating the experience of rhythmic thirdness.

In this way our work involves not only attention to dissociated self-states and the more entrenched enactments they engender but also to the micro-interaction that the study of infants and small children has delineated. Small moments of recognition can facilitate movement between self-states, shifts from complementarity to thirdness, or from dysregulation to regulation.

I think it has been insufficiently observed how playful behavior by the analyst can actually contribute to affect regulation and a sense of safety by finding a way to provide recognition while bypassing the head-on confrontation that evokes anxiety and shame (Ringstrom, 2016). Reactivity is diminished as one person is not meeting the other's negation with her own. And so, in a kind of circular process, playful communication may be a condition as well as an outcome of safety.

Play and affect regulation can function synergistically, as we saw in our discussion of marking, which is the prototype of playful responsiveness to disruptions. When we use marking to signal that the feared thing is not really happening this simultaneously serves affect regulation and establishing the symbolic function— rhythmic and differentiating thirdness are co-determining. The use of meta-communication, using the gestural and implicit marking to signal the nip rather than the bite, to express the negative without real consequences, both relies upon and creates a sense of safety: it conveys something about whether one's own or the other's feelings are being contained, framed and marked, not being received as threatening or impinging.

Rigidity, flexibility, multiplicity: qualities of motion

In theorizing the relationship between play and enactment, it is also important to distinguish the relationship to dramatization, which occurs in both. The content of the dramatized reality might be similar, but play entails a kind of open system regarding the drama, as in improvisation. Play, freed from the need to be equivalent to reality, suspends the need to resolve incompatible positions and the need for the inviolable rightness of one meaning. Indeed, where such rightness is at stake, where reality must be acknowledged because real transgression and violence have occurred, play is not possible.

In play the (potentially) opposing positions cease to be mutually exclusive. The distinctions that co-participants in play sense between them are not part of a split complementarity, but rather, they exist in the space of thirdness that we have understood as transitional experience. What this means is that the quality of movement itself varies between rigidity and flexibility. This quality of motion is something that we sense more than analyze. We are able to note how some dyadic or individual self-states can move or play together almost naturally, while others, those holding very painful, anxious, or shameful experiences, must go through an enactment, which only then gradually opens up into play.

Play involves and supports the experience of multiplicity of meaning. As with paradox, the wider implication of this position is that play is formally important because it develops and expresses the capacity to hold more than one reality (see Pizer, 1992). Play allows the player to hold antithetical positions, ideas or feelings.

Contradictions need not be resolved; in the willing suspension of disbelief, holding antithetical meanings constitutes part of what makes play therapeutic and suggests how therapeutic action is related to play.

A crucial point is that creating a space for multiple, disjunctive meanings may allow multiple self-states to be present or alternate in awareness. By simultaneously satisfying and giving recognition to states or feelings that ordinarily have to be unlinked, dissociated, *play allows selves that would otherwise be at war with one another to co-exist*, even co-create together. For instance, in playing a game about mother leaving, the child may be able, as First (1988) showed, to hold together the self-state that feels separation anxiety and the self-state that knows that mother will still be there. As play makes room for more than one self-state, more than one thing can be true, and hence multiplicity and plurality of perspectives can be true.

Just as the psychic work of play permits a negotiation or at least an acceptance of contradiction between selves (Pizer, 1998), so conversely a movement towards bringing together previously warring selves begins to permit play. This also obviates using projective identification to off-load the contradicting self into a complementary opposition with the other, as no one self need extinguish the other in order to exist. They and we can both live when we find a position of thirdness. Multiple realities are viewed as reflecting different self-positions who can exist without cancelling each other out. As we shall see later in the story of Jeannette, this can begin to meet the need for the experience of a lawful world in which "more than one can live."

Tolerance for multiple positions may also mean that no one mind has to dominate the other. In this context we underscore the significance of the idea that the analyst demonstrates her embrace of multiplicity by expressing her subjectivity without replacing, or substituting it for, that of the patient (Bromberg, 2013). She makes clear that she is speaking her truth, not the truth. Herein lies a kind of safety. Plurality and multiplicity, in which more than one subjectivity or view of reality can exist in the same space, can feel safer than a reductive pull towards a singularity of perspective, as it is neither coercive nor demanding.

The To and Fro of fruitful analytic work often reflects the movement of negation and recognition, an alternating pattern like that of disruption and repair, repetition and renewal. Thus we might view as transformational the repeated, reparative transitions in the dyadic system: from disjunction to joining, from polarizing to including, from stuckness to throwing and catching in a back-and-forth motion, and from avoidant withdrawal or impingement to a sense of effortless movement. In the space of thirdness each person can add something to the contribution of the other, neither through compliance nor cancelling out. This movement sets the stage for but cannot circumvent or dispense with the needed force of the negative; it does not obviate the question of whether the not-me, the not-spoken, can be taken out of the shadow of dissociation and given a recognized place.

Tarrying with the negative

Insofar as interpersonal trauma commonly involves non-recognition, the lack of validation that our separate mind is valued and known by the other, we may generalize that such trauma entails a lack of differentiation between minds. In the extreme, either it is only the abuser or neglecter who possesses the power to be right or make things right, or one is thrown back on one's own mind as the only place of safety and imagined control. In this way either the mind of the other or the self is figured as absolute, omnipotent, and the relationship is one of dominance or submission. Figuratively, only one person's mind can exist; one can reflect or be reflected only by the other. Expressed in terms of the axis of intersubjectivity that charts the relation between two minds, omnipotence means there is "zero tension" (Benjamin, 1988). Mistrust is the inevitable expression of such conformity, and yet its expression may be forbidden or suppressed.

In Zizek's interpretation of the Hegelian phrase, to "tarry with the negative," the moment of negation of such omnipotence arises through identification with that which has been excluded, forbidden, marginalized and thus contains the hidden truth of a social order. Analogously, we may consider the negative to be the dissociated feelings, perceptions, "truths" that were denied because of the necessity of conforming to the other's omnipotent control or misrecognition. Precisely the negative, then, must be recognized.

Initially, psychoanalysis may offer someone who has suffered from the sense of the other whose mind was omnipotent—Mother or Father God—the opportunity to negate: to refuse, to reject what is on offer, and thereby express the mistrust that was forbidden. Testing the offer of freedom to reject or "spit out" the mother's milk relates to an important aspect of experiencing the moral Third. If the analyst's milk is offered in a reliable but non-coercive fashion that permits rejection, the spitting out then implies the possibility of having one's own mind and body, aids in acquiring power and agency. If I can spit out, it means that I don't have to eat to affirm your goodness. Fitting and accommodation, vital components for our sense of a lawful world, can only help constitute the Third when it is clear that they are not motivated by a coercive demand to make the other good.

As it turns out, this relative freedom may be figured as playing with "the breast." Winnicott's idea of the creative illusion, the baby's sense that he has called the breast and now it appears just as he wants or expects it, is an evocative metaphor for how recognition of need confirms the belief in one's own agency in a lawful universe. But this rhythm of expectation and satisfaction, important and crucial as it is, does not go as far as identifying the playful use of the breast as a Third. When a baby is no longer simply being satisfied but becomes *playful*, interrupts sucking to make facial contact, fools around and teases the mother, nips to see what she will do—the breast (or bottle) can become a Third, not owned solely by mother. This is a vital moment of negation in the recognition process, an assertion of autonomy: Baby decides how he wants to suck, pause, dribble out or swallow the milk. He does not have to guzzle it down for fear it will be taken away before he gets enough. When mother allows the baby this freedom, lets him make the breast into a shared object that neither person owns or controls exclusively, nursing becomes an experience of thirdness.

Mother is not (or not only) the Goddess, the great provider; or, as Atlas (2015) puts it, the one who feeds is not or is no longer identical with the food. The breast can become a symbol rather than a symbolic equation, part of a triangular space between mother and baby (Ogden, 1986). So the early differentiating function of play manifests as part of the rhythmicity of "Our Third," our interactive patterns of expectation and lawful relating. Mother is now distinguishable in one sense as the one to whom the breast and body "really" belongs but since she does not unilaterally dictate how it will be used it can be experienced as shared. From this perspective, protests that have been interpreted as refusal of dependency on the breast or destructive envy of it, might instead be seen as contestations of rigid prohibitions and exclusive control. As a challenge that demands recognition of the child's need to share. A patient's contesting of the analyst's sole ownership of cooking the ' food" (making meaning) would suggest a reaction to an early attachment in which he was denied a chance to co-create the breast experience, enjoy the creative illusion, play with the object.

Here we might consider a story Atlas recounts of a woman, Sophie, for whom Mother is "God." Mother alone controls all nourishment and so the daughter is used to being helpless, waiting with desperation for the Mother-Goddess to provide for her and with no breast of her own, that is, no ability to feed herself. Atlas experiences her as always asking to be fed, told what to do by an omnipotent mother. Yet because this compliance does not let her feel her own feelings or desires, Sophie also rebels against swallowing whole what her mother offers. She responds to all her analyst's formulations with: "So what good does this do?" In the absence of mirroring with a difference—the differentiating Third—no idea or feeling can truly be her own, and thus there is an absence of reflective function or enjoyment in having her own mind. She herself cannot compete with the analyst, who now represents the Mother-God, whose mind is omnipotent.

Sophie's metaphorical solution to this dilemma—introduced in a dream—is to feed herself by going out to buy fast food, rather than wait patiently for the food the analyst cooks in the kitchen. At first the potential meaning of Sophie's "resistance" is not yet visible because neither analyst nor patient are aware of a dissociated, fearful child self state that does not want to admit her resentment towards the mother who owns everything.[2] Sophie either has to swallow everything the analyst gives her or reject and spit it all out.

2　Should we call the activation of a relationship to an omnipotent parental figure an unconscious fantasy, or should we rather say that since the child state is dissociated, its fantasy is not known to the presenting self? Donnel Stern, among others, has challenged the notion of unconscious fantasy. For me, it is still a useful description of the fact that even when the child state is present it doesn't normally have the ability to depict or convey this view of the parent except in behavior; dreams, hypnosis, allow this view to be expressed directly

In my view it is significant that what might appear as rejection of the analyst's thinking expresses the dual aspect of feeling dependent on the omnipotent mother (the mysterious kitchen the patient cannot enter) and the mistrust that Sophie solves by buying her own fast food rather than cooking. Ultimately, however, Sophie expresses delight in her dreaming—her own "cooking"—and the wish to be admired for it. Atlas relationalizes the metaphor of cooking (Ferro, 2009) by recognizing the patient's wish to cook for herself, come into the kitchen with her, become a partner in the shared Thirdness, participate in an activity of two different minds (Aron & Atlas, 2015).

As Sophie's protest so aptly illustrates, negation is a vital moment in the movement towards recognition. Rejection or dismissal, at first appears to negate the possibility of co-creation and enacts the previously experienced control by an other. The child mirrors the parental omnipotence, the omniscient claim to know and determine the future, and so demands that the other or oneself be equally knowing. Often, the complementary pull of this moment initially draws the analyst into expressing an equal and opposing force. In the effort to find a way out of complementarity the analyst might do well to tarry with the negative, seek the discomfiting "truth" of the excluded self. What emerges in recognizing the protest, the spitting out, often reveals implicit aspects of the analyst's dissociated reactions as well. If we envision the recognition of negation as a contribution to the moral Third, we may be more aware of the tendency to meet resistance to our mind with counter-resistance. It is tempting for the analyst to feel that the patient rejects thinking or his separate mind, but this misses the patient's "blackwashing" his own need to think.

The idea of recognizing the negative aids the analyst in the effort to dissolve the pathological accommodation often present in the compliant use of symbolization—the "split off intellectual functioning" that does not constitute real play but only a simulacrum of a symbolic Third. After all, the ideal of all-giving maternal power marks the place of lack—lack of a thirdness in which mother scaffolds and mediates the baby's growing ability to grasp, initiate and feed herself as well as relate to the world as an intermediate space (Winnicott, 1971a). The genuine symbolic Third arises when the triangle of mother, food and baby creates that space (see Benjamin, 1995a).

Thinking, symbolization and the Third

From these considerations I have formed a view of how symbolic thirdness arises in the original relation with mother that diverges from the conventional psycho-analytic view of the oedipal triangle and so has quite different clinical implications.[3] For instance, the analyst might theorize as Britton (1988) does in terms of oedipal

---

but the "daytime" mind does not usually access it. Hence I am comfortable with the messy formulation of both dissociated states and unconscious fantasies.

3   Such a misreading of my idea of the Third as simply triangulation is present in Altmeyer (2013).

exclusion when the patient resists the analyst's thinking (see also Aron, 1995; Brown, 2011). He might associate thinking with the link of the parental couple and the rejection of thinking with fearing the intrusion of another of whom the patient is jealous.[4] The Third, in this theoretical view, is the representation of the Other (Father) with whom the patient analyst (Mother) is conversing in her mind (Britton, 1988). As I see it, although the Third may be symbolized by imagining two minds in conversation, a true Third is not exclusive or persecutory nor is it embodied in a person or thing. If the Third is conflated with a person of whom one is jealous, I would imagine this reflects a lack of intersubjective space and differentiating thirdness, which depends on the baseline of the rythmic Third of attunement.

Brittons' idea of a shaky maternal container, reflecting the lack of attunement, seems a better direction to follow. The concretization of the Third as an Other—ostensibly expressed by the patient in hatred of thinking or theory—would suggest that there is a disconnection of thinking, symbolization and reflection from affect attunement and affect regulation. In other words, a decoupling of the symbolic and the rhythmic, which might indeed be figured as an opposition between father and mother (Aron, 1995). The dysregulation and feelings of alienation need to be addressed, rather than the analyst protecting his thinking while the patient feels the analyst is not resonating with his affective state.

Expressed rejection of the analyst's thinking might lead us to consider whether there is dissociation in both analyst and patient from a source of dysregulation not yet fully identified by either, the excluded part of the patient's experience. Thus the patient's objection to thinking might indeed reflect a sense of exclusion, but this might occur because the analyst is relating to a different self/part than the

---

4   Brown (2011) offers an explicit oedipal theory of the origins of the differentiating element that makes possible the sharing of thinking between separate minds. Differentiation is seen as accomplished by separation, accepting mother as "not-mine," rather than by experiencing the affective resonance modified by the difference of marking that implicitly contains two states, two separate but related minds. Viewing separation and ability to symbolize as impeded by oedipal jealousy and rejection of a third partner reverses the order in which we develop differentiation and then symbolization, or lacking it, fear of the other partner. When the Third is seen concretely as the mother's other love object who must be painfully accepted, this misses the point of studies that Brown himself references (Brown, 2011; see Von Klitzing, Simoni & Von Burgen cited in Brown, 2011). They demonstrate intersubjectivity rather than competition in the early triad: they observe the coordinated rhythmicity of alternating attention in infants who play in tandem with the parental couple. The triadic intersubjectivity of shared play between two parents and Baby illustrates the underlying principle of sharing a Third—as when the parents alternate with one playing with Baby, one leaning back observing, and then with implicit procedural choreography, switching. As Baby turns from the interacting to the watching parent, the second now leans forward as the first leans back. This coordinated dance shows how the observational position, which is initially that of the *other parent* who admires and appreciates, still involves sharing the Third: in this fluid movement the dance is shared, the baby herself is shared (a shared Third object of attention), the roles are switched and shared. Through this the baby comes to feel part of a We, in which coordinated interaction, observation, shared attention to an object—thinking together—is possible.

patient is currently inhabiting. In other words, the person the analyst is *speaking with*—"Me"—may feel that the unlinked self-state being *spoken of*—the "Not-Me" excluded part—cannot co-exist with "Me." This might be true with a self-state that is too painful and shameful for the presenting, protector self to acknowledge. For instance, when I spoke to a patient about how she had within her an abandoned little girl, she shot back with uncharacteristic vehemence, "I hate that little girl!" Surprising both of us, it was a particularly useful moment of negation, affirming the little girl's existence while defending her present Me against being overwhelmed by her.

When the analyst feels that the link in his mind, his thinking, is being attacked, a symmetrical sense of being attacked may arise in the patient. The analyst may not grasp the threat one self-state poses to the existence of the other that is felt to be "Me," and a complementarity push-pull may ensue, wherein each person feels controlled, done *to*. The patient may well feel and act as if something alien is being forced into his mind through the symbolic portal. At the same time, the feeling of being shut out, excluded, alone, may intensify for both analyst and patient. Thus the feeling of exclusion, we could say, becomes mutual. The analyst may try to mobilize his thinking to avoid the unpleasant feeling of disconnection, of being shut out, even as the effort to hold on to his own mind may exacerbate the disconnection and intensify the painful symmetry.[5]

In sum, when the analyst feels a lack of space for his own thinking this probably should not be theorized as the patient "doing" something, such as attacking thinking or linking. It is more useful, when we feel such inability to think or link, to imagine ourselves surrendering to what is—opening ourselves to a concealed message delivered by the acting part of the patient, the something unwelcomed, unthought, unrecognized. In the complementary interaction, the patient's experience of not being understood reactivates the template of early helplessness, "this other is not thinking about me"—non-recognition of early distress.

Oedipal explanations for such complementary binds were, for much of the last century, the only ones permitted in "real" psychoanalysis. This led to a scotomization of early developmental trauma related to unrecognized distress, specifically exclusion from the mother's mind. Bion was an important exception, inasmuch as he tried to integrate oedipal concepts with a theory of maternal failure to contain in infancy. Although he is known for writing about attacks on linking and the development of thinking, using gendered references to the container and contained, Bion seemed also to be gesturing elsewhere. He wrote equally compellingly of the catastrophe of being shut out of the mind of the mother (see Bion, 1959) who lives in a seemingly intact world and does not know about the terrors of life and death that actually happen for the infant.

5   As we saw in the case discussion by Feldman (1993; see Chapter 1) the analyst may be well aware that this is taking place yet feel he is required by his theory not to "fit in" and acknowledge why the patient feels controlled. The idea of sharing the breast, the kitchen, or in his case the ice cream with the patient is not recognized as an alternative.

Interestingly, Bion wrote somewhat ambiguously that the attack on the link originates in the analyst or breast, that is, that it lies in the mother's unreceptiveness. He said that her "comfortable state of mind" in the face of infant distress is what generates hate: "peace of mind becomes hostile indifference" (Bion, 1959, p. 313). It would seem that he indeed meant that the failure to link lies in the maternal mind, an effect of her anxious, helpless reaction to the heightened arousal of a distressed infant. In my reading of Bion's formulations, the consequent exclusion of the infant from the maternal mind, her failure to contain painful affect, generates intolerable frustration and hatred. Yet, ironically, such frustration caused by lack of containing is also associated with a demand for premature thinking, in the sense that thinking serves as a kind of frustration tolerance (Bion, 1962b). Thus the *demand for thinking* (not maternal thinking itself) corresponds to a lack of provision of affect regulation, a failure of the rhythmic Third. Consequently what appears as an attack on thinking may be seen as a reaction to this excruciating condition, and only the reverie that understands the protest against the demand to tolerate deprivation and live with agony will begin to provide recognition.

The demands for an observing self to function in the absence of soothing leads to a splitting of self or a complementary dynamic in the analytic dyad, where the mistrust of thinking opposes the demand for thinking. If the analyst persists in thinking, the mistrust is then expressed and projected more violently (Ferro, 2007), as Britton famously described (Stop that fucking thinking!) and the patient feels she cannot get in. This complementary dynamic would appear as a reenactment or evocation of early failure to recognize infant distress, the basic developmental trauma, along with demand for precocious self-care. Dysregulation prevails, because symbolic thirdness has been detached from the level of soothing, affect regulation, and emotional matching, which the patient desperately needs but is not necessarily primed to receive. The patient has no choice but to negate—covertly or overtly refuse the nourishment that does not satisfy, that demands choking down the sobs of pain in order to swallow the milk as one patient described it.

Aware of how an appeal to thinking appears as a refusal to give recognition of distress, or even a demand to renounce it, the analyst might find some way of conveying her awareness that her own "comfortable and peaceful state of mind" feels dangerous to the patient. In the middle of such a moment one patient responded with a broad grin when I said to her "I've been a stupid Mommy, such a stupid Mommy!" and responded "Say it again!" This marked response was a way to meta-communicate, to acknowledge how obtuse and unfeeling I seemed at this moment in the face of the patient's urgency or pain.

It can feel in such moments of extremity for the traumatized patient as if he were about to be set on fire (or remembering it) and the analyst is talking thoughtfully about the causes of combustion. As I came to see with Jeannette, whose story follows, the problem appears to be that therapists just don't get how much destructiveness there is inside and out; our ignorance is dangerous. This ignorance also replicates a person's experience of being left to "drown" unaided by those who are "saved." Attuning to and acknowledging the powerful difference between the witness and the suffering one is a necessary preliminary step. With some truth-fulness we even might move together towards affirming a lawful Third: through honesty about our limitations and about the reality of another's suffering.

Then again it may not be possible to bypass the enactment that conceals and reveals the absence of a lawful world, in which the suffering person finds no entry to a place of safety, peace. This is where the negative action, often under cover of a joint dissociative cocoon, evolves as a co-constructed part of the dramatization of traumatic experience and failed witnessing. Yes, the history of violent trauma imbues the struggle to get into the other's mind with rage and dissociative defenses against breakdown. But the war between selves can be violent too: *the self that speaks for Me is not necessarily the self I need you to know; and it feels like only one of them can live, so at least one must die.*

PART II. TRAUMA, VIOLENCE AND RECOGNITION OF THE OTHER (ME)

Turning the kaleidoscope again, another way to assemble the interlocking shapes of negation and recognition is this: in both developmental and acute trauma, faith in the other's recognition is shattered. Simply put, the sense of a lawful world that can be trusted is blown. And this in turn places yet another stress on the distinc-tion between play and reality, one we have not yet dealt with, between what is presented symbolically in psychoanalysis and what was and is a material threat, such as violence. But given this distinction, the question of how a primarily symbolic process—psychoanalysis—can build trust in a lawful world and in the possibility of witnessing is not a simple one.

In my view, the agency to interpret and act on one's own sense of reality, includ-ing recognition of terrible things, requires some experience of the moral Third, constituted in part by the analyst's reliable witnessing. This kind of experience becomes the scaffold for the transformation of raw, chaotic elements of trauma initially appearing as enactment into forms of dramatization and play that serve shared meaning making and affective connection. In the story of Jeannette that follows, I will try to show how the effort to provide analytic recognition, stumbling and groping as it often may be, helps to foster such transformation.

Among its many effects, violence is liable to make a child confused about inner and outer reality, to foster "the omnipotence of thoughts": the inability to dis-tinguish what is imagined from reality results from "knowing terrible things" (Bragin, 2007). This confusion involves the fear that destructiveness—"bad-ness"—lies as much within as without. Bragin (2007) has contended that victims of torture may begin to fear that some hidden badness in them, their own childhood fantasies of harm, is congruent with and corresponds to the destructiveness within the perpetrator. Hence, they must in some way resemble the torturer in their familiarity with "terrible things" that others are ignorant of. This "omnipotent" belief in the power of one's own badness intertwined with the unreliability of

attachment and the failure of witnessing, leads to a magnified sense of the unlawful, untrustworthy world. Nguyen (2012), however, points out that this fantasy of
knowing is perverted by its opposite: that the bond of intimacy between torturer
and tortured—knowing and being known "in one's abject fear and pathetic bodily
functions"—creates helplessness precisely because in this knowing there is still
"no possibility of mutuality or comprehensibility . . . What is borne of this
encounter is the helplessness of not being able to assimilate another's subjectivity"
(Nguyen, 2012, p. 311).

Perhaps this helps us to think about what it means to carry such an unassimilated,
unmetabolizable version of the intimate other's subjectivity inside oneself. To have
survived childhood abuse yet walk among others as if part of the normal world,
feeling alien and "other" with respect to those who seem to inhabit a "normal"
reality, yet unable to reveal the truth of what one has suffered. Such experience
intensifies a vital question: what could another person, a "normal" person, possibly
know that would offer any connection with one's own experience? This problem,
of trying to be in the world of others, makes it necessary to split one's own self
and further complicates the matter of dissociation, the knowing and the not
knowing. There are splits in the self, between the part/self-state who feigns
normalcy (what Jeannette would call the "created self") and the one who has
suffered abuse, as well as mistrust and fear of those who do not recognize the
pretence for what it is because seemingly everyone finds dissociation preferable
to sharing real agony.

More than one me

One day a rather remarkably determined woman entered my office. Looking
somewhat deflated and speaking in a small voice, she appeared laconic, affectless
and suspicious, but somehow also managed to convey right away that I might be
the Other whom she needed, whom she was deeply afraid she might adore, and
also whom she would have to try to destroy—and so, as I only vaguely sensed,
in order to protect this person from her destructiveness and ensure her survival,
she would hold her at a distance if not to say reject her from the outset. The very
first thing Jeannette had to tell me about was her childhood experience as a
religious obsessive, and the result, her absolute mistrust of all faith, hence lack
of faith in therapy. A foreshadowing of her attitude not only towards trusting me
but also towards "the law."

Jeannette had found her way to me through my book, which she found on the
shelf of her boyfriend who collected works on sadomasochism, since he was an
avid practitioner himself. She had been playing the role of his slave intermittently
for the past 2 years. Recently, she had tried unsuccessfully to separate from him
and fallen into a deep depression. Nonetheless, she could function well enough
to keep it together as a successful professional helping the disadvantaged in the
public health system. It seemed as though because I wrote about erotic domination
she might hope I knew something about the badness, inside and out, that afflicted

her. Although Jeanette was playing the role of someone submissive, her unassuming demeanor barely concealed an extraordinarily intelligent and strong-willed person. She had obviously been far more abused than her terse speech wanted to reveal. And though she eyed me suspiciously, readily admitting that she had nothing but scepticism about therapy and mistrusted me, she seemed to have made up her mind to be as frank and direct as possible. Jeannette wanted me to know certain things, despite the pain of recounting her story and her disbelief that anyone could in fact "know."

This was 25 years ago, and psychoanalysis was not practiced in the way it is now; ideas about trauma were not part of my then recent training. I knew that traumatic experiences are followed by dissociation, and I could feel that Jeannette was very frightened even though her affective expression came across not as fearful but tough, matter of fact, if despondent. I had as yet no idea what had frightened her, but when I sought advice from a colleague, she helpfully suggested that the kind of childhood self-punishing religious practices Jeanette presented as part of her childhood were probably a sign of abuse.

Jeannette launched her tale in the first sessions immediately with her own understanding, describing herself as two people: an "outside goody two shoes," an "inside rebel." Her parents were from large, violent and impoverished families in a New England mill town, of French Canadian descent. Her father, she said, had put her on a pedestal when she was small, taking her everywhere with him to show off her brightness. But she later lost all feeling for him as he was a violent, ignorant bigot who slept with his gun under his pillow (which, as I found out, he also took out to threaten the children for "misbehaving"). Her mother she described only as clutching her rosary when Jeanette wanted to leave home at 18, the most difficult act of independence in her life, tantamount to murder. The backdrop to her current submissive practices she identified in the obsessive religious practices of her adolescence, when she would stay up all night on her knees, cut herself and wait for death. It took quite some time before Jeannette told me about her mother's violent abuse of her, beginning in infancy. Initially she said that her mother had been fair and just in not liking her for being her father's indulged favorite.

In the third session Jeannette informed me that she believed the self she was presenting to be a created or artificial adaptive self; there was an "Other Me" who had been contained, but just barely, by "This Me." Other Me was evil, all-powerful, too much for This Me, and about to get out of hand and do something highly destructive. I suggested that her master-lover had been useful to her in containing Other Me. Jeannette agreed, saying that she had thought the beating, the handcuffs, the ritual abuse would exorcise that bad self, that it might even empty her out and make her totally self-less. But This Me, whom she saw as the "created" I, kept resisting becoming a slave. To show her gratitude for my understanding and willingness to know, Jeannette brought flowers to the next session.

She then told me there were actually three selves: In addition to the bad one, there was the outer, "real world," competent but submissive self whom she called

Jane, and a whimsical, creative part who "like a fairy godmother" saved her life by telling her not to kill herself. Interestingly, it seemed that this self-state may have been assigned a crucial role, as the playful and creative one, who understood the drama of selves best, but she, like a narrator, was not named. I came to think this fairy godmother part was a persona she assigned to me as well as to her own imaginative, symbolic capacities.

Eventually, with Jeannette's help, I was able to formulate the idea that since she would present more than one self, it was up to me to try to hold these disparate selves together in my mind. However, I had not yet encountered this kind of thinking about dissociation and unlinked selves. I ought to have been more worried than I was, but I noticed that something about Jeanette's belief in my power (to understand) was oddly reassuring. My only partially formulated perception was that Jeannette was testing me and that my job was to survive, to hang in there and to learn what I could while making constant mistakes. But I sensed that surviving destruction in the Winnicottian sense was only part of the story.

Being present with Jeannette was not consonant with being an analyst, in any way I had yet known. At the time, the notion of being an analyst who uses her own subjectivity was a newly minted idea. But being with Jeannette did not feel like a space for entertaining new ideas. She directed hefty contempt at what she perceived as my professional mask and obliquely sought signs of my real person-hood, which, paradoxically, she was determined never to believe in. This made it very important that I respond directly and not conceal my ignorance—or at least not be too uncomfortable about it; and strangely, I was not . . . or only a little.

In Jeannette's world it was probably unremarkable to be flying without instruments, as I was, peering into an unknown landscape—how else would she have gotten from "Milltown" to New York and my office? And there was no contradiction between such haplessness and the omnipotent knowledge that comes with terror—those were simply different worlds of being, self-states. I was mainly required to try—or as she would later write, "grope"—to find my way. In this play she held some (or most?) of the cards, and I should try to watch carefully and gain clues as she now and then passed me a card I needed. Because she did not really want me to lose, be at a loss, even though she needed to win many hands. And as she made clear that I could not behave and speak from my therapist identity, I had no choice but to play as the one who did not know what was coming next.

The other mind and the need for no

Jeannette's ongoing expressed negation of the idea that "this process" could work or have meaning, her mistrust and doubt, were tied to the highly uncomfortable reality of my existence as an Other. My simple presence in the room could never be background. At first, all I knew was that every minute of every session was for her an intense confrontation with intersubjectivity, with the fact of an Other. There was no sense that I could recede and she might talk in some state of only partial susceptibility to my presence. Jeannette's rejection of my existence as an Other mind was too explicit to be filed under inability to play or share reverie. Anyway she could, in her tough way, though under stress these capacities sometimes collapsed. But she could also feel and articulate the horrific experience of having to be in some form of dependency or relatedness, exposing her pain. "This process would be fine if it didn't involve another person." Thus the posture of omnipotence was associated with an explicit rejection of other minds, while also keeping alive and well the paradox that I was receiving the communication, the one listening.

I believe Jeannette marked her opposition in a way that let me palpably feel that this enactment was also a dramatization of power and protection. "I know that," was Jeanette's usual response to anything new I formulated. The negative was indeed "in play"; every moment we were engaged, the ball was in play with no stopping the clock. The constant effort to reverse roles or vie for power was a clear, often conscious part of Jeannette's intent. Yet this frank power play made it possible for me to work with her, because I could grasp the rhythm of the reversal, recognize her intent without yet knowing the story behind it. While we were enacting something not yet formulated, we were also playing according to a procedural choreography and signals I thought I could follow.

Thus we hovered between enactment and explicit play, allowing the danger itself to find some expression, even though terror of any closeness set constraints on our interaction. As if replaying a moment in child development, Jeanette and I needed to find a way to play with "No" together—she would negate, and I would affirm and recognize her negation. In this way, we worked to create a space of paradox. She needed to assert: "No one can get in!" and for me to respond: "That's right!" However, sometimes unexpectedly, the experience of marking and difference can turn simple joining into real play. One day, a few months into the therapy, Jeanette said as she was standing up to leave: "I don't trust you, and my instincts are usually correct." Standing as well, I replied: "Yes! But you err on the side of caution." At the next session, Jeanette walked in and immediately said with frank admiration: "Wow! That really surprised me; it really made me think."

This moment of play with the antithetical, the need to mistrust and yet be understood and trust that understanding, illustrates the way the movement of recognition and negation form the space of paradoxical thirdness. Jeanette could feel this "safe surprise" open the window of tolerance for the other's input just a little bit, and for a moment she could surrender the fantasy of omnipotent control. My challenge to the isolation and vigilance of her protectiveness felt like enough push back— survival of her deeply feared destructiveness—that she could link minds with me in recognition. For a moment, we shifted from the mode of object management to subject-to-subject recognition, from enactment to play.

Jeannette's narration of her different selves, her appreciation of being understood, and her articulate avowal of negation were all part of her reflective function, the part of her that was not concrete. Yet, as she herself reflected, the separation of selves was hardly a metaphor. What could be told "about" these selves was told with an absence of feeling, because the sharing of states, of feelings, was out of the question.

If the posturing in our ongoing enactment appeared to be in service of maintaining a dismissive attachment towards me, its real function was to wall off self-states that were too painful or destructive to be let out. The absence of symbolization is not what dictates the need for enactment, but the existence of self-states with unbearable feelings that cannot be symbolically expressed unlike the self-states that do speak—as Jeannette had informed me. Where feeling is intolerable, where dissociation is needed to protect us from, yet also damages, the links between emotion and ideas that represent events (knowing), dramatic action may be needed. With no reliable expectation of being held and recognized by another mind, symbolic meaning is drained from representations, hence the links must be "lived" with an Other. And since what must be given life is also unbearable, to live these links with an Other requires very complex action. Action that goes to the limit in testing the possibility of safety or faith in a lawful world.

Knowing and staging—enactment and ritual healing

As we have seen, in the course of ongoing enactment in the treatment there may arise a push for something more, a drama that enables a safe enough collision of self-states to allow a real negotiation between them in interaction with the analyst (Slochower, 2006; Stern, 2009; Bromberg, 2011). In this case, Jeannette needed a transformation of the relationship between her different selves *such that the existence of one self-state did not threaten the annihilation of another self-state (or the Other who represents it)*. This "kill or be killed" relation of selves began to seem quite nearly literal for Jeannette.

The overcoming of such an opposition, a virtual reality that may feel almost as intense as the violent harm that engendered the dissociation, requires gaining access to a different kind of experience with an other. This someone should be knowing of the dangerous world of death yet also connected to the world of life and loving. It is no abstraction to say that this experience must render palpable a form of thirdness that can contain the tension of different selves, allow them to live "in peace" rather than in violent opposition, without engaging in self-harm or externalized in submission.

In writing about the experience of child soldiers and survivors of torture in war-torn countries, the analyst Martha Bragin (2005; 2007) has provided invaluable reflections on the effects of violence and what it means to be knowing and not knowing at the same time. Bragin (2007) suggests that the victim of violence survives in part by denying the power of the aggressor and instead assuming responsibility for the aggression himself. In this way, the stance of power and all-knowing serves a deeply protective function. The therapist needs to grasp how "acts of terror or torture . . . can produce rage so enormous that one is reduced to the infantile omnipotent states . . . [in which] one can fantasize that one is the creator of the universe, and that the universe that one has created is violent and perverse" (Bragin, 2007, p. 231). These fantasies of control are well-known to us through comic book characters and their film representations, but victims right-fully assume that this is not true knowing and that non-victims are not-knowing.

Bragin proposes that knowing the real consequences of this state of omnipotence (the kind of state Jeanette would later come to name "Rage") results in a special "bond between tortured and torturer." For the clinician to be helpful it is important they not humbly emphasize that they have not suffered as much, but that they admit knowing about certain kinds of badness in themselves. To leave her master and be with me, Jeanette had to believe I could know something of what she knew—the hope she had felt when she read my writing on erotic domination. But this posed the terrible dilemma that she would have to show and tell what she knew, and so actually know it to be true herself.

Healing and knowing are of course not identical. Having the opportunity to work with a team in Angola that employed both Western psychoanalytic psychologists and indigenous healers, Bragin (2005) observed the complicated ritual of healing devised for one child soldier, Pedrito. This child, who had witnessed and partici-pated in horrific violence, returned to his village orphaned and depressed and could not reenter the human community. Bragin concluded that the healer made a link to the patient through shared knowing of the world of death and violence, but also through attachment, living with and ministering to the child. The healer provided complicated rituals involving the community, similar to those in other cultures where warriors are purified before returning home. The rituals involved bringing forth the dangerous part of the self to be known. Thus the knowing acceptance of the dangerous destructive self is part of what allowed the soldier to cease being haunted (Felman & Laub, 1992; Laub & Auerhahn, 1993; Ullman, 2006; Orange, 2011).

Being a healer of violence in this world entailed being more hands-on than the witnessing psychoanalysts have described. It also meant designing the means of dramatizing both the murder and the purification. The purification included the making of reparations to the community for the damage by feeding them and thus reestablishing the soldier's sense of belonging to a lawful world. In thinking about the healer and the creation of rituals described by Bragin, I wondered how we might imagine psychoanalytic work with violent trauma to substitute for the ritual dramatization and healing. How might we make possible the enactment and caretaking of the dangerous part?

After many years to consider and reflect on Jeanette's story, I can formulate the problem for her of needing me to know enough to witness while not exposing her in an unbearable way to her own terror, something I initially did not grasp. More important, I came to see that she was struggling to find a convincing representation of the lawful world in which such terrible things could be known and judged as wrong. The problem of knowing was, in my view, linked to the need for what I now call the moral Third, and directly related to the way she needed *me* to enact something. The question of what part would I play, and not only how she would represent her different selves, had to be solved. Seemingly a born dramaturge and creator of rituals, Jeannette would intuitively construct for me the part of healer.

While I could formulate the idea of surviving destruction, playing along with power reversals, my afterthoughts suggested to me that the relinquishing of omnipotence also involved a surrender in Ghent's (1990) sense of relinquishing the false, protector self in order to liberate the expansive self; a process Milner (1969) described in which a "force to do with growth," unleashes a "creative fury" that strives despite great fear of chaos to move beyond compliant adaptation (pp. 384–385; Ghent, 1990, p. 113). I surmise that this creative fury of anti-compliance becomes more violent in direct proportion to the submission and subjugation suffered earlier. What would it take for Jeannette to give up the all-knowing and all-powerful protector self, and not feel left alone in a separate universe, one which, as Jeannette said, was dominated by the evil "Other Me," who demolished everything? Seemingly it required, as with the healer, that some other power be dramatically embodied that would represent safe attachment and lawfulness, including the possibility of repair. Surrender would need some manifestation of the moral Third, a lawful world.

Enacting war of the selves

The dramatic singular Enactment that took place between Jeannette and me was markedly distinct from our moment-to-moment engagements in the ongoing enactment involving encompassing negation or disruption and repair. One day Jeanette made a bold move, making clear to me that we were now entering different terrain: the playing out of destruction and survival. Real violence had not only blurred the boundaries between reality and fantasy, but the present moment was also truly shaking the fault lines of dissociation that, as Jeanette said at one point, had been put there for a good reason. I have no doubt that part of what led up to this was her desperate sense that she must show me what I seemingly could not get, sheltered as I was in ignorance, holding on to a naïve belief that we were doing good work within our ongoing form of play with negation.

After some time in therapy, Jeanette's dreams, thoughts and memories about violence became increasingly intense, and she began writing a journal, which she printed out for me. She started doing this after a session in which she was trying to tell me a dream but became so agitated that she repeatedly got up to leave in the middle:

> I was in my mother's house with the other kids—I'm in the bathroom, the water is on, there is a tiny baby (she shows me, the size of a hand) on the edge of the sink, and I give it a rag with some soap on it, I wash its face and the soap gets in its eyes. The baby is now afraid of me, crawling away on the edge of the sink. I throw a towel over its head. "Why did you do that," the baby asks me. "I saved you, stupid!"

As she then told me, shuddering and breathless, that she had probably been going to drown the baby, Jeannette got up to run out of the room. Instead, she stood at the door, wringing her hands and saying: "That's not my mother, that's not my mother."

The next session Jeannette handed me the first entry in her journal, which detailed her mother's murderous attacks, her obsession with Jeannette's virginity, her attempts to keep her daughter from ever leaving the house alone, and the central memory of her early childhood: her mother coming home from working at night shift, discovering that Jeannette had gone to bed without pajama bottoms (which she'd not been able to find in the laundry), and throwing her with all her might against the wall yelling: "Only whores sleep without their pajamas!"

Jeannette seemed to be handing me these pages to keep; however, I was mistaken about this. Jeannette did leave the paper in my hand, but that night wrote down her feelings about my assuming I could hold on to them. In this writing "Other Me," now given the name "Rage," appeared. Jeannette wrote:

> JB makes mistakes. She borders on not being genuine or honest. When I asked her a question, she resorted to some evasion . . . , not straightforward enough to say I'd rather not tell you . . . endless panic . . . a trap. I hate that JB kept my notes without asking. JB is just a narcissistic case-hungry user of human beings . . .

Jeannette went on to detail the idea of my taking "intellectual and clinical pleasure" in her suffering, my illusions of helping her, her fear of me hurting her. She then ironically reflected: "It gives me pleasure to dismiss JB into the whole continuum of ineffective, dangerous do-gooders, just as she relegates all the suffering people she sees to Cases."

Jeannette then shifted to self-questioning: "Is this Rage? . . . an explosive, fiery, war-like word that has nothing to do with me and everything to do with Her. *She* is RAGE personified. It could be her name." Jeannette then provided a list of Rage's childhood acts of defiance: she stole from her mother, beat her siblings with the same belt her mother had used on her; she turned on the gas, thinking she could blow up the house, she cut her body with razor blades, and swallowed a bottle of aspirin but only threw up. As a young adult, Rage had put her and others in danger, with her car, with shoplifting, and had fantasized about more dangerous crimes. Rage was both the mother and herself, one might say, the violent perpetrator as well as the terrified, defiant girl who refused to cry when her mother beat her.

This passage was followed by the account of a dream in which a friend, also with the initials JB, insisted that it was possible for Jeannette to continue driving despite very deep, seemingly bottomless, potholes in the road. Her friend said: "This is New York, there are holes everywhere, you don't let them stop you, just find a way over the hole, the car will fall into it a little, come out again, and you keep going." At the bottom of the last page, Jeannette had written: "This is YOUR copy." We discussed my keeping the pages, a mistake that I acknowledged, and its meaning. It could be said that my neglect to ask permission as to how I touched her feelings, in my eagerness to receive, was perceived as sloppy disrespect for boundaries, since to own feelings proper to the self also means to respect the other, to know that one does not own the not-self. Could Jeanette have felt my mix-up of ownership meant that such possession meant the mother may devour the baby?[6]

Jeanette's dilemma was this: the need to involve an Other meant that the Other would have to show the impact personally and so would be out of her control, thus potentially harmful and dangerous. So my devouring her suffering for my own use would confirm her fears. How was she to negotiate this paradox, to receive something from the Other (the new and needed relationship) without actually being invaded or harmed (repetition of the old relationship)? The paradox threatened to split apart in this moment of collision, compelling a choice of one side. But by providing me with a separate copy of her writing, containing both her attack and the reflections, Jeannette had helped to restore the paradox of repetition and repair. I had to recognize the attack not as a refusal of shared thinking but as a demonstration of both sides, a powerful symbolic statement that she was interested in sharing her thoughts, but not relinquishing them. In writing, she could excoriate and then repair the disruption of misrecognition. She could even provide a dream whose prospective function was to state that she would get through the holes with my encouragement.

Of course, the dreamer and the rageful writer were not on easy terms. Two weeks later, in what had now become an ongoing journal, Jeannette reflected on her divided self and her "rigid orientation to the world," which caused her to assign every experience to "one of me." Maybe, she said,

> I could think of me as ONE life composed of concentric spheres . . . As ONE person, the trade-off is, I lose the separate people I've created to maintain balance, I may be unbalanced, but I won't feel invaded . . . I will have to seek out other humans for interaction instead of being so content with my one universe of selves. Seeing myself as one allows for paradox and ambiguity.

Jeannette was beginning to approach the problem with her analytic mind, but this thinking self was not able to hold the fear and panic that one part of her might

---

6   Charles Spezzano, commenting on an early presentation of Jeannette's story, said that Jeannette, presenting to me the murderous mother in writing, was angered that I tried to hold on to it because her belief was that no therapist really wants to hold that mother. The underlying issue then was possession of each other. He asked: "Does JB mean to own that powerful feeling in Jeannette's body variously called rage, me, and mother? Does JB own Jeannette in the ultimate sense that she can kill her if she wants?" Spezzano, grasping the level of omnipotence at which Jeannette lived, could see the symbolic meaning of the gesture. This amplified what I, in the moment's heat, felt as the procedural meaning: her reacting against my appropriation, my lack of care with boundaries and with her trust in writing to me.

annihilate the other. It burst through two entries later with: "A growing sense of panic. I awoke this morning with Rage thinking, go ahead and put us all together and see what happens . . ." (It seemed remarkable to me that Jeannette could explicitly formulate this danger of giving up dissociation.) But she ended her long rumination, about whether that reasonable self was fake or becoming real, with this counterpunch against the omnipotent one: "I'm not completely destroyed by the old internal Other Me who thinks she can do anything, destroy anyone."

Surrender, submission and destruction

A week later Jeannette expressed how her growing trust in me was creating a terrifying vulnerability and activating the furious protector:

> "J. is trying to disarm me by understanding me, but I feel that she's luring me into some trap . . . I remind myself calmly that this is not coming from J. and not coming from me but from my mother."

Jeannette decided to describe for me her memories in every detail, including the origin of the sink dream: as a baby she would cry violently until she was holding her breath; as her mother could not soothe her, she followed her father-in-law's advice to fill a sink with cold water and hold the baby's head under water until she stopped holding her breath.

I at that time imagined that with Jeannette's growing ability to speak to me, to narrate her life, to use the symbolic forms of analysis, we were containing the violence and pain. I was not sufficiently alarmed. Jeannette became preoccupied in almost every entry with the idea that this effort to integrate was merely an act of will, yet it could not occur by an act of will. As if she knew acts of will and surrender were antithetical. Something else had to happen, but she did not let herself think that the something else had to do with me, with something the Other alone can do.

For my part, I had my general theory about how she needed my survival without retaliation, and that she dreaded surrender. And while I intuitively knew that a war of selves produced by violence does not allow itself to be healed by an act of will, I had not yet grasped that it required something outside the frame of what I then understood as psychoanalysis.

Soon Jeannette reported a dream in which her therapist, an unknown woman, was flayin her alive, terrifying but not painful. She added: "Finally, I'm clear about something: I'm really afraid." I also felt her dread. I felt rather than formulated that surrender to such vulnerability and risk was much too terrifying entwined as it was with her experiences of being violated.

In session not long after, Jeannette began telling me about a dream that she was being hunted down, chased through dark streets by men with rifles who intended to kill her. The frightening mood hung over us. At the end of the hour, she told me in her most detached fashion that she had been considering a plan to buy a gun so as to shoot me, that she had actually even called gun stores. I felt genuine alarm, but I decided to hold back and not respond, waiting for a space when I could think and look into my own feelings. Then, consulting with a colleague, I concluded that this revelation was to be taken extremely seriously, however not so much as a "real" threat, but as a kind of drama in which my part was exceedingly delicate. My being scared, terrified, to feel something like what she felt with her father, was my first thought, but the idea of reenacting the past seemed to be only the obvious part.

I called Jeanette that night and said that I wanted to keep seeing her, but that we could only continue if we agreed that there were certain clear limits: she could not buy a gun, she could not leave a session and harm herself or anyone else with her car, and she must call me and let me know if she had any such ideas in the future so that I could keep the therapy safe and protect both her and myself. I decided to take the rest of the weekend to think about it before saying more.

Jeannette's journal entry after this call mentioned wishing she could die, but seemingly as a reaction to her humiliation at having lost awareness of limits. Also, I believed, her continued fear that one part of her would have to be destroyed. She went on to write:

> There was wisdom in constructing the wall between RAGE, the other, and me. Walls are built for a reason. Tearing them down may be exhilarating, but the people who tear them down are not those who built the wall in the first place. I HATE RAGE. She is nothing but a crying whining hysterical, histrionic, vengeful, demanding waste of a human being. My satisfaction in putting an end to her would be splendid. I just don't know how to do it without also putting an end to me and the other one.

As to my phone call, Jeannette was ashamed that she had forgotten she could choose to keep Rage corralled and that she had the power to do so. Indeed, she reflected on her pleasure and pride in recent changes she had made, which she attributed not to her fake but her real self who was more complex and had more possibilities than she had known. However, she said it was:

> Still irresponsible to have pushed RAGE into her own corner, to have denied and to have been afraid of my own rage so fiercely that it became magnified, intensified, and incarnated in another person. I know cerebrally that the rage is mine, but I don't know if I can claim it.

Most importantly, Jeannette called me back and left a long message on the answering machine saying that she needed me to confront her with limits, as no one ever had; but that she also needed me to act from my own instincts, authentically, not my therapeutic rules.

For my part, I did get in touch with fear—but not fear that Jeannette would act out the idea of buying a gun, rather because of how serious her gesture was.

I felt a sense of risk because she was calling me to be as truthful as possible, and I wondered if I was equal to this life and death struggle. This was the moment to honestly ask myself if I could be a healer who in some way did know about life and death, knew such terrible things could happen. I was not sure. Such knowledge may be beyond me, I felt. Yet to be a witness, not to fail, to try to embrace this knowledge—it seemed I was obliged to try my best. With a sense that this was a different kind of "not-me" experience, reaching beyond my own limitations, not trying to be "good" but surrender to something unknown I was called to do, I thought about what I would say to Jeannette. I was fairly sure that I could truthfully affirm our attachment, the principle of not abandoning her; I was thinking, I am meant to feel in my own cells and understand something about the terror of her father threatening her with the gun he used to hold to the children's heads. But this also meant that I too was responsible, I had flushed out monsters, caused pain and shame that led to violence. What had my dissociation and ignorance of my own violence or shame contributed? This was confusing to me at the time.

I did, however, think about how Jeannette had grown up in a world surrounded by useless religious "moral" authorities who offered discipline and punishment, whose ideas of right and wrong were absolute and disconnected from felt experience. They had provided her with no models of taking responsibility or of acknowledgment, of true lawfulness or repair of injury. I heard her telling me that she needed me to embody *some* limit, some principle of right and wrong that I truly believed in, and that she could therefore believe in, too. This message from her was my first encounter in the context of violence with what I later came to formulate as the moral Third.

The lawful world

I opened the next session by telling Jeannette that it was not our last session and acknowledged her fear that I would give up on her. I told her that I felt the effort she was making to induce this terror in me, letting her know that I had been deeply affected by her. I recognized her need to show me not only her terror of being shot but also her terror that I would flay her alive, take away all her protective skin—thus the terror of Rage, that she would be eliminated. I said: "No part of you has to die, it will not work that way." I said that she can hold these feelings inside her or in her communication to me without literally acting them out, since after all, she was given the gift of language by her fairy godmother to partly undo the curse.

Jeannette assented to my formulations, and told me that she felt less afraid of my power now that I understood. "Understand what?" I asked. "The complexity —that there is real danger." I took this to mean that Jeannette needed me to know the limits of my power by understanding her power, the degree of her destructiveness. At some point she said in a matter of fact but playful way that she was surprised when I accepted the Christmas cookies she baked for me. Didn't I realize she might have been trying to poison me? "Of course," she quickly added,

"I would never try to kill your children, I guess you knew that." Her next journal entry stated,

> I left J.'s office feeling extraordinarily warm toward her. A secret, smiling, grounded sense of connectedness. Yuck. A sense of finally making contact with her. This process is so slow, fragile, so feeble, people can end up dead before they finally make contact . . . sad to realize that so much struggle and risk has gone into the simple act of making contact, and all in this rarified "therapeutic" setting . . . I woke up yesterday and today with a sense of space around me. Not trapped, not panicky, not afraid to move. I could feel the rungs of my spine against the floor, but no sharp daggers holding me there. I've felt this sense of space before on occasion, but it never lasts.

The dimension evoked by the images of warmth and space and a firm ground beneath suggests to me both safety and surrender, not only the differentiating aspect of the lawful world but its harmony. Jeannette's violent fantasies have not killed me; there are limits on power and destructiveness because I, another person, actually exist and she can make contact. Her protector self weighs in with disgust at her surrender: "Yuck." But the No does not stop her or undo the feeling of liberation. The knowing that is false certainty, the omnipotent knowing of catastrophe that can only imagine repetition, has been displaced by surrender to the new: a sensation of security with a protective other person, who is trying to know the catastrophe with her.

Jeannette comments a short while later on negation and the need for an ideal, in relation to me:

> J thinks that I like to keep her uninformed, in the dark, stumbling amidst obstacles in this sense-making process . . . I'm just so amazed that she eventually always finds her way back on course, that she recognizes wrong turns and misinterpretations, has the courage, authenticity and confidence to acknowledge it, that she has the fortitude to continue in spite of the obstacles, and that in spite of this being an unreal relationship, she is insistently real . . . It doesn't give me pleasure to see her groping, but it's so fascinating to watch. Besides the fact that I think wrong turns are a source of many discoveries, J is not idealized at all when she's stumbling. And since idealization is the major obstacle in my life—at the same time that it's utterly life-giving—how I idealize her (keep her unreal) or realize her (keep her un-ideal) is very important.

After this intense collision of selves, Jeannette and I began something more like what I thought was psychoanalysis. This included not only sharing and making a narrative of scarcely bearable trauma, which was at the same time an "open book" on jealousy, envy, fear, hatred and attempts at reparation or self-healing, but also her discovery of new capacities: She could express and deal with loss directly, without literally or figuratively feeling she had to kill herself. Despite moments of realizing an excruciating discomfort of simply being with an "Other," Jeannette became less preoccupied with being more than one person, her different self-states somewhat uneasily coexisting, less dramatically "other" to each other based not on willing but surrender to feeling in my presence. By this time there were available to me more ideas about dissociation, multiple selves and trauma (Davies & Frawley, 1994; Bromberg, 1993; 1994), confirming the idea of creating links between split-off selves through my recognition and holding.

I had asked Jeannette during this period of analysis if I could share what we went through as well as some of her illuminating journal, and I did so at a few meetings. But I was reluctant to publish it, excepting a brief mention to demonstrate the vital role of the moral Third and the need for a lawful world (Benjamin, 2004). Jeannette's story, her own deep reflections and writing left me with the question of what it means to know terrible things. What she told me about how important it was that I should understand my limits, the danger, the power of her destructiveness—all assumed new meaning for me as I encountered other, collective forms of violence and trauma (see Chapter 7). I came to realize even more clearly that my own capacity for such knowing is limited: my tolerance for violence, my ability to bear the suffering it causes. Because of the great reorganization of our psyches and our analytic work on trauma in the aftermath of 9/11, I was able to perceive the conflict between those limits and the escalating exposure to terrible things, and appreciate the work of my colleagues in helping me to reflect more on working with traumatic violence (see especially Boulanger, 2007; Grand, 2010). Along with so many of my contemporaries, I learned about the meaning of witnessing: that at times the most meaningful thing we can do is to express some version of the moral power that acknowledges and affirms what is lawful, what is wrong, what should never happen to a child, to a human being. We can try to represent some version of the moral Third.

But Jeannette gave me a very special opportunity to co-create with her a dramatic play, the staging of which included my performing the action of calling a halt to violence. In this way I could represent and uphold the lawfulness, the moral Third, she was seeking. Our chapter of the story had to start out in dissociation and break into reality, finding a way out of the trance-like grip of the past. I think now that this breaking out requires confronting limits in the context of the analyst's own fears and tendency towards avoidance of danger through dissociation. It is a challenge to the core of one's own belief in the process, the possibility of recognizing an other while being frightened oneself. But this fear does not only pertain to the power of harm, it also pertains to the power of healing. In addition to my understanding destructiveness and suffering, Jeannette needed me to represent the protest and power that opposes harm.

As with any co-created thirdness, I felt the transitional quality of this very serious play, that is, the sense that the script we enacted was somehow being revealed to us as well as created by us, writing itself (Ringstrom, 2007). In one sense we try to work in the transitional space without breaking the "fourth wall," while in another sense we are dealing with real damage and harm, there is bound to be ambiguity and sometimes dire uncertainty. In any given moment we can try to use our own felt responses to track shifts between self-states, between enactment and play, danger and safety, dissociation and recognition. Following along, holding in mind both the symbolic multiplicity of meaning and the rhythmic feel of intersubjective relating—moments; attending to the cycles of safety and peril, trust and mistrust, clarification and confusion—is part of the process of "playing at the edge." The edge is the cusp of what is bearable or safe, where rupture and trans-formation meet. The edge on which we balance may also be thought of as the difference between knowing about something that has not yet become real to us and knowing as recognition of a shared reality that feels in accord with our need for a Third that makes the world sane, bearable, perhaps even more. The place where knowing definitively, where knowing as openness to what is and what has happened, recognizing an other person and ourselves in our vulnerabilities and our strengths, sharing in a lawful world of thirdness, begins. Here we may find an end to warring selves, a place where more than one can live.

Chapter 7

Beyond "Only one can live"

Witnessing, acknowledgment
and the moral Third

Strangely enough, this same thought ("even if we were to tell it, we would not be believed") arose in the form of nocturnal dreams produced by the prisoners' despair. Almost all the survivors, orally or in their written memoirs, remember a dream which frequently recurred during the nights of imprisonment, varied in its detail but uniform in its substance: they had returned home and with passion and relief were describing their past sufferings, addressing themselves to a loved one, and were not believed, indeed were not even listened to. In the most typical (and cruelest) form, the interlocutor turned and left in silence.

Primo Levi, The Drowned and the Saved

In this chapter I reflect on my theory of the Third in relation to experiences travelling in parts of the world where my colleagues are struggling with the effects of violence and collective trauma either in the present or its aftermath. In addition to psycho-analytic thinking I will bring some of my experience with dialogue in the Middle East to bear on these issues.[1] This represents an effort to show the possibilities for applying psychoanalytically derived concepts to social phenomena, and suggest

---

1   From 2004 to 2010 I worked with groups of Israelis and Palestinians in the mental health and community service fields to create a project for mutual acknowledgment (see Benjamin, 2009), a project under the auspices of the Gaza Community Mental Health Programme and with the help and inspiration of Dr. Eyad el Sarraj who served as co-director of the project. During that time I travelled repeatedly to both Israel and the Palestinian territories, visiting project members individually and in smaller groups, observing as they tried to work with difficult conditions on the ground. Despite the fragility of the connection between the groups caused not only by periods of violence but also the difficulties of travel and communication, which prevented most Gaza members from attending the actual workshops, a link was established that was maintained by participants continuing to write to one another even during wartime. I am deeply grateful to workshop leaders Judith Thomson and Adin Thayer, to Uri Hadar and Yitzhak Mendelsohn for leading the Israeli team, to Mustafa Qossoqsi and Bassam Abu Omar for leading the Palestinian team, and to Avi Berman and Miriam Berger for helping with the original proposal, as well as to the Norwegian Council on Mental Health and Foreign Ministry for the grant that enabled our meetings. In addition, to all the participants and the international team members who contributed to holding the enormous tensions of the group both in person and later on line.

ways in which recognition theory can be used to grasp deep psychological structures within both collective and individual processes. My thoughts about acknowledgment and witnessing could only take shape because of the opportunity to connect with those who embodied these ideas in their practice in conditions of extreme violence and suffering. This thinking about the meaning of witnessing has acquired a different cast since the recent election of 2016 and the ensuing crisis of democracy. As permission to express violence and hatred against the vulnerable has been delivered, it has become clear to many that acknowledging the present and historical reality of violent oppression in America requires active resistance. While only a few stood up when the images of militarized police in Ferguson, the use of force against Black Lives Matter, flashed on our TV screens, now, a whole new spirit of resistance has seized a great number, who refuse to be bystanders. The question that preoccupies me is whether this movement can show an implacable will to face the truth of our society and its history without engaging in violence ourselves. Can we be as radical and forceful as we must be without subscribing to the kill or be killed ideology of our opponents. In this light, I believe the analysis of "Only one can live" remains relevant. For his inspiration, wisdom, leadership in this vision of dignity and non-violence (Benjamin, 2016b), I will always be most grateful to my friend Dr. Eyad el Sarraj, to whose memory this chapter is dedicated.

The absence of an Other who can hear[2]

In relation to the psychological consequences of collective trauma I have conceived of the failure of recognition as the problem of the "failed witness" (Chapter 2). This idea refers to a failure of those not involved in the acts of injury to serve the function of acknowledging and actively countering or repairing the suffering and injury that they encounter as observers in the social world. Gerson (2009) has described this failure most evocatively as the experience of "When the Third is dead." The witnessing function, which includes both recognizing suffering and validating the truth of what happened, is a crucial part of what I call the moral Third. Witnessing makes the Third manifest and alive in the world, attempts to restore it to life when it has been violated or denied, and thus may require that individuals or groups become actors rather than bystanders.

The psychological position of the Third, from which the violations of lawful behavior and dehumanization can be witnessed or repaired, is a fragile one. Here I undertake to ask: what makes that position of acknowledgment possible, what prevents it? What perpetuates dissociation in regard to the suffering of others ("the Other"), or even in regard to the fate of those we claim to acknowledge, claim as our own people? When people risk their social bonds and assume the burder of

---

2 One of the most cited statements in the psychoanalytic and literary discussion of trauma is Laub's (Felman & Laub, 1992): "The absence of an empathic listener, or more radically, the absence of an addressable other who can hear the anguish of one's memories and thus affirm and recognize their realness, annihilates the story" (p. 68).

disloyalty to their group's self-protection in the name of revealing truth, what makes this possible? This chapter considers the obstacles to knowing and witnessing in terms of the psychological processes involved; it considers the breakdown and restoration of the capacity to hold the connection with suffering, including our own.

I also discuss how our identification with the suffering of others can be interfered with by the identity of victimhood, in which a dissociated fear of forfeiting recognition plays a great role. In the victim position it becomes difficult to discern the difference between that form of recognition that extends universally and that which privileges one's own self-protection. Overcoming this requires a trust or belief in a form of the Third that would make it possible to move beyond protecting the self to identification with the other.

But this is a reciprocal relationship, since lack of witnessing acknowledgment may be seen as the cause of such distortion of recognition (see Oliver, 2001), the belief that only one "side" or group will be recognized. Under conditions of competition for social recognition of just claims and victim status, the risk is that of further confirming the position that one group's legitimacy or need can be acknowledged only by cancelling that of another group. My reflections are intended as an initial step in reconsidering that bind, deconstructing that logic of competition between victims which at its worst is expressed in fascist politics, or even violence, by those who feel humiliated against oppressed groups (e.g., immigrants) and their demands for recognition. It seems to me that there is a gulf here between the pragmatic, psychological manner of analyzing this problem and political philosophy; between those who have been involved in witnessing of collective trauma, working as peacemakers in non-violent social movements post-conflict or conflict reconciliation and those reflecting theoretically (Honneth, 2007) on the quandary of victimhood: that those who make claims based on lack of social recognition do not necessarily do so from a position of sharing universal democratic values that grants rights to others. My aim is to show how the pragmatic psychological experience of those in the field can enlighten theory and transform the understanding of social recognition.

I will consider how certain forms of acknowledgment and remorse between perpetrator and victims transform relations of powerlessness into those of agency. Ultimately these efforts to dignify and heal suffering also serve to affirm the possibility of lawful social behavior and responsibility for fellow human beings; they have a political meaning. The social recognition of trauma is not only healing for individuals, it promotes agency and gives weight to ethical considerations within the social discourse. Public acts of apology for injuries and restorative justice, as for instance in the memorials to genocide, encourage the development of a civic consciousness that resists state terror, racism and denigration of the weak and vulnerable and advocates for facing painful truths. The insights of psychoanalytic recognition theory should ultimately contribute to both awareness of interdependence and attachment to the social whole as well as the respect for the needs of unique and different individuals to be confirmed in their self-understanding (Allen, 2008; see also Honneth, 1995). Recognition gives validation to victims that their injury matters; but also restores the connection to truth and the social bond with the larger Third that is inevitably denied during the exercise of violence.

Some of my thinking derives from my experience working with colleagues in the Middle East where I helped to facilitate some dialogues about violence and acknowledgment. The process of reflecting on collective trauma caused by political violence and oppression is part of the daily practice of my colleagues in Israel and Palestine. Working with some of them for the better part of a decade, I found there was not only much to learn from those who endured trauma as victims but also those who participated in harming, and have recognized their part in a social reality that denies the truth of that harming (Ullman, 2011). And as in the Truth and Reconciliation process in South Africa, some have tried to engage in social healing with and provide acknowledgment for their victims.[3] I can only refer here to the contradictory outcomes of this process and the debates about reconciliation. (Hayner, 2002; Thomas, 2010). As Hamber (Hamber & Wilson, 2002; Hamber, 2008) notes: the painful experiences of victims giving testimony to truth commissions where they feel perpetrators continue to be given a free pass and they feel insecurely held; the positive experiences of testifying and being heard, and even in some cases survivors of violence who have been transformed by encounters with their former enemies, or perpetrators being a vital source of acknowledgment for their victims (see Gobodo-Madikizela, 2016).

The question as to the responsibility of individuals who are not directly implicated in violence and suffering but nonetheless informed of it daily by the media is also too vast for this short moment. There are many questions raised by this notion of witnessing (see Margalit, 2002) social and psychological (Ullman, 2006), relating to how and whether attention is paid, how and whether testimony is enabled, and how witnessing would inflect our notion of recognition to include not only the identity or rights of victims but their right to an existence outside "our" definition or construction (Oliver, 2001). My scope here is more limited, asking primarily what psychological forces are in play when such attention is granted or withheld. I proceed from the pragmatic view that "we" (who are not suffering this violence) can fail or succeed in the call to confirm through witnessing

---

3   Such instances of confrontation and engagement have deepened our understanding of the healing of collective trauma (see Hetherington, 2008) despite their limitations, as revealed by critical discussions of commissions aiming at truth or reconciliation after civil war, genocide, dictatorship and terror (Hayner, 2002; Thomas, 2010). The literature on this subject is vast. I draw especially on the work of ILAS in Chile with torture survivors (Cordal, 2005; Cordal & Mailer, 2010; Castillo & Cordal, 2014); Bar-On (1995; 2008) Laub and Auerhahn (1989; 1993), Felman and Laub, 1992 regarding Holocaust survivors; Antje Krog, Hamber (2008), Gobodo-Madikizela (2002; 2003) regarding South Africa; Qouta and Sarraj (Qouta, Punamaki & El Sarraj, 1995a) regarding Palestine; Hetherington (2008) and Verwoerdt & Little (2008) regarding Northern Ireland; Herman (1992) and Van der Kolk (2014) on trauma, and the inspiration of psychoanalytic colleagues like Judy Roth (2017) who has had the courage to testify to the suffering of families with detained children, and the members of the Study Group on Intergenerational Consequences of the Holocaust (Hammerich et al., 2016) who have delved unflinchingly into their shared past.

the knowledge of terrible things that others have witnessed, whether or not we are in a position to provide justice for the victims. While moral injury, the denial of justice, has been understood in terms of our need for recognition to affirm our sense of self (Honneth, 2007; Bernstein, 2015), it is equally important that denying acknowledgment to others damages the social fabric and our own bond to the lawful world of the moral Third, fixing both sides in the complementarity of doer and done to. In light of this, I am considering what we can learn from witnessing about the restoration of the Third, about the effects of witnessing not only for victims but also for bystanders and possibly even perpetrators. How does the giving of testimony transform and heal suffering? (see Felman & Laub, 1992; Oliver, 2001; Boulanger, 2007).

Here I have considered this question in terms of the move from discarded to dignified—viewing the dignifying of suffering as the way out of the horror of the drowned and the saved. This matter of dignifying and validating with our bystander attention, or intervention, is so crucial, while acknowledgment is so often impeded by reactions of denial and dissociation that it seems well worth asking what this giving or denying of acknowledgment entails. What kind of connection between self and other is implied by this giving or denying? What are the obstacles and prohibitions on "knowing terrible things" (Cohen, 2001; Bragin, 2007)? What processes are involved in identifying with the injury of others, what determines whether such identifications are activated on behalf of witnessing or merely supporting violence, what determines how and when the world witnesses or denies the importance of injuries that are suffered "elsewhere?" What allows the suffering of the other to get through our defenses, how does our grasp of the terrible things become embodied, visceral, a matter of urgency?

Embodied and disembodied acknowledgment

Father Michael Lapsley was speaking at a conference (Bloemfontein, 2013) at the University of the Free State in South Africa on the sequelae of the truth and reconciliation process, "Engaging the Other". Father Lapsley, who had had his hands blown off by a letter bomb as retaliation for his activism in the ANC against apartheid, began his speech by saying that what every victim of trauma wants and needs is acknowledgment. I was surprised by my reaction, how relieving his "acknowledgment of acknowledgment" was for me. Even though I had already spent so much time writing about acknowledgment as an analyst and had even developed a project to create dialogues between Israelis and Palestinians based on the idea of acknowledging injury and injustice, I nonetheless received his statement as if it were a vital confirmation I had been missing. Or as if I were hearing the idea afresh, as if indeed his testimony and experience lent to it a vital, wholly embodied meaning.

Psychoanalysts are long accustomed to noticing whether words seem empty and hollow, or embodied and resonant, that is, whether they express something already "known" in an intellectual sense, or whether they seem transmitted and apprehended with the affective force of the new, a force that reverberates throughout the many chambers of the mind and even within the body (the right brain connection that directly links one mind with another). I was now having the experience that something I thought I "knew" and even promulgated could be charged with greater meaning through being embodied by a person who has lived his convictions in the midst of great suffering and conflict. Indeed, a part of his body has been sacrificed. It was clear that Father Lapsley himself was aware of how the very act of speaking his need and that of others for acknowledgment was performative, would have an impact on the listener who would be able to identify with him precisely because he refused to deny his suffering and insisted it be dignified. His desire to impose this dignity did not seem to me to make his claims any less vital or authentic.

The psychological theorist to whom I turn to think about such processes emerged from the post-Apartheid efforts at reconciliation with a vital perspective on how both victims and perpetrators can be transformed. Pumla Gobodo-Madikizela's reflections on her work as a psychologist at the Truth and Reconciliation Commission and subsequently with victims and perpetrators have provided a framework for thinking about the more radical possibilities of reconciliation. Her writing is known, in particular her work dialoguing with the security service chief Eugene de Kock, *A Human Being Died That Night* (Gobodo-Madikizela, 2002), but her process since then has included discussions of continuing efforts at dialogue. Some of her most powerful writing relates to the spoken narratives of affectively embodied encounters with people giving testimony in the form of their personal stories about the traumatic events during apartheid and its aftermath. Combining the experiences in the Truth and Reconciliation Commission (TRC) in South Africa with studies of other reconciliation processes and engagement between former victims and perpetrators led Gobodo-Madikizela to argue for the importance of personal narrative and the story-telling approach (Gobodo-Madikizela, 2008) also developed in relation to the Holocaust by Bar-On (1995; 1998; 2008). In this process people share their experiences with collective and historical trauma and oppression in small groups. This story telling becomes a way of testifying and allowing others to witness. I begin these reflections with a story which I decided to write about despite my hesitations because it seemed to resonate with Gobodo-Madikizela's (2011; 2013) perspective on the role of embodiment, that is to say identification with body connection and intimacy in the reconciliation of victim and perpetrator. My aim here is to understand the role of these identifications in overcoming the dissociation that charecterizes the helpless bystander position, active witnessing and acknowledgment, and thus to theorize the repair of the moral Third at a personal and social level.

These events occurred on the day shortly after Christmas 2008 on which the war on Gaza, that Israelis called Operation Cast Lead, began. It so happened I was supposed to be going to Miami to spend two days on the beach. My son reached me on my cell phone in a taxi on my way to the hotel; he wanted to alert me that Gaza was being bombarded, as he knew that I had connections with people there.

I immediately called Eyad el Sarraj, founder of the Community Mental Health Programme in Gaza, with whom I had spent the last 5 years working on The Acknowledgment Project between Palestinian and Israeli mental health workers. During that time I had travelled to Gaza where I saw the conditions on the ground and met with the colleagues who were going to join the project. But he and I had also met many times in Tel Aviv where Eyad was being treated for cancer and had developed a warm friendship. He was a man so extraordinary and admirable, even to his "enemy," that he could mediate between opposing factions in Palestine, speak with leaders of Israeli security, advocate for the Geneva Accords in the ministries of Europe and for non-violence with the militants in his home country. He was known for bringing to tears an Israeli soldier who was threatening to take away his identity card and beat him by standing his ground and demanding that the young man show him his face so he could see that a human being was doing this. Like other leaders who have attained a deep realization of the connection between all human beings he could easily engage in friendships that crossed all borders of difference.

When I called Eyad's mobile phone there was never any certainty of what would be going on at the other end of the line: for example, I reached him waiting in line to cross the checkpoint into Egypt at Rafah, but we were cut off mid-sentence as I heard voices in the background; on the following day he let me know by email that his phone had been confiscated by the soldiers as he passed through. But often enough, despite having a privileged pass, he like hundreds of others waiting in line simply had to turn back. Even when dangerous things were happening, he managed to sound contained and unflappable.

I was surprised that I managed to get through to Gaza on the phone, and within moments I was reassured that Eyad was alright, but I was hearing a different quality in his usually calm voice as he reported that the situation was indeed terrible, he was listening to the bombs falling, the windows were shaking and breaking as shells landed nearby, that it was devastating everything with a force far beyond anything they had lived through before. When we hung up I was shaken, all I could think of to do was go on line to see how to send medical aid through the Israeli Physicians for Human Rights. And then since I could think of no more, went out to the beach.

When I got to the beach I had a very strange and overwhelming experience: as I walked onto the sand I found myself uneasily scanning the beach which was full of White people, and realized I was looking for, as my internal voice seemed to be saying, "other brown people like myself." I felt something not quite verbalized like "I am all alone here, there are only White people, no other people of color on this beach." As I heard this thought spoken in my mind, a reply came, this also not quite in words, "Wait a minute, YOU are White not Brown"—but this did not alter my feeling, my self-state, or my search. The self-state in which I was identified with my brown-skinned friend, identified so completely that I was stepping inside his skin. I could be aware of this strangeness to my other self, to reality. I could witness it, but I did not cease to feel it.

I gathered afterward that I was undergoing a particularly intense form of dissociation due to my helpless feeling of being unable to protect a person I deeply cared for; finding myself outside or altered through a mechanism similar to the one that allows an abuse victim to leave her body and watch herself from the ceiling. In thinking about it now, I consider the exposure through identification with a loved person to such violence had a traumatic effect of dissolving the protective wall that normally stands between oneself and the events happening far away, even when they are felt to be quite horrible. True, after my visit to Gaza I had suffered physical shock and a powerful sense of alienation and separation from those around me who were sitting in safety—ordinary conversation in a café seemed unreal in the wake of talking with families whose homes had been blasted by missiles, whose child had been killed; after driving through no man's land in the dead of night not knowing if the tanks would shoot at us; passing through the enormous steel turnstiles of the checkpoint under blinding search lights while being yelled at through a loudspeaker. But that reaction was based on my own direct experience of fear; this was based on vicarious trauma, identification with someone far away, yet emotionally close to me.

Striking was the form my identification took, one that had a specific social context and meaning in terms of race, skin and the line between the drowned and the saved. It was as if a part of myself had been seized and transformed from a familiar "safe White self"[4] into one of the unsafe, unprotected people—young Black men, refugees, migrants, camp or prison inmates—who can be abandoned or attacked with impunity because the world does not value their lives, indeed may actively devalue them. I felt the world was abandoning the trapped people of Gaza to their fate, that they were written off as unworthy of saving, and that I identified with that position in some way without my usual defenses running interference.

I decided to write about this experience because I wanted to understand the meaning of this embodied identification, for I recognized that my reaction was not necessarily identical with people actually being bombarded or suffering being outcast, ignored or mistreated based on their color or social position. It was not even congruent with what I felt as a Jew living in Germany only two decades after World War II, because there, in fact, my anxiety, which was sometimes activated in uncanny ways related to the past, was mitigated by being in reality legally and socially protected. In this case my reaction had more to do with a specific alienation from those who live in the safety of denial on the sunny beach while others are cast into the horror of destruction. The safe group's obliviousness to suffering and atrocities—read by me as denial of them—was the threat to my emotional reality (see Cohen, 2001), a threat that felt as powerful as the denial of trauma I experienced in Germany (see Chapter 2).

---

4 Coates (2015), subsequent to my writing this, wrote about whiteness in the way I was thinking of it: as an illusion of protection, invulnerability and self-realization that functions to deny vulnerability and block identification with those being harmed: "this is not happening to people like me."

This experience of identifying with someone who has been deemed not worthy of being saved had changed my relationship to the line of demarcation between the saved and the endangered, one I was familiar with from working with those who have experienced severe trauma. That demarcation often prevents trauma victims from feeling the empathy or witnessing responses of those wishing to help them (the sense of alienation felt by combatants from those outside the battle zone is well known, as is the vicarious traumatization of those who work in the field of human rights or therapy with victims of abuse and persecution) (see Nguyen, 2012; Roth, 2017). What was important here was less the line between perpetrators and victims than the line created by denial, lack of acknowledgment, between those who live in a safe protected world and those who are left to perish "elsewhere" without recourse or resources: the drowned and the saved. This division, which has become a matter of intense scrutiny in contemporary Europe due to vast numbers of war refugees seeking safety, many of whom actually have drowned, (and in January 2017 as I edit this essay even more violently experienced in the United States due to the attack on immigrants) is what I now want to interrogate further. In particular hoping this moment of dissolving identification might shed some light on how we operate when "We" live as those who are relatively safe, protected, "not the Other."

For me, growing up in Washington D.C., a racially segregated Southern city in post-war America, the sense of some humans being marginal and imperilled while others are safe and privileged was a defining experience. Despite my family's own persecution for political radicalism (including the narrowly escaped threat of my father's deportation), the anti-Semitism openly directed at me at my elementary school, and my youthful activism, I also was still living as a White: where I went to school, where I could dine, which hospital I could go to when ill, and which neighborhood I lived in were all determined by race up until my late teens. In this situation there was ample opportunity to experience what it is to identify with the "Other" while still being privileged, to choose to be a bystander or an actor, to comply with or challenge the prevailing norms, and to feel guilty for doing too little while being made an outsider for doing too much. Even as I bore the hostility of my schoolmates for protesting racial slurs and discrimination, as part of a counter-culture I could mobilize my own anger to fight back the fear I felt of their hatred, and as children do, live with wrongs they cannot right.

During both the women's liberation movement as well in the civil rights movement, many problematic aspects of claiming victimhood or guilty efforts to divest oneself of being on the side of privilege and whiteness became apparent. I began to recognize how, in these movements, guilt and moral outrage could drive people to engage in actions that were frightening or defensive efforts to shame and "guilt trip" others. As a feminist I gradually grasped the politically damaging effects of the victim position, confirming my experience in the civil rights movement of the fruitlessness of guilt as an effort to counter a perpetrator identity. Once I became a psychoanalyst, I hoped to be able to investigate the problematic of victim-perpetrator-bystander relations in a more useful way.

This is a piece of work I first undertook in *Bonds of Love* (Benjamin, 1988). Responding to the historical juxtapositions of sex, race, and class that feminists like myself were conscious of, and caught in the duality of victimhood and guilt in relation to a politics of liberation, I sought a different perspective in psychoanalysis. I began to analyze the source of reversals in complementary relations. I looked to a way to deconstruct rather than reverse the binary of doer and done to and conceptualize a position in which victims of oppression can demand liberation and empowerment without retaliatory reversal of power relations.

The politics of liberation had begun to seem inextricable from such reversals, and thus I was drawn to the idea of reconciliation as introduced in South Africa, which suggested a different way of dealing with the collective trauma of oppression. The study of reconciliation processes offered a perspective that links up with a clearer delineation of the difference between guiltiness and guilt (Mitchell, 1993) between guilt that is self-referential, based in the fear of one's own badness, and that which is coupled with concern for the other as subject (Ogden, 1989; Fallenbaum, forthcoming). It clarified for me the distinction between the effort to override guilty identifications with the perpetrator or oppressor class by adopting a counter-identification in the form of moral indignation and the effort to form an identification with suffering as an empathic witness. Although some form of indignation and anger may be absolutely essential, it became clear how this moralism might become a manic defense, employed in the service of repudiating identifications with the aggressor. Intersubjective theory could be applied to the work of differentiating forms of healing collective trauma from actions that preserve the binary opposition between oppressed and oppressor through reversal, leading to cycles of victims becoming perpetrators.

So I am going to try to track my development of the moral Third as the basis for a theoretical framework for understanding more about that moment of changing my skin, re-aligning identification based on intimacy with the one who suffered. This state of what we might call "primal witnessing," will be seen as rooted in the primary embodied relations of recognition and attachment, that is, in the rhythmic Third. In this sense the roots of the moral sensibility that resists or is repelled by injustice will be seen to lie in psychological capacities for empathy and embodied identification with roots in early experience (Singer, 2014 cited in Benjamin, 2015).

Ullman (2006), an observer of the Checkpoint Watch, which documented the practices of the Israeli occupation as well as a psychoanalyst, has made a case for the action of witnessing by those who are implicated in the harming group, who acknowledge being part of creating the destructive web in which the other is caught. I want to recast our thinking about what might constitute an ethical position in relation to the other using a notion of the moral Third grounded in the rhythmic and not only the symbolic dimension of thirdness—one which includes the conditions for witnessing based on a level of primal identification rather than mere knowledge of what is right (Ullman, 2011; Benjamin, 2011a).

While the idea of the Third or thirdness was developed to characterize the position that transcends the complementarity of doer and done to, harmer and harmed, the idea of the moral Third specified the function of *acknowledging* violation of agreed upon patterns of interaction, the reality of some wrongness. I use the term Moral Third to refer both to the mental position and the interpersonal processes that enable the repair of such breakdowns in lawfulness through dialogue, mutual understanding or atonement. Holding the tension between Is and Ought, this mental position opposes denial which collapses that distinction. It affirms what is lawful even in its absence; it affirms the value of acknowledging the truth of violations even when they cannot be undone.

The moral Third is then a position from which we can witness the dehumanization and debasing of some humans to elevate others. Let us think about how this position would become an embodied one. How would it be related to the more general idea of the Third as holding the tension between opposites or transcending binaries? We shall explore this by considering how overcoming splitting, holding the tension of oppositions, containing identifications with goodness and badness, strength and weakness, perpetrator and victim, allow us to take up the position of embodied witnesses.

In order to define the moral Third as embodied, we must introduce categories that relate not only to moral goodness and badness, but to psychologically complex constellations, not merely right versus wrongdoing but clean, safe and pure versus abject, contaminating, dangerous. There is more implied in the ability to hold opposites than merely recognizing one's own capacity for destructiveness or wrong action. There must also be an ability to tolerate the possible incursion of the badness that has been identified with the Other into the good that has been identified with the self: the so-called primitive or early feelings of discarding and projecting that which is abject, faecal, disgusting in the human body have to be countered by an acceptance of bodily or psychological weakness within self and other. Otherwise what dominates is the powerful impulse to project it outward into a vile and dangerous Other who must be kept out of the self and excluded from the group at all costs (see Theweleit, 1987; 1988). Preserving the safe pure realm of Us against the impure, dangerous Them makes violent action appear "good" rather than "bad," and so confuses the notions of right and wrong.

These oppositions of goodness and badness, deserving and undeserving, structure our relation to the problematic of who can live, whose suffering matters, who is dignified and who is discarded. These considerations of purity and danger (Douglas, 1966), primal badness and goodness require developing a more complex notion of the moral Third. It is necessary to carry the concept of the Third further into the territory of other binaries shaped by unconscious fantasy and fears of bodily disintegration (see Theweleit, 1987; 1988). The idea of recognizing the Other must include transcending the binary between weak and strong, vulnerable and protected, discarded and dignified, helpless and powerful. The Other serves the subject—relieves and props him up—by embodying the discarded, abject elements, as in the scapegoat function. Too often the negatives in this binary are opposed by ostensibly positive values, vaunted by liberation ideologies that are actually defensive, for example, invulnerable, triumphant.

The projective identification of what is bad or impure inside the self thus accompanies the perversion of its opposite term and in its repudiation of the weak, vulnerable, discarded Other the Self is made grandiose, self-righteous, and devoid of empathy. That Self is then primed to violate the Other in the name of its own purity. In the common moralizing reaction against identification with that persecutor Self, those who engage in altruistic or political efforts on behalf of victims may still unconsciously attribute to the Other all helpless vulnerability, endowing the righteous Self with (apologetic and guilty) power and safety. It is even more shocking therefore when victims reject the Other position of weakness and try to align themselves with the strength and grandiosity of the powerful Self, rather than the empathy of the righteous Self.

However, by the same token the Self that does not discard or split off weakness and vulnerability and instead poses a demand for acknowledgment of humanity can *dignify suffering*. My experience suggests that this reversal whereby the visage of dignity disrupts the conventions of power and strength can have a surprising, even electrifying effect. Thus Father Lapsley or Eyad Sarraj exemplifies the action of dignifying: in a sense, they show the way in which the embodied subject, not purified morally or physically, can overcome the splitting into discarded and dignified. This perspective leads to a notion of an emotionally grounded or embodied moral Third based on a level of primal identification with the split off aspects of vulnerability and weakness rather than merely knowledge of "right and wrong." In avoiding the reversal of power relations, rejection of the defensive use of hatred or violence have often collapsed in the face of this incapacity to tolerate vulnerability.

The reclamation of vulnerability is a dialectical move, I would argue, in the historic evolution of self-assertion by victims. We can note that earlier demands for dignity in the form of political power and agency were affected by the need to legitimate themselves through erasing the specter of suffering. This erasure often involved the substitution of an image of the empowered male hero for the traumatized victim, a denial of one's own traumatic experience with violence (see Layton, 2010; Ullman, 2011; Grand, 2012). For instance, left wing movements in the last century characteristically embraced images of masculine workers as powerful, clean, even Herculean; post-Holocaust Zionism fortified itself with contempt for victimhood and images of male heroism and military strength (Kane, 2005); in the U.S. Black Panthers marched in military fashion and anti-imperialist followers adopted the slogan "Pick up the gun!" The claims made in the name of respecting victims of abuse differ in this way from liberation struggles half a century ago, directly confronting not only social oppression but psychologically motivated violence against vulnerable victims: attacks on transsexuals, Black men crushed by the police, female genital mutilation to name a few. I assume that the single factor most responsible for this change was twentieth-century women's liberation, with its insistence on "Our Bodies, Our Selves," which brought the oppression of bodies and emotions and the problematic denial of personal vulnerability into socio-political discourse. The way was paved for that move, of course, by the sexual revolutionaries and psychoanalysts of the earlier part of the century. Despite his strong identifications with paternal authority and masculine power, Freud, always ambivalent, did his great part in liberating us to claim the explicitly embodied affective needs of the subject (see Aron & Starr, 2013).

The shift into reclaiming vulnerability is associated with the contemporary recognition of the position of witness in relation to the shattering collective traumas of the last hundred years. The witness position, as the expression of the moral Third, means that we are observing not from a safe distance of dissociation but stirred by empathy and identification. It thus depends upon our ability to hold the identification with the suffering other (see Orange, 2011). The less able we are to genuinely identify with all parts of emotional experience, the more we leave unchallenged our own propensity to identify with one side of the doer–done to opposition, of weakness versus strength. The more abstract then becomes our entry into other's experiences and the more likely we are to turn the moral Third of seeking truth and lawfulness into mere moralizing. So the position of the embodied moral Third includes this capacity for accepting multiple identifications. My argument is that the penetration of our psyches with visceral binaries of weakness and strength plays a critical part in shaping our response to collective trauma and failures of recognition, one that is as important as the global psychic position of complementarity between doer and done to, kill or be killed. Indeed, we should note that whereas those complementarities admit of no positive reversal, the reversal of strength versus vulnerability in favor of dignifying suffering has potential for transforming social relations and restoring the moral Third.

Failed witnessing: the discarded and the dignified

The pivotal function of the moral Third in relation to collective trauma is constituted by the acknowledgment of violation by the others who serve as witness. At a social level this role is played by the eyes and voice of the world that watches and upholds what is lawful by expressing, at the least, condemnation and indignation over injustice and injury, trauma and agony endured by the victims. The suffering or death of the victims is thus dignified, their lives given value. Their lives are worthy of being mourned; as Butler (2004) termed it, they are grievable lives. In other words, they are not simply objects to be discarded. Discarded or dignified becomes, in this context, the essential distinction. Given the state of media proliferation, victims the world over know whether their suffering is seen and regarded; they can ask in despair, "Why is no one paying attention as we die here?"

I have introduced this chapter with Primo Levi's poignant assertion from *The Drowned and the Saved* that every camp survivor he had ever encountered had the same dream or fantasy of returning home and telling his loved ones of the horrors they had seen and suffered; and in every case the person would be disbelieved or ignored by those by whom they so urgently needed to be heard. Levi's account, like many others, suggests that this experience of the failed witness is a central component of trauma. Without an other to hear the testimony, not only the story but the teller's sense of self is erased (Felman & Laub, 1992; Laub and Auerhahn, 1993). In psychoanalytic therapy we are accustomed to the fact that the injured child feels as betrayed by the bystander parent as by the abuser parent (Davies & Frawley, 1994). The problem of the failed witness is directly related to the division between the discarded and dignified.

Samuel Gerson (2009), in a stunning paper on "The Dead Third," took the experience of failed witnessing to mean that the person or groups feels that the social world that ought to care has disappeared and so the values of a caring world have become lifeless. Instead of recognition, there is only the unresponsiveness of the heaven that does not weep. Both the witnessing Other and the Third are dead. Working with traumatized victims shows us that this despair makes it very difficult to revive the witness function, to acknowledge in a way that is useful, because the very divisions I spoke of earlier interfere. The person who ought to witness or help appears to be on the other side of the barbed wire, and even with good intentions unable to truly take in the horror or terror known by human beings exposed to such brutality. Levi's story implies the faint-heartedness, the reflexive self-protection and anxiety on the bystander's part that lead to denial. Such reactions are merely one form of denial (Cohen, 2001), one kind of non-recognition that causes an alienation that seems beyond healing. And the inability to recognize horror, combined with the alienation it produces, can be seen as one facet of the escape from anguish that we have identified as dissociation (see Howell, 2005). The problem of dissociation, the human mind's escape when there is no escape, plagues victims as well as bystanders, the accuser as well as the accused.

The issue of self-protection through dissociation, indeed dis-association, was addressed in characteristically hyperbolic language by Rousseau:

> Though it were true that co-miseration [compassion] is no more than a sentiment, which puts us in the place of him who suffers . . . [it is] active in the savage, developed but dormant in civilized man . . . In fact, commiseration must be so much the more energetic, the more intimately the animal, that beholds any kind of distress, identifies himself with the animal that labours under it. Now it is evident that this identification must have been infinitely more perfect in the state of nature than in the state of reason. It is reason that engenders self-love . . . that makes man shrink into himself . . . keep aloof from everything that can trouble or afflict him: it is philosophy that destroys his connections with other men . . . dictates that he mutters to himself at the sight of another in distress, *You may perish for aught I care, nothing can hurt me* . . . One man may with impunity murder another under his windows; he has nothing to do but clap his hands to his ears, argue a little with himself to hinder nature, that startles within him, from identifying him with the unhappy sufferer.
>
> (Rousseau, 1755/1992, p. 21)

What Rousseau's critique of Enlightenment took aim at is the so-called rationality of self-protection, of the self-interested individual that denies social connectedness as opposed to the involuntary, unbidden identification that may justifiably be seen as a first, untutored response of our nature. It is questionable perhaps to identify empathy with our animal nature rather than human sociability, but it is clear that Rousseau sees reasoning activity—that is, the Cartesian reasoning subject related to the other as object or it—as developing through dissociative processes in the service of disconnecting, or tolerating the disconnection one has already suffered. The capacity to dissociate, to disconnect and preserve the self when need-satisfying dependency is unsafe or unavailable, is doubtless facilitated by certain forms of intellectual activity (or so, at least, neurologically informed psychologists who start with connection via the right brain as a baseline concur) (Schore, 2003; McGilchrist, 2009).

Though we might well feel a similar despair at the inhumanity accepted as normal self-interest, a less polarizing psychological position, than Rousseau's (a third position) would argue that both these self states—compassionate and self-preservative—exist in most people, and that much of our social thought struggles with how to live the conflict between them. It is from the position of the moral Third that we may admit this conflict within ourselves and struggle to transform it—not by denying the self-protective urge to turn away but by examining its sources. A powerful impetus to dissociation of harming and denial of the other's suffering is the fear of living in a world of badness. As Fairbairn proposed (1952), in a most profound analysis, it is better for the child to feel that he is "a sinner in a world ruled by God than to live in a world ruled by the Devil." (p. 66) To accept the reality of living in a world without hope of redemption, without goodness, may be too terrifying. In this sense what we think of as self-preservation relates to protection from the terror of living in a lawless world. The conflict is not merely between altruism and aggression, but between believing that repair of the world is possible or rationalizing the despair we feel when helpless to make the world good and lawful.

Only one can live

Before considering the consequences of this conflict, I want to offer a more general perspective on the complementary opposition that underlies them. I suggest that we make use of an intersubjective psychoanalytic position to extend Klein's idea of the paranoid position of splitting between good and bad objects to include splitting the world into those who may live and those who must die. I want to underscore this refraction of the kill or be killed, doer–done to analysis: living in an imaginary world in which some are saved and others left to drown, or in which "*Only one can live*," is another version of complementarity that manifests when the lawful Third—"all deserve to live"—is missing. In essence, it is the opposing term to the moral Third, its challenge and its imaginary Other.

When the Third fails, there seems no way out of this imaginary in which some are left to die except what Sue Grand (2002) called "the bestial gesture of survival." The guilt attached to survival would then evoke persecutory anxieties in Klein's sense—it would not be the guilt of remorse and making amends based on the felt humanity of the other, but the guilty fear of being cast out for transgression. Interestingly, this fear begins with the original myth of "Only one can live," the Cain and Abel myth.

Here I am reminded of conversations with Eyad Sarraj about the difficulty Israelis had in acknowledging the Nakba, the painful reality of having taken the means of life from the Palestinians in order to live. Eyad pointed out that the Israelis were afraid that if they had done something wrong, been harmers, then they did not deserve to live. This insecurity could be seen as rooted in the Nazi genocide, which produced massive survivor guilt in those European Jews who escaped—the guilt of abandoning the others to their fate. This guilt would add a layer to the feeling of guilt at harming to survive: fear of being abandoned by the world. There are more paradoxes here than I can grasp. But it appears that the fear of not deserving to live is associated with the guilty feeling of having lived, as well as needing to harm to continue living. How to reconcile the contradictory correlates of "Only one can live" when historical conditions make this fantasy into a horrifying reality? I must harm to live, and, I lived so I am guilty of the other's death, therefore I do not deserve to live. If, however, one's suffering were greater, if one had already perished—then, one would not deserve blame and paradoxically now deserve to live. Thus we enter the psychic economy in which the moral capital of suffering rules. Whoever suffers most deserves to live. If the Holocaust remains the greatest suffering, then the Israelis could feel they are still the harmed ones, not the guilty ones, and thus deserve to live.

The complementary position of "Only one can live," of being either among the discarded or the saved is often associated with a protective shell of dissociative denial about the horror suffered by the other. That shell protects the bystander from inhabiting the part of self that would be evoked by feeling the other's suffering, but also from feeling the shame of recognizing the choice not to feel. But this experience belongs not only to bystanders, as I have shown, it is part of the response of victims and perpetrators as well.

The survivor response of disidentification with those who do perish is common. The response of disidentification is a reflexive aspect of self-protection that cannot be erased by moralizing. It can arise as a manic defense against vulnerability or as a reflexive shut down in the face of pain or fear. What clinical experience with manic and grandiose states allows us to grasp is the way in which individuals rationalize their survival or success precisely in order to uphold the dissociation of their fear—fear of being left to perish by their families or community. But another matter is the etching of such responses into the collective psyche as superiority or triumph: justifying the inflicting of harm and permitting avoidable suffering as the deserved fate of the unworthy, now defined as those who fail or don't keep up in the race. The disavowal of public social responsibility for helping over harming is part of a complex process of withholding acknowledgment of injuries to victims in an unlawful world. This constitutes a form of failure to dignify suffering through witnessing that perpetuates breakdown of the moral Third. It may be seen as the *avoidable* failure, the one which enshrines the complementarity of dignified and discarded and deprives those who suffer trauma a vital ingredient in reclaiming their sense of value and agency. I would argue strongly that in many cases this deprivation is not based on material necessity, which is merely the excuse, while the cause is the wish to perpetuate subjugation and segregation of the Other.

Still, this dissociation of the others' humanity, which supports the ongoing splitting between the discarded and the deserving, is occasionally disrupted by a violent breakthrough of the real consequences of this division. I saw this occurring in vivo in 2005 when reporters in New Orleans watched in horror the conditions under which Afro-American victims of Hurricane Katrina were herded and held in the convention center with no water or medical supplies. For one short and virtually unprecedented moment members of the official media who were live on camera expressed naked personal shock and horror at the treatment of fellow citizens who were clearly being abandoned by all agencies deemed responsible for saving them (the President, the army, the national guard, the governor, the police). These reporters became real witnesses, embodying emotionally the impact of what they saw, indeed more intensely in spite of the fact that the scene they could not turn away from flew in the face of what they wanted to believe about the lawful nature of our society. Their own lawful world, the goodness they also depend upon, was cracked. This shattering of self-protective goodness allowed them to step through the breach, out of their disembodied professional roles, the customary forms of pseudo-witnessing and pseudo-Third based on dissociation and protectively cloaking the authorities' failure. This rare crack in the façade of "fair and balanced" reporting simultaneously ratified for their viewers the truth of their experience; it was in itself shocking.[5]

The rarity of this event is underscored inasmuch as we know that the general response to natural disaster is more generous and acknowledging than catastrophe caused by human malfeasance or state/social failure: disaster resulting from harming or cruel indifference often immediately sparks denial. I am suggesting that in such moments collective breakthrough of dissociation constitutes a shift out of the unconsciously held convention according to which some Other(s) is not worthy of saving so that some responsible party (the parental force) can be protected, the illusion of lawfulness maintained.

The idea of the chosen, of course, played an important part in American intellectual history. The justification of being among the "saved," calls to mind

---

5 At the same time we should note that the people trapped in the city were there because white policemen and sheriffs stood with guns blocking the bridge that led out of the flood zone on the grounds that those who were trying to escape were going to endanger their communities—a clear fantasy that that they could only survive by letting these Others drown.

our Puritan ancestors who saw each moment of good fortune as a favorable sign of being among the elect, each piece of ill-luck as assignment to the damned—justification and condemnation being a constant obsession, as Weber (1905) remarked. This effort to maintain the fiction of a lawful world of a deserving elect meshes with the guilt at turning away from the other's suffering. Together they create the ideology that those who survive when others do not are justified, chosen to be saved (if not now, then after the "Rapture"). Thus the projective efforts to disidentify with the drowned by making them the ones deserving of their fate coincides with the sense of righteousness and an intact world. From an internal point of view, the Other who is discarded is guilty of breaking the law, of dis-obeying the Father and the morality of family, church and state, he deserves his fate (Lakoff, 2016), while those who obey the Father are rightly spared this fate. However, viewed from the outside, as Brickman (2015) pointed out in a critical commentary, the exclusion from full social membership—reduction to repre-sentatives of Agamben's "bare life"—should arguably be seen as constitutive of the repressive order of the nation state, a correlate of the need to have one perish for the other to live. In this sense, the psychological premise "Only one can live" is not accidentally materialized in nationalism and imperialism.

Attacks on the moral Third

The ideas I am presenting here seemed further confirmed when I had the opportunity to hear from Chilean colleagues of their therapeutic work with sur-vivors of the Pinochet dictatorship in Chile. They have particularly elucidated for me the relationship between such justifying ideology, torture and the imaginary of "Only one can live," as well as the destruction of the Third in the name of preserving social order (Castillo & Cordal, 2014; Gomez-Castro & Kovalskys, in press).[6] ILAS has been a strong proponent of the need for social recognition, integrating this awareness into their analytic work for over 20 years. In listening over time to their clinical reports of psychotherapy with women activists subject to torture and sexual violence by the security forces during the dictatorship, I came to think that part of the hatred manifested in this vast use of torture by the defenders of the old regime reflected their envy and fear in relation to the freedom of these young activists. They were part of an international movement of cultural and social liberation, on the side of history that believed "everyone can live." Everyone could have enough to enjoy life, not to speak of the sexual revolution. The activist's refusal to betray others even under torture also embodied their belief in the social bond, that more mattered than individual survival.

6   ILAS stands for Latin American Institute for Mental Health and Human Rights. The members of this group in Santiago have kindly shared their stories and their work with me since 2004, and I am deeply grateful to all of them. See also the papers by Cordal (2005) and Castillo and Cordal (2014).

Listening to these stories I began to imagine that part of the intention of the torture was to not only break down the person but to attack the ideal and their attachment to it, to prove the "truth" of the torturer's world view, that instead everyone must choose, either to live and betray others who would be killed, or to be destroyed themselves. The hatred manifested by this regime's torture of so many thousands cannot, in my view, be explained simply by the aim of maintaining economic power. It behooves us to keep in mind the unconscious motives behind the hatred: the envy and fear of the freedom and solidarity the victims had enjoyed, which in turn led to perverse sexualized punishment of the "liberated ones." In this way the moral Third, the commitment to a principle that connects us to others in their suffering and their aspiration to all live together, was attacked. It appeared, by the same token, that when the person who sacrificed her own physical and psychic body to this principle did not receive from her own comrades the witnessing, validation and loyalty she hoped for in return, this betrayal was as psychologically destructive as the torture itself.

Conversely, ILAS describes many instances in which the Third was restored through witnessing and testimony, highlighting the value of revealing the truth (Cordal & Mailer, 2010). Revelation and confrontation with truth also plays an important role in the experience of giving testimony. The story of Valentina, whose parents were young activists at the time of the Pinochet coup, and whose fate strikingly illuminates the attack on the Third. The security police came to Valentina's grandparents and threatened to disappear the baby who was in their care while the parents were in hiding unless the grandparents revealed their daughter's hiding place. The grandparents "chose" to save their granddaughter, while their daughter and her husband were disappeared, never to return. The choice, like "Sophie's choice," was intended to make the parents complicit in their child's death, as if to project the murderousness into them, but also to make horribly clear the "truth" of their worldview, the impossibility of having more than one live.[7] Growing up with her grandmother as her mother, Valentina could not tell if her grandmother's anger at times reflected a wish that she had made the other "choice." Through the release of giving testimony she becomes able to express to her therapist the feeling of not deserving to live. The burden of feeling chosen to be saved, living at the expense of those who had given her life, had spoiled her, was like a "hidden manufacturing defect." In addition, the disappearance had been like a trauma denied—it could not be recognized until it was realized. Only when Valentina gave testimony in the making of the film did she experience a breaking through of dissociation, an awareness of the need for a "live Third" (Gerson, 2009; Castro-Gomez & Kowalskys, in press) to touch the painful truth and dissolve the

---

7 In the case of Marcela (Gomez-Castro & Kovalskys, in press) who was tortured in order to obtain information about a leader of her group, she was forced to watch the police interrogate her sisters, again, forcing her to "choose" between her comrades and her sisters.

denial of what had happened. When the actual violation is confronted without such illusion and the embodied witness courageously comes forth there awakens a palpable, powerful wish to connect with the other's suffering and affirm the value of social attachment.

Dignifying suffering, restoring social bonds

To imagine a way out of the binary of deserving and discarded requires envisioning a world governed by the Third, in which our attachment to all beings as part of the whole is honored as real. That vision of social attachment is a condition of the ethical position of the Third, and it is central to *Ubuntu*, the South African tradition that so deeply informed the Truth and Reconciliation Commission. As defined by Desmond Tutu, *Ubuntu* means:

> A person is a person through other persons . . . "my humanity is caught up, is inextricably bound up in yours" . . . a person with *Ubuntu* . . . has a proper self-assurance that comes from knowing that he or she belongs in a greater whole and is diminished when others are humiliated or diminished, when others are tortured or oppressed.
>
> (Tutu, 1999, p. 31)

Our humanity depends on reciprocal recognition of each other and of our ineluctable attachment. The belief that one's humanity depends not only on the respect one receives but the quality of recognition one gives, that indeed one's own dignity is fostered by giving recognition, is a more radical part of the *Ubuntu* perspective, an ethos which explicitly represents the position of the moral Third. From a psychological standpoint, a person potentially has the power to resist indignity by initiating dignifying relations, as Mandela famously did, even as a prisoner with one's jailers, to become the representative rather than the recipient of the recognizing action. Or as exemplified by the Native American water protectors at Standing Rock, the resistance to injustice directly calls upon the witnessing world to recognize our interconnected responsibility, manifesting the Third, that we are all parts of a great, connected whole.

From the *Ubuntu* perspective, when the world fails to witness it harms us all, for this neglect represents a tearing of the bond of social attachment. The reciprocal dependency of recognition in *Ubuntu*, a fundamental tenet of recognition theory as I see it, not only encompasses the embodied personal function of empathy or caring, but also the social symbolic function of affirming what we might call the "law of interconnectedness." There Ubuntu ethos is a powerful way imagine our mutual responsibility for maintaining the attachment to a representation of the social order, one that preserves respect for all and links our individual actions to a larger picture of the lawful world (see the work of Antje Krog, author of *Country of my Skull* (2000)).

The social symbolic law, embodied by the witness who shows respect for suffering and affirms moral injury, corresponds to practical experience. This idea of interconnectedness might sound abstract to Western ears trained in individualism, but it is something the body itself recognizes through the attachment system. The witness validates the fact that there has been a rupture of the bonds of social attachment and responsibility. But there is more to this. As Ogden (Ogden, Pain, Minton, et al., 2006) following Porges, has proposed, the first best neurophysiological response to danger and pain is to activate the social engagement system of attachment, to move towards the other. When this activation fails in response to trauma, finding our way back to the world of meaningful engagement with others through the witnessing person or world—restoring social attattchment—is itself a healing at the level of the body and the nervous system. At times, a recognizing response can therefore cause someone to be released from dissociation into contact. In this sense the acknowledgment of violation and rupture literally restores the social bond and some sense of intact subjectivity. The action by which we ask for a response, for acknowledgment, is thus an essential form of agency that restores the self even as if repairs the relation of social recognition. The intersubjective movement towards recognition and reclaiming of agency is vital to the healing of trauma (Van der Kolk, 2014).

The reciprocal relationship between calling for and providing acknowledgment has been explored in detail by Gobodo-Madikizela in relation to *Ubuntu*. When the victims' protest, outrage or testimony are heard, their function is not only that of demanding acknowledgment but also of restoring the lawful Third, the principle that we are all human, that vulnerability and suffering must be honored and met with justice—dignified rather than disdained. When we demand witnessing as well as when we provide it, we are validating the Third.

In most cases of traumatic abuse, there has already been a failure of witnessing by the passive bystander (see Staub, 2003), an abandonment by the one who should have been there (Frankel, 2002). When personal or collective trauma has been denied and the breakdown of lawfulness normalized, the victims are often pulled into oscillating assertions of doubt as to the importance of their suffering and urges towards revenge (see Urlic, Berger & Berman, 2013). There is an inverse dependency relationship between recognition and denial wherein being denied recognition may intensify vengefulness and victimhood. Often, a kind of madness is created when people feel that the truth of what is being done to them is being denied and blacked out by the world, which can lead to further violence. This sense of betrayal and lawlessness creates an impulse to demonstrate to the world through the act of violence what you have suffered. The act of violence becomes an alienated version of the act of testimony, made in the face of the indifference: when the witness fails, the victim testifies *in spite*: through his actions or even vengeance he declares "I'll show you!" to the world which has turned its face from his suffering. And even as the denial of the importance of wrongdoing towards victims breaks the social bonds of attachment, the obligation of care, it reinforces the helplessness of the bystander. The alienation and despair felt by bystanders may escape notice, as the state of helplessness is so often taken for granted that it falls into the unremarked chasm of denial.

Experience in The Acknowledgment Project

In organizing "The Acknowledgment Project" in Israel and Palestine during the height of the Second Intifada (2003–2004) one guiding idea was that the abdication of responsibility by the world constituted the frame for both the violent actions on the Palestinian side as well as the Occupation violence by the Israelis. The passivity of the world powers who had claimed to be responsible for intervening, while apparently "favoring" the Israeli side was seen not as a favor but an enabling of further violence. We organizers tried to hold in mind both the highly asymmetrical power relations and exposure to violence of the two sides (moving forward during the second Lebanon war and accompanying assaults on Gaza) and the fact that no participants on either side felt in any way protected.[8]

This failure of witnessing by the world was meant to be addressed by the presence of a large international team in the project, whose role was to literally be the Third party, the eyes and ears of the world. But the scenario that was re-enacted in our large group meetings was closer to that of the failed witness. As we allowed a large group process to occur in which much was acted out, the international team were often pressured to play the role of the failed Third, who betrays and abandons (see Frankel, 2002). However, even as the dynamic of the failed witness was enacted in the large group, and members experienced the lack of protection they felt in the presence of the other, the small groups created a very different space for acknowledgment and attachment in which the experience of the other's suffering and reality could be taken in. It became clear how the predictable narratives and group identities expressed in the large group created a barrier to that primary empathy with the suffering of the other, and thus to acknowledgment of responsibility for injury. Such responsibility had to be integrated with the careful process of listening to and receiving the other's story not as a narrative of identity that meshed with the prevailing "Us versus Them," but as affective, embodied

---

8   The evidence that being given permission to "defend themselves" was not deeply reassuring might be seen as evidence in the speech given by Israel's Prime Minister Olmert gave a speech after the bombing of civilian refugees in Kfar Khana in 2006 in which he said "Any human heart, wherever it is, must sicken and recoil at the sight of such pictures" and yet he declared he would continue the bombing because of the Holocaust experience: "And that, ladies and gentlemen, leaders of the world, will not happen again. **Never again will we wait for bombs that never came to hit the gas chambers.** Never again will we wait for salvation that never arrives. Now we have our own air force. The Jewish people are now capable of standing up to those who seek their destruction—those people will no longer be able to hide behind women and children. . . . You are welcome to judge us, to ostracize us, to boycott us and to vilify us. But to kill us? Absolutely not." Ehud Olmert, *Jerusalem Post*, 13 August 2006. At this time I wrote an open letter to Merkel and the Germans suggesting that they might better serve Israel by admitting their historical responsibility and offering to protect both sides with their own soldiers than by allowing Israel to send young men to kill and die in Lebanon. However improbable in practice, it seemed crucial to address the way that unconsciously Germans were assuaging their own guilt by giving Israel permission to be aggressive rather than offering any genuine help in reducing violence.

experience. We concluded that the conflict between the demand for recognition of identity and the acknowledgment of injury is of extraordinary importance. (For a lengthier discussion see Hadar, 2013.)

For each group, the need for recognition by the other was always liable to threaten its own precarious sense of being recognized as deserving to have its own injuries acknowledged. A struggle for recognition between groups could be triggered at any moment. Each group was afraid of losing its moral status: the Israeli members felt their diligent efforts at making reparation, expressed through ongoing political protest against the Occupation and provision of services in the West Bank, were being devalued or unrecognized. Palestinians felt they would be renouncing their moral right to have their victim status, their suffering, truly acknowledged if they acquiesced in the Israeli's need to have their goodness or suffering sanctified. The underlying premise, "Only one can live" was translated, as it so often is, into "Only one can be recognized," as in Hegel's account the struggle to the death for recognition culminates not in death but only one subject retaining his life in freedom.

By contrast, in the small group a third position could be held in which members could reflect on their role as soldiers or militants, or listen as individuals described in detail the violence they had suffered, or the anguish they felt about family members who were involved in perpetuating violence. The zero-sum struggle over recognition diminished as the small group provided a better container for arousal, in direct proportion to the experience of exposure to the other's affectively embodied expression of suffering, which enabled individuals who might otherwise become caught up in defending their identity to empathize with the other—to feel it was valuable for oneself to give and not merely receive.

Gradually the attention to group process also made clear to us how much recognition was dependent on the self-states of participants, which in turn reflected the level of containing or flooding in large and small groups. While the large group was initially more likely to encourage narratives of group identity which activated familiar patterns of victimhood, non-recognition and helplessness, the small groups with their more intimate stories could often facilitate an embodied experience of witnessing in which an individual's conflict between loyalty to national narrative or group and connection to the enemy could be recognized. In the one-on-one conversations between members of the different nationalities even more powerful experiences of witnessing occurred. Members gravitated towards these conversations, seeking out partners for dialogue whom they felt to be exactly those others they were least likely to encounter in their ordinary life, indeed often a challenge to their identity. Still, how could the conflict between competing identities and narratives be reconciled with the identification with others as suffering human beings? Could these very different self states and orientations be integrated?

While we did not conclude our project with an answer to this question, we did have some meaningful experience of the identification with the Third allowing for "standing in the spaces" (Bromberg, 1998) between these states. The identification with and attachment to the group as a container, as a Third that holds and modulates conflict, whose leaders stay connected to the idea of repair, gradually overcame the fear and despair created by collisions. Most members could sustain the tension of conflict between their national group narratives and the project's symbolic function, that of enabling acknowledgment and respect for the injuries all had suffered. But this function changed over the course of time. Attachment to the group and its function of including everyone, all the different voices and feelings, began to take precedence over the specific idea of acknowledgment. As leader, I could feel myself shifting into the position of identifying with the multiple voices rather than being swayed by the need to identify one as right. While all members were committed from the beginning to awareness of the injuries of the Occupation suffered by the Palestinians, the violent intensification of those injuries during the period of several years in which we maintained the project became even more overwhelming. The group as a whole organically evolved to meet a challenge other dialogue projects had not undertaken, to sustain contact between meetings and during the height of hot violence. Our list serve and network provided a space for expressing heartfelt anguish and remorse, support and sometimes debate during the wars in 2009, 2012 and 2014 (for a more detailed account, see Hadar, 2013).

Creating a possibility for mutual acknowledgment under conditions of such asymmetry in power on one side, injury on the other, requires holding many paradoxes. Each person struggles in their own way with a hurt, unrecognized part of self that wants to deny the other's suffering, which feels that the giving of empathy will deprive it. Each struggles with some measure of guilt or shame about their impulse to self-protection, their unwillingness to receive the pain of the other. What we found was that the injured, self-protective part is more likely to be aroused by situations in which conflicts were addressed impersonally, intellectually or politically, through narratives of justification and attempts at self-legitimation. All of these contained some level of dissociation from the concrete suffering with which they were associated and thus blocked the reception of emotionally embodied witnessing.

As affect regulation theory contends, hyperarousal (fight-flight reaction) and dissociation prevent the actual feeling and communication of specific emotions as part of an intersubjective process (Fosha, Siegel & Solomon, 2009). When recognition is demanded on the "identity channel" where only one identity can live, it cannot actually be received from the other. The person captive to the doer–done to narrative seeks the self-affirmation of being right, not recognition. The failure of witnessing becomes a two-way process, as the shutting down of receptivity to the other matches the lack of empathy. The rhythmic thirdness of resonance and connecting through affect is missing. Despite much discussion about the varied success of truth commissions, the healing effect of testimony when victims feel they are truly listened to has been deemed an important transformation of the helplessness of trauma by any number of practitioners from all fields (Felman & Laub, 1992; Herman, 1992; Minow, 1998; Gobodo-Madikizela, 2000; Van der Kolk, 2014).

However, since the matter of how victims are heard is so complex, I do not wish to make a claim for one form of reconciliation, testimony or witnessing. Even though I am emphasizing a form of embodied, expressive acknowledgment and witnessing that functions to break through denial of suffering and vulnerability, I want to be clear that this does not replace nor is it commensurate with receiving officially legitimated acknowledgment of a symbolic kind.[9]

I do want to conclude here by remarking on the fact that restoration of democratic rights is supported by acknowledgment. Furthermore, as we learned in our Acknowledgment Project, it is possible to create social forms of thirdness that mediate between personal witnessing and attachment to identities and narratives, which otherwise become abstract and dissociated in the language of social rights. My conclusion is that political discourse aiming at social justice would do well understand how the language of justice and rights can be reconnected to the language of suffering and mutual acknowledgment. I do not believe it is possible even theoretically to sunder the psychology of reciprocal recognition at the level of individual attachment from reciprocal recognition at the level of social rights and obligations. Acknowledgment of wrong doing that needs to be put right is a common impetus in both the earliest individual experiences of repair and later reparation of social injustice. Thus a veteran of the Iraq war who went to support and join in the ceremony of apology to the Native Americans at Standing Rock spoke of his need to repair and help to right the wrongdoing that had deeply troubled him in his war service. The urge to repair the world proceeds from our earliest minute experiences with acknowledgment and recognition even though it may join us with millions. Thus, while there are surely grounds for differentiating between the individual and societal discourses on acknowledgment, the value of thinking of them as isomorphic will be illustrated in what follows as we take up the matter of creating or repairing the moral Third, as in the idea of repairing the world or moral community.

Dignifying suffering and restoring the moral Third

Gobodo-Madikizela's contention is that in the wake of injustice and oppression the victims' protest, testimony and claiming of the right of redress have a function not only of demanding acknowledgment but also of restoring the moral community. In this sense, the victim is able to repair the moral Third, to contribute to repairing the world, even though the loss of loved ones can never be undone. At least the loved one is not dishonored and demeaned by denial. The demand to

9 In 2004, when the Chilean Torture Commission interviewed and received the testimony of thousands of survivors of Pinochet's torture, a member of the commission relayed to me the story of a chief legal advocate, working closely with the President of Chile at the time, who said that despite even the President knowing what he had suffered during imprisonment, not until he told the commission his story did he feel truly heard and relieved. Many individuals were relieved when the Chilean army took responsibility and apologized after the Commission's report was released; others experienced the revival of painful memories as their truth was confirmed and testimony made public (Cordal, 2005; Cordal & Mailer, 2010; Castillo & Cordal, 2014).

be heard is reparative insofar as it affirms the principle that we are all human, that vulnerability and suffering must be honored and met with justice rather than disdained. Both in demanding witnessing as well as in providing it, the appeal to the moral Third affirms its validity.

In her extraordinary accounts of the meeting between perpetrators and victims Pumla Gobodo-Madikizela has shed light on the process of healing collective trauma and restoring the moral Third. Gobodo-Madikizela's work argues for the value of restorative justice over prosecution, calling upon Desmond Tutu's renowned promulgation of reconciliation and forgiveness. She believes that a new form of subjectivity is created in the intersubjective dialogue of the reconciliation process (Gobodo-Madikizela, 2015). Her direct observations of remorse and acknowledgment by apartheid perpetrators have led her to unusual convictions about the strength of the *Ubuntu* ethos and the embodied aspects of the rhythmic Third (Gobodo-Madikizela, 2013). Her primary study described her encounters with the security chief Eugene de Kock whom she wrote about in *A Human Being Died That Night*. De Kock was responsible for many deaths and did not receive amnesty, was sentenced to 200+ years of prison. Sometime after her work with him De Kock requested to meet wives of the men he had commanded to be killed and expressed his remorse to them, saying, "I wish I could bring your husbands back." One victim said she "was profoundly touched by him, especially when he said he wished he could bring our husbands back" (Gobodo-Madikizela, 2003, p. 17).

Gobodo-Madikizela shows how facilitating remorse through the offer of potential forgiveness changes the consciousness of the perpetrator but also the nature of the social bonds surrounding the violence. She describes a form of restorative justice in which the forgiveness is deeply appreciated by the perpetrators as restoring their bond with the community.[10] An ongoing story that has been shown in several films (see *One Day After Peace*; Laufer & Laufer, 2012) is that of a Black commander of an armed group of the ANC that attacked a café and killed a young White girl, whose mother wished to forgive him for her own peace of mind. The Black PAC commander Letlape and the militants who carried out the attack explain how this mother of the slain girl, Gin Foure, "gave us back our humanity."[11] The need to make amends in order to heal one's own monstrousness

---

10 The function of re-integrating individuals into community and healing social bonds is the leading argument for the Gachacha process in Rwanda as well. In regard to those processes there is considerable debate about effectiveness, whether perpetrators try to escape justice, and outcome. No system of justice has prevented some individuals from "getting away with it" while others truly repent or compromise. Here my purpose is to explore a psychological function within a social institution in terms of the effect on collective trauma and the sense of moral community.

11 From the film interviews and speeches in *One Day After Peace*, (Laufer & Laufer, 2012) a film about the Israeli peace activist from Bereaved Families, Robin Damelin, who went back to her native South Africa from Israel after her son, doing reserve duty, was slain by a sniper, in order to explore how reconciliation processed violence.

often becomes pressing and irresistible once the dissociative trance of combat is dispelled. However, the protective shell of ideology may continue to protect the dissociative stance. It is noteworthy that Letlape did not appear at the TRC because he refused to renounce his actions, arguing that even civilians were settler colonialists. Foure accepted his political position but insisted upon reconciling with him nonetheless. They agreed they would set up a foundation that would help young men, former militants, be re-integrated into society, and Letlape proposed that they name it after Foure's daughter. By the time he is shown in the film, Letlape is fully connected to Foure and her suffering; he is visibly moved when Foure tells her story publicly, despite having heard it so many times, and he tells us that each time it causes him pain on her behalf.

In the aftermath of these initial events Gobodo-Madikizela described (2006) how when the Gin Foure was invited by Letlape to give a speech at a ceremony welcoming him back to his rural village (a conscious process of re-integrating former warriors), she came with her sleeping bag as she was to stay in his sister's hut and did not wish her to have the arduous work of washing the sheets. But the next morning, after hearing that this was why the sheets were not slept in, the sister expressed disappointment "I did not intend to wash the sheets, I wanted to sleep in the sweat of the woman who forgave my brother."

The power of this story of forgiveness is its visceral metaphor of skin and sweat as recognition of the other's humanity and kinship, exemplifying the overcoming of bodily separation on which we found our dissociation from the other's pain. It links the power to confer dignity through the smallest gesture, a singular act of intimate aid or communication, with a moment of transgressing the ordinary boundaries and conventions of society—it is a striking metaphor for abandoning self-protection in favor of the intimacy between others, strangers. And it is a display of *Ubuntu* ethics that powerfully expresses the position of the Third: a challenge to the normal dissociation of the perpetrator's suffering and need for rehumanization and thus more broadly to the separation of individuals in which self-interest is paramount. It becomes clear how dignifying the suffering and its redress provides a different basis for humanizing both perpetrator and victim. It also shows how the effects of the TRC carried beyond its institutional reach, in lending power to the ethos of reconciliation.

Upon hearing my account of the story of Letlape and Foure as well as Gobodo-Makizela's analysis, which I presented to a psychoanalytic meeting in Israel a few months after the 2009 Gaza war, some Palestinian members of our Acknowledgment Project were inspired to articulate in a powerful way how they as victims had the power to forgive, to be a moral force, to become *agents*. The idea of transforming victimhood, that is, dignifying it as a position from which to recognize the other, emerged as we reflected through the lens of Gobodo-Madikizela's insights on the difficulties of the workshop process. This idea of the politically weaker side's power to give something the other side urgently desired—recognition of their efforts to repair, their pain at having harmed—had been difficult to grasp in the live heated action of our dialogue project, because it required a recognition of how being on the powerful side, as bystander or in some cases as perpetrator, compromises one's feeling of humanity. That is, it requires empathy with the perpetrator's loss, which in itself presupposes moving out of the complementarity of power-powerlessness where the goal is to reverse positions. The vision of dignified victims is one in which they draw upon the power of the moral Third, understanding that the one who has harmed needs recognition of his humanity. The dignified victim affirms that all necessarily participate in an interdependent system of reciprocal recognition.[12]

The idea of the perpetrator being "given back their humanity" by the victim's forgiveness may be usefully compared to the bystander being given agency by allowing her or him to serve as a witness and provider of acknowledgment. After the Gaza war one of the Israeli team leaders—whose members remained in touch across the lines by email all through the war—reflected on his need to witness and be allowed to give his solidarity. He spoke of gratitude for friends and colleagues in Gaza putting up with his persistent calls to find out how they were doing, his asking perhaps irrelevant questions, enabling him to feel his humanity, that he was not an indifferent bystander, and thus part of the harming.

The experience of moving from the paralyzing guilt of the bystander, the helplessness to protect those in harm's way, to the more active position of the witness may be seen as part of a wish to repair the world, even when it is no longer possible to repair the concrete injured other. In it lies a yearning to connect to the social world beyond one's own self-interest and validate the social attachment that can overcome enmity. These aspects of non-violent sensibility have been expressed repeatedly by activists who reach across the divide despite the overwhelming violence, injustice and lack of juridical resolution, because such actions lessen the feeling of helplessness through connecting with the other.

For perpetrators, acknowledging the human bond with the victim may allow them to feel partially returned to themselves, to inhabit a human status in which their own vulnerability is included. Such action, again, transforms the binary of powerful versus helpless, for when the formerly helpless can take action to recognize the vulnerable human being hidden within the killer their own dignity can be reclaimed. The "monstrous" side of the powerful, for whom the calculus of killing has been cloaked in the unquestioned justification of self-protection and survival, is exposed when the victims are no longer discarded "collateral damage" but real humans. In forging a new bond of empathy with the suffering and embodied other, however, those who have harmed are no longer protected by the dissociation from suffering their own monstrousness. Suffering arises not only

---

12 One member described going through a checkpoint in a car with his family, being harassed by and forced to wait unnecessarily by a soldier, despite having a "VIP" pass. When the soldier finally waved them through, the man's baby son who had been wriggling in the back seat waved back at him—causing a look of confusion and consternation on the soldier's face. After a moment's pause, in which he clearly tried to process how he could be perceived as a human in this moment, he waved back to the baby.

from being injured but also from being the one who harms—thus the binary that denies one's vulnerability is transcended. The horror associated with the realization of having "blood on one's hands," the sense of being contaminated, were expressed by one former combatant who asked: how could these hands ever hold a baby? What if a soldier like myself wanted to marry my daughter? (Shapira in Singer, 2014). This thought broke through his initial numbness at having killed. Accepting both the painful reality that the Other was human and his own self-hatred led this former combatant to struggle with how his body had been altered through killing, to realize that overcoming victimhood through violence had placed him on the side of the perpetrator.

Embodying the Third

Returning to the beginning of this chapter, I have tried to suggest how we might view the embodied, affectively realized rather than dissociated self-state as part of the reconstruction of the Third in the wake of trauma. Embodiment in this sense requires, as Gobodo-Madikizela (2013) has stressed, making public spaces intimate. She illustrated this with her discussion of the Gugulethu Seven mothers, who engaged with a Black police collaborator who had caused the death of their sons. The seven young men, the Gugulethu Seven, were shot after being entrapped in a situation where they believed they were going to become resistors, arms were given to them by the police agent provocateur, and they were then immediately killed. One mother of the slain sons spoke of feeling the pain in her womb even as the women and the perpetrator spoke of being parents and son. In expressing his remorse to them, the perpetrator addressed them as his mothers. Gobodo-Madikizela (2011) described the common use of the term for the bodily connection of the umbilicus, to describe certain kinds of relations. Relating to my conceptualization, she suggested that this aspect of the rhythmic Third founds the moral Third, representing in the language of the body the empathic connection to the suffering of others (Gobodo-Madikizela, 2013).

The move from dissociated to embodied language and affect creates a Third in which the binary of perpetrator and victim, invulnerable and vulnerable breaks down, as the suffering body itself is dignified through acceptance of pain. This dignity changes the psychic position in relation to the abject and the monstrous. Whereas, as Kristeva (1982) illustrated in her theory of abjection, the abject becomes the discarded, even faecal, part object that the controlling subject denies dignity, once pain is dignified and re-admitted to awareness it is the dissociated denier of bodily pain who is felt to be monstrous (see Grand, 2002).

However, we all have a monstrous side, a side that wants to escape and deny pain, as well as a side that identifies with inflicting pain and transgression. Bragin (2003) discussing clinical work with torture victims, speaks of the importance of the witnessing analyst also "knowing terrible things" so that the patient does not feel left alone with what she knows not only of what others can do, but of her own violent identifications with the aggressor. The shame felt by war torture and rape victims, she contends, may be not only a result of being victimized and degraded but also of perverse identification with the inflicting of bodily harm and degradation. In my view, such appearance of identification is part of a dissociative response to the helplessness in the face of horror, which nonetheless feels unspeakably shameful and frightening.

This psychoanalytic perspective suggests another powerful reason for the feeling of guilt, even monstrousness, as bystanders; we have to continually rediscover not only the remorse of failing to witness, but the fact that denial is based on the unwillingness to know these terrible things about ourselves: we monstrous humans. To reclaim the position of witness and restore the lawful Third ultimately requires a tension between "I could never imagine doing such a thing" and "I could imagine doing it." Accepting badness and the reality of hatred as a force in social life is a part of the journey for those who actually expose themselves to human rights violations, collective trauma and indeed horrors with the hope of witnessing or actively helping. Acknowledging the reality when hatred and destructive feelings threaten to overwhelm our polity seems especially relevant at this historical moment.

In the meeting between the Gugulethu Seven Mothers and the collaborator who turned them over to their murder at the hands of the police, the victim's mother shows her grasp of this difficult truth when she prefaces her forgiveness by saying, "We all are sinners." Her forgiveness comes from the position that it is human to harm, that everyone has to accept the potential within themselves to hurt another. We might notice that she is giving herself the moral authority to declare this universal dilemma in the very moment where she is called upon to forgive and thus surrender to the reality of What Is, what cannot be undone—a very compelling representation of the Third. To forgive in this way constitutes the acceptance that vengeance cannot restore what has been lost. But we notice that this acceptance is not an individual feat, it is highly dependent on the presence of the witness, the structured ritual intended to provide acknowledgment within the protective container of the group.

I observed the effect of integrating this aspect of witnessing when Eyad spoke to a meeting of the Israeli group in The Acknowledgment Project a few months after the Gaza war. It was clear that he was speaking both personally and also as a representative of victims to those who felt themselves to be representatives of the perpetrator group. The members of the group were paralyzed by guilt, what they consciously expressed were feelings of helplessness and despair of making a difference. Sarraj spoke from a place of connection rather than dissociation of his pain and that of his listeners. He stated that of course he was very angry about the destruction, but recognizing the terrible position in which they found themselves he wanted to share his conviction that the only way to deal with their feeling of badness and helplessness was to accept that each of us has bad and good within us—in effect, not to be immobilized by the part of themselves that identifies with the fear and self-protectiveness that motivated their nation's aggression. He said that knowing he also has this badness, fear, and potential for destructiveness it is his experience that when you truly accept both sides you will not be paralyzed, you will be able to act again in a positive way. His simple speech released the Israelis from their grim despair, because his self state of surrender to What Is helped shift their self states, from resistance and struggle to acceptance. This state based in a surrendered self-forgiveness implicitly offered a relation to the moral Third, including the capacity to see the subjectivity of the Other, that liberates the potential for agency.

His action came from a deep understanding that accepting both perpetrator and victim sides of self, goodness and badness, breaks down the fictitious line between those who deserve mercy and hence to live, and those who do not; those who consign others to die and those who perish. This is what generated his previous formulation of the Israeli fear that if they are guilty of being in any way like those who harmed them, they do not deserve life (see Benjamin, 2009). By contrast, the recognition of our victim and perpetrator identifications together, re-associated as it were, creates the equivalent of remorse for having denied the other's humanity without the complementary reversal in which now one's own person must take up the position of unworthy to live. True remorse takes us to the third position beyond "Only one can live."[13]

I am suggesting that the remorse of those who acknowledge harming sharply contrasts with the passive bystander attitude because it does embrace the identification with the precarity of the other. Where Butler (2004), following Levinas, argues that our response to the precarity of the vulnerable Other should, in order to be ethical, be free of identification, I believe the identification with our own precarity is part of what counters our inevitable tendency toward dissociation. Since, to paraphrase Rousseau, all the passive bystander philosopher requires as he flees from feeling the horror in imagining that he or his child could be murdered at will by any policeman who stops him in traffic is to think "This is not happening to me," I would argue that we might start by imagining, "This is happening to me." I do not see how we can bypass this identification if we accept the necessity of recognizing a shared human condition of vulnerability. The more so, since most acts of violence we would abjure proceed from the effort to escape that very identification. Remorse and recognition of our wishes to escape both the painful identification with vulnerability and the hateful projection of it into the Other seems to be a starting point for a psychoanalytically informed ethics of a world where more than one can live. In this regard there is much to be learned from those who have accepted the loss and suffering wrought by violence, who have experienced the reality of hatred and destructiveness on their own bodies,

---

13 In the film *Moving Beyond Violence* (Singer, 2014), a former Israeli soldier and a former Palestinian prisoner reflect on the complex emotional process whereby they came to renounce violence, recognize the humanity of their enemy as well as their own remorse at harming, and reject the victim status that has been part of the conventional narrative justifying violence. (For a discussion of Israeli soldiers "Breaking the Silence" see Botticelli, 2010).

whose narratives and testimony lift our dissociation and provide a dislocation from conventional positions along the line of doer and done to, dignified and discarded.

A conclusion in time of crises

Between the time of writing this essay and its editing, the election in America brought to power the frightening and destructive figure of Trump. This event has aroused an historically unprecedented surge of popular uprising, accompanied by powerful emotions regarding the need for a lawful world and recognition of our need for social protection and connection. The vigorous assertion of the need to resist, to overcome denial—or as we are currently calling it, "normalization"—especialy of persecution, hatred and destructiveness has made bystanders into activists. For this moment of crisis much of the business-as-usual dissociation regarding the fate of the marginal and vulnerable seems to be replaced by widespread concern, anxiety and urge to defend the lawful world where more than one can live. I can only hope that this will to defend and protect grows and transforms us. In closing this chapter and this book I will note that the tearing of the veil of denial to expose the painful truths of American history seems to be engaged in a way I have never previously experienced, even in the Vietnam war. The sentiment of the movement to resist the breakdown of democracy feels more like a reckoning, more an attempt to face a frightening reality than the blame or reproach that were indulged in safer times. It is in light of this that I have some hope that the idea of the Third by whatever name will find new, practical expression.

From the standpoint of psychoanalytic recognition theory, I would argue that efforts to think about repairing the world and restoring the Third require a psychological understanding, too often spurned by philosophical and political theory, of the effects of collective trauma and what it means to overcome splitting and dissociation in relation to harming and suffering, power and helplessness, humiliation and indignity. From this admittedly psychological point of view, the principle of repair through acknowledgment in individual attachments is isomorphic with that expressed in relation to social injustice, despite the language that assigns them to separate domains (as in Honneth 1995). The common thread of repairing ruptures and admitting violations that need to be put right, unites the healing of social and communal bonds. The rejection of wrongness or unfairness is an impetus common to early individual repair and later reparation of social injustice. For instance, a veteran of the Iraq war who went to support Native Americans at Standing Rock and join in a ceremony of apology for historical violations spoke of his need to engage in an action that would put right the wrongdoing that had deeply troubled him in his war service. The urge to repair the world, though it may join us with millions, is a response that originates in the same psychic impulse that manifest in early efforts to repair and restore the Third through acknowledgment and recognition.

While acknowledgment processes do not substitute for material justice, political resolution of violence, economic reparation and social responsibility for the fate of victims they can help to de-escalate political power struggles fueled by fears of being left discarded and unrecognized because some Other appears to be "cutting in line." The function of the Third—representing a lawful world in which more than one can live—needs to be socially embodied in genuinely protective institutions. Failing that, we will continue to struggle against persecutory anxieties attached to the fear that Only one can live.

On the one side, political efforts aiming for restoration of rights or reparations to those who have been harmed (slavery, colonization, persecution, genocide) need to be supported by acknowledgment that tangibly and incontrovertibly affirms that this wrongness happened. However, opposing this process is the intense fear, as in regard to race in America, of admitting the truth of harming because the loss of goodness is intolerable to the rigidly organized psyche. The fear of losing goodness expresses itself as a sense of being unfairly attacked, rather than being asked to take responsibility. And the consequent denial of harming then makes people vulnerable to a larger anti-democratic strategy to retain power by inciting competing narratives of victimization. Absent the social and political forms of thirdness that mediate between testimony of suffering and demands for justice while offering practical means of making amends, the attachment to identity becomes organized by the imaginary battle of "Only one can live." For this reason, even in the political arena, where this battle is inflamed and exploited by demagogues like Trump, the effort to counter dissociation of harming requires more than the abstract language of rights. It needs to include the idea of recognizing the humanity of the other and the fact of harming as respect for suffering, an invitation to redress harming. The movement of political resistance developing in this historical moment already shows interesting signs of uniting the discourse of justice with the dignifying defense of the vulnerable, the demand to have repressed voices heard, the anthem "I Can't Keep Quiet," that speak forcefully to the desire for recognition. What political movements for transformation can learn from social healing, witnessing and reconciliation is how to testify and witness as a shared process of strengthening our recognition of both psychological and material harm. Ultimately, when realized, the aim is to create agency and conviction on behalf of a lawful world and oppose the insidious effects of denial.

Efforts to create acknowledgment have allowed us to reclaim vulnerability, to understand how to dignify suffering, and so come to understand how acknowledgment helps to alleviate it. While acknowledgment can certainly be offered from above, and social recognition provided by public apologies is very meaningful to victims, embodied experiences of testimony that take place in an intersubjective matrix where recognition is demanded from below gives victims the possibility of recharging the bond of social attachment in themselves and others, exercising agency on behalf of a lawful world.

Conversely, denial of the effects of an imaginary based on discarding some while saving others reinforces the harming, erases the fact that the law has been violated, degrades victims. In social psychological terms we need to assert the reality of suffering, to dignify it with the recognition it deserves, to allow those who have suffered to move out of victimhood into agency. The limitation on this recognition is the acknowledgment of responsibility by the harmers, which alone can enable those who have harmed or acted out of self-protection to move out of paralyzing guilt into reparation. In this way, recognition, by reincorporating acknowledgment of responsibility, may help to own and ameliorate the suffering that comes from denial; help to mitigate the corruption of social bonds, and restore the moral Third that gives human life dignity beyond mean survival. To imagine a way out of the binary of deserving and discarded in which Only one can live requires the vision of a lawful world in which our mutual attachment to all parts of the whole is honored. Both harmers and harmed need the moral Third of "All can live" to replace the frightening world in which "Only one can live."

Bibliography

Adorno, T. W. (1966/1973). *Negative Dialectics*. E. Ashton (trans.). New York: Continuum.

Ainsworth, M. D. S. (1969). Object Relations, Dependency and Attachment: A Theoretical Overview of the Mother–Infant Relationship. *Child Development*, 40: 969–1025.

Ainsworth, M., Blehar, M. C., Waters, E. & Wall, S. (1978). *Patterns of Attachment: A Psychological Study of the Strange Situation*. Hillsdale, NJ: Lawrence Erlbaum Associates.

Allen, A. (2008). *The Politics of Our Selves: Power, Autonomy, and Gender in Contemporary Critical Theory*. New York: Columbia University Press.

Altmeyer, M. (2013). Beyond Intersubjectivity: Science, the Real World, and the Third in Psychoanalysis. *Studies in Gender and Sexuality*, 14: 59–77.

Ammaniti, M. & Gallese, V. (2014). *The Birth of Intersubjectivity: Psychodynamics, Neurobiology and the Self*. New York: Norton.

Aron, L. (1991). The Patient's Experience of the Analyst's Subjectivity. *Psychoanalytic Dialogues*, 1: 29–51.

Aron. L. (1992). Interpretation as Expression of the Analyst's Subjectivity. *Psychoanalytic Dialogues*, 2: 475–507.

Aron, L. (1995). The Internalized Primal Scene. *Psychoanalytic Dialogues*, 5: 195–237.

Aron, L. (1996). *A Meeting of Minds: Mutuality in Psychoanalysis*. Hillsdale, NJ: The Analytic Press.

Aron, L. (1999). Clinical Choices and the Relational Matrix. *Psychoanalytic Dialogues*, 9: 1–30.

Aron, L. (2006). Analytic Impasse and the Third. *International Journal of Psychoanalysis*, 87: 344–368.

Aron, L. & Atlas, G. (2015). Generative Enactment: Memories from the Future. *Psychoanalytic Dialogues*, 25: 309–324.

Aron, L. & Benjamin, J. (1999). *Intersubjectivity and the Struggle to Think*. Paper presented at Spring Meeting, Division 39 of the American Psychological Association, New York.

Aron, L. & Starr, K. (2013). *A Psychotherapy for the People: Toward a Progressive Psychoanalysis*. New York & London: Routledge.

Atlas, G. (2011a). The Bad Father, the Sinful Son, and the Wild Ghost. *Psychoanalytic Perspectives*, Fall 11, 8(2): 238–251.

Atlas, G. (2011b). Attachment, Abandonment, Murder. *Contemporary Psychoanalysis*, 47: 245–259.

Atlas, G. (2013). What's Love Got to Do With It? Sexuality, Shame and the Use of the Other. *Studies in Gender and Sexuality*, 14(1): 51–58.

Atlas, G. (2015). *The Enigma of Desire: Sex, Longing and Belonging*. London: Routledge.

Bach, S. (2009). Remarks on the Case of Pamela. *Psychoanalytic Dialogues*, 19(1): 39–44.

Baraitser, L. (2008). Mums the Word: Intersubjectivity, Alterity, and the Maternal Subject. *Studies in Gender and Sexuality*, 9: 86–110.

Baranger, M. & Baranger, W. (2008). The Analytic Situation as a Dynamic Field. *International Journal of Psychoanalysis*, 89: 795–826.

Baranger, M., Baranger, W. & Mom, J. (1983). Process and non-Process in Analytic Work. *International Journal of Psychoanalysis*, 64: 1–15. Also in L. Glocer Fiorini, (Ed.) (2009). *The Work of Confluence* (63–88) London: Karnac.

Bar-On, D. (1995). *Fear and Hope: Three Generations of the Holocaust*. Cambridge & London: Harvard University Press.

Bar-On, D. (1998). *The Indescribable and the Undiscussable: Reconstructing Human Discourse After Trauma*. Budapest: Central European University Press.

Bar-On. D. (2008). Toward Understanding and Healing through Storytelling and Listening: from the Jewish–German Context After the Holocaust to the Israeli Palestinian Context. In O'Hagan, L. (Ed.), *Stories in Conflict: Toward Understanding and Healing*. Derry, UK: Community Foundation for Northern Ireland.

Bass, A. (2003). "E" Enactments in Psychoanalysis. *Psychoanalytical Dialogues*, 13: 657–675.

Bassin, D. (1996). Beyond the He and She: Toward the Reconciliation of Masculinity and Femininity in the Postoedipal Female Mind. *Journal of American Psychoanalytic Association*, 44S: 157–190.

Bataille, G. (1976). Hegel in the Light of Hemingway. *Semiotext[e]*, 2: 12–22.

Bataille, G. (1986). *Eroticism: Death and Sensuality*. San Francisco, CA: City Light Books.

Bateson, G. (1972). *Steps To an Ecology of Mind*. New York: Ballantine.

Bateson, G. (1956/1972). Toward a Theory of Schizophrenia. In Bateson, G. *Steps to an Ecology of Mind*. New York: Ballantine.

Beebe, B. (2004). Faces in Relation: A Case Study. *Psychoanalytic Dialogues,* 14: 1–51.

Beebe, B., Jaffe, J., Markese, S., Buck, K., Chen, H., Cohen, P., Bahrick, L., Andrews, H. & Feldstein, S. (2010). The Origins of 12-Month Attachment: A Microanalysis of 4-Month Mother–Infant Interaction. *Psychoanalytic Dialogues*, 12(1–2): 3–141.

Beebe, B. & Lachmann, F. (1994). Representation and Internalization in Infancy: Three Principles of Salience. *Psychoanalytic Psychology*, 11: 127–165.

Beebe, B. & Lachmann, F. (2002). *Infant Research and Adult Treatment: Co-Constructing Interactions*. Hillsdale, NJ: Analytic Press.

Beebe, B. & Lachmann, F. (2013). *The Origins of Attachment: Infant Research and Adult Treatment*. New York & London: Routledge.

Beebe, B. & Stern, D. (1977). Engagement–Disengagement and Early Object Experiences. In Freedman, N. & Grand, S. (Eds.), *Communicative Structures and Psychic Structures*. New York: Plenum Press.

Beebe, B., Sorter, D., Rustin, J. & Knoblauch, S. (2003a). A Comparison of Meltzoff, Trevarthen, and Stern. *Psychoanalytic Dialogues,* 13: 777–804.

Beebe, B., Sorter, D., Rustin, J. & Knoblauch, S. (2003b). An Expanded View of Intersubjectivity in Infancy and Its Application to Psychoanalysis. *Psychoanalytic Dialogues,* 13: 805–841.

Benhabib, S. (1992). *Situating the Self.* New York: Routledge.

Benjamin, J. (1977). The End of Internalization: Adorno's Social Psychology. *Telos,* 32: 442–464.

Benjamin, J. (1988). *The Bonds of Love: Psychoanalysis, Feminism, and the Problem of Domination.* New York: Pantheon.

Benjamin, J. (1995a). *Like Subjects, Love Objects: Essays on Recognition and Sexual Difference.* New Haven, CT: Yale University Press.

Benjamin, J. (1995b). Recognition and Destruction: An Outline of Intersubjectivity. In *Like Subjects, Love Objects* (27–49). New Haven, CT: Yale University Press.

Benjamin, J. (1995c). The Omnipotent Mother, Fantasy and Reality. In *Like Subjects, Love Objects* (81–115). New Haven, CT: Yale University Press.

Benjamin, J. (1995d). What Angel Would Hear Me? The Erotics of Transference. *Psychoanalytic Inquiry,* 14: 535–557. In *Like Subjects, Love Objects.* New Haven, CT: Yale University Press.

Benjamin, J. (1995e). Sympathy for the Devil: Notes on Aggression and Sexuality with Special Reference to Pornography. In *Like Subjects, Love Objects* (175-212). New Haven, CT: Yale University Press.

Benjamin, J. (1996). In Defense of Gender Ambiguity. *Gender and Psychoanalysis,* 1: 27–43.

Benjamin, J. (1997). Psychoanalysis as a Vocation. *Psychoanalytic Dialogues,* 7: 781–802.

Benjamin, J. (1998). *Shadow of the Other: Intersubjectivity and Gender in Psychoanalysis.* New York & London: Routledge.

Benjamin, J. (2000a). Response to Commentaries by Mitchell and Butler. *Studies Gender & Sexuality,* 1: 291–308.

Benjamin, J. (2000b). Intersubjective Distinctions: Subjects and Persons, Recognitions and Breakdowns: Commentary on paper by Gerhardt, Sweetnam and Borton. *Psychoanalytic Dialogues,* 10: 43–55.

Benjamin, J. (2002). The Rhythm of Recognition: Comments on the Work of Louis Sander. *Psychoanalytic Dialogues,* 12: 43–54.

Benjamin, J. (2004a). Beyond Doer and Done-To: An Intersubjective View of Thirdness. *Psychoanalytic Quarterly,* 73: 5–46.

Benjamin, J. (2004b). Revisiting the Riddle of Sex. In I. Matthis (Ed.), *Dialogues on Sexuality, Gender and Psychoanalysis* (145–172). London, UK: Karnac.

Benjamin, J. (2005). From Many Into One: Attention and the Containing of Multitudes. *Psychoanalytic Dialogues,* 15: 185–201.

Benjamin, J. (2006). *Our Appointment in Thebes: The Analyst's Acknowledgment and the Fear of Doing Harm.* Paper presented at IARPP Conference, Boston.

Benjamin, J. (2008). *Mutual Injury and Mutual Acknowledgment.* Lecture in honor of Sigmund Freud's birthday, Sigmund Freud Verein, Vienna.

Benjamin, J. (2009a). A Relational Psychoanalysis Perspective on the Necessity of Acknowledging Failure in Order to Restore the Facilitating and Containing Features of the Intersubjective Relationship (the Shared Third). *International Journal of Psychoanalysis,* 90: 441–450.

Benjamin, J. (2009b). Psychoanalytic Controversies: Response to Sedlak. *International Journal of Psychoanalysis*, 90: 457–462.

Benjamin, J. (2009c). Mutual Injury and Mutual Acknowledgment Under Conditions of Asymmetry. In Heuer, G. (Ed.) *Sacred Violence. Essays in Honor of Andrew Samuels*, London: Karnac.

Benjamin, J. (2010). Can We Recognize Each Other? Response to Donna Orange. *International Journal of Self Psychology*, 5: 244–256.

Benjamin, J. (2011a). Acknowledgment of Collective Trauma in Light of Dissociation and Dehumanization. *Psychoanalytic Perspectives*, 8(2): 207–214.

Benjamin, J. (2011b). Facing Reality Together Discussion: With Culture in Mind: The Social Third. *Studies in Gender and Sexuality*, 12: 27–36.

Benjamin, J. (2013). Thinking Together—Differently: Commentary on Philip Bromberg. *Contemporary Psychoanalysis,* 49(3): 356–379.

Benjamin, J. (2015). "Moving Beyond Violence": What We Learn from Two Former Combatants About the Transition from Aggression to Recognition. In Gobodo-Madikizela, P. (Ed.) *Breaking Intergenerational Cycles of Repetition. A Global Dialogue on Historical Trauma and Memory*. Leverkusen: Verlag Barbara Budrich.

Benjamin, J. (2016a). Intersubjectivity. In Elliott, A. & Prager, J. (Eds.) *The Routledge Handbook of Psychoanalysis in the Social Sciences and Humanities* (149–168). London: Routledge.

Benjamin, J. (2016b). Non-Violence as Respect for All Suffering: Thoughts Inspired by Eyad el Sarraj. *Psychoanalysis, Culture and Society*, 21: 5–20.

Benjamin, J. & Atlas, G. (2015). The "Too Muchness" of Excitement: Sexuality in Light of Excess, Attachment and Affect Regulation. *International Journal of Psychoanalysis*, 96: 39–63.

Bernstein, J. M. (2015). *Torture and Dignity. An Essay on Moral Injury.* Chicago, IL: University of Chicago Press.

Bersani, L. (1977). *Freud and Baudelaire.* Berkeley, CA: University of California Press.

Bersani, L. (1985). *The Freudian Body: Psychoanalysis and Art.* New York: Columbia University Press.

Bion, W. (1959). Attacks on Linking. *International Journal of Psychoanalysis*, 40: 308–315.

Bion, W. (1962a). A Theory of Thinking. *International Journal of Psychoanalysis,* 43: 306–310.

Bion, W. (1962b). *Learning from Experience.* London: Heinemann.

Black, M. J. (2003). Enactment: Analytic Musings on Energy, Language, and Personal Growth. *Psychoanalytic Dialogues*, 13: 633–655.

Bohleber, W. (2010). *Destructiveness, Intersubjectivity and Trauma: The Identity Crisis of Modern Psychoanalysis.* London: Karnac.

Bohleber, W. (2013). The Concept of Intersubjectivity: Taking Critical Stock. *International Journal of Psycholoanalysis*, 94: 799–823.

Bollas, C. (1989). *Forces of Destiny: Psychoanalysis and Human Idiom.* London: Free Association Books.

Bollas, C. (1992). *Being a Character: Psychoanalysis & Self Experience.* New York: Farrar, Strauss & Giroux.

Boston Change Process Study Group [Stern, D. N., Sander, L. W., Nahum, J. P., Harrison, A. M., Lyons-Ruth, K., Morgan, A. C., Bruschweiler-Stern, N. & Tronick,

E. Z.] (1998). Non-interpretive Mechanisms in Psychoanalytic Therapy: The Something More Than Interpretation. *International Journal of Psychoanalysis*, 79: 903–921.

Boston Change Process Study Group [Bruschweiler-Stern, N., Lyons-Ruth, K., Morgan, A. C., Nahum, J. P., Sander, L. W., Stern, D. N., Harrison, A. M. & Tronick, E. Z.] (2005). The "Something More" than Interpretation Revisited: Sloppiness and Co-Creativity in the Psychoanalytic Encounter. *Journal of American Psychoanalytic Association*, 53: 693–729.

Boston Change Process Study Group [Stern, D. N., Sander, L.W., Nahum, J. P., Harrison, A.M., Lyons-Ruth, K., Morgan, A.C., Bruschweiler-Stern, N. & Tronick, E.Z.] (2010). *Change in Psychotherapy: A Unifying Paradigm.* New York: Norton.

Boston Change Process Study Group (2013). Enactment and the Emergence of New Relational Organization. *Journal of the American Psychoanalytic Association.* 61: 727–749.

Botticelli, S. (2010). The Politics of Identification: Resistance to the Israeli Occupation of Palestine. In Harris, A. & Botticelli, S. (2010) *First Do No Harm: The Paradoxical Encounters of Psychoanalysis, Warmaking, and Resistance.* New York: Routledge.

Botticelli, S. (2015). Has Sexuality Anything to Do with War Trauma? Inter-generational Trauma and the Homosexual Imaginary. *Psychoanalytic Perspectives*, 12(3): 275–288.

Boulanger, G. (2007). *Wounded by History.* New York and London: Routledge.

Bowlby, J. (1969). *Attachment and Loss: Vol. 1. Attachment.* New York: Basic Books.

Bowlby, J. (1973). *Attachment and Loss: Vol. 2. Separation: Anxiety and Anger.* New York: Basic Books.

Bragin, M. (2005). Pedrito: The Blood of the Ancestors. *Journal of Infant Child and Adolescent Psychotherapy*, 4: 1–20.

Bragin, M. (2007). Knowing Terrible Things: Engaging Survivors of Extreme Violence in Treatment. *Clinical Social Work Journal*, 35: 229–236.

Brennan, T. (1992). *The Interpretation of the Flesh.* New York: Routledge.

Breuer, J. & Freud, S. (1895). *Studies in Hysteria.* In Standard Edition, vol 2, London Hogarth, 1957.

Brickman, Celia. (2015). *The Law of Bare Life and the Alternative Oedipal Register.* Paper Delivered at Division 39 Spring Meeting, April 2015, San Francisco.

Britton, R. (1988). The Missing Link: Parental Sexuality in the Oedipus Complex. In R. Shafer (Ed.) (1997), *The Contemporary Kleinians of London* (242–258), Madison, CT: International University Press.

Britton, R. (1998). *Belief and Imagination.* London and New York: Routledge.

Britton, R. (2000). *Internet Discussion of Britton's Work.* Panel "On Psychoanalysis" sponsored by Psybc.com.

Bromberg, P. (1998). *Standing in the Spaces: Essays on Clinical Process, Trauma, and Dissociation.* Hillsdale, NJ: Analytic Press.

Bromberg, P. (2000). Potholes on the Royal Road – Or is it an Abyss. In *Awakening the Dreamer: Clinical Journeys.* Mahwah, NJ: The Analytic Press.

Bromberg, P. (2006). *Awakening the Dreamer: Clinical Journeys.* Mahwah, NJ: The Analytic Press.

Bromberg, P. (2011). *The Shadow of the Tsunami: and the Growth of the Relational Mind.* New York: Routledge.

Brown, L. (2011). *Intersubjective Processes and the Unconscious: An Integration of Freudian, Kleinian and Bionian Perspectives*. New York: Routledge.

Brown, N. O. (1959). *Life Against Death: The Psychoanalytic Meaning of History*. Middletown, CT: Wesleyan University Press.

Buber, M. (1923/1971). *I and Thou*. W. Kaufman (trans.). New York: Scribner.

Bucci, W. (2003). Varieties of Dissociative Experiences A Multiple Code Account of Bromberg's Case of William. *Psychoanalytic Psychology*, 20: 542–557.

Bucci, W. (2008). The Role of Bodily Experience in Emotional Organization: New Perspectives on the Multiple Code Theory. In Anderson, F. S. (Ed.) *Bodies in Treatment: The Unspoken Dimension* (51–75). New York: Routledge.

Butler, J. (1997). *The Psychic Life of Power: Theories in Subjection*. Stanford, CA: Stanford University Press.

Butler, J. (2000). Longing for Recognition: Commentary on the Work of Jessica Benjamin. *Studies in Gender and Sexuality*, 1: 271–290.

Butler, J. (2004). *Precarious Life: The Powers of Mourning and Violence*. London and New York: Verso.

Casement, P. (1991). *Learning from the Patient*. New York: Guilford.

Castillo, M. & Cordal, M. D. (2014). Clinical Practice with Cases of Extreme Traumatization 40 Years After the Military Coup in Chile (1973–1990): The Impact on the Therapist. *Psychoanalytic Dialogues*, 24: 444–455.

Celenza, A. (2007). Analytic Love and Power Responsiveness and Responsibility. *Psychoanalytic Inquiry*, 27: 287–301.

Celenza, A. (2014). *Erotic Revelations: Clinical Applications and Perverse Scenarios*. London: Routledge.

Chasseguet-Smirgel, J. (1985). *The Ego Ideal*. London: Free Association Press.

Chodorow, N. (1976). *The Reproduction of Mothering: Psychoanalysis and the Sociology of Gender*. London: University of California Press.

Christiansen, A. (1996). Masculinity and its Vicissitudes. Reflections on Some Gaps in the Psychoanalytic Theory of Male Identity Formation. *The Psychoanalytic Review*, 83(1): 97–124.

Civitarese, G. (2008). Immersion Versus Interactivity and Analytic Field. *International Journal of Psychoanalysis*, 89: 279–298.

Coates, T.-N. (2015). *Between the World and Me*. New York: Spiegel & Grau.

Cohen, S. (2001). *States of Denial: Knowing About Atrocities and Suffering*. London: Polity Press.

Cooper, S. (2000). Mutual Containment in the Analytic Situation. *Psychoanalytic Dialogues*, 10(2): 169–194.

Cooper, S. (2010). *A Disturbance in the Field: Essays in Transference–Counter-transference Engagement*. New York: Routledge.

Corbet, K. (2009). *Boyhoods: Rethinking Masculinities*. New Haven, CT: Yale University Press.

Cordal, M. D. (2005). Traumatic Effects of Political Repression in Chile: A Clinical Experience. *International Journal of Psychoanalysis*, 86: 1317–1328.

Cordal, M. D. & Mailer, S. (2010). *Social Recognition. ILAS Working with Trauma Survivors in Chile*. IARPP, San Francisco, April 2010.

Cornell, D. (1992). *Philosophy of the Limit*. New York: Routledge.

Cornell, D. (2003). Personal Communication with the Author.

Crastnopol, M. (1999). The Analyst's Professional Self as a "Third" Influence on the Dyad: When the Analyst Writes About the Treatment. *Psychoanalytic Dialogues*, 9: 445–470.

Davies, J. (1998). Multiple Perspectives on Multiplicity. *Psychoanalytic Dialogues*, 8: 747–766.

Davies, J. (1999). Getting Cold Feet, Defining Safe-Enough Borders: Dissociation, Multiplicity and Integration in the Analyst's Experience. *Psychoanalytic Quarterly,* 68: 184–208.

Davies, J. (2001). Erotic Overstimulation and the Co-Construction of Sexual Meanings in Transference-Countertransference Experience. *Pschoanalytic Quarterly*, 70: 757–788.

Davies, J. (2003). Falling in Love with Love: Oedipal and Postoedipal Manifestations of Idealization, Mourning, and Erotic Masochism. *Psychoanalytic Dialogues*, 13: 1–28.

Davies, J. (2004). Whose Bad Objects Are We Anyway? Repetition and Our Elusive Love Affair with Evil. *Psychoanalytic Dialogues*, 14: 711–732.

Davies, J. & Frawley, M. (1994). *Treating the Adult Survivor of Childhood Sexual Abuse: A Psychoanalytic Perspective.* New York: Basic Books.

DeMarneffe, D. (2004). *Maternal Desire: On Children, Love and the Inner Life.* New York: Little Brown.

Derrida, J. (1978). Violence and Metaphysics. In A. Bass. (trans.). *Writing and Difference.* Chicago, IL: University of Chicago Press.

Dimen, M. (2003). *Sexuality, Intimacy and Power.* Hillsdale, NJ: The Analytic Press.

Dinnerstein, D. (1976). *The Mermaid and the Minotaur.* New York: Harper and Row.

Douglas, M. (1966). *Purity and Danger: An Analysis of Concepts of Pollution and Taboo.* London & New York: Routledge & Kegan Paul.

Ehrenberg, D. (1992). *The Intimate Edge.* New York: Norton.

Eigen, M. (1981). The Area of Faith in Winnicott, Lacan and Bion. *International Journal of Psychoanalysis*, 62: 413–433.

Eigen. M. (1993). *The Electrified Tightrope.* Lanham, NJ: Jason Aronson.

Eldredge, C. B. & Cole G. W. (2008). Learning from Work with Individuals with a History of Trauma. In Anderson, F. S. (Ed.) *Bodies in Treatment: The Unspoken Dimension* (79–102). New York: Routledge.

Elise, D. (2001). Unlawful Entry: Male Fears of Psychic Penetration. *Psychoanalytic Dialogues*, 11: 499–531.

Ellman, S. J. & Moscowitz, M. (2008). A Study of the Boston Change Process Study Group. *Psychoanalytic Dialogues*, 18: 812–837.

Faimberg, H. (2005). *The Telescoping of Generations: Listening to the Narcissistic Links Between Generations.* London & New York: Routledge.

Fairbairn, W. R. D. (1952). *An Object-Relations Theory of the Personality.* New York: Basic Books.

Fallenbaum, R. (Forthcoming). *In an Unjust World: Race and History in Psychotherapy.*

Fanon, F. (1967). *Black Skin, White Masks.* New York: Grove Press.

Feldman, M. (1993). The Dynamics of Reassurance. In Shafer, R. (Ed.) *The Contemporary Kleinians of London* (321–344). Madison, CT: International University Press.

Feldman, M. (1997). Projective Identification: The Analyst's Involvement. *International Journal of Psychoanalysis*, 78: 227–241.

Felman, S. & Laub, D. (1992). *Testimony: Crises of Witnessing in Literature, Psychoanalysis and History.* New York & London: Routledge.

Ferenczi, S. (1933). Confusion of Tongues Between Adults and the Child. In Ferenczi, S. (1980). *Final Contributions to the Problems and Methods of Psychoanalysis* (156–167). London: Karnac.

Ferro, A. (2002). *In the Analyst's Consulting Room.* New York: Brunner-Routledge.

Ferro, A. (2005). *Seeds of Illness, Seeds of Recovery.* New York: Brunner-Routledge.

Ferro, A. (2007). *Avoiding Emotions, Living Emotions.* London: Brunner-Routledge.

Ferro, A. (2009). Transformations in Dreaming and Characters in the Psychoanalytic Field. *International Journal of Psychoanalysis*, 90: 209–230.

Ferro, A. (2011). *Avoiding Emotions, Living Emotions.* London: Routledge and The Institute of Psychoanalysis.

Ferro, A. & Civitarese, G. (2013). Analysts in Search of an Author: Voltaire or Artemischa Gentileschi? Commentary on "Field Theory in Psychoanalysis, Part II" by D. B. Stern. *Psychoanalytic Dialogues*, 23: 646–653.

First, E. (1988). The Leaving Game or I'll Play You and You'll Play Me: The Emergence of Dramatic Role Play in 2-Year-Olds. In Slade, A. & Wolfe, D. (Eds.) *Children at Play: Clinical and Developmental Approaches to Meaning and Representation* (111–133). New York: Oxford University Press.

Fonagy, P. (2008). A Genuinely Developmental Theory of Sexual Enjoyment and Its Implications for Psychoanalytic Technique. *Journal of American Psychoanalytic Association*, 56: 11–36.

Fonagy, P. & Target, M. (1996a). Playing with Reality: I. Theory of Mind and the Normal Development of Psychic Reality. *International Journal of Psychoanalysis*, 77: 217–233.

Fonagy, P. & Target, M. (1996b). Playing with Reality: II. The Development of Psychic Reality from a Theoretical Perspective. *International Journal of Psychoanalysis*, 77: 459–479.

Fonagy P. & Target, M. (2000). Playing with Reality: III. The Persistence of Dual Psychic Reality in Borderline Patients. *International Journal of Psychoanalysis*, 81: 853–873.

Fonagy, P., Gergely, G., Jurist, E. & Target, M. (2002). *Affect Regulation, Mentalization and the Development of the Self.* New York & London: Other Books.

Fosha, D., Siegel D. & Solomon M. (2012). *The Healing Power of Emotions.* New York: Norton.

Frankel, J. (2002). Exploring Ferenczi's Concept of Identification with the Aggressor: Its Role in Trauma, Everyday Life, and the Therapeutic Relationship. *Psychoanalytic Dialogues*, 12: 101–139.

Freud, S. (1896). Further Remarks on the Neuro-Psychoses of Defence. In Strachey, J. (Ed.) (1953). *The Standard Edition of the Complete Psychological Works of Sigmund Freud Volume III (1893–1899)* (157–185). London: Hogarth.

Freud, S. (1905). Fragment of an Analysis of a Case of Hysteria. In Strachey, J. (Ed.) (1953). *The Standard Edition of the Complete Psychological Works of Sigmund Freud Volume VII* (1920–1922) (3-124). London: Hogarth.

Freud, S. (1911). Formulations Regarding the Two Principles in Mental Functioning. In Rieff, P. (Ed.) (1963). *General Physiological Theory* (21-28). New York: Collier Books.

Freud, S. (1912). The Dynamics of Transference. In Strachey, J. (Ed.) (1958). *The Standard Edition of the Complete Psychological Works of Sigmund Freud, Volume XII (1911–1913)* (97-108). London: Hogarth.

Freud, S. (1915). Instincts and Their Vicissitudes. In Strachey, J. (Ed.) (1957). *The Standard Edition of the Complete Psychological Works of Sigmund Freud, Volume XIV (1914–1916)* (109–140). London: Hogarth

Freud, S. (1920). Beyond the Pleasure Principle. In Strachey, J. (Ed.) (1955). *The Standard Edition of the Complete Psychological Works of Sigmund Freud, Volume XVIII (1920–1922)* (7–64). London: Hogarth.

Freud, S. (1923). The Ego and the Id. In J. Strachey (Ed.) (1961). *The Standard Edition of the Complete Psychological Works of Sigmund Freud, Volume XIX (1923–1925)* (1–66). London: Hogarth.

Freud, S. (1924). The Dissolution of the Oedipus Complex. In Strachey, J. (Ed.) (1961). *The Standard Edition of the Complete Psychological Works of Sigmund Freud, Volume XIX (1923–1925)* (159–172). London: Hogarth.

Freud, S. (1925). Some Psychical Consequences of the Anatomical Distinction Between the Sexes. In Strachey, J. (Ed.) (1961). *The Standard Edition of the Complete Psychological Works of Sigmund Freud, Volume XIX (1923–1925)* (248–260). London: Hogarth.

Freud, S. (1926). Inhibitions, Symptoms and Anxiety. In Strachey, J. (Ed.) (1959). *The Standard Edition of the Complete Psychological Works of Sigmund Freud, Volume XX (1925–1926)* (75–176). London: Hogarth.

Freud, S. (1930). Civilization and its Discontente. In Strachey, J. (Ed.) (1961). *The Standard Edition of the Complete Psychological Works of Sigmund Freud, Volume XXI (1927–1931)*. London: Hogarth.

Freud, S. (1931). Female Sexuality. In Strachey, J. (Ed.) (1961). *The Standard Edition of the Complete Psychological Works of Sigmund Freud, Volume XXI (1927–1931)* (281–297). London: Hogarth.

Freud, S. (1933). New Introductory Letters on Psychoanalysis. In Strachey, J. (Ed.) (1964). *The Standard Edition of the Complete Psychological Works of Sigmund Freud, Volume XXII (1932-1936)* (1–182). London: Hogarth.

Freud, S. (1933). New Introductory Lectures on Psychoanalysis: Femininity. In Strachey, J. (Ed.) (1964). *The Standard Edition of the Complete Psychological Works of Sigmund Freud, Volume XXII (1932-1936)* (112–135). London: Hogarth.

Gadamer, G. (1960). *Truth and Method*. London: Continuum.

Gallese, V. (2009). Mirror Neurons, Embodied Simulation, and the Neural Basis of Social Identification. *Psychoanalytic Dialogues*, 19: 519–536.

Gerhardt, J. B. & Sweetnam, A. (2000). The Intersubjective Turn in Psychoanalysis: A Comparison of Contemporary Theorists: Part 1 Jessica Benjamin. *Psychoanalytic Dialogues*, 10: 5–42.

Gerhardt, J., Borton, L. & Sweetnam, A. (2000). The Intersubjective Turn in Psychoanalysis A Comparison of Contemporary Theorists: Part 1 Jessica Benjamin. *Psychoanalytic Dialogues*, 10: 5–42.

Gerson, S. (2009). When the Third is Dead: Memory, Mourning and Witnessing in the Aftermath of the Holocaust. *International Journal of Psychoanalysis*, 90(6): 1341–1357.

Ghent, E. (1990). Masochism, Submission, Surrender: Masochism as a Perversion of Surrender. *Contemporary Psychoanalysis*, 26: 108–136.

Ghent, E. (1992). Paradox and Process. *Psychoanalytic Dialogues*, 2: 150–169.

Gill, M. (1982). *Analysis of Transference*. New York: International Universities Press.

Gobodo-Madikizela, P. (2002). Remorse, Forgiveness and Rehumanization: Stories from South Africa. *Journal of Humanistic Psychology*, 42(1): 7–32.

Goboda-Madikizela, P. (2003). *A Human Being Died That Night*. New York: Houghton Mifflin.

Gobodo-Madikizela, P. (2008). Trauma, Forgiveness and the Witnessing Dance: Making Public Spaces Intimate. *Journal of Analytical Psychology*, 53: 169–188.

Gobodo-Madikizela, P. (2011). Intersubjectivity and Embodiment: Exploring the Role of the Maternal in the Language of Forgiveness and Reconciliation. *Signs: Journal of Women in Culture and Society*, 36: 541–551.

Gobodo-Madikizela, P. (2013, April). *Feeling with the Womb: Reciprocal Mutual Sense-Making*. Keynote address presented at the Lessons in Peace Conference, New York University, New York City.

Gobodo-Madikizela. (2015). Psychological Repair: The Intersubjective Dialogue of Remorse and Forgiveness in the Aftermath of Gross Human Rights Violations. *Journal of the American Psychoanalytical Association (JAPA)*, 63: 1085–1123.

Gobodo-Madikizela, P. (Ed.) (2016). *Breaking Intergenerational cycles of Repetition. A Global Dialogue on Historical Trauma and Memory*. Opladen, Berlin & Toronto: Barbara Budrich.

Goldner, V. (2003). Gender and Trauma: Commentary on Michael Clifford's Clinical Case. *Progress in Self Psychology*, 20: 223–230.

Gomez-Castro, E. & Kovalskys, J. (2013). *Reencounter with History and Memory Through a Therapeutic Process*. Paper presented at IARPP, Santiago, Chile.

Grand, S. (2002). *The Reproduction of Evil*. Hillsdale, NJ: The Analytic Press.

Grand, S. (2009). *The Hero in the Mirror: From Fear to Fortitude*. London: Routledge, Taylor & Francis.

Grand, S. & Salberg, J. (2017). *Trans-generational Trauma and the Other. Dialogues across History*. London: Routledge, Taylor & Francis.

Greif, D. & Livingston, R. (2013). Interview with Philip M. Bromberg. *Contemporary Psychoanalysis*, 49: 323–355.

Grossman, D. (2003). *Be my Knife*. New York: Farrar Strauss Giroux.

Guntrip, H. (1961). *Personality Structure and Human Interaction*. New York: International Universities Press.

Guntrip, H. (1971). *Psychoanalytic Theory, Therapy and the Self*. New York: Basic Books.

Habermas, J. (1972). *Knowledge and Human Interests*. Boston, MA: Beacon Press.

Hadar, U. (2013). *Psychoanalysis and Social Involvement: Interpretation and Action*. London: Palgrave Macmillan.

Hamber, B. (2008). Forgiveness and Reconciliation: A Critical Reflection. In O'Hagan, L. (Ed.) *Stories in Conflict, Towards Understanding and Healing*. Derry, UK: Towards Understanding and Healing, Community Foundation for Northern Ireland, YES!

Hamber, B. & Wilson, R. A. (2002). Symbolic Closure Through Memory, Reparation and Revenge in Post-Conflict Societies. *Journal of Human Rights*, 1: 35–53.

Hammerich, B., Pfaefflin, J., Pogany-Wnendt, P., Siebert, E. & Sonntag, B. (2016). Handing Down the Holocaust in Germany: A Reflection on the Dialogue Between Second Generation Descendants of Perpetrators and Survivors. (Sudy Group on Intergenerational Consequences of the Holocaust, Cologne). In Gobodo-Madikizela

(Ed.) (2016). *Breaking Intergenerational Cycles of Repetition: A Global Dialogue on Historical Trauma and Memory*. Opladen, Berlin & Toronto: Budrich.

Hartmann, H. (1958). *Ego-Psychology and the Problem of Adaptation*. New York: International Universities Press.

Hayner, P. B. (2002). *Unspeakable Truths: Facing the Challenge of Truth Commissions*. New York & London: Routledge.

Hegel, G. W. F. (1807). Lordship and Bondage. In O'Neill, J. (Ed.) (1996). *Hegel's Dialectic of Desire and Recognition* (29–36). Albany, NY: SUNY Press.

Hegel, G. W. F. (1807). *Phenomenologie des Geistes*. Hamburg, Germany: Felix Meiner.

Herman, J. (1992). *Trauma and Recovery: The Aftermath of Violence – from Domestic Abuse to Political Terror*. New York: Basic Books.

Hetherington, M. (2008). The Role of Towards Understanding and Healing. In O'Hagan, L. (Ed.), *Stories in Conflict, Towards Understanding and Healing* (39–54). Derry, UK: Towards Understanding and Healing, Community Foundation for Northern Ireland, YES!

Hill, D. (2015). *Affect Regulation Theory: A Clinical Model*. New York: Norton.

Hoffman, I. (2002). *Forging Difference out of Similarity*. Paper presented at the Stephen Mitchell Memorial Conference of the International Association for Relational Psychoanalysis and Psychotherapy, New York.

Hoffman, I. Z. (1983). The Patient as Interpreter of the Analyst's Experience. *Contemporary Psychoanalysis*, 19: 389–422.

Hoffman, I. Z. (1998). *Ritual and Spontaneity in the Psychoanalytic Process*. Hillsdale, NJ: The Analytic Press.

Hoffman, M. (2010). *Toward Mutual Recognition: Relational Psychoanalysis and the Christian Narrative*. New York: Routledge.

Honneth, A. (1995). *The Struggle for Recognition: The Moral Grammar of Social Conflicts*. Cambridge, UK: Polity Press.

Honneth, A. (2007). *Disrespect The Normative Foundations of Critical Theory*. Cambridge, UK: Polity Press.

Horney, K. (1926). The Flight From Womanhood. In Horney, K. (1967). *Feminine Psychology* (54–71). New York: Norton.

Howell, E. F. (2005). *The Dissociative Mind*. Hillsdale, NJ: Analytic Press.

Ipp, H. (2016). Interweaving the Symbolic and Nonsymbolic in Therapeutic Action: Discussion of Gianni Nebbiosi's "The Smell of Paper". *Psychoanalytic Dialogues*, 26: 10–16.

Jacobs, T. (2001). On Misleading and Misreading Patients: Some Reflections on Communications, Miscommunications and Countertransference Enactments. *International Journal of Psychoanalysis*, 82: 653–669.

Jaenicke, C. (2011). *Change in Psychoanalysis: An Analyst's Reflections on the Therapeutic Relationship*. New York: Routledge.

Jaenicke, C. (2015). *In Search of a Relational Home*. London: Routledge.

Kane, B. (2005). Transforming Trauma into Tragedy: Oedipus/Israel and the Psychoanalyst as Messenger. *Psychoanalytic Review*, 92: 929–956.

Klein, M. (1934). The Pyschogenesis of Manic-Depressive States. In Klein, M. *Contributions to Psychoanalysis, 1921–1945*. London: Hogarth, 1945.

Klein, M. (1946). Notes on Some Schizoid Mechanisms. In Klein, M. *Envy and Gratitude and Other Works*. New York: Delacorte. 1975.

Klein, M. (1952). Some Theoretical Conclusions Regarding the Emotional Life of the Infant. In Klein, M. *Envy and Gratitude and Other Works.* New York: Delacorte, 1975.

Knoblauch, S. H. (2000). *The Musical Edge of Therapeutic Dialogue.* Hillsdale, NJ: Analytic Press.

Knoblauch, S. H. (2005). Body Rhythms and the Unconscious. *Psychoanalytic Dialogues,* 15(6): 807–827.

Knoblauch, S. H. (2008). "A Lingering Whiff of Descartes in the Air": From Theoretical Ideas to the Messiness of Clinical Participation: Commentary on Paper by the Boston Change Process Study Group. *Psychoanalytic Dialogues,* 18: 149–161.

Kohut, H. (1971). *The Analysis of Self.* New York: International Universities Press.

Kohut, J. (1977). *The Restoration of Self.* New York: International Universities Press.

Kohut, H. (1984). *How Does Analysis Cure.* New York: International Universities Press.

Kojève, A. (1969). *Introduction to the Reading of Hegel.* New York: Basic Books.

Kraemer, S. (2006). Betwixt the Dark and the Daylight of Maternal Subjectivity: Meditations on the Threshold. *Psychoanalytic Dialogues,* 16: 766–791.

Kristeva, J. (1982). *Powers of Horror: An Essay on Abjection.* New York: Columbia University Press.

Kristeva, J. (1987). Freud and Love: Treatment and its Discontents. In Kristeva, J. *Tales of Love* (21–57). New York: Columbia University Press.

Krog, A. (2000). *Country of my Skull: Guilt, Sorrow and the Limits of Forgiveness in the New South Africa.* New York: Three Rivers Press.

Lacan, J. (1975). *The Seminar of Jacques Lacan, Book I: Freud's Papers on Technique, 1953–54.* New York: Norton.

Lacan, J. (1977). *Ecrits: A Selection,* A. Sheridan (trans.). New York: Norton.

Laing, R. D. (1965). Mystification, Confusion and Conflict. In Bozormeny-Nagy, J. & Framo, J. L. (Eds.). *Intensive Family Therapy.* New York: Harper & Row.

Laplanche, J. (1987). *New Foundations for Psychoanalysis,* D. Macey (trans.). Oxford: Blackwell.

Laplanche, J. (1992). *Jean Laplanche: Seduction, Translation, Drives: A Dossier.* J. Fletcher (trans.) & Stanton M. London: Institute of Contemporary Arts.

Laplanche, J. (1992). *Le Primat de L'autre en Psychanalyse.* Paris: Champs Flammarion.

Laplanche, J. (1997). The Theory of Seduction and the Problem of the Other. *International Journal of Psychoanalysis,* 78: 653–666.

Laplanche, J. (2011). *Freud and the Sexual. Essays 2000-2006.* New York: International Psychoanalytic Books.

Laub, D. & Auerhahn, N. C. (1993). Knowing and not Knowing Massive Psychic Trauma. *International Journal of Psychoanalysis,* 74: 387–302.

Laufer M. & Laufer, E. (2012). *One Day After Peace.* Featuring Robi Damelin. Israel/South Africa.

Layton, L. (2010). Resistance to Resistance. In Harris, A. & Botticelli, S. (Eds.) (2010). *First Do No Harm: The Paradoxical Encounters of Psychoanalysis, Warmaking, and Resistance.* New York: Routledge.

Lazarre, J. (1976). *The Mother Knot.* Boston. MA: Beacon.

Levenson, E. A. (1972). *The Fallacy of Understanding* New York: Basic Books.

Levenson, E. A. (1983). *The Ambiguity of Change.* New York: Basic Books.

Levenson, E. A. (2006). Response to John Steiner. *International Journal of Psycho-Analysis*, 87: 321–324.

Loewald, H. (1951). *Papers on Psychoanalysis*. New Haven, CT: Yale University Press.

Loewald, H. W. (1960). On the Therapeutic Action of Psycho-Analysis. *International Journal of Psychoanalysis*, 41: 16–33

Lyons-Ruth, K. (1999). The Two-Person Unconscious: Intersubjective Dialogue, Enactive Relational Representation, and the Emergence of New Forms of Relational Organization. *Psychoanalytic Inquiry*, 19: 576–617.

McDougall, J. (1989). *Theaters of the Body: A Psychoanalytic Approach to Psychosomatic Illness*. New York: Norton.

McDougall, J. (1996). *The Many Faces of Eros. A Psychoanalytic Exploration of Human Sexuality*. New York: Norton.

McGilchrist, I. (2009). *The Master and His Emissary: The Divided Brain and the Making of the Western World*. New Haven, CT: Yale University Press.

McKay, R. K. (2015). *Empathy reconsidered*. Paper delivered at IARPP, Toronto, Canada, June 2015.

McKay, R. K. (2016). *Bread and Roses: From Empathy to Recognition*. Unpublished manuscript.

Magid, B. M. (2008). *Ending the Pursuit of Happiness: A Zen Guide*. Cambridge, MA: Wisdom Press.

Magid, B. M. & Shane, E. (2017). Relational Self Psychology. *Psychoanalysis, Self and Context*, 12(1): 3–19.

Marcuse, H. (1962). *Eros and Civilization*. New York: Vintage.

Minow, M. (1998). *Between Vengeance and Forgiveness: Facing History after Genocide and Mass Violence*. Boston, MA: Beacon.

Mailer, S. (2010). *The Social Reproduction of Trauma: The Case of Chile*. IARPP Panel on Collective Witnessing and Trauma, San Francisco, February 2010.

Margalit, A. (2002). *The Ethics of Memory*. Cambridge, MA: Harvard University Press.

Mark, D. (2015). *Radical equality in the wake of enactment*. Paper presented at the International Association for Relational Psychoanalysis & Psychotherapy (IARPP), Toronto, June, 2015.

Markell, P. (2003). *Bound by Recognition*. Princeton, NJ & London: Princeton University Press.

Maroda, K. J. (1999). *Seduction, Surrender and Transformation*. Hillside, NJ: Analytic Press.

Mendelsohn, Y. M. (2003). *Complementary Relationships and Sustaining Cycles of Violence*. Unpublished.

Milner, M. (1969). *The Hands of the Living God: An Account of Psychoanalytic Treatment*. London: Hogarth.

Milner, M. (1987). *The Supperessed Madness of Sane Men*. London & New York: Tavistock.

Mitchell, S. (1988). *Relational Concepts in Psychoanalysis: An Integration*. Cambridge, MA: Harvard University Press.

Mitchell, S. (2000). Juggling Paradoxes: Commentary on the Work of Jessica Benjamin. *Studies in Gender & Sexuality*, 1: 251–269.

Mitchell, S. (1993). *Hope and Dread in Psychoanalysis*. New York: Basic Books.

Mitchell, S. (1997). *Influence and Autonomy in Psychoanalysis.* Hillsdale, NJ: Analytic Press.

Mitchell, S. & Black, M. (1995). *Freud and beyond: A History of Modern Psychoanalytic Thought.* New York: Basic Books.

Nahum, J. (2002). Explicating the Implicit. The Local Level and the Micro-Process of Change. Boston Change Process Study Group. *International Journal of Psychoanalysis*, 83: 1051–1062.

Nahum, J. (2005). The "Something More" than Interpretation Revisited: Sloppiness and Co-Creativity in the Psychoanalytic Encounter. *Journal of American Psychoanalytic Association*, 53: 693–729.

Nahum, J. (2008). Forms of Relational Meaning Issues in the Relations between the Implicit and Reflective-Verbal Domains Boston Change Process Study Group. *Psychoanalytic Dialogues*, 18: 125–148.

Nebbiosi, G. (2016). The Smell of Paper. *Psychoanalytic Dialogues*, 26: 1–9.

Nguyen, L. (2012). Psychoanalytic Activism: Finding the Human, Staying Human. *Psychoanalytic Psychology*, 29: 308–317.

Ogden, P., Pain, C. & Minton, K. (2006). *Trauma and the Body.* New York: Norton.

Ogden, T. H. (1986). *The Matrix of the Mind.* Northvale, NJ: Aronson.

Ogden, T. H. (1987). The Transitional Oedipal Relationship in Female Development. *International Journal of Psychoanalysis*, 68: 485–498.

Ogden, T. H. (1989). *The Primative Edge of Experience.* Northvale, NJ: Aronson.

Ogden, T. H. (1994). *Subjects of Analysis.* Northvale, NJ: Aronson.

Ogden, T. H. (1997). *Reverie and Interpretation.* Northvale, NJ: Aronson.

Oliver, K. (2001). *Witnessing: Beyond Recognition.* Minneapolis, MN: University of Minnesota Press.

O'Neill, J. (1996). *Hegel's Dialectic of Desire and Recognition. Texts and Commentary.* Albany, NY: SUNY Press.

Orange, D. M. (1995). *Emotional Understanding: Studies in Psychoanalytic Epistemology.* New York: The Guilford Press.

Orange, D. M. (2010). Recognition as: Intersubjective Vulnerability in the Psychoanalytic Dialogue. *International Journal of Psychoanalytic Self Psychology*, 5: 227–243.

Orange, D. M. (2010). Revisiting Mutual Recognition: Responding to Ringstrom, Benjamin and Slavin. *International Journal of Self-Psychology*, 5: 293–306.

Orange, D. M. (2011). *The Suffering Stranger.* New York: Routledge.

Orange, D. M., Atwood, G. E. & Stolorow, R. D. (1997). *Working Intersubjectively.* Hillsdale, NJ: Analytic Press.

Parker, R. (1995). *Mother Love, Mother Hate. The Power of Maternal Ambivalence.* New York: Basic Books.

Peltz, R. & Goldberg, P. (2013). Field Conditions. Commentary on "Field Theory in Psychoanalysis, Part II" by D. B. Stern. *Psychoanalytic Dialogues*, 23: 660–666.

Pizer, B. (2003). When the Crunch is a (K)not: A Crimp in Relational Dialogue. *Psychoanalytic Dialogues*, 13: 171–192.

Pizer, S. (1998). *Building Bridges: Negotiation of Paradox in Psychoanalysis.* Hillsdale, NJ: Analytic Press.

Pizer, S. (2002). *Commentary on J. Davie's "Falling in Love with Love".* IARPP online symposium.

Qouta S., Punamaki, R. & El Sarraj, E. (1995a). The Relation Between Traumatic Experiences, Activity and Cognitive and Emotional Responses Among Palestinian Children. *International Journal of Psychology*, 30(3): 289–304.

Qouta S., Punamaki, R. & El Sarraj, E. (1995b). The Impact of the Peace Treaty on Psychological Well-Being: A Follow-up Study of Palestinian Children. *Child Abuse & Neglect*, 19(10): 1197–1208.

Racker, H. (1957). The Meaning and Uses of Countertransference. *Psychoanalytic Quarterly*, 26: 303–357.

Racker, H. (1968). *Transference and Countertransference*. New York: International Universities Press.

Rappoport, E. (2012). Creating the Umbilical Cord; Relational Knowing and the Somatic Third. *Psychoanalytic Dialogues*, 22: 375–388.

Renik, O. (1993). Analytic Interaction: Conceptualizing Technique in Light of the Analyst's Irreducible Subjectivity. *Psychoanalytic Quarterly*, 62: 553–571.

Renik, O. (1998a). The Analyst's Subjectivity and the Analyst's Objectivity. *International Journal of Psychoanalysis*, 79: 487–497.

Renik, O. (1998b). Getting Real in Analysis. *Psychoanalytic Quarterly*, 67: 566–593.

Ringstrom, P. (1998). Therapeutic Impasses in Contemporary Psychoanalytic Treatment: Revisiting the Double Bind Hypothesis. *Psychoanalytic Dialogues*, 8: 297–316.

Ringstrom, P. (2001). Cultivating the Improvisational in Psychoanalytic Treatment. *Psychoanalytic Dialogues*, 11: 727–754.

Ringstrom, P. (2007). Scenes that Write Themselves Improvisational Moments in Psychoanalysis. *Psychoanaytic Dialogues*, 17: 69–99.

Ringstrom, P. (2016). *Paradox in Enactments: Double Binds and Play*. Paper Delivered at International Association for Psychoanalysis and Psychotherapy, Rome, June 2016.

Rivera, M. (1989). Linking the Psychological and the Social: Feminism, Post-Structuralism, and Multiple Personality. *Dissociation*, 2: 24–31.

Roth, J. (2017). Dwelling at the Thresholds; Witnessing to Historical Trauma Across Concentric Fields. In Alpert, J. & Goren, E. (Eds.). *Psychoanalysis, Trauma and Community: History and Contemporary Reappraisals* (44–63). London & New York: Routledge.

Rothschild, B. (2000). *The Body Remembers: The Psychophysiology of Trauma and Trauma Treatment*. New York: Norton.

Rousseau, J. J. (1775/1992). *Discourse on the Origins of Inequality*. D. Cress (trans.). Indiannapolis, IN: Hackett.

Rozmarin, E. (2007). An Other in Psychoanalysis: Levinas' Critique of Knowledge and Analytic Sense. *Contemporary Psychoanalysis*, 43: 327–360.

Rundel, M. (2015). The Fire of Eros: Sexuality and the Movement toward Union. *Psychoanalytic Dialogues*, 25: 614–630.

Russell, P. (1998). *Crises of Emotional Growth (a.k.a. Theory of the Crunch)*. Paper presented at the Paul Russell Conference, Boston, MA.

Safran, J. D. (1999). Faith, Despair, Will and the Paradox of Acceptance. *Contemporary Psychoanalysis*, 35: 5–23.

Safran, J. D. & Muran, J. C. (2000). *Negotiating the Therapeutic Alliance: A Relational Treatment Guide*. New York: Guilford.

Safran, J. D., Muran, J. C. & Shaker, A. (2014). Research on Impasses and Ruptures in the Therapeutic Alliance. *Contemporary Psychoanalysis*, 50: 211–232.

Saketopoulis, A. (2014). To Suffer Pleasure: The Shattering of the Ego as the Psychic Labor of Perverse Sexuality. *Studies in Gender and Sexuality*, 15: 254–268.

Salberg, J. & Grand, S. (2017). *The Wounds of History*. New York & London: Routledge.

Salomonnson, B. (2007). Semiotic Transformations in Psychoanalysis with Infants and Adults. *International Journal of Psychoanalysis*, 88: 1201–1221.

Samuels, A. (1985). *Jung and the Post-Jungians*. London: Routledge.

Sander, L. (1983). Polarity, Paradox, and the Organizing Process in Development. In Call, J. D. Galenson, E., & Tyson, R. L (Eds.). *Frontiers of Infant Psychiatry no 1*, New York: Basic Books.

Sander, L. (1991). Recognition Process: Context and Experience of Being Known. In Amadei, G. & Bianchi, I. (Eds.) (2008). *Living Systems, Evolving Consciousness, and the Emerging Person* (177–195). New York: The Analytic Press.

Sander, L. (1995). Identity and the Experience of Specificity in a Process of Recognition. *Psychoanalytic Dialogues*, 5: 579–593.

Sander, L. (2002). Thinking Differently: Principles of Process in Living Systems and the Specificity of Being Known. *Psychoanalytic Dialogues*, 12(1): 11–42.

Sander, L. (2008). Paradox and Resolution: From the Beginning. In Amadei, G. & Bianchi, I. (Eds.). *Living Systems, Evolving Consciousness, and the Emerging Person* (177–195). New York: The Analytic Press.

Scarfone, D. (2015). *Laplanche: An Introduction*. New York: The Unconscious in Translation.

Schore, A. N. (1993). *Affect Regulation and the Origin of the Self: The Neurobiology of Emotional Development*. Hillsdale, NJ: Lawrence Erlbaum Associates.

Schore, A. N. (2003). *Affect Regulation and the Repair of the Self*. New York: Norton.

Schore, A. N. (2011). Foreword. In Bromberg, P. *The Shadow of the Tsunami and the Growth of the Relational Mind* (ix-xxxvl). New York & London: Routledge.

Sedlak, V. (2009). Psychoanalytic Controversies: Discussion. *International Journal of Psychoanalysis*, 90: 451–455.

Seligman, S. (1998). Child Psychoanalysis, Adult Psychoanalysis, and Developmental Psychology: Introduction to Symposium on Child Analysis, Part II. *Psychoanalytic Dialogues*, 8: 79–86.

Seligman, S. (2012). The Baby Out of the Bathwater: Microseconds, Psychic Structure, and Psychotherapy. *Psychoanalytic Dialogues*, 22: 499–509.

Siegel, D. (1999). *The Developing Mind*. New York: Guilford Press.

Siegel, D. & Solomon, M. (2003). *Healing Trauma: Attachment, Mind, Body and Brain*. New York: Norton.

Silverman, K. (1990). Historical Trauma and Male Subjectivity. In Kaplan, E. (Ed.). *Psychoanalysis and Cinema* (110–128). New York: Routledge.

Singer, I. (2014). *Moving Beyond Violence, the Video*. Featuring Bassam Aramin and Itamar Shapira. MovingBeyondViolence.org.

Slavin, M. (2010). On Recognizing the Psychoanalytic Perspective of the Other: A Discussion of "Recognition as: Intersubjective Vulnerability in the Psychoanalytic Dialogue," by Donna Orange. *International Journal of Psychoanalytic Self-Psychology*, 5: 274–292.

Slavin, M. & Kriegman, D. (1998). Why the Analyst Needs to Change. *Psychoanalytic Dialogues*, 8: 247–285.

Slochower, J. A. (1996). *Holding and Psychoanalysis*. Hillsdale, NJ: Analytic Press.

Slochower, J. A. (2006). *Psychoanalytic Collisions*. London: Routledge.

Spezzano, C. (1993). *Affect in Psychoanalysis: A Clinical Synthesis*. Hillsdale, NJ: Analytic Press.

Spezzano, C. (1996). The Three Faces of Two-person Psychology: Development, Ontology, and Epistemology. *Psychoanalytic Dialogues*, 6: 599–622.

Spezzano, C. (2009). The Search for a Relational Home. In Aron, L. & Harris, A. (Eds.). *Relational Psychoanalysis Vol IV: Expansion of Theory*. London & New York: Routledge.

Spitz, R. A. (1957). *No and Yes: On the Genesis of Human Communication*. New York: International Universities Press.

Staub, E. (2003). *The Psychology of Good and Evil*. New York: Cambridge University Press.

Stein, R. (1998a). The Poignant, the Excessive and the Enigmatic in Sexuality. *International Journal of Psychoanalysis*, 79: 253–268.

Stein, R. (1998b). Two Principles of the Functioning of Affects. *American Journal of Psychoanalysis*, 58: 211–230.

Stein, R. (2007). Moments in Laplanche's Theory of Sexuality. *Studies in Gender and Sexuality*, 8: 177–200.

Stein, R. (2008). The Otherness of Sexuality: Excess. *Journal of American Psychoanalytic Association*, 56: 43–71.

Steiner, J. (1993). Problems of Psychoanalytic Technique: Patient-Centered and Analyst-Centered Interpretations. In Steiner, J. *Psychic Retreats: Pathological Organizations in Psychotic, Neurotic, and Borderline Petients* (131-147). London & New York: Routledge.

Steiner, J. (2006). Interpretative Enactments and the Analytic Setting. *The International Journal of Psychoanalysis*, 87(2): 315–320.

Stern, D. B. (1997). *Unformulated Experience*. Hillsdale NJ: Analytic Press.

Stern, D. B. (2009). *Partners in Thought; Working with Unformulated Experience, Dissociation and Enactment*. New York: Routledge.

Stern, D. B. (2013). Field Theory in Psychoanalysis: Part II – Bionian Field Theory. *Psychoanalytic Dialogues*, 23: 630-645.

Stern, D. B. (2015). *Relational Freedom*. London: Routledge.

Stern, D. N. (1974a). The Goal and Structure of Mother–Infant Play. *Journal of the Academy of Child Psychiatry*, 13: 402–421.

Stern, D. N. (1974b). Mother and Infant at Play: The Dyadic Interaction Involving Facial, Vocal and Gaze Behavior. In Lewis, M. & Rosenblum, L. (Eds.). *The Effect of the Infant on its Caregiver*. New York: John Wiley.

Stern, D. N. (1977). *The First Relationship Infant and Mother*. Cambridge, MA: Harvard Universty Press.

Stern, D. N. (1985). *The Interpersonal World of The Human Infant*. New York: Basic Books.

Stern, D. N. (2004). *The Present Moment*. New York: Norton.

Stern, D. N. (2010). *Forms of Vitality*. New York and Oxford: Oxford University Press.

Stern, D. N., Sander, L. W., Nahum, J. P., Harrison, A. M., Lyons-Ruth, K., Morgan, A. C., Bruschweiler-Stern, N. & Tronick, E. Z. (1998). Non-Interpretive Mechanisms in Psychoanalytic Therapy: The 'Something More' than Interpretation. *International Journal of Psychoanalysis*, 79: 903–921.

Stoller, R. (1975). *Perversion: The Erotic Form of Hatred*. New York: Pantheon Books.

Stoller, R. (1979). *Sexual Excitement: Dynamics of Erotic Life.* New York: Pantheon Books.

Stolorow, R. & Atwood, G. (1992). *Contexts of Being: The Intersubjective Foundations of Psychological Life.* Hillsdale NJ: Analytic Press.

Stolorow, R., Atwood, G. & Orange, D. (2002). *Worlds of Experience: Interweaving Clinical and Philosophical Dimensions in Psychoanalysis.* New York: Basic Books.

Sullivan, H. S. (1953). *The Interpersonal Theory of Psychiatry.* New York: Norton

Symington, N. (1983). The Analyst's Act of Freedom as Agent of Therapeutic Change. *International Review of Psychoanalysis,* 10: 283–291.

Taniguchi, K. (2012). The Eroticism of the Maternal: So What if Everything Is About the Mother. *Studies in Gender and Sexuality,* 13: 123–138.

Taylor, C. (2007). *The Secular Age.* Cambridge, MA: Belknap Press.

Theweleit, K. (1987). *Male Fantasies 1: Women, Foods, Bodies, History.* Cambridge, UK: Polity.

Thomas, N. K. (2010). Whose Truth: Inevitable Tensions in Testimony and the Search for Repair. In Harris, A. & Botticelli, S. (Eds.). *First Do No Harm: The Paradoxical Encounters of Psychoanalysis, Warmaking, and Resistance.* New York: Routledge.

Trevarthen, C. (1977). Descriptive Analyses of Infant Communicative Behavior. In Schaffer, H. (Ed.). *Studies in Mother-Infant Interaction.* London: Academic Press.

Trevarthen, C. (1979). Communication and Cooperation in Early Infancy: A Description of Primary Intersubjectivity. In Bullowa, M. (Ed.). *Before Speech: The Beginning of Interpersonal Communication.* New York: Cambridge University Press.

Tronick, E. (1989). Emotions and Emotional Communication in Infants. *American Psychology,* 44: 112–119.

Tronick, E. (2005). Why is Connection with Others So Critical? The Formation of Dyadic States of Consciousness. In Nadel, J. & Muir, D. (Eds.). *Emotional Development* (293–315). Oxford: Oxford University Press.

Tronick. E. (2007). *The Neurobehavioral and Social- Emotional Development of Infants and Children.* New York: W.W. Norton.

Tronick, E., Als, H. & Brazelton, T. B. (1977). Mutuality in Mother-infant Interaction. *Journal of Communication,* 27: 74–79.

Tutu, D. M. (1999). *No Future Without Forgiveness.* New York: Random House.

Ullman, C. (2006). Bearing Witness: Across the Barriers in Society and in the Clinic. *Psychoanalytic Dialogues,* 16: 181–198.

Ullman, C. (2011). Between Denial and Witnessing: Psychoanalysis and Clinical Practice in the Israeli Context. *Psychoanalytic Perspectives,* 8(2): 179–200.

Urlic, I., Berger, M. & Berman, A. (2013). *Victimhood, Vengefulness and the Culture of Forgiveness.* New York: NovaScience Press.

Van der Kolk, B. (2014). *The Body Keeps the Score: Brain, Mind and Body in the Healing of Trauma.* New York: Norton.

Verwoerdt, W. & Little, A. (2008). Toward Truth and Responsibility after the Troubles. In O'Hagan, L. (Ed.). *Stories in Conflict, Towards Understanding and Healing.* Derry, UK: Towards Understanding and Healing, Community Foundation for Northern Ireland, YES!

Weber, M. (1905/2002). *The Protestant Ethic and the Spirit of Capitalism.* P. Baehr, & G. C. Wells (trans.). New York & London: Penguin Books.

Winnicott, D. W. (1947). Hate in the Countertransference. In Winnicott, D. W. (1975). *Through Pediatrics to Psychoanalysis* (194–203). London: Hogarth, The Psycho-analytic Library.

Winnicott, D. W. (1965). *Through Pediatrics to Psychoanalysis*. London: Hogarth.

Winnicott, D. W. (1971a). The Use of an Object and Relating Through Identifications, In Winnicott, D. W. *Playing and Reality*, New York: Penguin.

Winnicott, D. W. (1971b). *Playing and Reality*, New York: Penguin.

Wrye, H. K. and Welles, J. K. (1994). *The Narration of Desire: Erotic Transference and Countertransference*. Hillsdale, NJ: The Analytic Press.

Yeatman, A. (2015). A Two-Person Conception of Freedom: The Significance of Jessica Benjamin's Idea of Intersubjectivity. *Journal of Classical Sociology*, 15: 3–23.

Index

abjection 243
abuse 16, 25, 61, 68, 92, 122, 201, 235
accommodation 84, 193
acknowledgment 6–7, 16, 55–62, 68,
154, 168–9; Acknowledgement
Project, The 221, 236–9, 241;
becoming real 62–5; beyond
"Only one can live" 217–18, 225,
231, 236–7, 244, 247; clinical 90;
embodied/disembodied 219–27, 239;
transformations in Thirdness 86–8,
90, 93–4, 104, 109–10
acting out 210
affect 156, 175–6, 196, 201, 237;
affective care 118; affective joining
185; arousal 115; attunement 32, 169,
196; shared 178; tolerance 87
affect regulation 9, 115, 117–18, 190–1,
196, 198, 238; in development 113,
137–8; mutuality 78–81; play/paradox
170, 172–3, 175; theory 8, 112, 238
Agamben, G. 232
agency 2–3, 50, 73, 88, 92, 130, 165,
188, 193; beyond "Only one can live"
217, 226, 231, 235, 244, 247
aggression 87, 121, 123, 148, 176, 204,
229
alienation 222–3, 235
Allen, A. 17
alpha function 162
alphabetization 190
altruism 99, 229
ambivalence 5, 94, 96–8
analytic relationship 7, 14–15, 20, 40,
174; excess 136–40; mutual
vulnerability 103–9
anger 38, 45–6, 58–9, 157, 161–2,
166–8, 207

anxiety 57–9, 113, 118, 120–1, 138,
189, 228; play/paradox 157–8, 160,
162, 168–9; separation 192; sexual
127, 136; social 157; transformations
in Thirdness 82–3, 89, 91–3, 105
apartheid 219–20
apology 43, 58, 166, 217, 239, 246–7
Aron, L. 11, 27, 32, 50, 74, 156–7, 164
arousal 126, 141, 148; fear 133; hyper
61, 82, 119, 128, 238; physiological
121, 123
asymmetry 3, 8, 11, 37–8, 61, 183;
responsibility 89–91, 101, 103;
rhythmic Third 75–9; transformations
in Thirdness 73–5, 80, 82–3, 92, 96,
103–4, 108
Atlas, G. 124, 133–5, 156–7, 164, 194–5
attachment 9, 44, 60, 79, 81, 116, 133,
235–6, 238; social 18, 234–5, 242
attunement 5, 7, 12, 81, 91, 169–70,
187, 196; intersubjective Thirdness
29–32, 35–8, 40; misattunement 5,
41–2, 44, 49, 51, 101
Atwood, G. 22
Austen, J. 163–4, 169
authenticity 37, 48, 165
autonomy 85, 193

babies *see* children
Bar-On, D. 220
Baraitser, L. 96–7
Bataille, G. 114, 141
Bateson, G. 144, 147–51, 165
Beebe, B. 31, 77
being with 76, 174
Bersani, L. 114
bi-directionality 103
Bion, W. 10, 64, 87, 96, 162, 197–8

philosophy 2, 246
physiological arousal 8
Pinochet, A. 232
Pizer, B. 23
play 31, 184–7, 191–2, 199, 203, 214;
    analytic 179; dialogic 162; enactment
    144, 148–50, 153–7, 163, 165, 170–9;
    face-to-face 188; interaction 75;
    interactive 178; intersubjectivity
    189–91; negation 206
plays 154
pleasure 124, 129
politics 16, 18, 20, 217–18, 223–4, 226,
    237, 241, 247; theory 246
Porges, S. 235
post-modernism 3
power relations 2, 14–19, 27, 39, 55,
    151, 193, 203, 224, 226, 247
powerlessness 135, 217, 242
precarity 48, 87, 127, 237, 244
privilege 223
procedural domain 178, 182, 186
projection 18, 40
prospective function 157
psychic equivalence 150, 171, 190
psycho-cultural templates 124
public spaces 243

race 14, 221–2, 224, 226, 247; civil
    rights movement 223; segregation
    223
Racker, H. 24, 55, 94, 101
radicalism 223
rape 244
reactivity 5, 64, 97, 165
reciprocity 3–5, 10, 12–14, 22, 25–6,
    49–50, 58, 234; transformations in
    Thirdness 72, 88, 96, 98, 100–2
recognition 1, 3–5, 7, 13, 19, 49, 60,
    64–5, 213; basic 4, 76, 113;
    beginning with No and Yes 182,
    187–91, 195, 198; beyond "Only one
    can live" 224, 227–8, 238; enactment
    145, 154, 162, 168, 170; identity 237;
    intersubjective Thirdness 24–5, 27;
    mutual 10–11, 72–5, 77, 80–2, 87–8,
    94, 97–8, 101, 103, 107, 110, 234,
    242; non 14, 148, 193; performing
    152–4; sexuality 117–18, 129–30,
    138; social 217, 235; theory 7–8, 10,
    14, 17–18, 74, 79, 95, 97, 113, 178,
    216–17, 234, 246

recoupling 155, 179
reflection 14, 65, 67–9, 73, 91, 101,
    196, 204, 208, 213; enactment 152,
    156, 170, 178; intersubjective
    Thirdness 37, 43; self 24, 38, 96, 174,
    224; shared 8, 35, 169, 178
reflexivity 76, 149
refugees 223
regulation 80–1, 117, 153, 191; affective
    124; maternal 129; mutual 56, 82–4,
    124–5, 137–8, 140, 173
reification 128, 137
rejection 33–4, 147, 162–3, 193, 195–6,
    203
relational analysis 1, 3, 7, 39, 55, 186;
    enactment 155, 162, 168, 174–5, 177;
    transformations in Thirdness 74, 95,
    110
relational dimension 115
relational dynamics 25
relational knowing 175
relational paradigm 63
relational pattern 140
relational reversal 123
relational theory 173, 176
relational turn 1, 39, 90
religion 83–4
remorse 217, 230, 238, 240, 244
repair 7–8, 16–17, 19, 50–2, 54–5, 70,
    186, 208; beyond "Only one can live"
    216, 229, 238–9; disruption and
    repair 6, 77–8, 84, 94, 98, 110, 175,
    192, 206; enactment 146–7, 154,
    156–7, 161, 168, 170, 173, 176, 178;
    intersubjective Thirdness 26, 39–43,
    47; sexuality 120, 138;
    transformations in Thirdness 86–7,
    90, 93, 96, 102–3, 105, 108
reparations 247
repetition 8, 147, 170, 175–6, 186, 208
resistance 17, 25, 34, 38–9, 52, 194–5,
    234, 245
responsibility 18, 25, 41–3, 45–8, 50,
    53, 58–9, 62, 74, 96–8, 102–4;
    asymmetry 75, 82–3
responsiveness 78, 113
revenge 235
reverie 87, 149, 156, 158, 162–3, 165,
    171–2, 186; dialogic 175
rhythmic Third 51, 57, 59, 64–5, 81,
    139, 240, 243; beginning with No and
    Yes 182, 185, 189, 194, 196, 198;

Grand Hotel Abyss

Stuart

Jeffries

. Infants need from the beginning to express love.

MIRIAM   AIMÉ   HÉLÈNE
BECKY
ELIZABETH   ELIZABETH
MARIA

The Psychology
for the People